NIGERIA

What Will My Mother Say

A Tribal African Girl
Comes of Age in America

Dympna Ugwu-Oju

Bonus Books, Inc., Chicago

99   98   97   96   95   5   4   3   2   1

Library of Congress Cataloging-in-Publication Data

Ugwu-Oju, Dympna. 1956–
    What will my mother say: a tribal African girl comes of age in America / Dympna
Ugwu-Oju.
       p.   cm.
    ISBN 1-56625-042-0 (alk. paper)
    1. Ugwu-Oju, Dympna, 1956–   2. Nigerian Americans—Biography.
3. Women, Ibo—United States.   I. Title.
E184.N55U37   1995
306'.089'9699073—dc20   95-35909

Bonus Books, Inc.
160 East Illinois Street
Chicago, Illinois 60611

Composition by Point West, Inc.

Printed in the United States of America

For Sherifa Omade Edoga
(August 5, 1970–March 12, 1994),
whose spirit runs like a river through many lives.

Acknowledgements

My niece Sherifa Omade Edoga wanted me to write the story of her father's family, but I always managed to come up with excuses about why I couldn't. There was so much to tell, and all of it passed down orally: Who would help me? Who would finish the story if I should die before it was completed?

Sherifa assured me with authority that she would finish the story if I couldn't. Still I did nothing.

On March 8, 1994, I was in San Francisco keeping a vigil over Sherifa, who was in a coma following heart surgery. That night, Harriet Beinfield, the oldest daughter of Dr. and Mrs. Beinfield, my brother John's American parents, ordered me to tell the story of our family, something we could tell Sherifa when she woke up. I began narrating the story then that has turned into this book.

Stories poured out of me—events I should have had no recollection of, incidents that took place before I was born were remembered. I was still telling our story when Sherifa died four days later, but it probably would have remained in bits and pieces had Harriet not taken over. Sherifa's voice became Harriet's, and it was she whose enthusiasm infected me and made me believe I could write the book.

When I began to write, the words kept coming. Some days, I couldn't type them as fast as they came. Harriet read, critiqued and offered solutions to problems that developed. She has been involved in every stage of this book, introducing me to Deke Castleman, whose editing brought much needed order to my rambling.

Others whose contributions are invaluable include Janet Clausen, Alexis Khoury, Agnes Akabogu, Leslie Barron, Melisande Brown, Gladys Ajaelo, and Anne Barthel, my editor at Bonus Books, without whose persistence this project might not be complete.

I owe a debt of gratitude to my family: my husband Charles and my children, Delia, Chuka and Obi, for their carte-blanche support and sacrifice during this past year; my mother and parents-in-law for the photographs, and John and Delia Edoga for bringing me to the United States and encouraging me always along the way.

Part I
Mama

Raising Delia

About a year ago, I walked in on my husband berating our daughter for wrestling on the living-room floor with her brothers. His voice showed both his anger and disappointment that eleven-year-old Delia had neglected some chores assigned her.

"But Dad, how come the boys don't have to do anything around here?" Delia asked, her voice devoid of the whininess that usually marked her complaints.

"Because they're boys, and you're a girl, and it's time you learned that."

"Well, being a girl doesn't make me different from the boys, right, Mom?" Delia dragged me into a conversation I was desperately trying to avoid.

"Not really, Delia," I responded, my noncommittal answer reinforcing neither my husband's nor my daughter's position, the vagueness reflecting my long-standing confusion and ambivalence about how to raise my daughter.

Later that day, my husband accused me of misleading Delia. "How can you tell her there's no difference between being a boy and a girl? Was that what your own mother taught you?"

"This is California, not Nigeria. She's an American child," I argued, not for the first time that month. "We'll be doing her a lot of damage if we insist on teaching her that her femaleness is all she's about. We have to stress that girl or not, she's as able as anyone else to accomplish whatever she wants." My voice sounded convincing, surprising even me; did I really say that gender was irrelevant? Wow! What would my mother say about that?

"Whatever you say," my husband snapped before retreating, clearly angry with me, too. "But you'll only have yourself to blame if she doesn't turn out right."

"Turn out right?" I fought an urge to yell. "She will turn out right, you wait and see!"

But I've said that many times, more to myself than to anyone else. Like my husband, and probably more than he, I worry constantly about what will become of my daughter, my Ibo-American child.

I wonder what my legacy, if any, to her will be. How can I be a good mother to a child whose world, scope, and experience are totally different from mine? Sometimes I am so consumed with my helplessness over the matter that I cannot think of anything else for days. I can't help but compare Delia's life to mine at that age, as well as comparing her mother (me) to my mother (Mama), whose constant admonition, "Remember, you're only a woman," was the refrain of my early life.

Inevitably, I arrive at the conclusion that my daughter is short-changed by my lack of a fully articulated vision for her. I would readily admit that I constantly vacillate between attempting to mold Delia by the rigid standards of Ibo womanhood, relying mostly on my experiences with own my mother, on one hand, and on the other hand instilling in her my Americanism, pushing her to assert herself and excel in everything. While I burst with pride when she receives awards for academic accomplishments, I cannot quell that inner voice, my mother's, which warns, "These things are not really important for a girl; they'll take her nowhere." When Delia won the presidency of her school's student body this past year, I experienced my greatest confusion yet. "My daughter, the president," I congratulated her, even as I saw Mama's index finger wagging, and heard her say, "Remember, first and foremost, she's a girl. She's only a girl."

So I try to provide my daughter with the tools of Ibo womanhood, to mold Delia into the sort of woman her grandmother would be proud of—the sort of woman I was raised to be. But even with those simple traditional tasks, my indecisiveness gets the better of me. I teach Delia how to cook, but by using cookbooks, not in the "real-women-cook-by-instinct" approach my mother insisted on with me. I tell Delia I prefer that she wear only dresses, but when she emerges from fitting rooms holding only the pants and shorts from the stack of clothing I sent in with her, I buy her the pants and shorts. I caution her to remember to speak softly, but I pretend not to hear her boisterous voice.

Two years ago, in an attempt to break away from the trappings of my Ibo-ness and my mother's pressures, I presented Delia the blueprint for her adult life. I told my daughter that right after she graduates from college, she's to proceed directly into medical school, do a residency in neurosurgery, and establish her own medical practice; then, and only then, she can begin to contemplate marriage. "And, yes," I told her, "strictly in that order."

Delia asked, "But what if I meet a man that I want to marry while I'm in college or medical school?"

"Both of you will have to wait."

"But Mom! I'll be at least thirty-five years old by the time I'm done," she reminded me. Her voice was suddenly the voice of my mother: "She'll be way past her prime by then; a marriageable girl must be married or at least spoken for before she turns twenty."

"You'll still be able to have children," I said, asserting myself, raising my voice to drown out my mother's and my daughter's protests. Ironically, Mama and Delia often sound identical, although they argue from the opposite ends of the spectrum. Neither experiences any doubts about her place in life; Mama is as traditional as Delia is modern. I'm the one caught in the cross-fire of two divergent cultures.

Minutes later, I began to worry about things my mother would consider important. Whom will Delia marry? Will she let me guide her to a professional Ibo man (even though she neither understands nor speaks Ibo) from a good family, as my mother did for me? Should I follow my mother's advice and send Delia home (to Nigeria) more often, so she'll be adept in the culture and noticed as one who'll be on the market in the near future?

Only my ambivalence remains constant in my approach to motherhood as far as Delia is concerned. For my two sons, Chuka and Obi, on the other hand, there is no ambivalence, no confusion. I am the mother that my mother was to her own sons, geographical and language differences notwithstanding. I've experienced no difficulties in raising male children; I nurture them and teach them exactly what my mother taught my brothers, "Go out there and do the best that you can." I'm confident that I teach them well, and I have no doubt that they'll succeed, whether in the American or in the Ibo context.

Why does raising Delia create such a difficulty? Because I sense that my success or failure as an individual ultimately rests on what becomes of my only daughter. Because each day, each activity, each decision concerning her is a tug-of-war between the old and the new, between my Ibo and American selves, between my mother and me. Because where and when I was growing up, children, especially daughters, accepted their parents' authority completely, without question or resentment. Therein lies my conflict, one that I'm sure is shared by millions of immigrant women who, like me, are raising American-born daughters. We are having to deal with situations that our mothers could not have anticipated.

Sometimes I envy my mother, her straight uncomplicated life. As much as she complained about "today's children" when she raised us, she had no cross-cultural confusions. Her sense of tradition remained intact and unthreatened by Western influence, as mine has become. With only two years of formal education, her frame of reference was limited by her culture: her own mother, aunts, cousins, the church, all spoke in unison when it came to the essence of womanhood. Mama had no ambivalence about her place and she taught her daughters all she knew about life—Ibo womanhood, marriage, children, death. None of what she learned contradicted anything else that she learned: that the essence of womanhood is marriage and children and a good woman knows her place and never leaves it.

That is what I grew up with, and to a great extent, still live with. But, unlike my mother, I continued my education beyond grade school and acquired most of that education in America, in the classrooms and on the streets, from television and books. I know enough not to continue to believe that God intended women to be inferior to men, but I'm so used to living with that understanding that it would be a struggle to do otherwise.

I am my mother in more ways than not. Despite my American education and liberalism, when I was ready to marry I allowed my family to choose a groom who came closest to pre-determined criteria. I let them negotiate and accept a bride price on my head. But I'm as American in my career pursuits as I'm Ibo in my relationship with my husband. While I manage to reconcile the two parts of my life for myself and embody them efficiently, I cannot seem to do the same for Delia. Instead, when I view them in the context of my daughter, those two parts seem to be on a collision course.

Today, I watch Delia racing her brothers on their bikes. She does not cede any ground to them, but actually finishes a hair's breadth ahead of the boys. My urge to cheer her gets caught in my throat as I imagine my mother shaking her head, saying, "That girl needs to be taught that men don't go for aggressive women."

"I finished first," Chuka claims.

"No, I did!" Obi asserts.

The boys argue, and I fully expect Delia to interject and claim her rightful prize, but she gets on her bike and rides away slowly. I catch up with her and ask why.

My Ibo-American daughter explains, "Mom, if it's that important to them, let them believe they won."

I look up and see Mama's face. It's not smiling, because Delia raced and beat her brothers, but it's not frowning either, because Delia let them have their place. I whisper to my mother, "She'll turn out right; your granddaughter will be all right."

Mama's Early Life

Mama need not have worried about me the way I worry about my daughter. Though I struggled and suffered and thought often of rebelling against it, I never had any doubts about how I was supposed to be. That's always been quite clearly defined by Mama. She reinforced it in me every day of my life. She was every inch an Ibo woman.

My mother grew up with no male protection. Her father, named Ani, died five months before her birth. Ogbu, her mother, had already given birth a dozen times when Mama was conceived, but only three girls and a boy had survived past infancy. Ogbu's daughters were already married when Grandfather, a prosperous farmer, fell off a palm tree and was crippled.

Neither Mama nor my siblings and I know much about Grandfather. If the tales I've heard from my maternal cousins are to be believed, Grandfather's physical strength and beauty and sexual prowess were much celebrated in Aku, a medium-sized town in eastern Nigeria where both my parents were born. His *ogbeje* (a man's hut; a woman's is called *ulota*) was a magnet for widowed and divorced young women. But lest I be left with an unfavorable impression of the man who sired my mother, my cousins always remembered to add that Grandfather was benevolent to a fault and couldn't refuse the pleas of the numerous husbandless females who lurked by his hut at night and implored him to father their children. When he became crippled, he was not good for anything. He could no longer walk, and the women sought more virile men.

Grandmother was devastated. Her husband's greatest asset had been his strong body, but now that he was confined to bed permanently, she had to toil and slave to support him and their son, my uncle Ezike. Then she found herself pregnant with my mother.

It should never have happened. Her husband could barely sit up straight. She cried from shame about what would be whispered about her: how she forced herself on a dying man, or even that it wasn't his baby (though everyone knew that no married woman, even those whose husbands were impotent, dared to take lovers). Only Grandmother knew the truth of what happened between her and my grandfather. She hadn't wanted him to do it, but he did it anyway; she couldn't say no and continue to live in his home.

Grandfather died in his sleep when Grandmother was four months pregnant. The life of an Ibo widow is almost unbearable in the best of circumstances, but Grandmother's circumstances were the worst. The women who sat the required twelve days of the initial mourning period scolded and nagged her until she threatened to kill herself. Then they relented, but each time they walked by her mat, they cut their eyes at her and clicked their tongues, a sign of disdain. When the village women's group performed the ritual shaving of Grandmother's hair, they deliberately cut her scalp; she accepted it without complaint, as a sign that her own life no longer had any value. She hardly noticed the hard floor she was forced to sleep on for three months. When she was allowed to leave her hut, she found that her yam and cassava farms had been harvested by someone else and that she and Ezike had nothing to live on. She scavenged for food. Sometimes, neighbors brought tubers of yam; her daughters' husbands helped, though somewhat unwillingly.

It was under this cloud of shame and desolation that Mama was born. Grandmother went into labor in the middle of a stormy night. Her son was fast asleep and she labored alone, too ashamed to ask anyone for help. Her daughter, Omade, was born right after the first cock's crow, but no one heard the infant's cries or her mother's groans. The pelting, unrelenting rain muffled all noises.

Widows lived at the mercy of the village heads, who dictated how their children should be raised. A woman had very little say over her own affairs, and Ezike was considered too young to speak for his mother. Mama's childhood was filled with hunger and abuse at the hands of the villagers and their children who taunted her, calling her the "child who killed her father." No one spoke up in her defense.

Mama's life would have continued without adventure, but the village elder decided, when my mother was five, that she be offered in marriage to *Ojiyi Aku*, the village oracle. Ogbu knew the fate of women who were betrothed to *Ojiyi Aku*. A marriage to the oracle was in name only, for he was but a spirit. It was what became of his wives that my grandmother dreaded. *Ojiyi Aku's* wives were barred from getting married to real men, and throughout their lives, they were the sexual property of all the menfolk of the village, no exceptions. Men would take turns with them, and they had no right to refuse. These women lived in poverty, for they were no one's responsibility. No laws

required that their lovers provide for them, and the women themselves were perennially pregnant with some man's child. No one could
say with certainty who the fathers were, so the children shared the
poverty and shame.

My grandmother had no recourse. Her protests were ignored. No
one listened to women; she was threatened with ostracism if she did
not acquiesce. Ogbu knew that Omade was chosen only because they
considered her helpless and unable to fight them.

In preparation for the "wedding" celebration, the older women in
the village arrived at Grandmother's hut early the morning before to
take little Omade to bathe and prepare her for the rituals. Her head
was shaved and a pinkish dye was rubbed into her skin and scalp, tint-
ing her coloring to a rosy blush. Grandmother knew that she had to
do something to save her daughter from certain doom. I come from a
long line of strong women; the villagers had underestimated my grandmother's resolve. She refused to "sit quietly as a good Ibo woman
should." Unknown to the villagers, she began to plot how to protect
her ill-fated youngest daughter.

Grandmother readied her daughter and together they stole out of
the village before sunrise, hours before the village women were due to
pick her up for the ceremony. They walked the dark pathways, hands
linked. It was still dark when they arrived at St. James Church—the
mission, it was then called. It was at this church that Mama would
later be baptized and auctioned off to her first husband, marry my
father, baptize her first two children, and sit through a requiem mass
for her husband. It is at this church that Mama herself is likely to
receive her own last rites.

Mama says she has only two recollections about this very important day in her life. The first is feeling extremely cold, colder than
she's ever felt in her life (even after spending a winter in New
Jersey). Unclothed as most children were then, she had nothing with
which to shield her shivering body. Grandmother wore only a *patari*,
a short skirt that barely covered a grown woman's pubic area. Her
chest was bare, as was the rest of her. My mother and grandmother
were huddled on the steps of St. James Church when the priest saw
them as he entered to begin preparations for the morning mass.
Sworn to silence until he held a mass each morning, he motioned to
a young seminarian who brought them into the kitchen of the parish
house. In the warmth of that kitchen, they waited until the priest
returned.

"They want to marry my daughter off," Grandmother told the priest through the catechist, a man born and raised in Aku who didn't disapprove of childhood marriages.

"Is that why you're here?" the catechist asked, irritated that a village woman would dare to challenge the men in her village and belittle her culture in front of a foreigner.

"I'm here because I want the white man to save my daughter from this marriage."

"Is your daughter baptized?" the priest asked. Grandmother did not understand what baptism meant, but after a long explanation, she knew that the church had no jurisdiction over little Omade.

"Then baptize her," she pleaded.

"What about your husband? Does he know you want the child baptized?" asked the catechist, acting independently.

"My husband is dead, and the men in our village want to condemn my daughter's life," Grandmother said, looking at the priest though she knew he didn't understand a word she said.

"Woman, there's nothing wrong with an early marriage; what are you saving your daughter for?" The catechist was intent on discrediting this woman, who had interrupted his morning routine.

"I'm not opposed to early marriages. They want my daughter married to *Ojiyi Aku*; you know what that means," she said directly to the catechist, who, after a long exchange with the priest, told Grandmother that they would keep her daughter temporarily, while they investigated the situation.

Mama says that when her mother knelt by her to explain why she had to leave her there, both of them began to cry. "But I want to go home with you," Mama said over and over, not really understanding what was happening. Grandmother held her tightly for a long time, then let go and ran away from the parish house, not looking back at the little girl who screamed for her. That was Mama's second recollection of the day—her immense sadness at watching her mother leave the mission without her.

The catechist and his wife provided a home for little Omade, but grudgingly. He was an "in-between," neither completely Christian nor pagan, and seemingly unable to decide which was more suitable for his needs. He treasured his almost celebrity status of being the catechist— thousands of parishioners and new converts hung on his every word and believed it all to be the gospel truth. He was the only person in a fifty-mile radius of Aku who claimed he could understand the white man. He would never admit to anyone that he didn't understand the priest, who spoke too fast for him to keep up with, more than half the time. No one knew of his fear that someday someone with a good elementary education would come to this town and discover how he improvised when it suited him.

No one could know how hard he toiled to prepare for the three-hour Sunday service sung in Latin, which he did not understand, although he could recite all the words in the Order of the Mass and could sing the Gloria, Credo, Sanctus, and Agnus Dei as well as the priest. But for Sunday sermons, he took matters into his own hands. Although he prepared a sermon that fit with the theme of the scriptures read that day, what he preached had nothing to do with the priest's sermon. According to eyewitnesses, there were many awkward moments. For example, the priest would ask the members of the congregation to raise their hands in response to a question he posed and would see nothing. The congregation would wonder why the priest was gazing at them so intently while the interpreter rattled on.

The catechist, himself a convert, still believed in his traditional practices. He was raised in paganism, and most of his relatives were still ardent followers. Unknown to the priest, he fraternized with men in his village who worshipped their totems and went to their farms on Sunday. He joined in eating the goats and cows used in the villagers' sacrifices; he relished his cavortings with *Ojiyi Aku's* wives in his own village. It was for that reason he was troubled by the situation he now found himself in with the pinkish child the priest had left in his care. He had nothing against the girl; she was only a child. It was the mother for whom he felt disdain. She dared to challenge not only the men in her village, but the whole culture. He considered notifying those villagers of the child's whereabouts, but decided against it. The priest would hold him accountable for her safety.

He watched the girl, the same age as his youngest child, as she groped her way in a strange household. She had stopped crying and spent most of her time outside, staring into the distance, waiting for someone who never showed up. Occasionally, she peered intently, as if she saw something. He had not heard a word out of her mouth and didn't even know her name. He was impatient for Sunday to come once again, so that his responsibilities to the girl would end. The priest had told him as much.

Mama recalls nothing of the days spent in the catechist's household, but the mass that Sunday is still so clear in her mind that it could have happened a few days ago. Early that morning, she was ordered to bathe and to put on a dress of beige calico, a simple A-line, crudely fabricated by an *ndi dua-dua* (a "seamstress" who had no training and whose only claim to the art was that she owned a sewing machine). It was the first dress my mother remembers ever wearing. At the church, she was seated in the front pew with the catechist's family. It must have been sometime between the communion and last blessing that she was ushered up to the altar. She remembers she was lifted onto a table to face the large congregation crammed into the long and narrow church. She shivered, but not from cold this time. She felt more than a thousand eyes boring into her, probing and devouring her.

"We come to you today with an unusual plea," the catechist began. Mama says that the quiet stillness of the church unnerved her. Not even babies were crying. "This child here—" the catechist stopped abruptly, realizing that he did not know Mama's name. "Tell our Christian brothers and sisters your name," he ordered, but if Mama heard him, she showed no sign of it. "Poor child, she's scared, and what girl wouldn't be? She's being forced into marriage to *Ojiyi Aku*. My brothers, can we allow that to happen?"

"No!" they shouted.

"We need a Christian man, an unmarried Christian man, to save this child from that fate. She needs a Christian man to speak for her and take care of her from now on. Do we have anyone ready to take on this work for God?"

The church remained silent. No one answered. Mama's fate hung in the balance.

"Look at her. Look at her face, those eyes, her European nose and those lips. My brothers, look at her color. This child will bear a man some handsome-looking children."

Silence still prevailed.

"Will you sit there while she's returned to her village to be condemned to the kind of life we all know she'll live?"

At that point a thin, haggardly dressed man rose and stood in the aisle. He couldn't have been any more than twenty, but to Mama's little-girl eyes, he seemed old. The man said nothing, but Mama could see everyone's attention had been diverted to him.

"Do you wish to speak, young man?" the catechist asked.

"I want to speak for the young girl," Mama's savior said in a shaky voice. Spontaneous applause followed his announcement.

"Are you free to wed her in the church when she's old enough?"

"Yes sir. I've never been wed. I vow to wed her according to the rules of the church," he stated, his voice strengthened by the support he felt from the congregation.

That same day, five-year-old Omade's custody was turned over to her would-be husband. She was taken back to the parish house where plans about her life were made. Her betrothed promised to perform the necessary traditional ceremonies, including the payment of the bride price on her head. The priest extracted promises that Mama would be enrolled in catechism classes. It was at that gathering also that Omade was given her Christian name. The priest chose it himself after Mama continued to refuse to tell them her name. "Let's just call her Rose, Rosaline," he said, explaining that the name was fitting because of Mama's color (that dye lasted a good three months).

So it was that Mama became Rose, a name she was later baptized with. She was told she was a new person and that her past was expunged. Her Ibo name, *Omade* (My Mind Is Now At Rest), was completely forgotten until Mama was reunited with Grandmother almost ten years later.

Rose walked to her new home. Her betrothed's mother took her around to neighbors' homes, singing the praises of church for finally making her son choose a wife. The older woman treated Mama like her own child, and in a matter of weeks Mama had settled into the household. She neither saw nor heard from her mother. After a few months, she had forgotten everything about her previous life. For three years she was content with what she had.

When Mama was eight, her prospective husband got tired of waiting for her to grow up. He confessed to a church full of worshipers that from the onset, he had watched her as anxiously as one would watch a garden full of precious plants. Each morning, he had looked at her, but she didn't seem to grow—at least, not as much as was necessary to meet his immediate needs.

"My brothers and sisters," he pleaded, his head lowered in penance, "I ask you to relieve me of this obligation, so that I may marry a woman I can live with immediately."

No one said anything at first, but then the catechist asked if anyone else wanted to take over the girl. "She's used goods already!" someone shouted from the back of the room.

"I swear to you that I've never laid a hand on her. She's still a child," her husband replied.

But no one spoke for Mama, even after the catechist gave an extra hour for soul searching. She was once again returned to the parish house where, at last old enough to understand what had happened, she cried, out of shame and loss. She was unwanted: out of hundreds of people in the congregation, no one had taken her in. Worse yet, she was again separated from a woman who had mothered her for years. She had grown to love the woman who bathed her and rubbed palm oil into her skin every night. Mama had not been told when she left for church that day that she would not return to the home of the woman she called nne (mother). Mama never said goodbye and never saw the woman again in her life.

As young as she was then, Mama was nevertheless deeply affected by the disruption in her life, even more than when her own mother left her. Her life was not worth much to anyone, it seemed, and as she once again awaited her fate in the kitchen of the parish house, she wondered what they would do to her next.

Had Mama been taught that she could think for herself, she might have chosen to go home to Ogbu at that point. But she wasn't even sure she had relatives; she may have been told that she was orphaned and believed it.

And then someone came to her rescue. Mama says it was fate, that nothing else could explain what happened. My father, Bernard Edoga, then a college student, was in church that day. He was the first person in the whole town to have gone beyond primary education and was the pride of Aku. The townspeople held him in high regard and were apt to listen to his every word. Bernard was reportedly troubled by what he witnessed in church that day. Try as he might, he could not get the picture of the frightened girl out of his mind. He told people that when he closed his eyes, he could see her fear-ridden face, and that he would not be able to live with his conscience unless he did something.

He returned to the parish house late that Sunday evening. As he waited to be let in, he saw the girl sitting on the steps of the side entrance, the small door that led directly into the kitchen. She was completely immobile, with none of the fidgeting that fills little girls' lives. She seemed deep in thought, but he wondered what an eight-year-old could possibly be thinking about. If she saw him, she gave no indication of it.

Papa told the parish priest that he knew of a convent home for girls in Nsukka, a much larger town, twelve miles from Aku. The

Immaculate Heart sisters ran the home and provided their wards a Catholic upbringing. The girl, he argued, would be given some education, as well as some of the skills she needed in life.

"If she's never to marry, she'll be able to fend for herself," he stressed, convincing the priest that since the church had found it necessary to intervene in her life earlier on, it couldn't abandon her now. From his meager funds, he offered a shilling, enough to get the girl settled in her new home. No one knows if Bernard was just being kind that day, nor does anyone know when he determined that he'd marry and provide for Rose. Mama herself did not know until after Papa died that it was he who saved her from whatever fate awaited her that Sunday.

For Mama, the convent was just another stopover in her transient life. The sisters ran a dormitory-style lodging, and Mama and nine other "orphaned" girls, ranging in age from five to twelve, lived in a long narrow room. Their pallets lined both sides of the room and they were dressed in uniforms at all times: white dresses for school, blue-cotton shifts after school and on weekends. On Sundays, they wore light-blue dresses made from soft poplin. They lived a rigid schedule, waking up at five in the morning, bathing, and getting to church by five-thirty for morning prayers and mass. The orphans then swept, mopped, and dusted the church, and did chores around the grounds of the convent before sitting down for breakfast at the kitchen. They then ran across the soccer fields to the all-boys school, where, by special arrangement, they were allowed to attend classes.

Mama thrived in the convent atmosphere. The quiet life suited her well, for she had grown into a withdrawn, uncommunicative child. She did not like going to school, but no one asked what she wanted; she was the only girl in her class, and no one let her forget it. Math came easily, and though the other subjects were difficult, she labored, knowing that the sisters did not tolerate failure. Her teachers mostly ignored her, concentrating on the boys as they were expected to.

Mama passed through the two years of pre-primary and then started first grade, the real tough part, she was told. She never found out if she could have handled the rigors of elementary school. In her second grade, my father, done with teacher's college and newly appointed headmaster of the very school she was attending, rediscovered Rose and created new turmoil in her life.

Mama's Marriage

Mama still shudders when she remembers the first time she encountered my father. Not quite twelve, she was a second grader in the school where my father had become the headmaster. She recalls how imposing and intimidating he was. She had no way of knowing that she had been promised to him well before their first meeting.

Mama's class was in the middle of an arithmetic test when Papa walked in. As was the rule, everything stopped; the children rose, curtsied, and greeted him in unison. He waved to them to be seated, but remained in the classroom. Mama didn't dare look at his face, but she could tell exactly where he was because of the noise made by his shoes.

His presence unnerved her so much that she stopped writing. She had a feeling, she says, that he was there for her, for something that she had done, and she waited for him to approach her, which he did. More than six feet tall, he towered over her, his shadow cast wide over her notebook, saying nothing. She began to cry out in fear of him.

"Why are you crying?" his voice boomed, alerting the whole class to her state. She said nothing, completely stripped of the power to utter even a sound.

"Rose, isn't it you the headmaster is addressing?" her teacher scolded, trying to score a point with his boss. Still Mama remained quiet, except for her tears, the sign of her long suffering.

"Class stop!" Papa commanded. All pencils were dropped and all eyes turned to where he stood over his future wife.

"I want someone to go to the chalkboard and work out the fourth problem," he announced. But no one stirred. His presence intimidated everyone.

"Rose, go up and do it!" he ordered. Mama says she wished she had died. Her sweat rings were down to the skirt of her dress by then, but Papa was merciless.

"What's gotten into you today, Rose?" her teacher asked, which didn't help matters. But Mama couldn't have gotten up even if she'd wanted. By the time he left the class that day, she was deathly afraid of him. His visits to her class became more frequent from then on; he

seemed to enjoy his power over her, tormenting her. Each visit was
like the one before it: he paced the floor of the classroom and then settled behind her where he stayed until her sobs became too loud. Then
he left the class.

Mama found no solace in her home at the convent, because Papa
became a fixture there too. His presence had never been explained to
her, and it wasn't until the day before she was to leave the convent
that she was told. They informed her then that her tormentor, the
man she feared most in the world, was to be her husband. He had paid
a bride price on her head and owned her completely. There was nothing she could do; there was no running away from it.

My father wanted Mama to leave the convent, the only home she
had known since she was eight, to move to Enugu, the main city in
east-Central Nigeria, 30 miles south of Aku, to live with Mama
Helena, a barren woman who had devoted her life to training other
people's daughters in the art of being a wife. Mama was to be a woman-
in-waiting, a term used to describe adolescent girls, already betrothed
but not yet wedded in church. She was to take lessons in sewing, knit-
ting, cookery, and baking—domestic science, they called it. Mama
Helena, whose sternness was widely known, was already elderly and
walked with a cane when Mama moved into her home. No one consulted Mama; she was to do as she was told.

The driver of the jalopy that transported her from Nsukka to Enugu
took pity on the scared little girl who rode in the bed of the truck.

"Who died?" he asked over and over, yelling to Mama through the
glass that separated them.

"It's her father. Her father died. It's for her father she cries," Papa,
who shared the front seat, told the driver, who shrugged and then left
Mama to her tears.

Mama endured two torturous years with Mama Helena, the woman
who shaped her. She was reminded every day that she was lucky to
have been chosen over others to be the headmaster's wife. Mama did
not feel lucky; rather, she was consumed by a dread of the life with him
that she knew she would have to live. She was told she had to work
extra hard, harder than all the other women-in-waiting. She was told
she was destined for an unusual life, a life of glamor, one that she
didn't deserve. She toiled from cock's crow, when they were awakened,
to darkness. Complaining was out of the question. Mama didn't dare.

My father came to visit one Saturday each month. On those days,
Mama was made to work extra hard; the chairs in Mama Helena's

parlor had to be polished with warmed palm oil and the bare cement
floors were colored with a red polish. She also wore a special dress
that Mama Helena insisted my father purchase for her. Mama
remembers those days with special dread. For a week beforehand, she
was unable to sleep and would cry if anyone so much as looked at her
the wrong way.

"I was scared, really terrified of what could result from any one of
those visits," Mama now confides. She knew that the monthly visits
were Papa's way of checking her progress, not only her learning, but
her physical development as well.

My father had secured her hand by tradition, but he was in no way
obligated to make good on the marriage. He could have decided at any
point before the church wedding that Mama fell short of one of his
requirements. It wasn't unusual then, nor is it unusual now, especially
in instances where the girls married as young as Mama. "I thought she
would grow taller when I married her." Or "Look how her arms swing
too wide when she walks." Or "I don't like the shape her mouth takes
when she talks." These were and still are sufficient reasons for men to
reject their young brides. The man would simply ask that the girl be
returned to her family and he would commence a search for a wife that
suited his needs.

For the young women, however, a rejection could mean the end of
their lives. They were branded "used property," even though it was
known that these girls had never been wives in the real sense. Any
other man who expressed an interest would be told, "Are you the only
man who hasn't heard that she's married? What do you want with
someone else's wife?" The girl, in fact, stayed "married" to the man,
unless her family had the resources to refund the bride price and all
the other money expended on her behalf.

Even if they could return the dowry on their daughters' heads, many
families chose to let the rejected bride "stay for the man" unless there
was another suitor willing to make the refund himself. It was considered safer for a woman to be married, even in name only, than to be a
spinster. What if she took a lover, became pregnant, and had a child?
That concern also kept many girls married to men who had long since
wed other women. If a spurned woman bore a child, the child belonged
to her husband and was entitled to his name and estate as much as any
other child borne in a church-sanctioned union. If, on the other hand,
the woman refunded the bride price, any child of hers was illegitimate,
entitled to nothing from her family, for there were no maternal rights

to inheritance. The child would take on her family name, but he would be followed everywhere he went by rumors of his birth. "*Nwa mkpuke* (A child without a father)" everyone would call him.

Rose lived with the threat of rejection. The fear that the headmaster would find her too short, too slow, or lacking in any of dozens of ways and leave her doomed to a life of rejection and uncertainty nearly overpowered her. But incredibly, Mama labored under an even worse fear: that at each visit, the headmaster would decide that she was grown enough and was finally ready to live with him as his wife.

Her eyes were almost always red before he appeared, like clockwork, at exactly nine-thirty in the morning at Mama Helena's front door. Mama had to open the door to his distinct knock. She fought her instinct to run to the back room and hide, and bravely opened the door. "Good morning, sir," she always greeted him as she curtsied. Her curtsy had to be full, her right knee almost touching the ground. Mama was instructed by Mama Helena, who often witnessed the encounter, to hold the curtsy until Papa authorized her to rise.

He never touched her or showed any desire for her—not that Mama would have recognized it. She allowed him to pass by her to shake Mama Helena's hand. Then, because he was considered an important person, the other girls-in-waiting, in line behind their mistress, cried "Good morning, sir," in unison, before disappearing to do their chores. Papa and Mama Helena would retire to the parlor where she updated him on Rose's progress. Later, from the closed door where she was instructed to wait, she would hear her name called and would open the door and go through what seemed like her death sentence.

Papa chose to consummate his marriage shortly after Mama's four-teenth birthday (she may have been younger or older; her real birth was never recorded and is estimated, based on natural occurrences at the time). Mama was not told of this beforehand. Papa visited on his regular day, but soon after, Mama Helena's household seemed to explode with activity. Mama was dragged to a seamstress who took her measurements for a wedding gown. Since her parents were in no posi-tion to play the part that was expected of them in her wedding, Papa deputized Mama Helena to buy the necessary tools for the *Idu uno* cer-emonies, the part of the wedding reception where the girl's family endows her with the requisites of her household: a set of pans, a mor-tar and pestle, a kitchen knife, cooking spoons, a set of porcelain basins for laundering, later to be used for bathing the children when they came, a sewing machine if the girl's family was comfortable, and a marital bed, the center of her existence, in which she would conceive and nurture the numerous sons she is required to bear. Papa spared no expense for his bride, and on the eve of the wedding, she made the journey back to Aku, her hometown, in a dilapidated lorry with Mama Helena and one of Mama's fellow women-in-waiting in tow. It was only the day before their departure, when Mama Helena called Mama to her room, that she was told what was about to happen.

"Rose, tomorrow we'll leave for Aku; you'll get married to the headmaster the day after," Mama Helena announced outright, not deeming it necessary to break the news slowly or gently.

Mama started weeping and didn't stop till the second week of her marriage. Her tears were not shed because she did not desire to be wed. She cried from her bountiful fear of the unknown. She had been moved from home to home throughout her life and had never felt as if she belonged anywhere. She was moving yet again to another household, a new set of responsibilities and expectations that she wasn't sure she could meet. "A headmaster's wife? So much was expected of me, at home, in his school, in the church, and I was still a child, no older than a majority of his students," Mama explains.

At the altar of St. James Church, Rose collapsed in a satiny white heap when the priest asked her if she took my father as her husband. When she awoke, she was seated in a folding chair and her dress was soaked with the water they threw to resuscitate her. Someone told her that the ceremony was over and that she was now the headmaster's wife.

Witnesses report that Mama's cries were drowned by the noise of the celebration. Because Papa was the headmaster of the only school in town, and the most influential of Aku's citizens, my parents' wedding was attended by all the townspeople as well as those from neighboring towns. Numerous dance and masquerade troupes provided entertainment while thousands of guests helped themselves to the abundant food. Only Mama seemed miserable. She remembers that when the celebrations were over and it was time to follow him to the school quarters where he lived, she fainted again in trepidation, for she then realized that the duties Mama Helena had alluded to were at hand.

Women of Mama's generation were both aware and ignorant of sex. All she knew was that she'd heard of girls who "untied their wrappers too often and too soon." She also heard of women who actually had sex for reasons other than procreation.

Her mentor had a sex education program of sorts. Because a large number of her wards were still too young to menstruate, Mama Helena kept a watchful eye, looking for some indication of a change in their bodies and countenance. She did this for one reason: she was adamant that none of her girls be wed until she had gone through three cycles of menstruation. She reported every detail of the girls' development to their husbands, who then made wedding plans accordingly.

Mama's first menstruation occurred a mere four and a half months before her wedding. Mama Helena, who had calculated and recalculated when Mama's fertile period was likely to be, had told my father when to fix the wedding date. If all went as planned, Mama Helena reasoned, Mama would get pregnant on her wedding night. With any luck, exactly nine months later she'd deliver a boy. The headmaster deserved that at least.

Every first Friday of the month, right after the girls-in-waiting returned from morning mass, each girl had to give a report of her menstrual situation. It could have been funny had the girls only known they were entitled to enjoy themselves.

"Janet!"

"Madam, my visitor came on the 30th and left on the 3rd."

"Agnes!"

"Nothing yet, Madam!"

"Grace!"

"My visitor came yesterday!"

Mama Helena would go down the list to the last of the girls. When she completed her survey, she called on the oldest of the girls to demonstrate personal cleanliness during menstruation. Mama said there were no sanitary pads then, and the designated demonstrator showed them how to tear, fold, and shape perfect- sized rags from their old dresses and wrappers.

"You place it between your legs and you have to walk slowly with your legs tight or it could fall," the girl advised, her voice so faint that all the other girls had to strain to hear.

"You should count yourself blessed if you menstruate once a month. It is a sign that you're ready to start fulfilling your duty in this world," Mama Helena added, ending the session.

Mama did conceive on her wedding night. Her intimate relationship with my father is an area that she never discusses, except to imply that she only did what was necessary to bear children, and that she was lucky and conceived on the first try each time. Like most couples of their era, my parents slept in separate bedrooms. A man who shared a room with his wife was scorned. "He's soft in the head. He sleeps in the same bed with a woman. No wonder he's always preoccupied," people would snicker. A husband, the master of his home, had a big bed in the largest bedroom in the house. His wife slept in a smaller room with the relatives who helped her around the house. When the children came, the mother shared her bed with the latest baby until he or she was weaned off her breast at about fifteen months old. Usually, weaning the baby was a signal to an Ibo woman's husband that she was ready to be invited to his room once more, to begin trying for another child.

There was very little sexual contact between husbands and wives in those days. Parish priests warned against "the sins of the flesh." They admonished husbands to "respect their wives' bodies" and to remember that contact between a husband and wife should be for procreation only. My parents were strong followers of every Sunday's sermon and honored the church's rules. Mama's children were spaced at least two years apart. It was like clockwork. Mama says now, "I don't understand what women see in it (sex). I only let Master do what was necessary when I was ready to have children." I am almost certain that my mother and father lived exclusively by that rule.

Mama says that in their marriage, there were none of the strains and conflicts that mark new marriages. "I knew my place and I never contradicted my master in any way." He insisted that she be a full-time housewife and mother and refused to allow her to take up one of the trades for which she'd been trained at Mama Helena's. Although he had servants to help out, it was understood that everything that had to do with him was to be done by her. She prepared all the food that he ate. She did all his laundry.

"I wouldn't let anyone touch my Master's clothing," Mama boasts. "Even when I was very pregnant and couldn't bend properly anymore, I would place the laundry basin on something and stand up while I washed his clothes." She was the only one allowed to touch his bed, a black four-poster iron bed which had been Papa's first investment after he graduated from teacher's training college. His bed was much grander and more comfortable than the wood bed Mama slept in initially, but it didn't bother either of them. Mama would have felt insulted had he given up his bed for her. "It was his home," she now explains simply.

If he wanted a glass of water and she wasn't there, he would tell a steward to look for her and tell her, "Master wants a glass of water."

She would literally drop whatever she was doing and race to the clay water pot, but only after she'd made double sure that the tumbler was squeaky clean. She would carry the water to his room and curtsy before she handed it to him. While he drank, she waited a few feet away from him, her eyes dropped to the floor the whole time. A clearing of his throat would inform her that he was done and she would inch closer, both arms stretched to take back the glass (she would never extend only one arm, which was a sign of disrespect).

Mama remembers that the worst day of her marriage occurred when Papa refused to eat the lunch she had made for him. She had gone to the market square to purchase a few vegetables for the meal and had run into a friend whose husband was deathly ill. Mama's soft heart had taken over, and before she knew it she had allowed the woman to convince her to stop by to see her husband. Mama admits she didn't think what she did was improper, but would never encourage any woman to openly defy her husband. Everyone in town knew that the headmaster had strict rules for his new bride, which she was not to deviate from without his permission, but Mama had followed the weeping woman home. Unbeknownst to her, she had been sighted by others who felt it their duty to report her trangression to headmaster.

"Where did you go?" Papa, sitting in his recliner at the verandah, asked.

"To the market, sir," she responded without thought.

He let her in without an additional word, but refused to eat his lunch when she laid it out. He merely shook his head and indicated, by a wave of his hand, that he wanted nothing to do with it.

Mama dropped to her knees and started bawling. At first, she didn't even know what she had done wrong, but she knew the exact implication of his refusal to eat the food. Mama Helena had warned her girls. "Never ever create a situation where the man refuses to eat what you cook." It spoke a thousand words, and would be interpreted in many different ways. Mama knew that even as she begged him to forgive her for a crime she wasn't aware she had committed, word of his rejection of her was circulating around town.

"Did you hear what the headmaster's new wife did?" someone was sure to whisper to a friend or neighbor.

"Didn't I know it? Didn't I say that she was too fair for him, a mere child who doesn't know his value? Tell me what the little upstart did," the neighbor would reply.

"Whatever she did, he refused to eat her meal; you know what that means."

"Who doesn't? It's too soon for her to start disobeying him; someone ought to straighten her out."

Mama retraced her steps of the morning and could find nothing wrong. "Master, please forgive me. I'll never do it again." she pleaded, even though she didn't know what she'd done.

"You lied to me. Why did you tell me you went to the market?" he barked at her in front of the large crowd that had gathered to watch the headmaster chastise his wife.

"Tell your husband where you went," one of the gathered interjected, compounding Mama's humiliation. The gathering wasn't unusual; nothing was private between husband and wife, and what concerned one person concerned the whole town.

"Tell your Master, did you go anywhere else?" someone in the swollen group of spectators suggested.

Suddenly Mama remembered what her transgression had been. A feeling of relief overwhelmed her and she broke into a fresh sob.

"Forgive me, Master, I disobeyed you today." She was genuinely contrite as she begged to save her marriage. She remembers the humiliation and fear she felt, kneeling there before him in front of the jeering crowd, crying, petrified her husband would send her away. "How could I have faced Mama Helena?" she wondered, but she was lucky and Papa forgave her. After that, she became extremely careful about where she went and with whom.

Another time, Mama overstayed at a church function. She was aware of time, but she reasoned her Master would certainly understand because she was at the church. A heavy rain started falling as she went home, but she dared not stop for shelter and risk showing up even later than she already was.

"Stand right where you are!" my father's irate voice yelled as she climbed the three steps that led to the verandah. She froze in her spot, torrential rains pelting her scarved head. She made no attempt to get out of the rain until he told her she could go into the house, a good thirty minutes later.

When Mama tells the story, she insists that there was nothing unusual or cruel about his treatment of her. "He was my husband and he was doing what was best for his family. He had to set boundaries." Mama says she would have remained outside in the rain through the night if he had ordered her to. "A woman has to obey her husband at all times."

"The Headmaster Has a Son!"

Mama gave birth to her first child nine months after she was married. She told my father of her labor pains, but in such euphemisms that only skilled ears would understand. A woman never referred to her body in any way. "There's something wrong with me," she claimed.

Papa too recognized the signs and instructed some of the older girls in his household to walk the three miles to the maternity with her. Although Mama was only fifteen years old, it was a relatively easy birth; her wide hips, she was told, were made for delivering many, many children.

"It's a boy! The headmaster has a son!" The midwife on duty was beside herself. What good fortune—to be married and in nine months deliver a baby boy! Although it was two in the morning, she dispatched the maternity messenger on a rickety bicycle up the hill to the secluded area of the school compound where my parents lived. She couldn't wait another minute; it was a boy and the headmaster had to know he had a son. She would not have gone to any trouble for in a girl. In that case, it wouldn't have hurt to wait till morning when she would have probably passed the message along through the school children who attended Papa's school.

Mama's first son was named Charles, for Papa's alma mater, St. Charles Teacher's Training College in Onitsha. Mama remembers a glorious child with a permanent smile fixed on his face. Charles was a golden boy, several shades lighter than Mama's yellowish tinge, and perfectly round.

Mama immersed herself completely in her motherhood and went beyond what was required of her. She doted on her child, and it broke her heart when she had to leave his side, even for a moment. Papa's total care was still her responsibility, and she had to drop even Charles if Papa asked for a glass of water. But she also acknowledges that something began to happen in her relationship with my father. She didn't feel quite as scared of him anymore, and his voice grew softer and gentler, especially when he addressed her.

Papa loved to show off his son, and many afternoons he would return from school during break and instruct Mama to dress Charles up. Then he placed him on his shoulders and took him along on his rounds. My father was over six feet and built as straight as a pole; those who remember back then tell of the tenderness between father and son and of how strange he looked with the drooling baby perched on his suited shoulders. Ibo men are not expected to be involved in their children's lives, and people joked about the headmaster and his son.

Mama says that her son's life became hers and her life became his. Many nights, she was too overwhelmed by her happiness to stay asleep, and she would lift him from his place in her bed and cuddle him in her arms, smothering him with kisses and hugs.

People began to warn her about her relationship with the child. "You're too close to him; you shouldn't get too attached to a child." She was also told that her closeness with Charles would preclude other pregnancies. "Think of the future."

Charles went through a normal infancy, free of even childhood colds. But when he was almost two years, he died suddenly. Mama to this day is heartbroken over it and has never told us the story herself. Rumors have it that Charles was poisoned, although I'm disinclined to believe it, for who would poison a round-cheeked, babbling 20-month-old, who was always surrounded by doting relatives? But in those days, death was very common and most children were lucky to survive infancy. Also, it was easier to explain death by pointing accusing fingers at suspicious-looking neighbors or relatives for whom no one cared.

My cousin, Mama's niece, Mary, told us what happened. Mary, who was considered unlucky because she had a bad marriage, says that Mama was newly pregnant with her second child at the time, and was passing through the vomiting and lethargic stage. Mama turned over the care of Charles to Mary, who, forced to give up her own son to her ex-husband, worshipped the ground upon which little Charles walked. She took the toddler for their morning stroll, for Papa insisted that his son be exercised regularly. They took their regular route, through the yards of the teachers' homes in the Quarters. All the wives expected and waited for them on their verandahs. Not only was Charles a cuddly child, he was also the headmaster's son, and it didn't hurt to be seen paying attention him.

Mary says that all she did was blink, and when she looked around she saw that Charles had wandered into the yard of the only house in the Quarter that they had been told to stay away from. She ran to her ward, but too late. The woman, whom Mary still calls the "barren witch," had Charles enveloped in her arms. She watched while the woman poked and tickled the baby, whose giggles could be heard rows of houses away. She thought it would be cruel to Charles to snatch him away from a woman who was giving him so much joy.

As they walked home, Mary noticed a pasty black substance in Charles' mouth and wiped him clean, believing that he had picked up dirt from the dark soil. He fell asleep soon after they got home and stayed asleep past his lunch and Papa's rounds with him. Mama became alarmed when she felt how hot his skin was. She summoned the neighbor wives, who gathered in Mama's room, offering jars of their most potent *ude aku* (an oil extract from palm kernels, which is mixed with potent extras like garlic, onions, and snake fat). The odor was guaranteed to chase away any illness, but not baby Charles'. When he began to convulse, the stronger of the women held him down, prying his gritted teeth open with a spoon, pouring jar after jar of *ude aku* down his throat.

Someone remembered to send for my father, but by the time he arrived, Charles was laid out, tiny hands folded together and resting on his chest, in Mama's bed. He was dead, gone from their lives, taking from Mama the only happiness that she'd known in the sixteen years of her life.

It was on the day her first born was buried that Mama committed her first act of defiance. She watched from the sidelines, numb and in shock, as her baby's body was bathed and his chubby face, strangely drawn in death, was oiled and powdered. It wasn't really happening to her, she thought. My son, my pride, isn't really dead. She rose, to the protests of all the people in the house, and walked up to where he lay, flattened on a cloth spread over Papa's eating table. His eyelids were held down by a strap of green yarn, as if he were in a blindfold. She stretched out her arm to touch him as if he were alive, but she was grabbed from behind.

"Are you crazy, woman?" an elderly neighbor hissed. "You're carrying another child; do you want Charles to be reincarnated and appear again? Somebody take her away from here."

"The damage is already done!" someone else yelled. "You refused to listen when you were told you shouldn't be so attached to this boy. See, he found out you were having another child, and that's why he's gone, so he could come back again and always be the center of your life."

Mama was dragged away from her child, refused the chance to say her goodbyes. She was told it was the best thing for her; she had to think of the next child she'd bear, not the *ogbanje* (a child who rein-carnates) who was dead. "Let me touch my child!" she wanted to yell out, but even in the midst of tragedy, she had to remember the rules.

Then the issue of his burial clothes arose. Mama instructed Mary to go to the bottom of her trunk, where her wedding dress lay folded, waiting for her own death (Christian Ibo women are buried in their wedding dresses).

"I want him wrapped in this," she said, holding out the satiny dress toward the leader of the women.

"Are you out of your mind?" the woman asked. She looked around the room, acknowledging the support of all the others.

"I want him buried in it," Mama shouted. Unused to insisting on her way, her raised voice was quite unlike herself. Papa, as well as the other men who sat with him, heard her.

"Have you gone mad?" someone yelled just as my father walked in.

"Do exactly as my wife says," he ordered and left.

The room fell silent, and the women worked furiously, readying lit-tle Charles for his journey to his maker.

She watched as the men took him, his arm hanging awkwardly by his side; he was too young for a casket. The wedding gown trailed after them. For months afterwards, that was all she remembered, her child being carted away in the shiny satin on that sunny afternoon.

In those days, children who died before their mothers had another baby were considered too young to be mourned. There were none of the usual wakes or ceremonies. They were buried only hours after their deaths and their mothers were supposed to proceed as if nothing had happened. Mama went through her pain alone and in silence. Her only child was taken suddenly, and she was ordered not to mourn him. Used to obeying all orders, she tried very hard, but her pain was so enormous it almost killed her. Neighbors felt it wise to not sit with Mama, so she'd forget sooner, as if it were only a bad dream.

Despondent over her loss, Mama became sick. Her sickness was rooted in her fear that what happened to her first born would happen to all the other babies who'd follow. Her tears came on the third day and stayed for months, but she only cried alone, in the privacy of her room. No one could find out that she was mourning the "wicked child." Even my father was unaware of the gravity of her pain and offered no help. In his presence, she performed her duties without fail. Nothing had changed as far as he knew, but when Mama was alone in her room, the space that little Charles had occupied stared at her, vacant, and nothing she did could fill the vacuum. She says that whenever she closed her eyes, she could still see him, and every once in a while she heard his laugh in the distance or his attempt to call her name, "Hoz," as he heard his father say.

John was born five months after Charles was buried. Everyone who came to the maternity cringed when they saw him. He was Charles' exact image.

"It's he! Wicked child, hasn't your mother suffered enough?" they said as they backed away from the hospital bed, convinced that Charles was reincarnated and that he was there to torment his mother.

Mama, now 16, was told by older women that unless the child went through an exorcism, he too would die and return again and again. She went along as John was taken to a native doctor, who dipped the three-day-old infant in a gourd full of a greenish substance. He slashed the baby's cheeks with a rusted, dulled razor, leaving two vertical lines, rubbed herbs into the cut, and proclaimed the child cured.

The marks are intended to put the child on notice that everyone is on to him. The common belief is that if the marked child dies and then reincarnates, the marks will be on the newborn and, depending on the region of Iboland, the child could be either discarded or treated as evil all his life. In many cases, when a child suspected of being *ogbanje* dies, his body is mutilated: hands and feet chopped off and ears trimmed before he's buried. Stories abound of newborns sporting the same marks that were made on their deceased sibling. It's strange but true. There isn't an Ibo who doesn't know an *ogbanje* child.

John prospered, but the innocence with which Mama had loved her first son was gone. As much as she tried, she couldn't dive into mothering John with the same zeal and enthusiasm that she had given her first born. She couldn't bear to lose him, too. Mama thinks it ironic that John, the child to whom she gave the least of herself, has given the most back to her.

Mama gave birth to identical twin boys, Anthony and Christopher, two years after John. John was vindicated; he wasn't Charles after all, or if he was, he was scared too early in the game to continue playing.

Mama was extremely lucky she got to keep her twins. At that time in most parts of Iboland, twin children were considered an aberration and were thrown away in the bushes, where they were left to starve or be ravaged by wild animals, or dumped in a well. The rationale for this barbaric act was simple: only animals such as dogs, goats, and cats had multiple births, not humans. If a twin birth occurred, the midwife would call the elders and they would take care of the situation in as hush-hush a manner as possible. The mother had to go through a cleansing ritual to drive off the evil that had possessed her body. If neighbors wondered what became of the pregnancy, they would simply be told that it resulted in a still birth, which raised no eyebrows: still births were more common than live births at the time.

When Mama tells of her luck that her twins' lives were spared, she remembers an incident from her childhood, when she was no more than seven. Mama was on an errand when she encountered two evil-looking men, each holding a newborn, by the legs, upside down. She said it reminded her of chickens ready to be slaughtered for dinner because the men held knives in their free hands and were being led by a group of other strangely irate men into the deep woods. Mama overheard the crowds of women discussing the situation and, without anyone's notice, crawled into the hut where the woman who had given birth lay alone, crying quietly. Mama says she could only understand a question the woman repeated over and over again. "Why me? Why me?" She felt the woman's pain in a way that she had not felt anything before and claims she knew then that it was her destiny too, to give birth to twins. She did twice.

By the time the first set of twins was born, my parents no longer lived in Aku, their hometown. Papa had been transferred to a larger school district where paganism was threatening to drive away the forces of Christianity. He was a tough man and if anyone could control the situation, it was he.

Enugu Ezike, their new station, was a sprawling town of more than a hundred thousand people. My parents lived in the school compound, but Papa's influence went beyond the school gates. Many remember him as a stern-looking man who walked around town holding a cane in his hand. He used the cane on errant children, his pupils or not. "The headmaster is coming" became a favorite saying of mothers who wanted their children to do their chores or simply toe the line. Papa didn't wait to be invited into a home. If he sighted boys running aimlessly, he gave them six whips of the cane before dragging them to their grateful parents. In no time, he captured the heart of the town.

Mama's twin pregnancy had not been diagnosed. There was really no way of knowing. Yes, her tummy did seem excessively large, but the midwives had not attended her previous births and had nothing to compare it with. There were no doctors within an 80-mile radius of

Enugu Ezike, and the midwives in the maternity had little training, not much beyond a primary education, and six months of internship with another midwife. They couldn't tell a baby's heartbeat from the mother's.

The midwife went into shock when it became apparent that there were two babies, but she quickly recovered. Soon thereafter, Papa's only sister, Alice, who had brought Mama to the maternity, walked into the delivery room. Whatever thoughts crossed the midwife's mind about notifying village elders about this birth were pushed to the background; her patient was the headmaster's wife and she would let him deal with the situation himself.

"Two boys," she said calmly to Aunt Alice.

"Two? Are you sure?" Aunt Alice was as aware as anyone of the implications of this birth.

"Send for the headmaster before news of this birth spreads; I'm getting off duty right now," the midwife said as she fled the scene, fearful about what the villagers would do to her if they found out. Other patients in the maternity followed suit, afraid of what might befall them.

Mama says that the time she spent alone, still on the delivery table, while Alice ran the six miles to get Papa, was the longest of her life. She lay on her side, her eyes glued on the two boys lying in the cot next to her. The twins were swathed together, head to foot, in one of Mama's wraps. They whimpered intermittently, but she was unsure of what to do. She knew she had to wait for her Master to come and decide everyone's fate. All she could do was pray that God would give her husband the courage to stand up to the villagers and fight to save their twins' lives.

Papa arrived in good time. He burst into the delivery room just as the villagers started trickling in. News spread fast in those days, and it was known throughout town that the headmaster was about to engage in a showdown, a ferocious battle of wills with the elders.

Papa had come well armed. He brought the entire school population, hundreds of boys ranging in age from ten to twenty and more than twelve teachers. They circled the maternity, forming a barricade, shielding Mama and her infants with their bodies. The school choirmaster thought it wise to keep the students occupied and started conducting church songs. The children's raised voices were heard miles away by villagers who pondered the disaster the headmaster's stunt would bring on their town.

But the anticipated battle did not ensue. The villagers who had come dispersed, shaking their heads in amazement. They had never seen anything like that before. Indeed, Papa's foresight in bringing his students meant that many villagers could have had to battle their own children. When nightfall came, Mama rode home in a makeshift stretcher which rested on the shoulders of four of the biggest boys in the school. Her twin boys were nestled in the warm arms of adoring relatives. She couldn't believe her good fortune. Her twins' lives were spared. Her husband saved them—and her.

Mama Wants a Trade

Mama, who was eighteen when the twins were born, says that's when she finally began to feel secure, if not comfortable, in the fifth year of her marriage. She had not one, not two, but three living sons and the prospect of having many more. She started to gain Papa's confidence, and many evenings after the protracted evening prayers and dinner, he invited her out to the verandah to chat with him. She mostly listened, unless he asked her a direct question, but even then, she only provided as many words as were necessary, for as Mama puts it, "What good is a woman's input?" She still wasn't completely at ease in his presence and preferred her children's company to her husband's.

This was when Mama began to think about what she wanted out of life for herself. Her husband was the headmaster, the most prosperous man in town. He clothed her in finery. He spared no expense with her, and she had more than she could ever use, but she wanted more. She wanted to do more than keep the headmaster's home and raise his children, but she was still afraid and didn't know how to approach him.

Mama was already skilled in a general sense. Her two years at Mama Helena's had prepared her for many of the trades that were open to women. Her housekeeping skills were impeccable. Important people in town raved about her cooking. She was better trained than most seamstresses in town and she knew that her position as the headmaster's wife would bring her business.

Mama finally found the courage to ask and she had orchestrated the occasion skillfully. She cooked Papa a special dinner, came in after he finished, and knelt by his uncleared table.

"Is something wrong?" Papa was baffled by her behavior. Mama was extremely shy and not one for theatrics. She had to be troubled.

"Please forgive me for interrupting your evening, but there's something that I want to ask you." Mama kept her eyes lowered and her voice down. "I want to start doing something!"

"You don't think you do enough?" Papa either misunderstood or pretended to misunderstand her request, prolonging her agony.

"I mean like trading or sewing."

"Why? What's wrong with things as they are now?" He looked puzzled as well as irritated at her.

"Nothing, sir, but I finish all my work in no time, and I have a lot of free time on my hands."

"Who put you up to this? Which of the women is teaching you to disobey me?" He rose from his seat shouting, alerting the entire household that something was amiss between Master and his wife.

Upon sensing his anger, Mama said no more and fixed her stare on the floor, awaiting his judgment. Mama espouses the virtue of patience as the most important ingredient in any marriage. She boasts that she never showed impatience with my father even in moments when others felt she was justified to. "A woman must always remember that her husband is the man of the marriage, no matter how angry she is," she says in explanation.

Two weeks passed before Papa addressed the issue again. "Tell me exactly what it is you want." His voice had an edge that Mama notes was not anger, but a kind of frustration. She believes that he desperately wanted to understand the needs of his teenage wife.

"Nothing, sir," Mama replied, not quite sure what answer was expected of her.

"What is it that I've not provided you that you wish to obtain by pursuing your own trade?"

"Nothing, sir. I have more than any woman can hope for."

Mama started crying, but as much as all her instincts demanded that she apologize and tell him she no longer had any interest in a trade, she held on. Something outside of her took control of the situation.

"What trade would you take up?" Papa asked at last. Those who knew my father well believe that was a major step for him. He was a traditional man who strived all his life to provide his family with the best of everything. His wife was to do as he pleased, be available to attend to his every demand, and dote on his children. Papa may have agreed to Mama's demands to teach her a lesson about life, for he extracted promises from her that his household would continue always, without disruption, and that if he should at any time be inconvenienced by her profession, she would abandon it. She agreed wholeheartedly for she truly believed she could do it all.

Mama's first daughter, Virginia, was born when she was twenty, two years after the twins, soon after she began her career as a seamstress. Her Ibo name, *Oliaku* (One Who's Born to Enjoy Her Father's Wealth), was a statement both of my father's joy and of his economic status.

Mama was truly glad to have a girl, because people were beginning to wonder if her tummy held only boys. "What a shame! No one will be bringing bride prices to your family," they teased her. An Ibo woman's life is complex! If she had no boys, she would have been sent home, but not having girls had its own problems. It's always the woman's problem, never the man's.

Mama offered a mass in thanksgiving; she'd fulfilled more than half of her obligation to her marriage. All that was left for her to do was to raise those children while continuing to serve her husband.

She took only a few weeks off from her seamstressing when her daughter was born. In fact, Mama's shop was right in her verandah. That was how Papa wanted it; no wife of his would sit in the market all day like a common hawker, soliciting clients. Anyone who required Mama's service would come to her house; that was that. And come they did. Women arrived in droves to be measured and outfitted by the headmaster's wife. Mama sewed simple attire, mostly women's blouses and children's dresses. She did not sew for men or boys; it just wasn't appropriate. Soon, Mama was so busy she began to need help in her business. At first, the solution came from within the household. Mama simply recruited female cousins who, due to bad marriages or their parents' poverty, lived with the headmaster's family, and started teaching them the trade. But before long, people from the outside sent their betrothed daughters and wives to Mama to train, not only in sewing, but also in the art of wifely duties. She was on her way to becoming a "Mama Helena."

Mama says that at first she was terrified of this enormous responsibility. She was barely out of her teens and felt inadequate; how could she, only six years into her own marriage and still groping to find her niche, take on such a challenge? Papa encouraged her to start the program, like the one she had gone through herself.

Still, she was unsure. But then Mama Helena stamped her approval. "It's an honor that you shouldn't refuse," Mama Helena told her.

Mama's training school for girls began when she was pregnant with her second daughter. She started with seven resident girls, all betrothed to local men. It was a great challenge for Mama to impose her will on others. At night when she retired, she practiced being stern in front of her hand-held mirror. It was extremely difficult for her because she had never been in a position of any authority. She had always done as she was told, even in her own household. But with a house full of girls who completely depended on her direction, she had to assume a toughness, an intimidating countenance, as she had seen in Mama Helena. The girls had to be afraid of her, of what she would tell their husbands.

With Papa's permission, Mama opened a shop in the center of town, not so far from the school that Papa or his surrogates couldn't spy on her, but at a strategic location, which every woman who was likely to want a blouse made would surely see. She prospered; the shop grew and the number of Mama's trainees increased at such a rate that she kept a waiting list of applicants.

She didn't accept just anyone. The woman's husband had to be an upstanding Christian, a regular dues-paying member of the church, who was seen receiving sacraments on a regular basis. The girl herself had to meet Mama's own requirements. On the day her husband brought her for an interview, she would be given a bucket and a rag and told to clean the house. Then, she cooked lunch for the other trainees, whose comments would count towards Mama's final decision. Twenty girls were under Mama's care when Martha was born. Her Ibo name is Uzoamaka—literally, My path is well paved, but a name which expresses that for the child's parents, life is perfect. "We have everything we could ever want." Mama was then twenty-two years old.

At the end of each month, when Mama completed her accounts for the business, she delivered what amounted to her profits to Papa. She asserts that it was, and is, the right thing to do. "Your husband owns you and everything you own," is her simple explanation. Although there were times when her net profits were almost as large as Papa's headmaster's wage, she never forgot her lowly position. "Because it was by his authority that I did whatever I did. If he chose to, he could have closed down my shop any time he wanted."

She always took the money to him late at night when everyone else was asleep. It was one of the rare occasions on which she would go into his room, uninvited. As was her practice, she would knock and wait for his permission to enter. She always remembered to kneel before him first, and then hold out the saucer containing the pounds and shillings and pence in her two hands.

At first, Papa refused the money. "What would I do with a woman's earnings?" He acted insulted, although he was pleased that his wife didn't make it necessary for him to ask for it. Mama insisted, leaving the money in his room for days, until he relented.

It was 1951. The seven Edogas lived in the school compound at Enugu-Ezike. Papa's influence was growing. Mama had a successful business. John was six years old and already showing signs of his brilliance. Anthony and Christopher were four years old; Virginia was two, and Martha was a baby.

"The Honorable"

Papa, naturally a politician, decided to vie for political office. At this time in the early 1950s, wheels were in motion to gain Nigeria's independence from Britain. Each of Nigeria's four regions, including the eastern area of Nigeria where we lived, set up an Assembly. Our region, which later came to be known as Biafra, is east of the Niger River, which separates it from the crowded southwestern section of the country. Lagos, the former capital, is located in the southwest and is populated by Yorubas. The north is populated by Hausas and Fulanis.

Members of the assembly were chosen in elections held every two years. Papa and Mama campaigned hard, canvassing villages, talking to elders and everyone else who would listen. Mama says she spent the entire year of that campaign in the kitchen, cooking for and serving delegation after delegation of possible supporters. Politics in Nigeria is much more than who can do a better job. It is everything: who serves you the better meal, whose wife curtsies more humbly, and who doles out the most money.

Papa lost that first election because he refused to offer bribes. He told people they should vote for the better candidate and they did; the other candidate was better at handing out money. Mama says he was devastated and humiliated. His arrogance had cost him a position he desired, so he regrouped and waged a fiercer battle the second time around. He won, and their lives changed forever.

Papa became "Honorable," and Mama Nwunye Honorable (the Honorable's wife). In addition to his duties as headmaster, Papa had to travel sixty-five miles each way to attend Assembly meetings at Enugu, the regional capital, two weekends each month. He was gone a great deal, for even when he was home, he was busy meeting with his constituents or running voter-education programs throughout the area he represented. He took the job very seriously.

By the time Mama realized it, Martha was more than two years of age, well past the acceptable time to begin trying for another child. Papa seemed too preoccupied to notice, and Mama, had she wished things different, knew it wasn't her place to address the situation. She waited and waited, and Martha turned three. It was at that point that she decided she wasn't going to have any more children.

It was a hard decision, for a woman didn't decide such things; a woman didn't own herself and therefore couldn't decide to stop having children. Five children were too few for most families at that time, but maybe, Mama reasoned, it was the way God wanted it. She dove into her work and her motherhood, spoiling Martha excessively. When people asked her why she was letting the child do things that were potentially harmful, she dismissed them with a wave of her hand. "Let her be a child. It's not as if I'm going to have another one."

People wondered about their situation. Why wasn't the headmaster's wife pregnant yet? Maybe she had a problem, they whispered. Many suggested that she consult a native doctor; others offered her mixtures that would guarantee a desired result. She listened politely, but discarded their advice or potions the minute they left.

Mama Helena arrived without notice. "Is something wrong with you? When was your last monthly visitor?"

"Madam! My monthly visitor came last Wednesday!" Mama answered with affectionate good humor, thrust back to her sex-education classes more than a decade before.

"Is something wrong between you and Honorable? Rose, you're not refusing to fulfill your marital duties, are you?"

"No, Madam, nothing is wrong. Maybe this is just the way God wants it." She had almost managed to convince herself of it. Mama Helena left only after Mama promised to offer a novena for the situation. No one bothered to consult Papa; everyone took for granted that it was a woman's problem.

Meanwhile, Papa bought, as Mama calls it, a pleasure car. It was a two-door Opel, the only car available to would-be buyers in eastern Nigeria. His was the first and only car in town and almost in the entire region. Everyone knew who owned the car and where it was last seen or heard. The villagers even composed a song about the noise generated by so small an object.

Then Martha turned four, and several nights later, Papa invited Mama to his bedroom. She thought he had something to discuss with her, but he told her to blow out the lantern, his code for her to get into bed. Mama remained standing where she was, saying nothing, doing nothing.

"Do you have your monthly?" he asked, unsure of her behavior. In the number of times they'd shared his bed, she always did as he commanded. If she derived any pleasure from their encounter, he was unaware of it. He never asked, and she would rather die than say a word about sex. He read her shrug as an affirmation and sent her back to her room.

He allowed her five days and invited her back. Mama did in fact have her period on the second invitation and told him so. He looked puzzled, but said nothing. On his third invitation, Papa exploded in anger. "Do you want me to beg for what is mine?" Mama said nothing; her downcast eyes filled with tears.

Papa summoned Mama Helena, who was now livid. "Are you aware of what you're doing?" She circled Mama's seat, waving her finger in her face. "You're committing a mortal sin; you're causing Honorable to harbor evil thoughts in his mind." Mama lost her composure and began to cry loudly, her sobs shaking her body.

"God filled your tummy up with children, Rose," Mama Helena continued. "Do you know how lucky that makes you? Look at me, past the age, yet the one thing I would give everything for is a child. You, who are so blessed, refuse to allow the children to form and be born. I've begged the Honorable to give you another chance; after that, he'll send you packing. Is that really what you want?"

Of course that wasn't what she wanted, but no one had sought to find out why she had disobeyed her husband. Mama says that if she'd had any hopes about a woman's worth, that incident dashed them for good. She was her husband's property to do as he commanded, no questions asked. The next time he invited her to his room, she dutifully turned out the light and quietly slid next to him in his bed.

She didn't get pregnant after the first try, as was her experience, nor after the second. She began to wonder if she had become barren, or if it was really God's will after all. But then she became pregnant after the third cycle of trying and my parents returned to their celibate state.

From the onset, this pregnancy was different from all the others. She first blamed it on the gap between this pregnancy and her last, and then on her age: she was the ripe old age of twenty six. Everyone who remembers says that Mama was sick the entire length of the pregnancy. It began with the normal morning sickness, but her nausea lasted all day long and for six months. Then she was always out of breath and fainted constantly.

Papa took her on a journey to Enugu to see a "specialist" physician who treated members of the Assembly. No one remembers what this doctor was a specialist in, but probably in everything, since Papa himself went to him for his ailments. It was the very first time Mama was attended by a physician, and his gender made her uncomfortable. No man other than her husband had ever seen or touched higher than her knees. But this doctor, a red-faced European whom Mama remembers as speaking through his nose, had her lie on her back with her legs spread and held back. This was certainly worse than trying to conceive a child, for the light was bright and an attendant peered down at her. Mama said she closed her eyes and took deep breaths, which worked then, as it always did on the nights she performed her wifely duties with Papa.

"You're going to have twins," the doctors told her through the nurse interpreter. She was also diagnosed with raised blood pressure, gestational diabetes, and carrying two breech babies. Unable to understand the gravity of her situation, Mama was ecstatic at the chance of having another set of twins. Two babies were twice as desirable as one and she would attain her dream of ten children sooner. Also, she was no longer worried about her twins being taken from her. Since her first set of twins, the Nigerian government, still under British rule, had not only banned the slaughtering of twins, but had aggressively enforced the new policy. Midwives had been retrained and villagers were threatened with hangings if any infants were killed.

In her seventh month, Mama swelled up from head to toe. Family members remember how she looked: like a helium-filled balloon that was ready to burst at any minute. Her joints disappeared and even the easiest tasks became impossible. She could no longer close her hand to grasp anything. Her lips puffed out to the size of sausages, making speech impossible; to communicate, she gestured with her arm, when she had the strength to lift it. My oldest brother John, who was then ten, says Mama's coloring changed from her usual yellowish tinge to a pale watery gray. She looked like death.

Papa once again sought help, and this time she was taken twenty-five miles away to the Bishop Shannahan Hospital in Nsukka, the only hospital in the division. (Nsukka town was the headquarters of the Nsukka division which included Enugu-Ezike, Aku, Adani, and Ogrugu.) Mama waited out the rest of the pregnancy. Mama says that something happened to her as she was lifted out of the house that had been her home since John was an infant. Her body felt chilled, as if someone had dumped a bucket of ice water on her. She felt like she was leaving her home permanently, that she would never return to it again. As much as she could turn her neck, she did, taking in her gardens tended by her Master's students, especially the pink roses planted by a visiting school inspector in honor of the headmaster's wife. She looked at her children, holding on to the relatives that would take over their care. No one, not even the doctor who visited her at the hospital every Monday, thought she had a chance. Neither he nor the nurses could remember ever seeing anything like it or reading about anyone else with similar symptoms.

Mama says my father was beside himself. "I should have left you alone. Maybe God is punishing me for insisting that you have more children," he confessed at her supposed deathbed.

But Mama, long since reconciled to her fate in life and totally accepting of it, no longer resented his impositions. What now mattered was the end result, and who could ask for more—her twins were worth everything. The twins, of whom I'm one, were to be her crowning glory, the symbol of her fortitude. My father promised her that if she came out alive, with or without live babies, he would never again impose himself on her. In fact, he promised to perform the *efi ukwu* ceremony to honor her fertility. *Efi ukwu*, still an honored tradition in most parts of Iboland, is usually done after a woman has delivered her tenth live child (as long as at least one of them is a boy; if a woman has ten girls there is nothing worth celebrating). For most women, it is a signal to stop bearing children, for people would say of her, "What else does she want? She's had her cow." A cow (*efi*) is slaughtered and used in the celebrations. My father could, if he wished, declare that his wife deserved such honors. It was rare, but some men, especially prosperous ones, have cut corners and celebrated before the tenth delivery. Papa was ready to declare Mama's seven babies, if she survived with the twins, equal to ten children.

But then, a month before the twins were due, my father died suddenly. He died without warning. He just died.

Mama loves to tell the story of their last occasion together. It was on a Thursday, two days before Papa died. He had come to visit her in the hospital as he did every few days. She really didn't expect him to come daily because Enugu-Ezike was twenty-five miles of unpaved road away, a stretch of road known to be infested with dangerous robbers. She was content with his twice-a-week visits.

On the last day he came, Mama says he didn't look well to her. She had nothing to compare it with, since Papa had never had so much as a cold in the thirteen years they'd been married. Besides, she wasn't likely to trust her eyesight, since her lids were practically swollen shut. Papa moved his chair closer to her bed than usual and took her puffy hand.

"Rose, I have to tell you what you've meant to me, just in case I never have a chance to tell you this again." Mama said his face was very intense and that he leaned over her, displaying love for her, his wife, in a way that he'd never done before.

"You were a child in more ways than one when I brought you home, but you've held up, in spite of all the ups and downs. I could never have asked for a better wife." He continued to hold her bloated hand, even to caress it, which filled Mama with embarrassment.

"I have a strange feeling that one of us has to go. In fact, I've felt this way for several weeks now. I've prayed a great deal, Rose, not to thwart God's will, but to plead that if one of us has to die, let it be me."

"How can you wish that? What do you think will happen to me and the children if you should die? How can you think that I, a mere woman, can raise these children without your support?" Mama became charged with energy she didn't know she still had. She was defiant, refusing to accept whatever he said, as was her practice.

"Listen to me carefully, Rose. I've given this a great deal of thought, and there can't be any other way. You're a very strong woman. You're a stronger person than I am. You have the kind of strength that will last you a lifetime. I know that if I die, you'll raise the children just as well as we would have together. I'm not sure I could raise them by myself and get the same results."

"None of us is going to die. The doctor says that as soon as I have the babies, I'll be all right." She was becoming scared by his talk. He had never spoken to her like that before. Something must have happened to him in her absence.

"Have faith in God. Let that be your guide, and don't change!"

Those were his last words to her. He said them as he was walking away from her bed. He almost didn't say them; they occurred to him almost as an afterthought, after he had opened the door to the isolation room where she was kept. She remembers him standing there in his dark suit, as erect as if he were conducting a students' assembly. Only his eyes were soft and, if Mama could trust her sight, clouded with tears.

On that day, she hadn't strained to look at him with a particular interest. She believed something might be wrong with him, but she had no way of knowing when he walked out of her hospital room that he would never come back, that she would never again see him, that Papa, her husband, my father, would be gone from her life forever. Papa died on Saturday, barely thirty-six hours after he opened his heart to Mama.

"My Life Ended When They Buried My Master"

On Sunday, the day after my father died, Mama was still immobilized in her hospital bed with no real hope of recovering. Because it was a Sunday, the hospital was full of relatives visiting their loved ones. Mama was not allowed any visitors other than Papa, because the nurses felt that it would exacerbate her high blood pressure. From the window of the isolation ward, where only she lay, she could see throngs of people passing up and down the passages that linked the different buildings. Their chatty noises drifted to her, intensifying her loneliness. Mama remembers crying for days on end in that hospital because she so missed her children. Only John, the eldest, had been brought by Papa once. The others were too young to visit an isolation room. Papa usually visited on Sundays, but he hadn't come yet.

Mama waited, her eyes glued to the window, from which she could clearly see the only paved street in Nsukka. Right after lunch, she saw my father's car drive past the hospital, heading into town. She waited for him, but hours passed, and he did not show. When she saw the car pass several more times, she became concerned. Why would he be in town and not come to visit her? Had something happened to one of the children? Maybe he didn't know how to face her.

Mama waited anxiously, but all she could do was cry. About two hours after she first saw the car, the matron of the hospital came into her room, closely followed by nurses. They tried to make small talk and tease her about her tears, but Mama suspected something was terribly wrong. The nurses took their assigned positions, surrounding her bed, watching her every move.

Then Marcel, Papa's nephew who had doubled as his valet and driver, stumbled in. Marcel was a young boy when Mama married and had lived with them ever since, so although only a few years separated them, Marcel was like one of her sons, and she cared deeply for him. His swollen face told a different tale than the one his lips insisted on, but Mama played along.

He brought a note, he said, from Papa to her. The note merely said, "I want you to come with Marcel to Enugu to see another doctor."

Whoever had planned the deception was obviously not aware that Mama did not read English and that her master would have known that. If he had a message for her, he simply passed it on orally. He had never written a note to her, and if he had, it would certainly have been in Ibo. The handwriting was clearly not Papa's, even Mama could tell that, but before she had a second chance to look at it, one of the nurses snatched it out of her hands.

"Marcel, tell me what has happened!" Mama cried from her hospital bed, fear gripping her, racing her heart. She still does not know where her strength or voice came from that day. She, who had not risen from her bed for weeks, even for the basic necessities, suddenly had to be restrained by six people.

"Nothing, madam; nothing happened," Marcel said in a well-rehearsed tone.

"Who died? Is it one of the children? Which one of them is it?" Her voice rose steadily until it became hysterical, and passersby started to gather. All of a sudden, she felt as if she were in a bowl and thousands of people were hanging over its rim. She kept screaming, not really knowing why or for whom. It was all she could do to keep from going crazy. Her heart felt as if it would burst, and she wished someone would end her torment and tell her what had happened. It couldn't have been worse than anything she'd been through before.

She felt a syringe jab her upper arm as a nurse explained that she had to be sedated. The medication worked fast; seconds later, she was staring, unfocused, straight in front of her. Then her mind began to play games with her. She knew exactly what questions she wanted to ask, but every time, just before she framed the question, it disappeared. Her lips and eyelids felt weighted, and moments later, she caught herself dozing against her will.

She woke in the back of a converted Land Rover, a vehicle donated to the hospital for use as an ambulance. The stretcher in the back took up most of the room, but in the haze, Mama could make out two nurses with her. The terrain and the bumpy unpaved road told Mama that they were not headed to Enugu.

"Marcel said the Honorable wanted him to pick up someone who would help you at the hospital," one nurse explained when she noticed the confusion in Mama's eyes. She closed her eyes again and waited.

They got to Aku at sundown. Mama said that although she was strapped down to the gurney and could barely see through the window, she could sense that hundreds of people lined the roads, as they would for a celebration. Occasionally, she could make out people wailing, but she didn't hear what they said. The Land Rover came to a stop at Papa's family compound where not less than twenty thousand people had gathered, and as if on cue, everyone started wailing. It was thunderous, like nothing she had heard before, although she had been in many death houses.

The nurses helped Mama to sit up. It was then that she knew her husband had died. Maybe somebody told her. Maybe she heard the songs of death in their cries. Or maybe she knew that the throngs couldn't be for anyone else. Mama doesn't remember. She just knows that all of a sudden, she knew that her husband, my father, the man who had raised her and given value to her life, was dead and her own life was over.

She does recall the strong arms that supported her as she was led, past the screaming throngs of mourners who surged to touch her, to the room where Papa lay in state. She remembers the brightness of the candles and the shadow they cast on Papa's face.

It's not he, she remembers thinking. This isn't the man I married. "Your father couldn't and wouldn't just lie there."

She looked at him intently, searching for clues that everyone was wrong and it was someone else's husband, not hers. Although no one is certain, and there are no records to confirm it, Papa died from a massive infection, resulting from a ruptured appendix. But before she knew it, and she was being led away, taken to another room that had been prepared for her. In her state, she was not expected to sit on the bare floor at the foot of her husband's deathbed, as was customary; all that would come later. Even the villagers agreed that her condition demanded some exceptions, until she was free of the load she carried.

Mama says that her heart broke when she saw John, her oldest son, at the head of Papa's bed, standing guard over him as first sons do. He was pensive, older than she remembered, his dried tears leaving chalky white lines on his face. John did not show any signs that he saw Mama, so she let him be.

Mama never got to say goodbye to Papa. She never saw his body again. She was in shock and in a daze. It may have been the lingering effects of the tranquilizers, but she says that in the first hours following her discovery that Papa had died, she felt nothing—no pain, no fear, nothing. Her children were brought in to see her, and she remembers thinking, "Poor things, your lives are really over, but you don't know it yet."

They clung to her swollen limbs, and although a part of her wanted to reach out to them, she was too numb to do so. She watched as her attendants dragged the children out of the room, although they cried that they wanted to stay with their mother. She let her mind focus on other things. She worried, but not about what everyone would expect her to worry about, about how she would continue living now that her master was gone. Mama worried about whether her children had been bathed and fed dinner. Her mind simply pushed the bigger worries to the background and she waited.

John sneaked into her room late that night, when he was told to take a break from his watch. Mama lay in the dark, for the only candle that lighted the room was by the window, closer to the door. The nurses were all gone, leaving Mama alone with her thoughts.

John went straight to Mama's bed, and sat at the edge of it, as an adult. Mama says that it was her son, not she, who spoke first. He was several months away from his eleventh birthday, but Mama recalls that on that night, he seemed much older than his years. John put his arms around Mama's middle, as much of it as he could reach, and started to cry quietly. Mama joined him, at first because he sounded so pitiful she couldn't help herself. But when he began to speak, she started to cry in earnest, for the gravity of the situation cut through the numbness and shock and she became fearful.

"What are we going to do, Mama? What are we going to do now?" John asked repeatedly.

Mama did not answer. She had not even begun to ponder the question and had no idea what would happen to her and her children.

Mama knew it was customary that a widow mourn her husband by literally sitting at home for at least a year. *"Ikwadi"* (mourning a husband) is a tedious process, designed specifically to punish the widow, who is assumed to deserve nothing better than her husband's fate, death. It begins the day the husband dies, while he lies in state. The wife, in many parts of Iboland, must pass the night in her husband's bed, beside his cold, stiffened body. In full view of curious onlookers, the widow is taunted and commanded to put an arm or a leg across her husband. "Show us how the two of you did it!" the onlookers may jeer. Sometimes, a widow is locked in the room alone with her husband's corpse.

After the man is buried, her head is shaved and she sits and sleeps on the bare floor for the first year. She eats (very reluctantly) there and is only excused, not too frequently, to take trips to ease herself. The woman is not allowed to bathe or change from the black clothes she buries her husband in. In more lenient areas, she is permitted to take occasional baths, but only at night when everyone is asleep.

The ritual has proven too strenuous for many widows, who die within weeks of their husbands. Ibo women have a saying: "If I can survive my first year of widowhood, I can do anything." Mama was quite sure that in her bloated state, no one would force her to perform any of the rituals, but she was also aware that she had no one to speak up in her defense. Her husband was gone and her sons were too young to take his place. Who would make all the decisions about their lives?

John stayed with her through the night, mother and son crying together. She had no clue about what to do next. Who takes over the care of her children while she's in the hospital? Who makes sure that they're fed? What happens to the furniture in Enugu Ezike? Her mind was filled with a hundred questions, and there was no one she could ask. Her Master had taken care of everything. She didn't know how she could go on.

Mama had to be rushed back to the hospital early the next morning, before Papa was even buried. The nurses said that her blood pressure had risen past the acceptable level during the night and that she could have convulsions or, worse, a stroke. They carried her past thousands of mourners to the dilapidated Land Rover.

"Where are you taking her?" many from the crowd called. Mama could hear comments about how she'd connived with the hospital to save her from the traditional ceremonies.

"She's very sick. We need to get her back to the hospital," one of the nurses said to the crowd that surged toward the car.

"Isn't that her husband's body lying there? So what if she dies? She wouldn't be the first widow who died mourning her husband. She certainly is no greater than her dead husband," one of Papa's relatives said as he blocked the door of the truck with his bulky frame.

"The headmaster made this nobody female into somebody, and she doesn't even stay to see him buried?"

"Look at her fancy clothes and hair. Why isn't her head shaved yet?" Several people wagged their fingers in Mama's face as she lay on the stretcher beside the truck, as the teeming mob became more threatening.

But Papa's older brother, Uncle Crescent, saw the commotion, and it was he who contained the situation. He explained to the crowd that he'd authorized her return to the hospital and that they need not worry about the ceremonies. Mama would go through every single one if she survived childbirth.

"She has to be alive first, doesn't she?" He winked in their direction, and the crowd moved away slowly, somewhat appeased.

Mama claims she was not afraid of what the crowd would do to her.
She didn't care if she ever got back to the hospital or lived another
day. What she felt was shame, shame from the public humiliation. It
would never have happened if Papa had been alive, for no one would
have dared insult the Honorable's wife. But he was dead, so now she
was fair game.

She wished, but didn't ask, to be allowed to see my father again.
Mama says she doesn't know why, but she longed to see him one more
time. But not used to asking for anything, Mama waited for someone
else to suggest that she say goodbye to her Master. No one did, and
Mama left Aku without telling Papa goodbye. The man who'd been
her life was to be buried and she could not be present; she didn't even
know if anyone had explained to her other children that their father
was dead. Only John had been allowed to say goodbye to her; he had
clung on, fighting the tears Mama knew were there.

Boys were supposed to be strong, and as the eldest child, John, ten-
and-a-half years old, had suddenly become the literal head of the family. It was his responsibility to take care of his mother and siblings;
Mama wondered as she nudged him away what that awareness would
do to her son. She hadn't managed to say a word to him since the previous night; she still didn't know what to say. As the truck negotiated
its way out of the packed compound, she could have sworn she saw her
twin boys wandering aimlessly, like orphans. At that point that was
what they really were, for Mama had decided that she too would die.

Mama's tears came after she was resettled in her hospital bed. Once
they came, there was no way of stopping them. Mama would cry
almost nonstop for more than three years. My earliest memories are
dominated by my mother, then a plump, yellow-skinned madonna,
covered in black from head to toe, sitting on her canopied iron bed,
her back leaning against a white-washed wall, tears streaming down
her reddened face.

Mama refused to eat or drink anything for days afterwards. The
matron and nurses begged and preached, but she was adamant.

"What's the purpose? I'm better off dead," she said between sobs.

"But what about the children you're carrying? Don't they deserve a
chance?" They appealed to her sense of responsibility and then her
sense of guilt. "If they die, it will be your fault." None of it changed
her mind.

For the first time in her life, Mama gave up hope, no longer wishing that things would get better. All her life, her entire 27 years, she had been told what to do and how to do it. She had obeyed every command, believing that things would be all right for her and her children. But now nothing was right and it was hopeless to believe otherwise. What was an old woman with five, possibly seven, children going to do?

There are no logical explanations for why she did not die. As I grew up, I was told time and time again that my mother's survival and the birth of my twin brother and me were signs that miracles do exist.

Physically, her blood pressure and other vital signs were continuously in the red zone. She was also lying in a hospital that had no equipment to speak of and no medication to treat the ailments. The hospital did not have electricity, for it was still in the '50s. Nsukka got its first electric power in the '60s, years after I was born. If someone really was dying, that person had the option of trusting the instincts of the poorly trained assistants who passed as nurses or resorting to the native doctors. The latter were ruled out for Mama because she was a Christian; her reputation would be damaged by pagan medical rituals.

Emotionally, Mama was forlorn. Many who knew her then say that there was nothing more pathetic than the sight of her in that hospital bed, hoping to die. She only stirred when someone talked about her children. They caused her the most pain. She knew there was nothing she could do to help them, but she couldn't stop thinking about them. She mostly pondered their future without a father and a mother, and the hard life she knew awaited them.

Days came and went and Mama lay crying. No one was sure if she slept at all, for every time someone came into the room, they heard her sniffling. When the nurses could no longer hear her because of her weakened state, they decided to begin force-feeding her. When she clenched her teeth and refused to open her mouth, they pried it open and spooned in *akamu*, a creamy corn custard. If she refused to swallow, someone held her nose in a pinch until she gulped it down. Mama regained a little strength, but only so she could cry some more.

As if Mama didn't have enough to worry about, the doctor who visited weekly told her that her babies were lying in a breech position, feet first, and that even if she carried them to term, they would be delivered by caesarean section. To bear a child by "caesar," as Ibos call the process, was not only rare at that time, but even now continues to be looked on as an aberration, a phenomenon associated with women who are less than able, less than women. *Awalawa* (cut up good), as such women are called, hang their heads in shame. Other women actually tell them, "You don't know what bearing a child is all about. Yours was cut from you; normal women push theirs out." The doctor did his best to ready himself and Mama for the operation. Surgery had never been performed there, so the facility lacked even the most basic equipment.

And now Mama cried in earnest, from fear, shame, and disappointment. Nothing more could go wrong. She had prided herself on the ease with which childbearing had come to her. Hadn't she given birth to six hefty babies and gotten up to do her chores the day after? God had clearly turned away from her. As sure as she was that she didn't want to live, she was equally certain that she wanted a dignified exit, not for herself, but so her children would be spared the additional torments. She convinced herself that she would only live long enough to give birth, for she believed that if her twins died, she would be guilty of two murders. Afterwards, she could die quietly. It wouldn't do if she died on the operating table, under the knife. People would surely ask what she died from.

"Eh, did you say she died when they cut her open?" She could hear the inquisitors already. Later, the news of how she died would cause her children shame, and her poor little daughters might never get married. People would remember that their mother had to be cut up to deliver her babies.

Mama's niece, Mary, who was the closest we had to a nanny, came to Nsukka to stay with her at the hospital. Mary was convinced Mama would die, for she was swollen beyond recognition, and her eyelids no longer opened. Mary says Mama was constantly soaked in sweat and that she stood by the bed and fanned Mama constantly as the nurses instructed her. Mary remembers it being exceedingly hot. The temperature stayed over 100 degrees for weeks at a stretch and the humidity stagnated the air. One could hardly breathe, and in Mama's situation, things were critical.

Finally, my twin and I were born at seven o'clock on the evening of February 20, 1956, exactly four weeks to the minute since Mama laid eyes on Papa's dead body. No one, not the nurses, nor the doctor who was set on cutting us out of Mama, could explain how it happened. It was almost magical.

Both Mama and Mary tell it similarly. The temperature had dipped slightly below 100 degrees; a breeze was blowing. Mama had been able to say a few words to the priest who had come to pray by her bed. They were simple words. "We're still alive today," she replied to the priest's inquiry about her well-being. Around four o'clock, Mama seemed charged with a dose of energy and told Mary that she wanted to go for a walk.

Mary could not believe her eyes when, aided by nurses, Mama stood on her own feet and started walking. At first, she walked unsteadily, out of breath. Then she convinced everyone to let her walk the grounds of the hospital. At that point, Mary began to cry, convinced that Mama's death had come, since Ibos believe that a dying person gets an unusually high burst of energy just before dying. She followed Mama, who waddled down the corridors, calling attention to herself. Other patients' visitors stopped and stared openly at the balloon woman.

The nurses were waiting with several warm buckets of water to bathe her when she returned from her walk.

A hospital bathroom in those days consisted of a small building, a few feet from the wards, where a closet-sized room was set aside for bathing. It was usually a bare room with slippery cement floors that stunk of ammonia, for the gutter at one wall of this room also served as a receptacle for urine. The nurses made Mama sit on a short stool while they scrubbed her and dumped bucket after bucket of warm water on her body. Mary said she looked almost human after she was oiled, dressed, and propped back in her bed.

There was no preamble to the births. After the nurses left, Mama cried out suddenly, startling Mary.

"Call the nurses," was all she could manage, and Mary ran to get help. Mama says that it must have been the force with which the bag of water broke that pushed out the first of the twins in the rush of warm liquid. All she knew was that as the water soaked her newly cleaned body and linen, she felt her legs immobilized, almost numbed. When she tried to shift her weight slightly, the first baby slid out. I had arrived.

Mama calls it the greatest surprise of her life. There I was, feet first, but facing down, so she could see neither my face nor my sex. She watched in horror as I slid to within a few inches the edge of the bed. Mary and the nurses were still gone and she feared that I would fall from the high hospital bed onto the floor. I had not cried out as babies are supposed to, so Mama could not tell if I was alive. Then the nurses rushed in, and in a frenzy of activity cut me free and helped deliver my twin brother. It all took no more than ten minutes from start to finish, and we were declared healthy, albeit small. Neither of us weighed more than five pounds.

Mama was made comfortable. The babies were secured. The nurses left. And then Mama began to cry. For a long time, she cried harder than she'd ever cried in a life full of tears.

"Who Will Take Care of My Children?"

Between her convulsions of grief, Mama was able to manage a few words.

"He's dead. My Master is really dead. What am I going to do?" It was like a new consciousness for Mama, as if the pregnancy had buffered her from a full awareness of the cruel truth.

"He always came after each of the babies was delivered. He always seemed very pleased with me. He loved his children. Where is he now? Why did he leave me?

"Look how helpless they look; they don't even want to cry. It's as if they know no one is there to protect them."

When it appeared to Mary that Mama was totally out of control, she called the nurses.

"Don't speak like that!" Cousin Mary tried to talk some sense into her. "The God who protected them while you carried them will provide for them; you wait and see."

"Rose, how can you show God no gratitude? Didn't He just give you two healthy infants? What else do you want?" one nurse admonished her. "If you continue to cry, you will not make breast milk. How are you going to sustain those tiny things without milk?"

The nurse gave her a shot and she was asleep in minutes. Not long afterward, my twin and I woke at the same time, screaming for food. A nurse placed one of us in the crook of Mama's arm to nurse, but nothing came out, not even colostrum, the yellowish cream that usually came soon after birth. Mama's breasts were declared empty, not ready to nourish the babies she bore.

The nurses were in a quandary. They had never had such an experience and were unsure of what to do. After the matron failed to recruit a nursing mother to breast-feed us, she brought a can full of powder that had been donated by relief agencies. This Ostermilk supposedly could take the place of a mother's milk. Unfortunately, no one had ever seen or heard of a baby bottle, so the formula had to be spooned into our mouths. We were not given much chance of survival. Mama watched us squirming in hunger, but that was all she could do. Her body refused to cooperate. We didn't gain any weight for weeks and looked smaller than we had at birth, and there was no telling if we had ailments other than the malnutrition. We rarely cried those first weeks; we were too weak to cry.

Mama held one or both of us as often as the nurses let her. She says it was our helplessness that gave her the will to live. Mama herself made an amazing recovery right after we were born. Her swelling literally disappeared overnight, and she seemed like a different person. She was able to get in and out of bed without help and hovered over the crib where we lay. The sight of us, tinier than any babies she had ever seen, forced Mama to view her condition in a new light. She could not think of anything else but our well being; she was consumed with a passion to heal us, to make us normal. Today, she believes it was God's plan, His way of giving her the will to live. She stopped seeing herself as a victim and started focusing on our needs. She prayed to God to spare our lives, promising Him that if He did, she would fight hard to provide all that we needed.

Mama stayed in the hospital an additional month after we were born. When people asked, she told them it was so we could gain some weight and strength, but now I know it was more for her. She had no idea what would become of her. Also, she delayed going home for as long as she could to avoid the traditional rituals she had to go through.

Finally, she had no excuses left, no other reason not to go home to her children, whom she hadn't taken care of for half a year and hadn't even seen for two months since her husband died. She was filled with anxiety and fear. The hospital sent her off in the same Land Rover that had taken her to see her husband's dead body. She and Mary sat in the back of the truck, each holding a baby; each woman cried silently as the hospital disappeared from view.

Grieving

The *Umuada* (Daughters of the Land) were sitting in the family compound when Mama arrived. Their reception seemed to say, "The party is over." They made sure that Mama would now begin the actual mourning process immediately. They only allowed her a few minutes to see her children, whom she barely recognized. Their clothing was caked with dirt and it looked as if they hadn't bathed in weeks. John ushered Anthony and Christopher, Virginia and Martha into the little back room where she'd spent the night on the day Papa had died. They seemed timid and shy, staring at her vacantly, almost as if they didn't know her.

The children had been left in the custody of Papa's older brother, Uncle Crescent, and his wife. Crescent, a farmer, had pushed the responsibility of raising his own children onto Papa, and he did not relish the burden of raising his own children, let alone five very young nieces and nephews who were used to fineries that he himself had never had. He treated my siblings as he did his own, which meant that they were not entitled to breakfast. The children, including Martha, who was only five years old, went hungry till lunch, which was served about three o'clock in the afternoon.

Uncle Crescent and his wife left home for the farm at sunrise and were not there when the children rose from their sleeping mats. John took charge of his siblings as much as a ten-year-old could. Their education was forgotten while Mama was gone. When John raised the issue with his uncle, the older man told him that he'd already gotten as much education as he was likely to get.

Mama arrived home around two o'clock, before the children had eaten anything that day. Her helplessness in the situation caused her more agony. She quickly realized, however, that there was nothing she could do at that moment. She had no idea about the state of her husband's affairs; she didn't know if there was any money left to sustain her and the children. Meanwhile, the Daughters of the Land were waiting. Before returning to the Umuada, though, she lingered an extra minute with John. With encouragement, he walked into her arms and held on to her tightly.

"Don't worry, Mama, I'll take care of you, you'll see," he uttered, meaning it. Mama says that there was a seriousness in his voice that went way beyond his age. He seemed truly determined to provide for his mother and siblings. Mama nodded her assent before leaving him.

The *Umuada*, grown daughters of men in Papa's village, had gathered to fulfill part of their obligatory burial process. They seemed to take some delight in this particular duty. Many of them thought Mama undeserving of the position she attained through her marriage. My father had protected her when he was alive, shielding her from their fury. Papa's death, however, brought Mama down to their level.

"Explain to us again why you were not here to bury your husband. Wasn't he good to you when he was alive?" the leader of the female group asked. They had formed a circle around Mama, who was seated on a stool. The speaker moved into the circle with her, wagging fingers at her and spitting at her feet.

"Yes, tell us, 'the Honorable's wife,' why you were not here when your husband, our brother, was swallowed by the earth?" she repeated, her voice sounding harsher.

By that point, Mama's tears had taken over and were gushing down her face. She stung with anger and humiliation. Wasn't it enough that her husband had died? Why did she have to suffer through the insults? But Mama also knew she had to tread lightly with the *Umuada*. They were so powerful that they could determine what course her life would take from that time forward. A mere wife was defenseless against the Daughters of the Land. Mama had never been defiant and did not know how to begin, so she let her tears speak for her.

"The Honorable's wife, tell us why you were not here for our brother's burial." Another woman entered the circle, hovering over Mama's bent head.

"It wasn't my doing, my husband's sisters. It was the nurses at the hospital who insisted that I return for the babies' sake," Mama managed in spite of her tears.

"So you believe that the children's lives were more important than that of your husband?"

"Our brother married you when you were nothing. There was nothing to you then as there's nothing to you now. Do you understand that?"

Mama merely nodded, too choked up to speak. The women took turns berating and taunting her, but Mama would not take the bait. She was much smarter than that. She knew of new widows who had allowed themselves to be coerced into a no-win fight with the *Umuada* and had lost a great deal more than their pride. Mama could not afford to antagonize anyone at that time; she needed everyone on her side. She remained as she was, her eyes closed and her head leaning forward, to avoid their eyes. Only her flowing tears told of the pain they were causing her.

But as debilitating as this degradation was, it was only preliminary. When the Daughters tired of their warm-up, they got down to the main event. The ritual of shaving a widow's head is as old as the Ibo themselves. Every widow shaves her head when her husband dies, no exceptions. It symbolizes that the woman's life, too, has ended. She has to look as undesirable as possible for the length of the compulsory mourning period.

The *Umuada* in Mama's case, delighted in their function. Mama swears that the numerous razor cuts she had on her scalp were not accidental. When they were done, her scalp was as smooth as the skin on her face and it had a sheen to it. The village women then produced an outfit of black mourning clothes, a crude blouse with openings for the neck and arms and a set of wrappers. Right before every watchful eye, they lifted the blouse that Mama wore, baring her chest, and put the black one on her. The mourning clothes became Mama's uniform for seven years.

Later that afternoon, a station was created for Mama in the room where Papa's body had lain in state. The *Umuada* spread a bare raffia mat where Mama would remain for a whole year. It was normal practice for widows to sit stationary during the mourning period. A woman only got up to perform bodily functions, which she tried to accommodate at night, when it was dark and neighbors couldn't witness her rising. Mama could only bathe at night in the fenced-off area of the yard. If her mourning clothes needed a wash, she would do so at night and hope that they dried by the next morning. She had to be totally dependent on others for all her needs; she couldn't get up to get herself a drink of water even if her life depended on it. Mama says that she almost welcomed the monotony, for she was at a loss about what turns her life should take. She sat at her designated place day after day, talking to her children only if someone brought them to her. Even the care of the twins was turned over to Mary.

One night, John stole in to see her. He seemed to have been watching for a moment when she was all alone. He crawled in beside her, snuggling close. Mama waited for him to speak.

"I heard *Nna Anyi* (Our Father, which the children had taken to calling Papa's brother) telling someone that Papa only left 100 pounds in his bank account. He said there's no money to support us." John carefully avoided telling Mama that his uncle had also made denigrating remarks about his parents' extravagant lifestyle.

"We'll find a way," Mama reassured her son. "God will provide for us." But for the rest of the night, she was unable to sleep as she wondered how she could possibly support her children.

"What am I going to do?" Mama cried to herself over and over after her son left. Her very successful husband had not provided for her or their children; in fact, he had left them penniless. Papa had been a great philanthropist, contributing generously to the community, school projects, and programs designed for needy people. He believed in the notion that given support, anyone can redeem himself. "If I help other people's children, others will help mine," had been Papa's favorite response to those who criticized his openhandedness. Ironically, very few came to the aid of his destitute family after he died.

Mama still had a long way to go to reach the bottom of her fall from grace. Her famous husband and she had been revered by the villagers, and the other wives sought her opinion regularly, especially about seamstressing and matters concerning their marriageable daughters. Now, however, she was no better than a common village woman who'd never been anybody. The issue of what to do about Papa's car was one such indication. When Papa died, his family decided that Mama and her children were not deserving of a car. Although Mama would never have insisted on keeping a car that she couldn't possibly afford, no one asked her opinion on what should be done with it. Papa's brothers decided among themselves to sell the car. Mama never asked what became of the car or of the money that it brought. She waited for someone to tell her. No one ever did.

What became of her husband's other property Mama discovered by accident. One of Papa's cousins, Elias, without so much as a word to Mama, decided to travel to Nsukka, where Papa owned a lot of land and had stored wood and cement blocks to build a house. The cousin determined that since Papa was dead, the house would never be built. He proceeded to help himself to every piece of building material stored in the makeshift shed. Had he been able to, he would have lifted the plot of land.

His return with the loot triggered a celebration, for neighbors routinely celebrated each other's fortune. Everyone had thought that cousin Elias had purchased the material with which to build his own house. It was John who noticed that cousin Elias' wood and cement blocks were distinctly marked "Honorable Edoga" and told Mama about his suspicion.

It enraged her that her husband's assets were shared by his relatives when he had male children who were his rightful heirs. Even if they felt she should not be consulted because she was a woman, John should have been part of the decision. He was already past his tenth birthday and could understand that what was his was being taken from him. She was also angered by the fact that everyone assumed she and her children were finished and did not deserve even a roof over their heads. She sought the intervention of Uncle Crescent, but his response further demonstrated her lowly status.

"But why should the wood and things be allowed to sit there and rot when there's someone who could use them?" he asked her, his face in a frown, as if baffled by her expressions of concern.

She wanted to ask him how she and her children were supposed to fend for themselves, but she knew he would view her inquiries as a transgression, so she kept her mouth shut. Her voice was silenced the day they buried her husband; all she had to hope for was that her sons would grow healthy and strong and would speak for her when the time came.

Mama cried most of the time she spent alone on her raffia mat. Though she was becoming desperate to figure out how she could extricate herself and her children from their dreadful lives, she was no closer to knowing what she could or would do to accomplish it.

And still things got worse. Men began to sniff around. Mama thought they were stopping by to inquire about the children, and flattered by their attention, she presented them with cola nuts. It was only after their intentions became known to her that she started making serious plans to get her children away from their wretched predicament.

"The Headmaster's wife," her pursuers began, for although Papa was dead, Mama still had no right to her own identity. "My youngest wife has her monthly and I want to invite you to my bed tonight." The first few times she was thus propositioned, she was so shocked that she was rendered speechless, which the men misread as agreement.

"I understand if you're shy or even afraid about this; it's normal for you to feel that way," one and then another would reassure her.

Mama says that the sexual advances presented her worst predicament of all. She had never been comfortable with her sexuality, doing only what needed to be done to bear children. Her husband was dead, leaving her to care for seven children. Why would she want to engage in sexual activities? Certainly not for any pleasure derived from it, for as far she knew, there was none. There was also the issue of her religion. Did these men really think that she would commit the acts they were asking of her? How could they think so little of her and her dedication to her Master?

The men became bolder, and one even dared to move close to her mat, almost touching her. Mama's problem was compounded by the fact that the Ibo culture allowed and even encouraged widows to maintain sexual liaisons and continue bearing children well after their husbands were gone. Widows could not bear children within a year of their husband's death, but after that, they were fair game. In fact, a widow's continued sexual activity guaranteed her maintenance, since her dead husband's family would not carry the full weight of her and her children's upkeep.

Even today, in situations where the man dies before he's had his desired number of children, it is the widow's responsibility to guarantee that her dead husband's line grows. As soon as the mourning time requirement is met, she gets to work to keep the family name going. She continues until she's too old to bear children; all the children resulting from the liaisons bear her dead husband's name and share his estate equally as if they were his biological children.

Mama did not want to antagonize any of her suitors because she was essentially at their mercy. At the same time, she wanted it known that she would not carry on a relationship with anyone. As far as she was concerned, that part of her life was over. The problem was communicating it without turning the men into enemies.

Mama had to lie to save her honor. She could not just tell them she had no interest in what they were proposing; it would not do to insult the men of her husband's village.

"The nurses at the hospital told me I shouldn't do anything that could cause a pregnancy for at least three years," she told one very persistent neighbor who had made himself a permanent fixture in Mama's mourning space, ignoring Mama's more subtle signs of rejection.

"*Nwunye* Headmaster, you know I harvested ten and a half barns of yam last year. I can help you with your children," the man needled, making promises that no one would hold him to. He listed all his assets, the tons of rice, the vegetables, his wives and children.

"Because of my illness the last time, the nurses said another pregnancy will kill me." Mama feigned a regretful voice, hoping that he

would not only leave her alone but also spread the news of her affliction to others. The harassment didn't completely stop, but having
found a lie, Mama used it so frequently she almost believed it. When
she needed to, she explained that she couldn't risk dying and leaving
her seven young children without any parents.

Mama lived in Aku for the entire year following her return after our
birth. She observed fully the rituals of mourning and met all the obligations without complaint. Her children, the ones who were old
enough to be enrolled in school, were registered at the only school in
Aku, a good five miles away, which they trekked to.

Just before her year of mourning was up, Mama Helena visited her.

"Where are you moving to afterwards?" Mama's mentor asked
matter-of-factly.

"I don't know what to do," Mama said, throwing her hands up.
"There's no money anywhere. As far as I know, Master left nothing."

"Have you thought about what you could do? You can't sit here forever. You have seven children to take care of."

"What can I do that does not require money?" Mama replied, her
voice showing the strain under which she labored.

"You're a good seamstress and could . ."

"I know that, but I also know that I need money to start anything,"
Mama interrupted, the very first time she was even remotely disre-
spectful to Mama Helena.

"There are ways; I can ask friends who may be willing to help you
make a start."

"Really?" Mama allowed herself some hope. She saw the possibilities in what her mentor suggested. Yes, she was once successful as
a seamstress and could learn the new styles. Her sewing machine
was safe; she had confirmed that one night when she had sneaked
into the room where the remaining items from her household were
kept. It was enclosed in its case, and Mama was almost overcome
with a longing to open it and feel the cold machine. But it would
take a lot of money to relocate the family to a town where she could
start a business and develop a clientele. Aku's female population
consisted mostly of farmers' wives and did not need more than one
set of clothing for occasional outings. Besides, the marketplace was
teeming with newly graduated seamstresses whom she'd have to
compete against.

When she considered the details, Mama couldn't imagine how,
even with Mama Helena's help, she could possibly raise the money she
needed to pull her family out of its dire situation. Her oldest child,

John, was in his last year of primary school and was eligible to take entrance examinations to "colleges" (high schools). But the fee for secondary schools was twenty pounds a term, not including expenses. Twenty pounds, the equivalent of eighty American dollars, was more than a high school graduate earned in a year during the fifties. Mama charged her customers six pennies for a blouse and a shilling for an elaborate dress.

Her despair mounted. She wanted her children to continue with their education. That's certainly what her Master would have wanted, and she would be letting him down if she did not find a way to pay for it. She searched her mind for names of Papa's friends or contacts who could be of help, but none came. Ever aware of her place, she had not cultivated any relationships beyond what was expected of her as Papa's wife. Mama would have been overstepping her bounds had she spoken a word to anyone outside of her family without her husband's prior knowledge and consent. Her options seemed exhausted and she was almost ready to ask Uncle Crescent for a piece of land for farming.

Mama's first relief came from a group of people of whom she knew very little, twelve men who were members of the House of Assembly; they were Papa's colleagues and had known him well. Mama later discovered Mama Helena had appealed to them to help rescue Papa's family from their situation. She convinced them that they would be helping one of their own.

Mama received their two delegates warmly, more generously than her station allowed. She saw something in them, their refined clothing and manner, and sensed that they could help her tremendously. Because she was still limited to her mourning space, Mama instructed Cousin Mary to present them with cola nuts in the good dishes (the few unbroken ones) that were hers and to prepare pounded yam to serve them.

She felt almost in control of the situation. Because they asked and seemed genuinely interested in knowing, she told them her plans and fears. She revealed her dream of returning to a township, possibly Nsukka where she had lived for a few years. She would set up a sewing business and sell other materials in her shed. She could, if she had the capital and help, start a small eating place. Many people had told her what a great cook she was. But the men shook their heads in disapproval of that option. It wasn't a befitting trade for an Honorable's wife or any reputable woman. They knew that an eating house was a euphemism for a brothel and that the "diners" were married men who were not content with what they were served at home. Mama, who had never eaten away from home, had not been aware of that. She thanked the men for clarifying it for her.

"I don't have a penny to my name, so none of this may materialize," she concluded.

When the visitors asked her about the plans she had for her children, Mama began to cry quietly. Her tears were so sudden, so unexpected, that the men first stared at her and then left the room while she composed herself.

"John is finishing elementary school this year; we don't know what to do with him afterwards," she said when they returned.

"Have you asked him to register for college entrance exams?" one of the men asked.

"I haven't. John is very intelligent and will surely pass the test. But I don't have the three pounds to pay for the college registration fee. How can I let him take the test and then tell him he can't go to the college?"

Mama made a favorable impression on the men. Before they left, they counted out, on the bare floor next to Mama's raffia mat, the three pounds she needed for registration, plus an additional ten pounds which they told Mama should be used at her discretion. They left her with a promise that the group would return in a month, for the first anniversary of Papa's death.

Mama was beside herself with joy. She felt as if a lifeline had been thrown to save her and her children from drowning. She told herself over and over again that she would hold on to it until she was safely onshore.

She began to make earnest plans to move to Nsukka and start a trade there. Mama Helena reminded her that Papa had a second cousin, known as Tailor, who owned his own house in Nsukka. Tailor and his wife could provide the needed accommodations.

Tailor supported his family as a tailor, a trade that made him the butt of many jokes. Sewing was a woman's business, even though Tailor refused to touch women's clothing and only specialized in men's wear. "The lazy no-good man," people would say about him, "he has no shame."

Mama had John write a letter asking for Tailor's help. "Your cousin's children and I need a place to stay for a few months. I wouldn't be asking if we had anywhere else to go." John translated Mama's Ibo words into English as closely as he could and took the letter to the motor park where he found someone willing to deliver it.

Tailor responded promptly. His own letter, written by a school child who lived in the compound next to his, contained numerous errors that made it nearly impossible for John to understand or translate. He and Mama assumed that Tailor was offering them a room in his two-and-a-half-room shack whenever they wanted to move. Had the letter been more readable, Mama could have sensed Tailor's reluctance and might have planned differently.

She chose a Sunday to invite Uncle Crescent to her mourning space to discuss her plans. His wife was not invited to the meeting; it simply wasn't a woman's business. Mama waited until the usual after-mass crowds left before sending John to the verandah where her brother-in-law spent most of his free time. Mama knew that Uncle Crescent had little say about what she did with her own life, but he did have the power to refuse to let her take the children anywhere. They were his brother's children, and by extension his, especially now that his brother was dead.

She had one of the children position a folding chair directly across from where she sat. When Uncle Crescent entered, a good half hour after he was summoned, Mama attempted a curtsy, a difficult feat given her position on the floor. She tried to rise, but Uncle Crescent waved her down while taking his seat. She waited for him to open the discussion, although she had summoned him.

"What's so urgent that my Sunday has to be interrupted?" he sounded agitated, irritated by her presence.

"*Nna anyi*, it's three weeks to a year since my Master left us, and I want your advice on what to do afterwards," Mama began. Ever so aware of the thin line she walked, she spoke haltingly, pausing between words, not only for effect but so he could interrupt at any point should he see fit.

"What's there to do? My wife and I could use more hands around the farm. As soon as you no longer have to sit here, you could start going to the farm with us. John is old enough to join us at the farm also. If things go well, by next season, we may give you your own piece of land, land that belongs to the Headmaster and should pass on to his sons. If you're strong enough, the harvest from that land should keep you and the children going."

Uncle Crescent rose to leave, his response suggesting to Mama that he had given it a lot of thought and that Mama's task of convincing him was even harder than she had thought it to be.

"Thank you, sir. We're grateful for the way you've taken care of us all these months, and for the way you continue to think about our future," she stalled, looking for an avenue to present her own plan. Mama had to think quickly while she still held his attention.

"*Nna anyi*, Master bought me a sewing machine on our wedding day, and later, he allowed me to begin to practice the trade that I learned many years ago. I still have the sewing machine, and with your support and God willing, I think I can make a living sewing."

"When was the last time you went to the market? Do you think Aku needs another seamstress when there isn't any business for the existing ones? What makes you think you'll succeed when all the other ones already in business are failing?" Uncle Crescent was pacing the floor, his voice raised in anger. His wife, though uninvited, walked into the room and leaned against the wall, watching the exchange.

"I've thought of that, sir."

Mama told me many years later that that statement was a turning point in her life. A woman in her position simply does not think. To think would be to assume powers that she obviously did not possess, to underrate the influence of her husband's brother, who had taken over her care. She says now that she felt that the moment had come for her to take charge, not of her whole life, certainly, but at least a part of it.

"You have?" he asked, eyebrows raised.

"I know how big a burden the children and I have been to you and I thought I could relieve you of some of that." Mama was well versed in the ways of Ibo culture. As often as a woman can, she turns the tables and makes herself and her desires as little of the issue as possible. The issue, as she put it to Uncle Crescent and his silent wife, was the heavy burden she put on them and her willingness to help relieve some of it. Put that way, she made her plan sound more palatable.

"Do I ever complain about supporting you all?"

"No, sir," Mama answered, although she heard him ranting almost daily about the Headmaster's lazy children who ate all the food in the house.

"I see. Do you think we're not supporting you adequately, like you were used to? Is that it?"

Again, Mama knew she had to return the exchange to safer ground. "We're grateful to you, sir, for without you we wouldn't be alive today." Mama's voice broke as she began to cry.

Maybe it was the tears, or the stares of the group of spectators who'd congregated, or even the sad faces of Mama's children, who'd joined the crowd, that calmed Uncle Crescent down. As he walked away, he called to her, "You can do whatever you want with your life; just let me know when you're all leaving."

Ironically, Mama didn't feel that this was a victory for her. She had not intended to antagonize him, since she still needed his input in major decisions involving the children. Uncle Crescent found out in bits and pieces that Mama was moving to Nsukka where she planned to set up a sewing shop. He didn't ask her directly and she never attempted another discussion with him.

A widow's outing ceremony is elaborate. It is called an outing because it is the first time she leaves her mourning space for any outside activity. In it, the widow is escorted into church for her cleansing before she re-enters society and a mass celebrated for the family. On the day before the outing, she's presented in her new set of clothes, less somber than the pitch black that's mandated for one year, but still dark. The material has a mostly black background mixed with patterns of navy, brown, and black, with no bright colors. The *Umuadas* perform the ritual, which requires the woman to bathe (the first officially permitted bath after she's widowed). She's stripped of the black garb, usually browned at the edges and frayed at the seams, and dressed in the new material. Many view it as a progression from total darkness (as symbolized by the black) to some glimmer of life.

Mama, however, refused her new outfit. "I don't want to take off the black ones yet," she said, astonishing all fifty women who were there to share in the happy moment.

"It's a year since our brother died."

"I know that, but it's not been enough time for me to mourn my Master. I was told I could continue to wear all black if I chose to, for as long as I want," Mama said defiantly.

None of the women challenged her. They had seen many widows come out of their year with more than a little dementia. They thought Mama needed more sun to warm up her brain, to get it functioning again. What widow in her right mind would refuse a chance to remove her black clothes? Most could not wait for the day to arrive, but this one had to spoil their ceremony! Well, they always thought that the Honorable's wife didn't have it all together.

Mama's mourning space was cleared. It was rather unceremonious. A representative of the *Umuada* rolled the torn rectangular mat, which was her bed, chair, and table for the past year, into a pipe and took it out to the yard for burning. Mama's black mourning clothes, had she agreed to discard them, would also have been cast into the burning pile.

Only the women watched, and Mama says that the day held mixed emotions for her. The mat burning was one more separation to endure, one more thing she had become attached to and had to leave behind. Having been stripped of her position on the mat in the corner of the parlor in the house, she wondered how and where she would fit in. In retrospect, her life in the past year seemed so simple. She had risen and retired in the same spot, and there had been no confusion about her place in her brother-in-law's household. The next day, she and her children joined the crowded procession into church where they were blessed at the altar by the priest. The sermon was about Papa's life and his great contribution to Aku, even though his life had been cut short.

As promised, six of Papa's colleagues from the House of Assembly arrived at the church in two cars that held everyone's attention: the chrome finish glistened in the sun whenever they moved. The men were led to the pew behind Mama and her children, and they lent a grandeur to an occasion that would have been graced only by townspeople.

They presented their gift directly to Mama, with John, the man of the family, by her side. Mama said she could hardly restrain herself from screaming with joy at their gifts. John silently read the promissory note, a pledge to pay five years of college tuition to the school that admitted him. John started hopping up and down, shouting, "Thank God! Thank God!"

Then they gave Mama five hundred pounds, and she lost all control. She sobbed openly, restraining her urge to hug the men who offered her a chance at life. Her first child would have a chance to become somebody, like his father. He would then be in a position to help her with the other children. He would, in fact, be able to take care of her the way he'd always promised he would.

The after-mass ceremonies were at the family home where hundreds of people gathered to mark the anniversary of their hero's death. It was as grand as a marriage. Dancing troupes and church choirs kept the crowd entertained, while the Christian women cooked for the spectators.

With the five hundred pounds safely tucked away in her money belt, Mama left Aku for Nsukka two weeks after the memorial service. There was little else to pack. The only marital property in her possession was Papa's four-poster iron bed, the bed she had shared with him only to conceive their children. She was also allowed to take her sewing machine and other personal effects, but she was initially denied the right to take the wood tables and chairs that she had delighted in polishing to a high gloss every week, with palm oil that she prepared herself. But she did not allow even that to bother her.

On the day of the move, she and the children climbed atop the bed of a lorry, the only transport between Aku and Nsukka. As they rode the bumpy roads, Mama was filled with expectations, of things she knew she could and would accomplish, of the decent life she could provide her children. Papa's colleagues, along with his cousin Tailor, were providing the opportunity. Mama knew how cramped their accommodations would be, but she was undeterred. They'd manage. She'd find a way to reclaim her own life and provide direction for the lives of her children.

After all the living that she'd done—thirteen years of marriage to the most powerful man in a geographical region larger than many American states, seven children, a year of mourning her master, her meteoric rise to power and her crashing fall from grace—Mama amazingly still had never been her own person. She'd always been dependent, on her mother briefly, then on the mercy of the church, then on Mama Helena, then on Papa. So it wasn't until Papa died that her real life started. Even so, Mama continues to credit her long-departed master with her successes.

"It's all due to my Master, his good name, the great works he did," she says when someone congratulates her on her accomplishments. "I'm only a woman, and what can a woman do?" She smiles demurely, casting her eyes down. She then continues in a lecture, to any women who'll listen, that a woman is worth nothing. "We only have our husband's good name if we're lucky." She believes herself to be one of the lucky few.

No Room for Women's Dreams

Nsukka in 1957 was no place for a widow alone. There was very little room for a widow with seven children. It was, as it still is, a man's world. Mama came with dreams of making a living and providing her children with the kind of life that her master had desired for them. She was armed with the one tool she thought she needed to make her dreams come true—her sewing machine. But during her first months at Nsukka, Mama learned a bitter lesson, that there was even less room for women's dreams than there was for women themselves.

Nevertheless, Mama arrived with her seven children and my cousin Mary, who remained a steady influence in our lives until she remarried in 1968, during the Nigerian-Biafran War. Mama's first disappointment was Tailor's house. The one room that eight of us moved into was not much of a room, but then, the house wasn't much of a house either. It was a narrow three-room shack; the outside walls rose only as high as a grown man's middle, as if the builder had run out of mud blocks. The three openings did not have doors, and at night Mama improvised, taping an old mat to block outsiders' views. One could say we had a great view of the moon and stars through the gap between the dwarf walls and the roof, from our beds or pallets on the floor. But Mama's pain knew no bounds as she worried about her children's safety.

Mama says it was not snobbery on her part: after all, she had lived only in mud huts with thatched roofs until she moved into the convent. Besides, most of the people she knew still lived in mud huts. She insists it was about the condition of the house. On sunny days, and there were plenty of those in tropical Africa, there was no shade, and the sun beat directly on us as if we were outside. If it rained, we were ankle (at times calf) deep in filthy mud that often contained excrement. Then there were the insects that feasted on us, day and night. Mama said the mosquitoes were so brazen and large that often she and cousin Mary swatted them all night. The flies that surrounded us were the size of large bees, and their buzzing was so disconcerting that Mama preferred to spend her days outside. She saw nothing good in that house; it was not a suitable environment in which to raise any children, her children especially.

On top of her accommodation problems, Mama was troubled by Tailor's wife, whom we called Mama Ngozi. She initially dismissed her hostess' hostility as petty jealousy, since Mama had been married to the most influential man in the whole area. Mama Ngozi had never known contentment in her life, not in her childhood nor in her marriage. In addition, she lived with the stigma and shame of bearing only daughters, no sons. The tormented woman resented Mama for the good fortune of a prestigious husband and healthy sons. She didn't feel any pity for their guest, widowed or not.

Mama Ngozi was most angered by the way her husband had treated the Honorable's wife's decision to move in with them. She had not been asked her opinion, which would have been that their three-room shack was hardly large enough for the five of them, let alone the eight Edogas. Instead, Tailor had treated Mama's impending arrival as if she were visiting royalty. "I feel honored that she chose to live with us when she could have asked many others," he told his wife.

Mama sensed Mama Ngozi's displeasure soon after she arrived. Thus she stayed confined in the room she was assigned. In the mornings when she stepped outside to greet her hosts, Tailor's wife answered under her breath. When Mama tried to make a little conversation with the woman, she was rebuffed.

"I don't understand what you're talking about. I've never been married to a great man, I'm not a widow, and I don't have sons." Mama walked back to her room and stayed in her place. Mama also had to deal with the way Mama Ngozi treated her children. On the first few occasions, she looked away, lest she offend anyone. But her hostess became more and more brazen, seizing every little opportunity involving the children to insult Mama. On a particular day, it had to do with Virginia, Mama's first daughter, who had been terribly scarred by the events of the past year and had withdrawn into a shy, quiet child. Virginia was then eight years old and sat, as was her habit, by herself in a corner of the dirt courtyard, playing with stick dolls. One of Tailor's daughters had gone over to Virginia, and before anyone knew it, the two girls and Tailor's wife were screaming hysterically. The only voice Mama could make out was her hostess: "Leave my children alone, you wicked girl. Did your mother put you up to this? Does she want my daughters dead so my husband can throw me out and she can have him? Doesn't she know I'm on to her?"

Mama froze in her place, completely surprised by the depth of Mama Ngozi's anger. She says she realized then that Tailor's wife truly believed those accusations and wouldn't consider anything to the contrary, even though Mama's intentions were nothing but honorable and chaste.

All these concerns compounded Mama's most pressing worry: her children's safety. What options did she have? Not many. What other relative would accept a widow with six children (John had left for boarding school) into their household? She could think of none. Where else could she go? She had only been in Nsukka for a few weeks and was quite sure that few landlords would rent a room to a woman alone with children, fearing that she would attract undesirables, men who sought the pleasures of her body. Besides, Mama did not have the money to pay any rent. She had used nearly two hundred of the five hundred pounds to settle her first born in school and reserved the rest to establish the sewing business for which she had come to Nsukka. Meanwhile, she was not earning any income with which she and her children could live. She wondered if she hadn't made a mistake in bringing the children away from the family home at Aku where they were at least safe in a real house and were fed with some regularity.

Finally, she arrived at a decision: she would, if nothing else, limit the children's suffering. She couldn't bear the thought of keeping the children in Tailor's home for one more day. Her heart broke as she began to make plans to settle her children elsewhere. Mama admits that giving away her children was the hardest decision she ever made in her life and that nothing she had ever experienced prepared her for the pain.

She sent word to Papa's sister Alice, who arrived three days later. Together, the two women worked out a detailed plan as to where the children would go. Virginia was the first to be claimed. Our older cousin, Cecilia, a married nurse, took her. Cousin Cecilia had two sons and promised Mama that Virginia would be the daughter she never had. Mama cried as she readied her first born daughter, packing her dresses, most of which were from Papa's days and were too small for her tall frame, into a small polythene bag. She nudged the reluctant child toward her cousin and retreated to her own pain, remembering in vivid detail the day her own mother left her in the care of the priest.

She cried that entire night, terrified that she was not doing the right thing for her children. But she girded herself for the next day, when her twin boys, Anthony and Christopher, were to go to their new home.

The twins were the hardest to place, for no one wanted to feed and take care of two active boys. Some relatives offered to take one of the boys, but Mama insisted that they stay together. The boys were inseparable, and she felt they would wither without each other. They did everything together, including going to the bathroom; consequently, they'd fared the best after Papa's death.

The only person willing to provide a home for the twins together was an uncle-in-law, a man we called *Di Kathy* (Kathy's husband). Kathy was Mama's "sister." She was born, not to my grandmother, but to a wife that Grandmother acquired for her dead husband. After Mama was given to the mission, the chasm left by the absence of her last child was too wide for Grandmother to bear. She was also determined to prevent further victimization of her family, and she knew that the only way she could do it was by bearing more sons, so her only biological son would have brothers. It is a widely held belief that having one son is the same as having no sons at all. For one, that son could die, leaving his parents sonless. Secondly, a son needs backup, someone to stand up for him at village meetings and speak on his behalf. Sisters cannot perform that role, only brothers.

By this time, Grandmother could no longer bear children herself, being well past menopause. But even if she wasn't, she would not demean herself by sharing her bed with men who had mistreated her and her daughter and had caused her child to be removed from her life. Despite constant pressure from the men from her village, she had not had relations with any man since her husband had died and she had no intention of doing so.

The Ibo culture permits and often encourages the kind of arrangement my Grandmother sought. What she did was legal and traditionally sound. With the support of her children and relatives, she pursued a teenage, once-married woman who was anxious to get married again and paid a bride price on her head. Grandmother provided for all her needs and built a mud hut, directly across from hers, where she installed her new *nwunyedi* (husband's wife). She fed and fattened the woman so she looked fresh and appealing to strong virile men. Within months of her arrival, the young woman became pregnant and later bore a son, Bonaventure. When Bona was weaned, Grandmother took over the child's care, and the younger woman continued with the task for which she was acquired. This woman, whose name I don't even know, bore three children, two boys and a girl, for my grandmother.

The children called my grandmother *Nne* and their biological mother by her given name. There was no bond between the children and their biological mother. If they were injured, it was to Grandmother they ran. Likewise, when they were hungry, it was Grandmother who provided for them. The arrangement worked perfectly both for Grandmother and her husband's wife. The children, although they're not biologically related to my mother, are Mama's siblings. They're as entitled as she is to her father's name and inheritance. When Grandmother died in December 1983, her only biological son, Ezike, had already preceded her to his maker, and it was Bona, the first son of the surrogate, who performed the ceremonial dancing and clearing of the path after the burial, rituals reserved for a woman's first son.

Kathy, the only daughter of the surrogate, was sent to live with Mama briefly, shortly after she was betrothed. She passed through the domestic science and sewing training and got married in the church shortly before my father died.

Her husband, a low elementary teacher (uncertified teachers who do the job only because there aren't enough teachers) had no more than a grade-school education and suffered a serious inferiority complex. On top of that, he was a slightly built man, no taller than five feet, weighing about one hundred pounds, if that much. His bald head shone like a vulture's scalp, but he paraded around as if he owned the world and bossed his wife mercilessly. I'm quite sure that Mama was so desperate, she deluded herself into believing that Kathy would protect the twins. But I wonder how she could have believed that when Kathy was clearly terrified of her husband, who was poor, mean and physically abusive.

To such a man my nine-year-old brothers Anthony and Christopher first went. Kathy's husband insisted that both boys walk the seven miles to his home, and although Mama had serious objections to it, she acquiesced, crying silently as the boys left.

Martha, then six years old, and the most boisterous of Mama's children, was the last to be claimed. Martha was Mama's baby for five long years. She was her sweetheart, the child who always drew a smile from her, the one that constantly sought attention. She was sent first to Lagos to a couple who weren't even blood relatives, but who had known my father and had taken pity on Mama. Martha needed to go to Nigeria's former capital city to receive treatment at the only hospital in the entire country that provided orthopedic services. She had broken the bone in her right arm during the period right after Papa's death, before Mama even returned from the hospital. Uncle Crescent first ignored her, but when the little girl's cries persisted, he took her to a *dibia*, a native doctor who specialized in setting broken bones. The *dibia* formed a splint and tied it too tightly around her arm, so the bones didn't heal properly. In addition, Martha developed a severe infection in her arm.

Mama remembers that Martha's predicament caused her a lot of grief, especially during her year of mourning, when she could not even rise from her spot on the mat. Martha was dragged from *dibia* to *dibia*, but each one seemed to make the situation worse. A relative took her to the hospital at Nsukka where my twin and I were born, but they missed the doctor's once-a-week visit and Mama could not afford to pay for her to go back. Martha's little arm, set at an awkward angle, waited until we moved to Nsukka and became Mama's first priority. By that time, the doctor at the hospital pronounced Martha's arm beyond his capabilities; it required the expertise of an orthopedic surgeon. This complicated placement plans for Martha, who first had to get the necessary treatment.

Lagos seemed a faraway land to which few dared go. There was no telephone and few communication channels to keep in touch with relatives who lived there. The family that took Martha had many children and they assured Mama that they would treat her like one of their own. So Martha left, and it was many years before any of us set eyes on her again. I did not know of or see Martha until I was almost eight years old, and by then, she spoke no Ibo and very little English.

With John, Virginia, Anthony and Christopher, and Martha gone, it was just Mama, Cousin Mary, Ogbonna and I, as Mama set out on a quest to reclaim her life. It was a long and arduous journey, and many nights she cried out of frustration and, though she'll never admit to it, loneliness. There was no one to share her pain with or to confide in. A widow as young as Mama was scorned by women afraid that she would ensnare their husbands. Men only sought her for their own pleasure and they resented both Mama's constant rejection and her attempts to "be a man."

For these reasons, though Mama was determined to start a life for her children and herself, but she was careful not to step on any toes. She did not want to appear threatening to anyone, so she began her journey with a trade that met with everyone's approval. Mama recognized that the seamstressing business was her eventual goal, but she had neither the resources nor the connections to start up only a few weeks after moving to Nsukka. Besides, she was concerned that Tailor would think she was taking business away from him, even though they would service different clientele. Mama, therefore, started traveling to markets in Adani or Ogurugu, about thirty miles away, where she purchased food items in bulk. She bought yams, rice, and condiments, then brought them to the local marketplace the next day, where she set up a stall and sold at retail. She haggled, bantered, and nagged and was as common as the most common market woman.

After making a little profit and building up a clientele, Mama started a different sort of trade. In the mornings, before she left for the market, she made *akara* (fried bean balls) and *akamu* (corn custard). Mama's cooking was so good that even though seven other women served the same dishes, customers bought up Mama's *akara* and *akamu* faster than she could make them. Though everyone's praise was gratifying, it also caused Mama problems. Some women accused her of employing witchcraft and adding a secret ingredient to her *akara* balls that stole other women's customers. But the simple truth was that my mother never did anything in a haphazard manner and this cooking trade was no different.

For example, to secure the finest ingredients, she had to travel in the bed of a lorry to the market at Orba, fifteen miles away, where she purchased black-eyed beans and dried corn kernels. Both the beans and corn had to be grated, and the skin washed off. They were soaked overnight and Mama rose at two in the morning to start grinding the beans, using a large flattened slab and a smaller stone. She then mixed the ground beans with crawfish, salt, and a carefully selected hot pepper, one with an aroma that appealed to a thousand taste buds. She arrived at the local market around five in the morning, and heated red palm oil until it turned from yellow to a thin gold color. Then she dropped her bean mixture, one scoop at a time, into the hot oil. The *akamu* was made as customers demanded it, so it stayed fresh through the morning. When she sold out, usually around seven-thirty, she came home where cousin Mary was watching us, cleaned up her wares, and readied for the market to sell the uncooked foodstuff.

Her efforts paid off, but very slowly and at a high price to her health and sanity. Mama did not get more than two hours of sleep on any given night, and even to this day, she cannot sleep for long. She sat up in her bed many nights, even when there was nothing immediate troubling her. Mary says that Mama probably kept herself so occupied that she barely had time to think about the children she gave away and no longer saw. Every once in a while, she was allowed glimpses into their lives, but all the signs pointed to their maltreatment. Still, there was little she could do for them then, so they stayed with relatives who barely fed and clothed them and many times nearly killed then.

John went off to boarding school the year I was born, and because Mama could not afford the transportation money, he spent most of his holidays with relatives who lived in Enugu, where his school was. I remember seeing him three times during my childhood, once when he was in his final year in high school, another when he returned for a family portrait, and the last when he was leaving for the United States and our family had a send-off party for him. In my child's eyes, he was the most handsome and brilliant person in the world. Everyone thought the world of him.

Mama tells many stories of John's childhood, especially of the period following my father's death, of how he took charge of his mother and the situation. Mama says that many times when she was overcome by her despair, he assured her that he would take care of her. He insisted that she be strong for his siblings—always for others, never for himself. John's childhood ended on the day his father died, for every decision he made thereafter was meant to help out his family. He never went out to play as ten-year-old boys did; if another child invited him to play, he responded, "I have other things to do." He studied his books, memorizing every word in voluminous texts. It was as if the books held the mystery of his life. There was a time when neither Mama nor John had known if he could continue with his education and go on to secondary school. Mama says that although he was desperate to continue with his education, he showed no anger or resentment toward anyone who might prevent him from doing so. But when Papa's colleagues at the House of Assembly awarded him a scholarship, he cried from relief and joy. Mama says there wouldn't have been a worse fate than John's inability to obtain his education.

Virginia lived with cousin Cecilia until she finished grade school, but she was the house maid—cooking, scrubbing, polishing, while Cecilia's children sat around not doing much. She was beaten whenever anything was wrong. If the house was not swept properly, Virgy got a whipping. If dinner was late, she was slapped. When cousin Cecilia's children forgot to do their homework, it was Virgy's fault. She slaved over the hot coal stove with one of her cousins tied on her back, although she was but a child herself. Once when Virginia visited home for Christmas, Mama noticed that she was getting knock-kneed. My poor sister's legs were growing crooked from the weight of the buckets of water she drew from the well, from carrying the heavy chunks of coal, from kneeling in front of a basin full of soaking clothes that she had to scrub, from polishing the floors of her guardian's quarters to a shine. My oldest sister never complained of her suffering; she learned well from Mama what Ibo womanhood was all about. Virginia continued to live in an oppressive household until she went into boarding school. She visited us for holidays, so I knew her as my sister. She was so used to giving herself that I was able to manipulate and take advantage of her. But even if she knew, she never showed anger toward me or anyone. She acted like someone whose spirit had been sucked away. Virginia is the daughter who lived Mama's life, down to her quiet suffering.

Martha's life with relatives was smooth, for bubbly Martha would not have had it any other way. When she arrived at Lagos, she waited months before she could be admitted into the orthopedic hospital, where she had a series of operations to correct her arm. Unfortunately, most of the damage was done and no amount of skill or equipment could rectify a rotted bone. The bone between her right hand and elbow was replaced with an artificial one, and she suffered through many skin grafts. She spent more than a year in the hospital, healing and regaining use of the arm that everyone thought was useless. Mama remembers worrying most about Martha. The others had their good health, but only God knew how poor Martha was faring. There was no way of communicating with anyone in Lagos, unless you got lucky and ran into someone about to visit there. She wished she could be there to soothe Martha's pain, to hold her and comfort her and talk to her sweetheart, but all that was impossible.

Mama was afraid that Martha's hosts were too busy with their own lives to devote too much time to someone else's child, and she prayed every minute that God would provide someone to watch over her sick child. But from all indications, Martha did not lack love or attention, even while she was in the hospital. She became the darling of the doctors and nurses only a few weeks after she got there. Martha spoke only Ibo when she arrived in Lagos, but two months into her stay, she was fluent in Yoruba, the predominant language in Nigeria's capital; a few months later, she'd forgotten all her Ibo. She endeared herself to everyone she met; the hospital staff and her host family were sad to see her leave.

After leaving the hospital, Martha moved in with our first cousin, a barren woman we called "Aunt Monica." She lived in Jos in the northern part of Nigeria, where only Hausa is spoken. Martha could not communicate with her at first. But less than a month later, Martha was fluent in Hausa and was able again to wrap everyone around her little finger. Mama says of Martha, "She's so different from me, I really don't know where she came from."

Martha is the child that Mama was never allowed to be; she's free-spirited and enthusiastic about life, even when her options seem limited.

The twins, Christopher and Anthony, lasted all of two weeks with *Di Kathy*. The two children retraced their steps and trekked back to Tailor's house, arriving late one night when everyone was asleep. Mama heard their approaching footsteps and peered through the cloth that served as the door in the room where we lived. She cried out when she saw her twins, bare except for their *obante* (tailor-made briefs that most boys their age wore then), looking hungry and disoriented.

"Tell me what he did to you," Mama sobbed as cousin Mary first bathed the boys and then treated them to what must have seemed like a feast. They told her that their guardian refused to enroll them in school, despite receiving the registration fees from Mama and promising her that they would start school as soon as they got there. Worse, he treated them like slaves and had taken to calling them "Steward 1" and "Steward 2." They only ate what was left over from Di Kathy's dinner. Kathy stole some food for them one day while he was at work and he found out. He made them stick out their tongues so he could search for traces of palm oil and food particles. When he found the necessary evidence on their tongues, he beat them and Kathy with a strap and denied them all food for the next few days. Then he began measuring the food in his house. He used a ruler on the yam and noted exactly how many inches of it was left after each use; he kept a good account of the remaining cups of rice. The boys said that he stopped just short of counting the *grains* of rice and individual beans.

He got the boys up, hungry as they were, early in the morning to sweep, not only his yard but all the neighbors' yards. He dragged them to the farm to weed and harvest his crops and kept them there from morning till sundown. It was almost as if the little man had a vengeance against Mama and wanted to take it out on the twin boys. She still cries each time she remembers the state the boys were in that night, their dry scaly bodies covered with welts from beatings with his cane.

Long after the boys were settled and snoring, Mama continued to cry.

"Master, why did you do this to me and the children? Why did you abandon us to the mercy of this wicked world? Would anyone have dared do this to your children if you were alive? What am I going to do now?" Her sobs must have woken Tailor and his wife, for by the next morning, the news was all over the neighborhood that Mama's twins had returned in shame from their guardian's home.

"See? What did we tell you?" neighbors commented. "She spoiled those children rotten and surrounded them with fineries, but now the tables are turned. Let's see if they can survive."

The twins' experience only served to put more steel in her resolve. She became more determined than ever to right the wrong that she felt her husband's early death had done to their lives. She did not let even a day pass before she set out on a search for another home for the boys. I now know that concerned friends and relatives suggested to Mama that she move from Tailor's house. But she refused, arguing that a nice cozy house would just make her complacent and delay her own plans. She figured that Ogbonna and I were too young to be affected by the exposure.

Meanwhile, another teacher, a man whose wife had been one of Mama's trainees before Papa died, offered to take the boys in. They lasted several months with the second foster family before they went running home again. After that, no one wanted them together, and Mama was forced to separate her inseparable twin boys, the sons who were almost snatched from her at birth, the children she credits her master with saving. She did not let her emotions sway her; she sent off Christopher to live with my grandmother and Anthony to live with Uncle Bona, the first son borne by the wife Grandmother got for her dead husband. The boys stayed in these foster homes until our cousin Isaac returned from England and agreed to take Anthony.

Mama Picks up the Pieces of Her Life

With her children relatively secure, if not comfortable in their guardians' homes, Mama pursued her goals with a vigor that no one had ever seen in a woman before. There were no days off for her, except for Sundays when she spent most of the day in church, praying for God's graces and thanking Him for having mercy on all of us. On the other six days, she left early in the morning and returned late at night, and although I knew who she was, I did not know her. The few moments I saw her each day, she had tears in her eyes, for although Mama was busy and often worn out from the hard work she endured, she was not too busy to remember her master, to mourn him and the passing of the life they'd shared. Those were hard days, according to cousin Mary, and many times Mama was tempted to give up the fight and return to Aku to the family house; at least then she could have had her children living with her.

Other women, her competitors in the *akara* trade, detested her success and many times tried to sabotage and undermine her. Once, someone threw a handful of sand into Mama's ground beans, which ruined the entire day's work. When Mama discovered the sand, she quietly packed her wares and left; she refused to sell less than perfect products and ruin her good name. As she says, "That's all we really have in this world."

At home, she meticulously washed out her pans and mortar with tears in her eyes, but she didn't curse or complain to anyone. When her regular customers expressed disappointment that they would not get their favorite breakfast that day, Mama answered simply, "It wasn't meant to be, but by God's grace, I'll have your breakfast tomorrow." To Mary, who was distraught over the incident, she said, "It is the work of the devil; we'll pray harder so God will not allow Satan to cross our path again."

The next day, she was more careful and guarded her wares with hawk eyes. The women, disarmed by her quiet acceptance the day before, shook their heads in amazement, and kept away from her from then on. She even beat Tailor's wife at her own game. Mama killed her with kindness and generosity, and the two women eventually became friends. In fact they became so close that when Tailor's fourth daughter was born, Mama was asked to be godmother to the child she called *Chikaodili* (It's All in God's Hands). She never raised her voice or became visibly angry at anyone.

When her trading began to pay off and required more attention than she alone was able to give it, Mama brought in a couple of cousins to help her. The two girls helped her not only with the morning *akara* business but with the market stall, where her stand continued to grow. When she felt confident enough, she went to larger markets like Otu Onitsha, one of the largest markets on the West African coast, where she purchased bales of assorted clothing material. She started her cloth trade with plain colored material, manufactured and marketed by United African Company (UAC), the trademark under which the clothing materials were recognized. The cloth came in all shades and colors of the rainbow. It was used mostly for school uniforms and play clothes for children. Then she expanded into the adult market, buying not only the cheap prints made in Nigeria, but also the more expensive Dutch and English waxes of *abada*, the traditional prints, plus silky Georges from Asia, and laces from all over the world.

The more customers she acquired, the more confident she grew and the more risks she was willing to take. She expanded her business into sewing women's blouses and children's dresses. The intricate cutting and sewing proved very demanding, because she did all the work, from the measuring to the hemming, by herself.

Then someone suggested that she resume her women-in-training business, but Mama was hesitant. She still lived in one room in Tailor's house, and there wasn't space for an additional person. Besides, she didn't think it would be fair to take other people's wives into another's household. That would have to wait until later. However, Mama was able to put five apprentices to work. They arrived early in the morning and left late in the afternoon, after the market shed was closed. Mama trained these girls to become seamstresses in exchange for their help in her dressmaking business.

Her enterprises continued to grow at a pace that no one would have thought possible for one so young and inexperienced, but she did not even pause; she continued to labor as if her children's lives depended on the proceeds of each minute's business. No one can explain how she achieved all that she did—the *akara* business, the food stall, and the cloth and dressmaking trade—in less than a year, except to say that it was the way God wanted it.

But knowing Mama as well as I do, I'm sure that her success was a result of hard work, not sorcery, not even luck. It was sheer sweat, hers. Mama still attributes it to my father, his good name, and the doors that were opened to her simply because of him. It's true that my father's posthumous influence didn't hurt, but the path that she chose was not even one that required another's influence. Mama's goal could only be achieved with hard work and unyielding dedication to quality. People remember Mama in those first days of finding herself as very polite and kind, unusual for a trader. She did not hesitate to extend herself to others, even when she was not able to earn enough to support her own family.

Finally, Mama began to think the unthinkable. She started planning to build a house, a house of her very own. She says the thought emerged slowly. Her brother-in-law, the one who provided for her in her year of mourning, suggested that it was time to move out of Tailor's house, for Mama had clearly outgrown the one room she moved into less than two years earlier. Mama asked, "Where would I go? A woman alone?"

She understood her society's attitude toward women in general, and herself in particular. While living in Tailor's house had its limitations, it provided more than shelter. She lived under her husband's relative's roof, in an extended family. She thus felt herself protected from the unwanted advances of men who would have otherwise taken advantage of her. She would have been perceived as a woman alone and fair game to anyone who desired her. Even while she lived in Tailor's house, she had to fend off the advances of men, and there was no doubt in anybody's mind that without Tailor's presence, the situation would have become disastrous for her.

It was also the thought that she could be inconveniencing her hosts that firmed the idea of a house in her mind. The more she thought of it, the more sense it made. She wouldn't have to pay rent to anyone and she could use that money to improve other undeveloped plots of land bought by her husband. It wasn't practical to move into someone else's yard and rent at most two rooms when she could move into her own house with as much room as she wanted. Still, Mama did not know how to tell her brothers-in-law of her plans. She knew that if they chose to, they could oppose her plans and squelch her efforts. She had to tread lightly until she was adequately prepared to finance the project herself.

Mama Starts to Build a House

Mama still lives in the house she built. The house, completed around my third birthday, means everything to Mama. It was her declaration of independence and the beginning of her long journey to becoming the most respected woman in our region.

No other Ibo woman we've heard of built or even attempted to build a house until at least a decade after Mama completed hers. There were probably only two or three homes on the same scale as Mama's at that time. Today, the house is out of style, but its importance in Mama's life is undiminished.

Mama's house was built in the popular style of the day: simple, square and perfectly symmetrical. The walls are made of mud blocks, plastered with cement to give them a smooth finish. The floors are still glossy smooth and very slippery. The roof is aluminum zinc that glistens when the sun is out. At first, there were no ceilings and one could look straight up to the frames of the roof. Occasionally, bats flew in and terrorized the entire household. Later, Mama installed white sheetrock ceilings, which gave the house a more finished look.

The front entrance to the house is up three crudely shaped steps to a verandah, raised several feet off the ground. A disproportionate amount of my childhood was spent sitting on the dwarf walls of the verandah, looking over the neighbor's fence to keep tabs on who was approaching our house. Double wooden doors open from the verandah into the parlor, which is the largest room and the center of the house. Directly facing the front door is another door that leads to the back-yard. Four doors open from the parlor into four bedrooms.

Immediately to the right of the front door is Mama's room; it has two tiny windows with iron bars and wood shutters that open out. I don't ever recall either of the windows being open. Mama's room was never fully lighted. Its dark shadiness added to Mama's mystery. The iron four-poster bed that she had shared with my father and upon which she conceived all her children dominates the room. In recent years, Mama has added a chest of drawers and a table for her knick-nacks. In the years of my childhood, stacks of metal and cardboard cases sat at the foot of the bed and contained all our clothing and trea-sured belongings.

Directly across from Mama's room is the most famous room in the house. It mostly served as a guest room, but was occasionally rented to boarders Mama felt she could trust. Rose, Mama's first and favorite godchild, who never got married because of her choosiness, lived in this room. It was also this room that harbored Emma, my first known suitor, who caused me a lot of misery in my growing years. I was standing in this room on the day that Mama first told me she had selected my husband for me.

Closer to the back door are two other doors on opposite sides of the parlor, leading to two bedrooms. The room on the same side as Mama's is a utility room where cousin Mary slept and we children ate and did most of our schoolwork. Before Mama built a separate house for her trainees, they also shared that room. The last room was claimed, on the same day that Mama moved into her house, by Papa's half brother, our uncle Cyril, for his wife and seven children.

As originally built, the house had no electricity, running water, or plumbing. The kitchen shack, about fifteen yards from the back door, was no more than six by five feet and had a low roof, low enough to be compared to a chicken coop. The center of the kitchen was the stove, formed with three huge rocks that served as a tripod on which most foods were cooked. We had neither kerosene nor gas and used only wood, which we gathered from nearby forests. There was no furniture in the kitchen, which was doorless and open. When it rained, whoever had dinner duty and was confined to the kitchen would get drenched. The fire was often put out by the flood that flowed freely through the kitchen.

The outhouse consisted of two pits enclosed in a zinc shack that was blown away many times in my childhood. Because of the smell that came from such setups, the latrine was located at least one hundred yards away from the house, on the far fringe of Mama's property. It created numerous problems for us. We had to walk past the kitchen, through another fenced gate, down a crudely constructed stone path to an area that was surrounded by banana, guava, and mango trees that cast a dark shadow at all times. If we had to go at night, we had to plead with someone to come with us.

Years later, when Mama built a seven-room house in the backyard, she put in a four-stall bucket latrine. Though this set-up was much more conveniently located, it caused other problems. One was its proximity to the cooking area, and the other involved the complexities of negotiating for disposal of the waste. Mama had to contract out the disposal to a faceless individual who refused to be viewed in daylight by a woman. *Ndi obulu nsi* (men who carry feces) were considered to be the dregs of society and they performed their despicable profession under the darkness of night.

However, it was virtually impossible to negotiate or award contracts because no one would admit to working in that line of business. Even if they admitted it to their fellow men, they wouldn't to a female. Mama had to deal through third and often fourth parties in order to keep the bucket system working. We had many overflowed buckets and unpleasant experiences when the men forgot or plainly neglected to pick up the load. Eventually, Mama closed down the system and we fell back on the faraway pits once more. It's only in the past few years that Mama has added a flush toilet to her house, but even that is not always functional; the water service is neither reliable nor predictable. As late as 1992, the last time we traveled home, the pit toilet was the only reliable system near Mama's house.

Building the house was not easy. Mama suffered a great number of insults hurled in her direction. Neighbors and friends decried her determination. "Did you hear what the Honorable's widow is trying to do?" people asked with raised eyebrows as Mama's plans took shape.

"Doesn't she know women don't do such things?" Tailor's wife said to another woman, which Mama overheard.

"To think that her husband died a few years ago, and she's destroying his memory," the other woman commented.

"Well, she's crafty. My husband says she's taken care of everything; even the papers are in her oldest son's name."

"But isn't he only thirteen? Who does she think she's fooling?"

Even her own relatives told her she was making a big error. "Wait for your sons to be old enough to claim their rights. Everyone knows it's you who desire this, not your sons," they warned.

"But it's what my master would have wanted," Mama insisted. "He already bought the land and was ready to start the building before his death."

"Then wait for a decent amount of time to pass, five years, long enough to appease everyone," Mama's own brother begged her. No one supported Mama's quest to build the house, which she felt was the first step to reclaiming her children. But she marched on, ignoring the insults and name-calling. She felt she had waited long enough and couldn't wait another minute.

As much as she put up a brave front, however, Mama suffered from the isolation her community imposed on her. I remember her pain through the long nights in that room, although I could not have been more than three years old. Her quiet sobs were reserved for when she thought we were asleep; she had no other way of expressing her frustration with a society that stood squarely in her way.

Mama lived for the evenings, the period between her return from the market and dinner, when Mama, Ogbo, and I walked the unpaved paths to the unfinished house. Each evening, as we got closer to the house, Mama's pace would quicken, forcing my twin and me to trot. "How great it looks! See, doesn't it look like they're almost done?" Two three-year-olds were the only ones with whom she could share her joy. From the distance in the golden glow of the setting sun, the house looked larger and more impressive to me than it really was.

"Hurry!" she urged. "I need to take a good look before the sun falls." She seemed charged with new energy and looked radiant in the glow of the bronze sunset, transformed from her timid public self to a more confident woman. She invariably left Ogbo and me to play in a heap of sand while she circled the work site, checking for faults, throwing questions at the workmen.

"Isn't this window frame a little crooked?"

"What window frame?" The chief mason's voice barely hid his contempt for her. It was humiliating enough that he allowed himself to accept work offered by a woman, but she was stepping on his toes, questioning a man's job.

"I mean this one," Mama pointed out, unafraid, "and you should do something about this first thing tomorrow, before anything else."

"What else, Madam?" the leader of the workmen mocked Mama. "Any more suggestions?"

"Still looking; don't rush me."

Mama was meticulous in her inspection. She ran her hand along the mud blocks that had been laid, checking for misalignments. She peered into cracks and pushed the walls, reassuring herself that her dream was near attainment. "I'll see you tomorrow, and thank you for a great job," she finally conceded to the men, stroking their egos, knowing she needed them to bring her dream to fruition.

"Doesn't it look grand? Isn't God great?" I knew she was talking more to herself than to my twin and me, but I always nodded my assent. On those visits, Mama, who didn't believe in displays of affection, would pick us both up, hugging us so tightly that the wind rushed out of me and I struggled for breath. Even her perpetually wet eyes were dry. "It will be so nice when we all live here, with all this room. We'll be together, just what your father would have wanted."

From my early childhood up until today, I've always referred to it as "Mama's house," never "our house." Although I grew up in that house and most of my memories were created there, it was and has always been my mother's house. I knew, even at a very young age, that only to Mama could that house belong completely. To others in our community, it was just a house, a possession, but to Mama, the house was everything. It symbolized not only her hard work but her defiance and rebelliousness, traits that she'd never exhibited in her life.

As the house neared completion, neighbors smirked in the street at "the woman who thinks she's a man." They began to circulate stories about Mama. These lies made their rounds and eroded whatever support Mama thought she could have counted on. One story told of how Mama had hidden my father's sizable wealth from his family and had instead preferred to give everyone the impression that he died penniless. How else could she do what she was doing? Others speculated that Mama had brought about Papa's death by either poisoning him or arranging for someone else to do so. As pained as she was by the false allegations, Mama had no plans to back down in this, the most important fight of her life. It was her destiny to suffer, but certainly not her children's destiny, and she was prepared to sacrifice her good name, and even her own life, if that was the price to be paid.

It hailed on the day we moved into the new house. Cousin Mary interpreted the weather as a bad omen and begged Mama to postpone the move, but Mama was adamant and proceeded. Rain drops the size of pebbles pelted the shiny zinc roof, making a horrendous racket. Because the house had no ceilings then, the noise on the roof made conversation impossible, but Mama's spirits were not dampened. The smile was fixed on her face as she moved from room to room, shifting and readjusting the meager furniture, left over from her life with my father after her in-laws had taken their pick. Of the four bedrooms, only Mama's, contained any furniture, the iron canopy bed. The parlor had four wooden seats—their cushions had been claimed by another relative. The rest of the house remained bare for months, but Mama walked on clouds. "My house, my house, for my children," she whispered over and over as if she could not believe that her dream had been realized.

The parish priest arrived in his aging Volkswagen just as the sun emerged from the dark clouds, soaking up some of the wetness. The front verandah, with its cold, slippery cement floor, which had stayed muddy all morning, was wiped in readiness for the priest. In one corner of the verandah leaned a white-lace-covered table with a statue of the Virgin Mary on top.

We formed a line on the other side of the verandah, opposite the makeshift altar. Two mass servers in their white robes and red capes walked ahead of the priest, shaking the chimes that proclaimed the presence of the holy Eucharist. We knelt with our heads bowed until the priest started the blessings.

"Come, O Holy Ghost, and fill the hearts of the faithful," he intoned.

"And kindle in them the fire of thy love," we responded.

The exchange went on for several minutes and then we recited the rosary, the litanies, and the Catena. When the priest rose from his kneeling position, we all followed as he walked from room to room, sprinkling holy water and uttering prayers in Latin. This ritual involved exorcizing whatever evil spirits inhabited that area. (Mama's house is adjacent to a burial ground for indigents or others whose relatives refuse to claim them. It was believed that the spirits of everyone buried there terrorized that entire area. All through my childhood, I was convinced that we shared the house with many spirits, some friendly and some clearly hostile.)

"By the power of our Lord Jesus Christ, I command all evil spirits to depart from this house, and may this house shield and protect all that live in it, and may its inhabitants continue to serve the true Lord, Jesus Christ."

"Amen."

By the time the ceremony was over, a number of spectators had gathered, curious about the mid-day event. "Come share in our blessings; the good Lord has smiled on us today," Mama greeted onlookers, offering cola nuts and palm wine. There were none of the speeches or music that one would expect in a town that celebrated neighbors' good fortune. But then, no one considered Mama's house an accomplishment. It was viewed as a sign of defiance of her culture, not a cause for rejoicing. What I remember is a somber ceremony, closer to a funeral than the loud festive celebration it should have been.

But even on a day that should have belonged to Mama, she was reminded of her lowly place as an Ibo woman. It happened after the crowd dispersed and we were seated on the dwarf walls of the verandah, from which we could see anyone approaching from as far away as half a mile. The smile on Mama's face disappeared suddenly, and in its place was a deep frown. We all noticed her peering intently toward the road. She stared as if transfixed, then started shaking her head.

"It can't be. This can't be happening now," she muttered. The rest of us looked and saw our uncle Cyril, Papa's half brother, walking ahead of his wife and six children. All except our uncle carried loads on their heads and we knew what that meant.

Uncle Cyril was a likeable individual, but a drunk and lousy provider for his family. When our father was alive, Cyril and his family had followed Papa to his postings and occupied the servants' quarters of his residences. When Papa died, Cyril latched on to another cousin, moving into their two-room residence with his wife and children. I saw Mama gird herself, retying her wrapper as if she was readying for a fight. Then it must have hit her that she needed a man by her side, so she beckoned John, who had come home for the move, to stand by her. All we could do was wait.

"My wife, I've arrived to protect you," Uncle Cyril muttered, his voice blurred by his drunkenness. His wife and children, still weighed down by the load they carried, stood a good distance from the line of fire.

"Thank you, but I've managed this far without your protection." Mama's voice was cold but wobbly, and I saw her tighten her grip on my brother.

"What is this? You dare to question my words? Or have you forgotten that you're a mere woman?"

Mama kept her silence.

"Don't you realize that in the absence of my brother, your husband, I take his place? I'm his closest relative in this town. This house needs a man's presence," Uncle Cyril said.

"I have my sons," Mama uttered through her gritted teeth.

"You know as I do that your sons are still children. Besides, this house belongs to the Edogas. It's my house, my brother's house, and you have no say; you're only a woman," our uncle claimed.

"It's my sweat. I built it!" Mama cried.

"A woman owns nothing," Uncle Cyril chuckled. "Or have you forgotten that we own you and everything that belongs to you?"

Mama's face drooped as she realized that her half-brother-in-law spoke the truth. All of a sudden, her hard work seemed worthless, and her attempts to redeem herself futile.

Retreating to the privacy of her room, Mama allowed tears to flow down her face. She felt very angry and bitter, so much so that she could taste it in her mouth. Finally, she reconciled herself to the situation, and realized she had to make the best of it.

Feeling in control, Cyril ordered his family into the parlor while he surveyed the house. "You and your children can use the two rooms on that side, and mine can stay on the other side," he called to Mama in her bedroom, gloating in his victory. Mama emerged red-eyed, but in a mood I had never seen her in (and have only seen her in once since). Later, she explained that she was acting out of pure desperation, attempting to salvage what she could of the predicament.

I'll let you stay, but only on my terms." She paused for his comments, and none came. "You will stay in the room I give you. When you're drunk, I insist that you not come home; I will not expose my children to your drunkenness." Her quivering voice almost betrayed her fear, but Mama mustered whatever courage she had left and marched out of the room. Thus, Uncle Cyril and his brood were relegated to a room that faced the back (a separate entrance was added later).

Uncle Cyril's presence, it turned out, was beneficial. Like Tailor, he warded off men who would have made sexual advances toward Mama and was present, even when drunk and drooling, at major events in all our lives. But except when we addressed him directly, we never called him "Papa" as we traditionally should have, since he was the oldest man in our household as well as our uncle. The Ibo language has no words for "uncles," "aunts," and "cousins," and what children call a particular relative (or non-relative, for that matter) depends on that person's age, his respectability, and his importance.

We referred to our uncle as "Papa Li" (His oldest child is Linus) throughout his residence with us. He died suddenly during the Nigerian-Biafran war, but his wife and children continued to live with us. My cousins were an immediate part of my childhood and young adulthood. Mama extended her authority over them and ruled Papa Li's household like hers. We ate together, and because our uncle was frequently out of work, Mama provided all their necessities, including clothing, school fees, and even medical bills whenever Mama Li had another baby. Mama Li had seven children live past infancy. She had several stillbirths and miscarriages.

And so thirteen people slept in Mama's five-room house that first night. Mama was as protective of her house as she was of her children.

She guarded it with constant hawk eyes. She also worried—many things could go wrong. She even worried that one day she'd wake and find out that it was all a dream.

In fact, that day actually arrived, and Mama once again was called upon to demonstrate that woman or not, she could take care of herself.

The Okafor Deception

When my father purchased the plot of land Mama's house sits on, he bought it in partnership with Mr. Okafor. As Mama tells it, Mr. Okafor had been Papa's friend for many years and they had served together in the House of Assembly. In fact, he and his wife were sponsors of my parents' marriage. My mother treated the Okafors, who were older than she, with the same deference that one gives to parents.

Mr. Okafor had seen the land first and approached my father with a proposal to purchase it together. They would build identical structures and raise their children in close proximity to each other. Mama is convinced that my father alone came up with the money with which the land was purchased, since Mr. Okafor loved the good life and squandered his money on food, drink, and parties. My father had, without question, advanced the money needed to secure the two parcels of land—one for our house and the other for theirs. The Okafors took care of the surveying and division of the two plots.

My father died before all the details were completed, and the Okafors presented my mother with the final papers while she was recuperating from our birth. With her limited literacy, Mama had no way of knowing that she received less than her fair share of the land or that her lot had no access from the main road except through the Okafor property. This was a cleverly designed ploy to keep Mama subservient to them. It was only after Mama finished building her house and moved in that the problem exploded in her face.

Mama says she was completely taken by surprise when Mrs. Okafor, whom she still calls *Mama Nwunye Okafor*, casually told her that they were installing a fence to separate the two compounds. Mama did not understand the full implications even after the older woman added, "You will have to find another way to get to your house."

Several days later as she walked home from the market, Mama saw several ropes running the length of the property, demarcating her land from the Okafors'. The ropes were held in places by wood pillars, already dug into the ground and cemented in place. Mama was shocked and outraged at what was being done to her. The "boundary" was so close to the house that it allowed no way off the verandah. Mama pondered her options all night long and finally got an idea.

Early the next morning, she set out to find the man who sold the land to them. Mama had never met the man and had only once heard Papa mention his name and his village. She trekked the three miles with our cousin Marcel, Papa's valet, who had been with Papa throughout the negotiations. Marcel recognized Ezema Attah in front of his hut, mixing *utaba* (tobacco snuff) with his grinding stone.

At first, the man was hesitant to deal with Mama.

"I did not sell land to a woman," he told her.

"But my husband to whom you sold the land is dead, and I don't have any way of claiming what belongs to my children without your help," Mama pleaded.

With a promise that his help would be compensated, Ezema returned to Nsukka where another shock awaited Mama. The boundary wall, although not completed to its final height, now ran the entire line of the property, and Mama's house was locked in. There was no way of getting to it without scaling the fence.

This incident is legendary in the area. The stories that I've heard about it paint Mama as a reluctant heroine who, even in her most helpless state, singlehandedly took on a powerful adversary.

Once she recovered from her initial speechlessness, Mama charged up the steps leading to the Okafors' verandah. There, she threw herself on the floor and began to cry, not quietly as was her usual fashion, but in loud shrill screams.

"Everybody! Come and see what the Okafors are doing to me and my children! People, gather and see how they take advantage of a poor widow! My people, be witness to their attempts to erase my husband's name from the face of the Earth!"

Mama was unstoppable and her entire household, all the children, cousins, and various relatives, jumped over the low wall and joined her on the floor of the Okafors' verandah. Some even dared to open the front door that led to the Okafors' parlor, and Papa Li stood defiantly in the doorway, forcing the door to stay open so Mama's tormentors would no longer be shielded from the spectacle they had deliberately created.

The entire town heard Mama's cries and hurried to her rescue. There, they found Mama sprawled on the floor, her voice rising above the chorus of relatives who echoed her song of woe. When she started thrashing her arms and legs, some spectators climbed the already crowded steps of the Okafors' to restrain Mama from hurting herself.

After what seemed like several hours, Honorable Okafor emerged and stepped over the bodies on his verandah to stand on the steps. He stood awkwardly, waiting for calm to prevail before he addressed the crowd, but it never happened. When he began to speak, his voice was drowned out by Mama's wailing.

"Is there any truth to what this widow claims?" a neighbor called above the noise. In our society, one does not need to be called on or asked to intervene in any situation. Mama's wailing was an open invitation, and in a place and time when everyone's business is everyone else's, there was no way of preventing a public hearing on the matter.

"Are you going to listen to the voice of a mad woman? A woman who forgets her place? Her husband was my best friend, godfather to my children. I would have gladly sacrificed my life for him! But her actions today do her dead husband a dishonor." Okafor addressed his inquisitor directly, trying to appeal to the common bond among men: women's irrationality.

"Do you then say that the place of this fence is the rightful boundary between her husband's and yours?" another man spoke. No women in the audience felt it their place to interrogate a man. Mama's pitiful cries had most of them shedding tears in silent solidarity, but they dared do nothing that would anger their menfolk.

"I have the papers to prove it," Okafor answered, reaching into his shirt's breast pocket for the papers. As he did, Ezema Attah, the original owner of the land, stepped forward and walked toward him. Okafor saw him and froze, his right hand still grasping the papers that stuck out of his left breast pocket, unsure of what to do or say.

"I'm the man who sold the land to this man here and the woman's dead husband." When Ezema began to speak, the crowd hushed, and his voice rang out. Although several hundred had rallied to Mama's cries, everyone could hear Ezema clearly from every corner of the Okafors' front yard. He pointed at Okafor.

"This man lies. How dare you stand before God and man and tell lies? Are you no longer afraid of what the dead could do to you?"

A gasp escaped Okafor's lips and he turned around as if to flee into his house, but my relatives formed a barricade between him and the verandah, so he turned again to face a crowd that he knew would soon turn hostile.

"This woman's husband told me Okafor was his best friend. It was the man who's now dead who paid for the land, without insisting that the deal be completed before him. He trusted his friend. My brothers and sisters, he trusted this man to take care of his family! The fence infringes on this woman's son's land. I know the boundary." Ezema walked toward the fence, stopping several feet before he got to it. All eyes were on him when he pointed at stubs of trees that the Okafors uprooted in their effort to support their claim. "This here is the rightful demarcation between the two plots."

The crowd exploded in fury, their anger directed at Okafor, who remained where he stood.

"When your friend brought you to me," Ezema now faced Okafor, "you two talked about a common entrance. Would he have taken the inner piece of land with no entry had he an inkling that you would turn against him later? This woman's husband will be turning in his grave now."

"You're not speaking the truth! Here, I have the papers to prove it." Okafor, seemingly recovered, offered his evidence to the crowd who booed him. No one accepted the papers that he held in his hands.

During the exchange between Okafor and the crowd, Mama rose and walked to the wall and began digging frantically with her bare hands. She seemed like someone possessed as she lifted the hardening cement blocks and threw them in different directions. She demolished several feet of the fence before her family and then other women in the crowd joined her. They worked furiously until the last of the blocks was uprooted and the only evidence of the fence was the dug-up soil of the foundation. The crowd cheered and then began to disperse when they felt that justice had been done. The Okafors, afraid of inciting the people, could do nothing except watch, helplessly.

But no matter what they did, the Okafors would have come out of it looking bad. Everyone in that town knew of the bond between our family and the Okafors. My father had been godfather to not one but two of his friend's sons, and had helped raise his oldest son, Francis, who was the only member of their family to speak against their actions.

Clearly, the Okafors had misjudged Mama. They saw in her an easy victim and did not hesitate to take advantage of her. Then again, they were not about to let Mama, or any woman for that matter, get away with humiliating them in public. They were not finished with

Mama, but they chose a less plebeian arena to try to exact their revenge on her. Unable to live down their shame, they took their case to court, a very unusual step at that time in Ibo culture. Armed with the documents that legitimized their claim, they registered a complaint, charging Mama not only with damaging their property but also with assaulting them. The court papers were served at Mama's stall in the market two weeks before the scheduled trial. As soon as she fully understood what the papers involved, she became horrified at the thought that she could go to jail.

Mama had had no prior dealings with the court. All the stories she heard were of European magistrates and Ibo interpreters who took the side of the complainant each time. She was told that the Okafors, who had money and prestige, would bribe the interpreter to tell the judge only what they wanted him to hear. She pondered her options. The most sensible seemed to be to swallow her pride, proceed to the Okafors, and prostrate herself before them, begging for their forgiveness. But ultimately, she rejected that route. She would have been unable to live with herself. She was convinced her master would have wanted her to continue to fight.

So she readied for the court battle, taking steps that surprised most of the townspeople. Even though she had recovered from her deathbed and delivered a second set of twins, survived her year of mourning, moved to Nsukka, farmed out five of her seven children, started several successful businesses, and built a house—all of it by herself, a woman alone—still few of her neighbors could have guessed that she had it in her to put up such a battle.

Her first defense was an appeal for help to the members of the House of Assembly to which Okafor belonged. Her emotional letter, written by John, confided every detail of her situation to them. She told them that she did not stand a chance without their intervention.

While she waited for their response, she made several trips to Ezema Attah's village, armed with cola nuts, gallons of palm wine, and other gifts. She pleaded with him to be her voice and testify at the court hearing. Ezema, who himself was illiterate and fearful of having to deal with the government, was reluctant at first. In exchange for what she lost to the Okafors, he offered Mama an adjoining piece of land that would guarantee the needed access to the house. Mama refused the land and explained to Ezema that it was necessary that she protect her children's rights. At that, Ezema yielded under her pressure and agreed to be her key witness. While Ezema had no documents, he had his memory, as well as stories passed on to him through his father who had owned the land before him. He also brought relatives who had witnessed the land deal.

Mama's letter from the House of Assembly arrived two days before the court date. In it they condemned the actions of the Okafors and reassured Mama of their solidarity with her. Five of the members appeared at the trial, which was presided over by a well-known magistrate.

The courthouse was full and spectators spilled into the courtyard; some looked in through the sides of the dwarf walls, and many sat in the shade of trees, waiting for the verdict. The Okafors laid their case before the court, presenting the documents to support their claims. Their children, except their first son, Francis, testified to Mama's irate behavior on the day she destroyed the fence. Mama, in her mourner's black, sat quietly in the defendant's box, her trademark tears rushing down her face.

Mama was called to the stand, and in a barely audible voice, punctuated by her sobs, she told all she knew to the interpreter who spoke in English to the magistrate. No, she had not been witness to any of the negotiations. No, she had never seen the land before her master died. No, she did not know exactly where the correct boundaries should be. But she knew in her heart that what the Okafors were doing was simply not right.

"Do you have any evidence that the land where you built the house even belongs to your family?"

"Sir, Papa and Mama Okafor (she still called them Mama and Papa even in the face of all that was happening) gave me these papers a few days after my husband died. This is all I have."

"Who drew up the papers?"

"The Okafors," Mama answered, eliciting a sigh from the crowd.

"Is there anyone else who knows and can testify to this matter?" the interpreter asked.

It seemed like several minutes before Ezema Attah stood and walked gingerly toward the witness stand. In a manner common with Ibo villagers, he started talking about evil and exploitation, in very general terms. Then he pointed to the Okafors and declared in a voice that almost everyone in the courtroom could hear, "These are the evil ones. They deserve to be punished for what they've done to this helpless widow.

"I wish I never saw this man's face or sold him any land. But this woman's husband introduced him as his best friend and convinced me to sell the land to them together. I showed them the division of the two lands, but the dead Honorable said, `We don't really have to worry about it,' and this man here agreed. I know that this man took advantage of that friendship by changing the papers after his friend died."

"Can you show us the land yourself?" the court asked, and Ezema Attah rode in the magistrate's car to show him the boundary line. Mama and her adversaries remained in court.

When the session resumed, two of the House of Assembly members recounted Papa's service to his country and fellow man and his premature death. They told stories of how Papa spent his pay on the needy, took in homeless children, and devoted his life to the service of others. Another witness concentrated on Papa's friendship with the Okafors, of weekends spent together, of discussions about the land and the purchase, and of how Papa had said on his dying bed that he had nothing to worry about because his friend, Mr. Okafor, would guarantee that his wife and children were taken care of.

By this time, what started out as sobbing had turned to vocal anger that disrupted the court hearing, which had to be continued much later that day. A hundred voices chanted in unison, "Who is evil? The Okafors!" over and over while those outside the courtroom formed a circle and were clapping and stamping their feet to create a rhythm.

It is always at this point, every time the story is told, that I ask Mama what the Okafors were doing while the mayhem was going on. Always, she tells me she's not sure, for she never allowed herself to look at them or in their direction.

When it came, the court judgment astounded everyone who heard it, not because of the opinion rendered, but because of its language. The magistrate first called the petitioners to the front of the court and asked Mr. Okafor to identify himself over again. Then he said, "I'm ashamed of you and what you represent. You stand before me asking that we punish this young woman when you knew all along that you were misrepresenting the facts. You deserve to be punished for what you did, and were it in my power to do so, I would like nothing better than to see you in jail for exploitation."

It was ruled that the documents be redrawn to show the correct demarcations and that the Okafors not put up a wall between the two properties, even if it meant that Mama and her household used their front yard as an entrance way.

It was a complete victory for Mama, who was mobbed by a jubilant crowd. The Okafors left the courthouse with their heads hanging in shame. An interesting exchange transpired as they entered their car, the same car that my father had helped them buy. The leader of the Honorables led Mama toward them, in a last-ditch effort to settle the dispute and save whatever face the Okafors had left. He said to them as they entered the car, "Take this woman home and settle this problem; don't let the bad blood fester and spill to your children."

He was starting to help Mama into the car when Okafor said, "I don't want this woman in my car now or at any other time. I'll live with the court's decision, but I won't say another word to her until I die."

That defined the state of the relationship that existed between us and our closest neighbors throughout my childhood. We were never to enter their house or go beyond polite conversation with them.

Ezema Attah gave Mama a piece of land, almost as large as the one her house was built on, through which a driveway was carved and then widened as time went on. Even though the court had given us access through the Okafors' yard, we walked around their property, adding at least another block's distance between our house and the main thoroughfare. This assured Mama a peace of mind that she wouldn't have had otherwise. Months later, the fence between the properties went up, without anyone's opposition; its presence solidified the two families' anger toward each other.

Years passed without any contact between the Okafors and Edogas, except for occasional visits by Francis, who believed Mama was greatly wronged by his family. As a child, I was fascinated by their glamorous life, for Mr. Okafor continued to serve in the House of Assembly until the military takeover of the government in January 1966. An array of politicians paraded to his home, including Dr. Azikiwe, the first president of Nigeria. We were forbidden to attend or even watch those occasions, but when Mama was absent, we stood on the short walls of the verandah and had a clear view of whatever ceremonies were held in the Okafor home. I saw my first television picture in their house, but that was in 1966, after the feud between us had abated somewhat and Francis, their eldest son, had begged Mama to allow him to take my twin and me to view their television.

Interestingly, it was the Okafors who initiated several attempts at reconciliation between the two families, all of which were rebuffed by Mama. Once, when Ogbonna and I were about five, we returned home with our arms laden with presents from the Okafors. In spite of our age, Mama made us return all the gifts.

Then, in 1963, at a send-off party for John, who was leaving for the United States, the Okafors showed up uninvited, which, for people of their stature, was unusual. The man took the floor and spoke eloquently to John about his friendship with my father, adding, to the surprise of most present, "Anyone who tries to take from you what is rightfully yours will never know happiness. Like your father, you're headed for glory, and we're happy to be part of the celebrations."

They left soon after, and Mama, worried that they might have come to cast an evil spell on her son, brought out her bottle of holy water and sprinkled it all over, making the sign of the cross a few times.

When the Nigerian-Biafran war ended and we returned to Nsukka from our hiding places, we saw that the Okafor home had been leveled by a mortar, but Mama's house and the boundary wall remained standing. Mama is convinced that had the wall not been there, her house would have been destroyed alongside the Okafors'. The wall was God's own way of shielding her from the evil of the Okafors, and the evil that befell them.

Part II
My Childhood

Ifeoma Chukwa Melu Anyi

The names that my twin and I were given, like most Ibo names, are significant to the history of my family. A child's name reflects the family's circumstances at the time of the birth. There are names for every imaginable circumstances, and in the rare event that one doesn't exist, the parents can always make one up.

My two sisters' names are celebratory. My oldest sister, Virginia, was born at the height of my father's prosperity. Thus *Oliaku Nnaya* (Born To Enjoy Her Father's Wealth) was a befitting name for her. Martha's *Uzoamaka* (My Path Is Glorious) reflects my father's confidence in the future. John, born only a few months after Charles' death, was called *Chi-Edozie* (God Has Repaired The Wrong That Was Done To Us). Anthony's and Christopher's Ibo names tell the story of their birth and how they were nearly lost. Anthony is *Chikelu* (Only God Creates Life), implying that only He can destroy it, and Christopher is *Onyebuchi* (Who Can Be As Powerful As God?). Their names, like most children's names, are chosen by their fathers or, in their absence, surrogates. Mama did not have any say about what her children were called.

I've often wondered if my life would be different had I been given a name like Mary, Jane, or any other that is familiar. Mama says that I became my name from the very first day, that I assumed the personality of a "Dympna" even though no one had ever known a Dympna or what to expect. All she knows is that my personality was as different from a normal Ibo girl as the name Dympna was different from a normal Ibo name. And the Celtic Irish name Dympna was as difficult to the Ibo tongue as it is to the American. I refused to be identified by my Ibo name and much preferred the strange Irish name I was given. The name put me between cultures—not quite Ibo, not quite American, and certainly not quite Irish!

Through my years in elementary and secondary schools in Nigeria, my name was the first thing anyone noticed about me. Invariably, I was always the first child to be called up to the teacher's desk, so she could hear the correct pronunciation from me and not risk making a mistake in front of the whole class. In my college years, the combination of my first and last names was the most unusual sound most of my American professors had heard. Everyone was fascinated by the name and asked me about its origins—and by extension mine. Today, my first and married names are unapproachable. Whenever I go anywhere, like a doctor's office, where names have to be called out, I know it's my turn when I notice a nervousness in whoever is doing the name calling. Most never even try; they simply say, "Is D-Y-M-P-N-A Oo here?" If I'm in a good mood, I rescue them as soon as I notice their discomfort. My name has served me well, and I can't imagine my life without it.

Mama says that the day following our birth, the matron of the hospital approached her, inquiring what names she wanted to call us. All Mama managed was a shrug, for she really didn't care what we were called. She had done her part, carrying us to term and giving birth to us, and as far as she was concerned, there was nothing left for her to do.

"But they need to be baptized as soon as possible," the matron argued. Our baptism was urgent because of our frail health. It was necessary that we be baptized, just in case. It wouldn't do to have our souls floating in limbo indefinitely. Even Mama couldn't disagree with saving our souls.

The priest came to the hospital for our baptism when we were two days old. From the bed, Mama watched the nurses hold us up while the priest said his prayers. When the priest asked what our names would be, she offered the boy twin's first, without much consideration.

"Bernard. He'll be named for his father."

"What about the girl?" the priest asked, and again, Mama shrugged. "Why not Rose, after you? They'll both be called after their parents," suggested cousin Mary, the only relative to witness our christening. Mama said nothing, her attitude suggesting it didn't matter to her.

"Call her Dympna," the matron spoke from the doorway. Everyone turned to look at her. Her own name was Sister Mary Dympna, but the name Dympna seemed more strange than most names they had heard before.

"Please call her Dympna," the woman repeated more emphatically.

"Why? What does Dympna mean?" cousin Mary asked, for Mama remained uninterested.

"Saint Dympna is the patron of the emotionally disturbed, and if you give her the name, every time you call your daughter, you'll be calling on St. Dympna to give you the strength you need."

What Mama remembers hearing through the Ibo translator is that St. Dympna helps mad people. Had she thought more about it or been more interested, she might have understood the implications, but again she shrugged, and the priest, already growing impatient at the delay, baptized me with the name. No one could say my name correctly, and the family developed variations of it over the years. I was called "Dympu," "Dymp," "Dee Dee," and "Dy," as it suited the occasion and the nicknamer's whim.

I was given several Ibo names: *Nwagboliwe* (Only A Child Can Soothe My Pain—losing Papa), *Ifeatu* (A Thing Of Mystery—referring to the fact that we survived), and *Ifeoma* (A Great Thing Has Happened To Us—by itself, a curious name, given our circumstance). Mama cannot explain how that last name came about, especially since it is the one that was chosen for my baptismal certificate. Mama thinks that the Irish priest confused Ifeatu with Ifeoma, or that our family was trying to be positive in spite of our bleak prospects. How else could I have ended up with a celebratory name? It was not until I was almost seven and required my baptismal certificate for my first Holy Communion that I saw my Ibo name listed as Ifeoma, not Ifeatu and Nwagboliwe as I had believed all along. We went along with the entry; it would have been unusual to question the priest's entry or to demand that it be changed at the time.

Ironically, today Mama and everyone are pleased that I had ended up with Ifeoma, since it is most fitting of my life. My family delights in saying the full name, Ifeoma Chukwu Melu Anyi (The Great Thing That God Did For Us).

My twin's Ibo names were easier to select. He was called Onochie (He Has Replaced The Dead). It was the only fitting name for a male child born posthumously. To this day, however, everyone calls him Ogbonna, His Father's Namesake, a direct reference to his baptismal name, Bernard.

The Education of an Ibo Girl

Ogbonna and I were unlucky in that we never saw our father, but we were extremely fortunate to have been too young to be subjected to the innumerable hardships our family suffered after Papa's death. We were never far from Mama, even in her darkest moments. Mama desperately wanted to die after we were born, but eventually, we became her reason for living.

Even the trying first year of our lives at Aku, did not affect Ogbo and me adversely. We were the babies who brought the much-needed laughter into that dreary household and occasionally distracted even Mama from her sorrows. We were given the best of the little that was available. If anyone went without, it was never us. My siblings, however, tell a completely different tale of childhood after Papa was gone: they remember the bleakness and hopelessness and hunger. I remember feeling warm, secure, loved. They recall a despondent mother who seemed incapable of saving even herself, but I remember a take-charge woman, driven, as if pursued by a dozen demons, to provide a good life for her children. Because they were old enough to notice, they remember in vivid detail their riches-to-rags turnaround in the days after our father died, the squalid conditions in Tailor's shack, and the many stormy nights they too kept vigil, although Mama believed they were sleeping.

Most importantly, after Papa died, my siblings were convinced that they too would die. That was what everybody seemed to be saying. "These children's lives are finished. How can they survive without their father?" Mama's refrain, "What are we going to do?" did nothing to allay the fears that tormented their child minds, and they lived with this fear through the rest of their childhoods.

For my part, I never knew life with my father or their lavish lifestyle. I've never known a father's love (although I feel a special bond with my father). I could not miss something that I never had. I had nothing with which to compare my life with Mama, and I found it no less than anyone else's. When Mama returned to Nsukka and farmed out our siblings to relatives, we were only one year old—too young to be taken by anyone or to be affected by the removal of our brothers and sisters. We remained with Mama, and in the evenings when she returned from her market stall we were the only recipients of her love and attention; it was almost as if we were the only children she had. She was obsessed with protecting Ogbonna and me from harm. It's also important to remember that my twin and I were the only children she raised from scratch, without her master's dictates about what and how things should be done. I believe that this in part is why Mama was adamant that we both succeed and why she was more involved in raising us than she had ever been with her other children; she could point to us as signs of her parental efficiency.

Mama tells the stories of my early childhood a little differently than I would. She remembers me as a restless child who skipped from one activity to another, dictated by a hyperactive imagination. She thought my loudness and aggressive nature unsuitable for a girl. My twin was my opposite: extremely shy, quiet, more likely than I to sit through an entire activity. Our "switched" identities worried Mama. She said many times, even in my hearing, "Dympna should have been the boy and Ogbo the girl."

In those early years, Mama occasionally tried to live out her fantasy and she cross-dressed us, putting Ogbo's short pants and collared shirts on me, while Ogbo wore my frocks. One time, I could not contain my excitement and ran around the rooms of our compound, showing off my strange clothing. "See?" she said. "The girl has no shame. What are we going to do with her?"

I, on the other hand, remember myself as I was and still am: outgoing, revved up, overly friendly, even to strangers. I skipped rather than walked, most times "always in a hurry to get somewhere."

I also remember the distress and pain my "unwomanly" behavior caused Mama. Some of my earliest memories involve Mama trying to get me to act like a good Ibo girl.

"You need to begin acting properly," Mama warned me constantly. "Don't you see how other girls behave? Why are you acting like a boy?" She was concerned that I would not learn the rigid boundaries that separate boys from girls—that dictate our code of behavior, that embody all the expectations accompanying us through life. This pattern of maternal worry has followed me all through my life, even to this day.

I don't have any memories of when I could not read, and I don't remember being taught by anyone. Learning was the center of my life. My "education" was not limited to the long hours spent in school each day. It occupied my every waking hour. Mama filled whatever gaps were left by the teachers of the convent school, focusing on the art of Ibo womanhood: my behavior, my walk, down to the swinging of my arms.

"Don't you realize you're a woman!" she yelled, both in desperation and exasperation, more times than anyone can remember. "It will not matter that you're number one in your class; what will matter is how you conduct yourself," she berated me many times. Nevertheless, Mama sent me off to school a month before I turned three. "She's too restless and needs some discipline," she explained.

My twin was kept home for two additional years. This puzzled many people in our small town. Families then (and now) placed little value on a girl's education, and a school was not the proper place for a mother of that time to send a gender-confused child. A more proper step would have been to send me to a stricter relative who would prepare me for my lot in life. Mama chose not only to send me to school, but also when I was much younger than the acceptable age.

I remember bits and pieces of my first day at Holy Rosary Convent School. I had no first-day jitters. I wasn't a stranger to the school environment, for I had followed older cousins to school before that.

In the absence of birth certificates, the nuns who ran the schools used size as the admission criterion, and I didn't measure up. I was thus refused admission and shoved to the side, where I watched in disappointment as the hordes of other children filed into the classrooms. I was forgotten there in the burning sun that scalded my scalp until a passing nun mistook me for a child visiting a sibling. She engaged me in a conversation. By the end of that talk, I had sold myself and she was eager to convince the headmistress that I belonged in school despite my age.

I was a show-off. Presented with the opportunity, I counted to a hundred, recited my ABC's, identified all the letters of the alphabet, and sounded some words that were flashed before me. I rattled off the Apostle's Creed, Our Father, and Hail Mary, and would have done a lot more had the sisters not stopped me. They let me sit in a class, with the stipulation that I would not be promoted until I turned six. Even that condition was waived at the end of my first year when they realized that I was well ahead of the other, much older children in my class.

The three-mile walk to school was too much for me to negotiate, so Mama devised ways to ease the hardship. Older cousins alternated between carrying me on their backs and carrying a bucket of water, pouring a cup at a time in places where I would step. This was to prevent the burns that many children suffered on their feet from the intense heat and the scorching soil.

School became my life. Much to Mama's credit, she encouraged me to excel and insisted that I always come first in my class ranking, although she must have been aware that my academic prowess would create problems in the future. My performance in school was superlative for several reasons. First, I could no more control my natural abilities than I could my breathing. Learning came naturally, and it was the most fulfilling part of my growing up. I never had to strain or labor over textbooks as did a majority of my classmates. All I needed to maintain my first place in my class was to be present at a lecture or discussion on any subject. Second, I felt compelled to succeed to reward my mother for all her hard work. Excellent grades were the best acknowledgement I could offer for her sacrifices on our behalf. Third, I wanted my dead father to be proud of me from wherever he was. I wanted him to see that I was worthy to be his daughter and that I carried his name proudly and suitably.

Ibo children of my age and class did not usually spend time with their parents. A child who hung around in the presence of adults was considered too bold. "Aren't there any children your own age?" such a child would be asked. Children spent time with other children; adults spent time with adults.

In between were the needy disadvantaged cousins who lived in our household and doubled as our playmates and house help. When we rose in the morning, Mama was already gone, first to morning mass, then to the market. Who ensured that we were up and readied for school? In our case, cousin Mary, the unlucky one, our oldest cousin on Mama's side. She ran our household with more iron in her fist than even Mama would have used. She was warm, loving, and generous with her affections, but Mary was so consumed with not disappointing Mama that she overdid it. If we slept late by a couple of minutes and didn't jump up from the mat the second we heard her calling our names, she walked into Mama's room where my twin and I slept and swung the cane a few times, unmindful of where it landed. The stinging welts on the skin where the cane landed not only woke us up, but made us toe the line for several days following.

After waking up, depending on our age, we went about our morning chores. Everyone had responsibilities in Mama's household. For years, mine included sweeping fallen orange and guava leaves from the entire front yard, an expanse of unpaved land covered with gravel that made my chore nearly impossible. There even had to be a style to my sweeping. I had to be bent from the hips (boys could stand up when they did the same job).

After Mary's inspection, I was bathed, for I was not trusted to wash my own body until I was living away at school, and dressed in my starched-white dress uniform. Our breakfast usually consisted of left-over foods from the previous night, which I often refused to eat. Consequently, I walked the three miles to school and sat in class till almost three o'clock on an empty stomach. By the time I got home, I was ready and eager to eat whatever was offered me. Mealtime, the same as every event in our lives, no matter how routine, was an opportunity to teach us a lesson about life. Our mealtimes at home were not what most Americans might imagine. I never once sat down to a meal with my mother, or any adults for that matter, before I left home for the United States. Children ate with other children, usually from one plate of food shared by as many as four children who sat around it on the bare floor. The food's position in the center should have ensured that it was the focus of our attention, but Mama insisted that we try to look at anything but the food. We were only supposed to glance at it when our hands made contact with it.

She explained that if we didn't look at the plate, we were less likely to get into mealtime battles, because we wouldn't notice who was taking how much of the food.

Mama stressed over and over that food was not to become the center of our existence, no matter how little of it we had. A few times in my life, during the Nigerian-Biafran war, for example, when we didn't have food, I began to appreciate Mama's lessons. "People who dwell on food," she warned, "never get anywhere. They're so consumed with their obsession that they spend all their time scheming how to eat behind everyone's back.

"What do you think happened to Grace's mother?" she lectured us once after a particularly gruesome fight for food. Fortunately, the fight had very little to do with me. Another girl on my "eating team" had deliberately and craftily lifted the only piece of meat in our soup and smuggled it into her mouth. Before anyone was the wiser, she tried to swallow it whole (chewing would have given her away). With this act, she committed the most grievous of food crimes. We usually saved the meat for last and shared it among all the children eating. Often, the size of each portion was no larger than a red kidney bean, but we held it in our mouths for as long as we could, savoring the moment. This girl had, in a single impulsive act, denied us all the only pleasure of the meal. Another girl in our group noticed the larceny and pounced on the thief, grabbing her by the throat in a choke. In the ensuing struggle, the bowl of soup was overturned and the rest of us joined in beating the errant girl. Then cousin Mary walked in.

"Have you all lost your minds?" Mary miraculously produced her cane and went swish, swish, swish, her blows landing on random arms, backs, legs, and heads. The thief was the luckiest of the bunch, for she was so buried under our bodies that not one stinging blow landed on her. But such was Mama's brand of justice, and cousin Mary administered it faithfully. Her contention was that one erring person should not have caused the rest of us to get out of control, for then we were no better than the perpetrator. After we all cleaned up the slippery floor resulting from the spilled okra soup, we waited for Mama and the lecture we knew was imminent in the parlor, our almost empty tummies rumbling in protest.

"You all know Grace's mother?" We nodded our heads. Everyone knew the woman who allowed her love for food to damage her relationship with the whole world, including her husband. At the time of our food fight, Mama Grace still lived alone on an uncleared plot of land in an unfinished round mud hut with thatched roof. Smoke was always rising from her hut, evidence that she cooked around the clock. So great was her love for food that she couldn't bear to put out her fire, probably from fear that she wouldn't be able to start it again. No one visited her, not even her daughter Grace, who lived with her father. Mama Grace was so obsessed with food that she was said to have refused to share her food with her visiting mother-in-law. She simply told the older woman there wasn't enough food to go around.

Mama repeated what we'd already heard about Grace's mother a dozen times, and concluded with the moral. "Cooked food is not worth making enemies over. You'll have only regrets to show for it, certainly not the food." Most Ibos believe that *ihe oku gbulu buzi nsi* (anything that's been cooked is already in a decaying stage). Food can only satisfy a temporary craving, nothing more, and it should never take the place of friends.

The only food we ate with any utensils was rice. Everything else was scooped up with our bare hands. There was always enough to eat (except during the war), but the eating system resulted in a lot of anxiety and fights. At many different times in my childhood, I was grouped with girls who were as much as five years older, whose wider hands could hold more food. When we ate rice, I used a teaspoon, while they were assigned tablespoons with which they shoveled home more than their share. When we ate *foo-foo* the bigger girls molded larger balls faster than I could. *Foo-foo* is an everyday staple in the Ibo diet that is made of cassava or yam. It is dough-like in color and texture, and is molded into round balls to be eaten, with bare hands, with soups of different kinds.

Meal times became a major source of frustration in my life. But I was forbidden to complain about food, even on the occasions when I barely got enough to sustain me. If I made the mistake of complaining to Mama, I was lectured about Mama Grace and sent away without the satisfaction I sought. On some of those occasions, I retreated to the kitchen area, where, if cousin Mary was in a charitable mood and noticed my discomfort, she would sneak some food to me. While I ate, she would mutter under her breath about Mama's generosity. "Even she must see that these animals she fills her house with are depriving her own children."

This is not to say I was a deprived child. On the contrary, Mama struggled to provide well for all of us. Most times, we were well fed. Compared to other families in our town, we were in heaven. We never went without meals; we ate simple staple foods, depending on the season and what was selling cheapest at the market. Breakfast was always whatever food was left over from the night before. If our dinner was beans and yam, so was the next day's breakfast. I suspect that it was more out of practicality than punishment or frugality. Mama bought her first refrigerator in 1974. Before then, we had no way of preserving already cooked food, and we didn't throw food away. If we didn't finish the leftover dinner for breakfast, we started lunch with it. That happened rarely, for our home was constantly filled with either trainees or poor cousins who were always hungry.

Lunch was consistently *foo-foo* and a vegetable soup, the heaviest meal of the day, as it deserved to be. The children returned from school around three o'clock in the afternoon. The school authorities did not permit snacks at school for several reasons: the school did not have the facilities to set up an eating area, and allowing us to eat while standing would undermine all our teachers' efforts to turn us into civilized Christian ladies; more importantly, only a few children could have afforded to bring snacks, so our teachers were guarding against the problems that such a situation would create. Because of all that, we were usually ravenous by then. Dinner was eaten late, between eight and nine, depending on Mama's agenda and how late the nightly prayers ran. Although we were hungry and sleepy during the prayers, we dared not show it. We had to kneel on the bare cement floor, our backs erect, without flinching or resting on our elbows. Then, we laid out Mama's dinner, the only meal she ate at home. Unlike us, her food was served on a small low table, no larger than a lamp table in an average home. The table was placed in front of Mama's chair. We held a bowl of water in front of her so she could wash her hands, and we stood guard while she ate, ready to antici-pate and meet her every need. It was only after she was done that we were allowed to eat. It was a torturous ritual, but no one dared to oppose it.

Dinner provided some variety. It was alternately yam-with- tomato stew, yam-with-spinach stew, yam mixed with vegetables, porridge yam with plain red oil, *akidi* (fresh green beans if in season), *akidi na oka* (with corn), *akidi na ji* (with yam), *ngbugbu* (pidgeon peas if in sea-son), *ngugbu na achicha* (with dried cocoa yam, beaten into chunks), rice and stew (tomato or spinach), and jollof rice. Rice was a treat, a delicacy eaten only on Sundays, if we were lucky. I can still smell the frying tomatoes and onions that greeted our return from church on Sundays, for on Sundays alone, we ate the heavier meal at dinner time. Families who ate rice frequently were described as *ndi ocha* (Europeans). If any of us was ill and out of school for several days (usu-ally from malaria, the most common ailment), Mama or cousin Mary served the sick child whatever food he or she wanted. The food of choice was always rice, so if someone visited our home midweek and was offered a plate of rice, she would most likely ask, "Who's sick?" Every once in a while, I still need to remind myself that I can have as much rice as I want, not on Sundays only.

Foreign foods like tea were a luxury. In fact, I recall my first cup of tea. We called every hot beverage "tea": cocoa and coffee, as well as actual tea. My oldest sister Virginia came to visit from Aunt Cecilia's house where she lived. Cecilia gave us the tea as a gift. The first morn-ing of her visit, we watched with fascination as Virginia poured boil-ing hot water over a pot of tea leaves which she then let sit for what seemed like hours. She added just enough sugar (in cubes) to the pot to remove the bitterness, and then a can of condensed milk. The tea was interspersed with black leaves which remained in the cups when she shared the drink. I didn't know then that the leaves should have been removed with a sifter. We were each given a piece of bread, which we dunked into the hot tea and bit off a little piece at a time. Virginia told us that tea was part of the European diet and that if I enjoyed it, I had to work exceptionally hard to be able to afford it.

Later, after I went away to secondary school and began to associate with children whose parents had been educated in Europe or America, I became aware of other foods like corn flakes. I thought it was the best food on Earth and had it several times each day.

From the very beginning, there was something about me that warned Mama my life would not follow the normal path of Ibo girls. She says I exhibited an awkwardness even in the ordinary chores that to my sisters and other girls came automatically. It was as if I felt myself cut out for a different line of work than the one she was grooming me for: turning me into the kind of woman every Ibo man would want to marry. She was a strict parent, with unwavering determination, who never allowed herself to be bettered by any of us. She read our minds before the ideas even formed in our heads. She insisted that things be done properly at all times.

"No cutting corners," she preached. "What you have to do, you have to do well."

It almost became her motto. She did not tolerate failure in her children, whether it was in school or at home doing everyday things. She pushed us relentlessly, telling us there was no room in her life for anyone who didn't come first in everything. And she was always seemed geared up for a lecture, grabbing every opportunity to teach me lessons on obedience, and how I would end up if I didn't start to accept my mother's every word.

Luckily for Mama, she and the nuns at school were of the same mind. They not only kept us challenged academically, but they strictly guarded our virtue. A barbed-wire fence separated our school from the boys'. Our lessons followed a comprehensive curriculum, encompassing not only the three R's, but also the traditional Ibo beliefs about womanhood, which we were convinced originated from the Bible and could not be questioned. Our academic lessons were just as rigorous as the boys', but we had the additional burden of learning domestic science and the other areas that helped mold us into well-rounded Christian Ibo women.

Even at the tender age of six or seven, there was no getting away from my Ibo womanhood, not even in the convent primary school where all my teachers were either nuns or unmarried Catholic ladies who lived in all-women's dormitories run by the nuns. If I walked briskly or broke into a trot in the school corridors, someone was sure to admonish me, "Have you forgotten you're a girl?" or "What kind of girl are you?" If I spoke too loudly in class or seemed overly eager to provide the answers to a teacher's questions, she yelled, "Calm down; you're a girl, for Christ's sake."

With every breath and every step I took, I was reminded of my gender and all its implications. I was to know all the answers but not seem to do so. I was to speak loudly, but not so loudly that I called attention to myself. I was to be friendly, but not seem too open, for a "good woman stays within her own house." Much of the time, I walked around like someone in a daze, truly unsure of what I could and couldn't do.

The main difference between school and home was that while Mama raised me to be a woman, with a clearly defined purpose (my eventual marriage and motherhood), the school did not extol marriage. All references to it were made in connection with our religion classes, especially the sacraments. We were told in school, in many different ways, that the Lord much prefers a life of purity, and that our greatest gift to ourselves would be choosing the convent life, a life of celibacy and poverty. I alternated between desiring to be a nun and desiring to be a wife. Either way, I would be married to someone: to Christ or to an Ibo man. My life would stay very much the same, and I knew with certainty that I would succeed in either one.

Mama announced many times that she would die more happily if one of her children became a priest or a nun. It would firm her position as a leading church lady at St. Theresa's. She would be known as "Mama Father" or "Mama Sister," instead of simply "Mama John" or "Mama," as more and more people were addressing her. A seat in the front pews would be reserved for her permanently. She would no longer have to fight her way up the aisle to secure a seat close enough to the altar.

Without his consent, my twin brother, Ogbonna, was designated as the sacrificial lamb who would bring Mama the honor she sought, and he was groomed to be a priest from his childhood. She even encouraged us to call him "Father Ogbo." But when he discovered girls, he told Mama he didn't wish to continue his education at the seminary. I remember both Mama's gloom and tears and Ogbo's glee that the burden of this holy life was lifted off his shoulders.

Our play time and activities were equally monitored. To play in the yard, we changed from our pleated white dresses to what we called a "games dress," a blue dress with elastic leg drawers sewn into it. Later, I understood it would have been inappropriate to play in the yard with dresses on. What if someone fell and revealed her thighs and underclothes? Worse still, what if the fallen child in question was not wearing the appropriate underclothes? When I was growing up, panties were still considered foreign, and many parents preferred that their little girls wear *patari*, little skirts, under their dresses, instead of the contraption that made contact with a woman's most intimate parts.

A pair of shorts worn with a shirt would have been the most suitable play clothes for us, but that would have been blasphemy, declared the nuns. "If God had meant for little girls to wear shorts, He would have made them boys." Shorts were deemed too form-fitting and revealing of our little-girl endowments. At school and at home, our bodies were guarded more closely than most governments' top secret files. Since we didn't know any other life, we accepted it.

Mama's Virtuous Life

Of course, though our bodies were theoretically sacred, it didn't always work quite so neatly in practice. Mama, through no conscious fault of her own, was utterly blind to some of the traumas of my early childhood.

When her master died 38 years ago, Mama's sexuality died along with him. She has not known another man since, not because she's not been propositioned; in fact, she was approached by hordes of men who were drawn by her beauty and status. Mama turned every one of them down, not in a haughty, moralistic way as she might have been expected to do, but in a gentle, soft voice in which she explained her poor health. Mama says she was not tempted, not even for a fleeting moment, to become involved with another man.

There are moments when I cannot believe that a woman, widowed at twenty-seven, could shun all male attention for the rest of her life. How did she do it? How could she? The reasons are numerous. My mother, like most women of her generation, was circumcised, severely diminishing her sex drive. If there was pleasure to be derived from sex, Mama never attained it; she saw sex as a duty, a necessary function in a woman's quest for motherhood. Mama was religious to a fault and whatever physical desire she might have felt while married was more a topic for confession than obsession. She believed with all her heart that the union of man and woman was for one purpose only: procreation. Nothing else. She's told me many times that she got pregnant during the first attempt with all her children except for my twin and me. She also accepted completely that sex outside of a marriage would send her to hell. Perhaps most importantly, Mama was intent on preserving my father's good name and would not have engaged in anything that would bring disgrace to him.

By itself, Mama's virtuous life was fine, but for us children, especially for me, whom Mama seemed most interested in controlling, it posed numerous problems. Mama's virtuousity was evident in every activity in her life, from the moment she woke to the moment she retired: in her clothing, her friends, her walk, her talk, and all other aspects of her life. That meant that we had to mimic Mama's strait-laced life as closely as we could. We were subjected to the hour-long morning prayers, the mandatory morning mass on weekends and holidays, the constant novenas, adorations, and Angelus; we prayed from morning to night. In addition, Mama's outlook was utterly conservative. I was always one of the last children in my class to wear the latest styles, if I ever got to wear them at all. The necks on my dresses were high and the hems low. My walk could not have any of the hip swaying that was characteristic of my age mates.

Most importantly, Mama was blind to many things that were going on both in her household and around her. For instance, she did not believe that anyone else was sexual. She never saw the many incidents of abuse in my childhood that involved male relatives or tenants.

One particular male relative, Godwin, tormented my childhood with his persistent touching and poking. He even attempted to penetrate me. Even at the young age of seven, I sensed there was something terribly wrong with what Godwin was doing to me. But I dared not tell, for I would be blamed for it. So great was this fear that many times I suffered silently, even though my twin lay on the other side of me and could have gone for help. Godwin was not the only man to violate me; he was just the first one in my memory. Many others followed, even into my teenage years, but I never said anything to anyone.

We did not talk about our bodies, and mentioning them in connection with men was blasphemy. In fact, I did not see the men as the guilty parties until I became a mother and began to fear that the same fate might befall my daughter. Ibos believe that a man who violates a child is committing an offense, but his act is not deemed so grievous that he's shunned or ostracized by the community. It is looked upon as a minor transgression, almost a misdemeanor, like driving on the wrong side of the street. Even relatives and well-meaning neighbors still ask, "But what was the girl doing there? Why did she go into his room?" To this day, people counsel the girl's parents, "Don't let this story spread. Think of the girl's future. Who would want to marry her after this gets out?"

I believe that's what Mama would have said had I or anyone else gone to her with stories of sexual abuse. She believed the best about people and would not allow herself to see the evil side of things. Mama would not have thought it possible that another human could be so possessed by evil. She couldn't imagine that someone would let his mind wander into areas where her own mind couldn't.

This is not to say that these things only happened because Mama's religion caused her to see only good in people. At times, she seemed to have deliberately closed her eyes to the truth, maybe because it was less painful that way.

One incident that convinced me Mama hid from the truth was when cousin Mary became pregnant while she lived under our roof. Everyone, except Mama, knew of the pregnancy, for how could one not know? Mary had a pendulous protruding stomach. She had been separated from her husband almost since Mama was married and had lived with Mama ever since. Mama found out when Mary's husband, a man she had not seen or lain with for years, brought his family to claim his wife and their unborn child. Mama had summoned cousin Mary to the parlor to counter their contention, but when she appeared, Mary's silence and tears told her side of the story. Mary left with her husband and was gone for several months while Mama walked around, hanging her head in shame. Mama must have felt she had failed in her duty somehow and accepted the blame for the pregnancy. When she was asked how she could live in such proximity with Mary and not have known she was seven months pregnant, Mama shook her head and said, "I simply did not expect it of her; I was not looking for it." I was eight years old when Mary had Christopher, whom she brought back to live with her in our home.

The most constant thing about Mama is her religiousness. The center of her existence, it guides her every action on a minute-by-minute basis. Her day begins with morning mass and ends with her rosary beads clutched in her right hand. Although Mama's knees are arthritic and she can no longer kneel and rise at will, she still insists on the hour-long morning and the doubly long night prayers, even when she's ill. Today, she allows herself to be more observant of things, probably because she's now dealing with other people's children and can be more objective. I still feel that our lives would have been less complex had she allowed herself more view points other than the one offered by her very strict church.

Our Male Role Models

Only some of the men in our lives were abusive. Others, though not entirely positive with their influence, weren't entirely negative either. The fact was that without some male presence in our household, life couldn't have gone on. Mama was the true leader. She provided for all of us and made all the important decisions concerning our lives. But she never once held the title of the head of household. It wasn't a woman's place, and Mama knew her place exactly. She was always concerned about perceptions and how her financial independence would be perceived by outsiders. She did not want to seem to be her own person; rather, she was intent on seeming subservient to men, even if the men were completely dependent on her for their upkeep.

My uncle Cyril, Papa Li, who took up residence in Mama's house on the same day we moved in, turned out to be a great asset in that regard. To Mama, it was like having a husband in the house, so she did not need to go far to obtain whatever male input was required. Ironically, both the best and the worst part of Uncle Cyril's presence was his drunkeness. He was unable to be sober long enough to assess whatever requests Mama put before him. Always caught at a bad moment, he eagerly gave Mama his approval, often without listening to the details. If Mama had been the conniving type, she could have claimed at any time that she had obtained his permission beforehand; he could never dispute any of it since he had no way of remembering. Even so, Mama insisted that he be privy to all major developments in our lives. In addition, we had to accord him the respect that was due a man old enough to be our father, which included marching into the room he shared with his wife and children every morning to greet him before anyone else and making sure his food was laid out for him even if he was never around to eat it. Mama never failed to remind us that in the absence of our father, Uncle Cyril, in whom I found little to be proud of, was our father and that we had to treat him as such. When we addressed him directly, we called him "Papa," and when we greeted him, we had to remember to curtsy.

This respect that Mama insisted on, so contrary to my personal opinion of him, baffled me no end. It was not until I was an adult that I began to understand what Mama had been trying to achieve. Apart from the cultural requirements, she needed a male role model for her children. This imperative also helps to explain her decision to place my siblings in other homes. Mama's reasons for sending them off to live with relatives were not limited to economic hardship. Not one of my brothers or sisters was sent to a home that did not have the proper set-up of husband and wife. They were thus accorded the opportunity to learn about relationships and the proper form between an Ibo man and woman. Mama did not want any confusion in their gender identity. It was so important to her that she sent them away to learn it. My twin and I had our uncle, Papa Li, and as unacceptable as I found him, he functioned as a role model for that aspect of my education.

Though we had to be on our best manners no matter how useless or offensive a man was, interacting with boys was definitely out of the question. I could not play with boys or associate with them in any way. Not that I would have wanted to if I could, but it was rather a difficult challenge, given the close presence of my brother. We did go to different schools and were engaged in gender-appropriate after-school activities, but we were twins. We ate from the same plate, were bathed together, and slept together; we fell asleep together and woke up together. Though Mama argued that I could avoid them totally if I really wanted to, it was inevitable for me to come in contact with Ogbo's friends occasionally. If his friends visited, I was supposed to leave whatever area of the house they settled in and go somewhere else. I wasn't supposed to exchange more than a few unavoidable words with them, answering questions such as, "Is Ogbonna home?" with a "Yes, come in." If I went beyond the pleasantries, I did so at my own risk, because anyone in our house could report me for engaging in conversation with boys.

No one ever bothered to tell me what was so offensive about boys and why even talking to them could lead to my destruction. So, from as far back as I can remember, I learned to avoid members of the opposite sex without really understanding why. As I got older, I began to pick up bits and pieces about men from friends. But I learned practically everything I knew about sex during the war when we lived in the farms with villagers whose daughters were raised differently. These girls, some younger than I, were already married and well on their way to having children. They described, in vivid detail, the art of copulation and conception. Mama tried to disabuse my mind from the pagan and carnal aspects of life they were showing me, imploring me to remember that "These people have nothing in common with us. They're villagers; they don't know any better." For my part, I was enthralled by the picture of life that these girls painted for me. As the war progressed, I longed to become part of the existence they were offering me, to marry a farmer and become one of them. But it was not meant to be, for the war ended and we returned to our Catholic lives and convent schools and my door to "real" life was closed.

Our Catholic Lives

It was the potent combination of Catholicism and the Ibo tradition that sealed our fate. As if being Ibo was not bad enough, we had to be Catholic also; one finished what the other started in eroding whatever pride we might have had in our womanhood. Both traditions were surprisingly similar, even while seeming to be at opposite ends of the spectrum. They reinforced each other, especially in their institutionalizing the mistreatment of women. Like the Ibo tradition, Catholicism, at least the brand that was practiced in Ibo land, treated women as second-class citizens who, contaminated, did not deserve human respect or dignity. Females had no place in the church's hierarchy and were not consulted about its affairs. They were expected, nevertheless, to assume responsibility for the cleaning, maintenance, and fund raising. Women did not read the liturgies, nor did they play any visible role during mass. Women had to cover themselves when they entered the church; even young girls were not spared the degradation. Men and women were separated both in church and at social gatherings. They could not be trusted to be together—lest the women contaminate the men. Unfortunately, our parents accepted without question the teachings of the church. Even when they had no biblical roots and did not make any sense, the church always managed to convince the congregation that its position was God's and anyone who held a different opinion was damned. The few who dared to challenge the church were in fact doomed—to be ostracized by the entire community.

Also, our Catholic culture was very controlling of its congregation. Members' lives were dictated by the church, so much so that it was not up to parents to decide to what schools to send their children. The rule was that a practicing Catholic who attended a non-Catholic school was committing a mortal sin, punishable by hell. That rule did not leave parents many options, since there were only two Catholic schools in town, one for boys and the other for girls. The church even dictated whom we associated with and how. If, for instance, we were seen associating with a family deemed undesirable for any reason, someone was bound to warn us away from them "before the catechist or Father hears of it." If we didn't heed the warning, every community member who was aware of this unsuitable relationship would feel it to be his or her duty to report us to the church hierarchy. At that point, we were either visited by church elders or simply warned during confession to cease and desist the association or else. The "else" was often more than most members could bear, and no one I know ever dared to learn the consequences.

The church intruded into familial relationships and forced parents to cut off their children if they were deemed to have sinned. One such incident involved Dorothy, the daughter of my oldest sister's brother-in-law. Virginia's husband's brother reluctantly consented to a marriage between his first daughter and a man whose trangression was that he was a Protestant. This man, Samuel, was successful in his field of architecture and had set up a lucrative business. At the time he sought Dorothy's hand, he had just finished the construction of two homes for himself and a prospective bride, one in Enugu where his business was located and the other in Aku, our hometown. Had he not been Protestant, Samuel would have been a serious contender for many girls' hands. But his religion severely limited his options to the few marriageable Protestant girls.

Our town discovered that Samuel was not one to stay within rigidly dictated religious boundaries when he widened his search for a wife to include girls from some of the best Catholic families. And that was the beginning of the problems for Virginia's in-laws. They liked Samuel's wealth, and without publicly seeming to do so, they encouraged their daughter to pursue the union. But the word leaked out, and before anything could be sealed, Dorothy's parents were summoned by the parish counsel and read the rules. "If you support your daughter's cavortings with a Protestant, you will be excommunicated," the priest told the father.

"But we've tried to forbid her from seeing him, all to no avail," he said.

"Then throw her out of your home. You must decide which is more important to you." Dorothy's parents made a choice to stay with the church and did not attend their daughter's marriage to the Protestant man. Though they were rumoured to be communicating with her and seeing her at other people's homes, publicly at least, they severed all ties to their daughter. So imposing was the church on all our lives.

In my own family, a cousin became pregnant without the benefit of wedlock. Her mother was at a loss about what to do and sought the counsel of the Christian Mothers group, which told the priest about it. My poor cousin found herself the subject of a Sunday sermon. The priest identified her, giving not only her name and address but also that of the supposed father of the child. My aunt, the girl's mother, was called up to the front of the church and berated before the entire congregation for raising a "loose girl." "It's all your fault," she was told, first by the priest, and then by the congregation, which chanted the words, "Shame on you." After her public humiliation, her daughter was subjected to an open confession, heard by all who attended mass that day. My cousin was institutionalized in a convent where she spent the rest of her pregnancy. I remember the day her baby daughter was baptized. It had been announced weeks ahead of time, and the church was packed; not even standing room remained. Mama forced all of us to attend so we'd learn what happened to girls who did things they weren't supposed to do. My aunt and cousin, dressed in black as they had been ordered, knelt in front of the church, my aunt holding the baby girl in her arms. If their knees or arms hurt, they showed no evidence of it and remained still, intent on reentering the good graces of the congregation. Much later, after an exorcism had been performed in which the baby was absolved of all the sins she was born with, they were able to walk down the street without fear of someone calling out their names or throwing dirt on them.

We all lived with the threat of excommunication hanging over our heads. Mama begged us on numerous occasions to be forever watchful of our manners in public and not cause her to be barred from the church community. Any parent could be ostracized by the Catholic community if the children were found wanting. It was always the mother who received the brunt of the punishment. The husband even joined the congregation in pointing an accusing finger at his wife. If a child was bad, it was only because his mother did not teach him what he needed to know. And of course, the community was harder on girls than on boys. Girls were taught early in the game that our bodies were the temples of the Lord and could not be defiled with unclean thoughts or actions. Many times in school, our principal, a reverend sister, would declare a special week during which we were encouraged to report our own, or our friends', evil thoughts and deeds. We even competed for prizes that were awarded to the girl whose confessions led to the discipline of the greatest number of other children. We betrayed our closest friends' trusts and even our own innermost thoughts, believing that if we knew something and didn't tell, we were just as guilty as the sinners. When we ran out of information, we embellished or made up stories to our confessors. I still wonder how we could have continued to trust each other, knowing fully well that whatever confidences we had were certain to be betrayed to the authorities. It must have been a difficult situation for a child, but it was all we knew, so we didn't call it oppressive.

Number One in My Class

I read voraciously. By the time I went into the 4th grade, I had read all the books in our limited school library. I sought and received special permission to use the county library and the one at the nearby secondary school. My teachers insist that my writing was always a part of me and was not taught. My first grade teacher still tells the story of the first composition I wrote for her class. She remembers that she had asked us girls to write about our fathers and had expected childish, incoherent scribbles, for we had only completed two full years of kindergarten education. She says that had the essay not been done in class and before her watchful eyes, she would never have believed that I wrote it myself. My essay explained that although he died before I was born, my father was the most influential person in my life. I wrote about what my relationship with this unknown father might have been and how that kept me motivated to do well in school, so he'd be proud of me.

I was highly competitive and led my class academically through elementary and most of secondary school. I simply never could allow anyone else to do better than I did in any subject. If the school needed a representative in any competition, I was always the one to be selected. That didn't sit well with a lot of parents, especially those who felt they had more clout than my widowed mother and could buy the school's favors with money, but our headmistress could not be swayed. She said repeatedly, "It's simply an issue of which child would represent our school best."

I received a first-class education, and by the completion of sixth grade, I had studied most of Shakespeare's tragedies, plus numerous other British poets. I memorized Coleridge's "Rime of the Ancient Mariner" long before I completely understood it. My teachers knew my capabilities and pushed me to the limits, allowing me no room to slack off. When we were ready to take the national exams to graduate out of elementary school, I scored at the Distinction (highest) level. The result actually surprised me somewhat. I had taken my school report cards for granted, even after disgruntled students concocted a story about how the teachers favored me. The test result confirmed my belief that I could succeed in whatever field I chose.

Mama would never have permitted less than an excellent performance from me. She told me many times that I was capable of great things. If I returned home with less than a perfect score on my tests, Mama punished me. She ordered me to kneel on the bare floor of her room so I could think my life through. Many times I was left there for more than an hour, my knees smarting from the grains of sand on the cement floor.

"With everything I'm sacrificing for you, this is how you pay me back?" she said when she finally joined me. "Why didn't you get a hundred on the test?"

"Mama, mine was the highest score."

"Did I ask you what the highest score was?" she took on an angry tone. Sometimes she rose from her bed and paced the floor, wagging her index finger close to my eyes.

"No."

"Why did you not score a hundred on the test?" she repeated, her voice more calm.

"I don't know, Mama; I'm sorry to fail you again," I said, knowing it was what she wanted to hear.

"Have I ever denied you anything?" Mama threw that question at me every time she felt I fell short of her expectations. I always answered no, although I could provide a long list of things that I asked for but never received.

"I'll never score less than a hundred again," I always ended up promising, usually on the verge of tears. At the end of each of the sessions, I vowed to myself that I would do well even if it killed me.

Mama never demanded the same kind of performance from my twin brother, who, though a good student, never came close to my level. Once I made the mistake of asking why I was held to a higher standard than Ogbonna. Mama told me I was never to compare myself to Ogbonna or anyone else, but that I should concentrate on myself alone.

All my friends were carefully selected and regulated: Cecilia's father was the headmaster of the boy's school; Regina's father worked for the church; Vivian's father was an administrator at the district office and her mother was a teacher; Franca's father was employed by the county office. Our teachers and parents encouraged these friendships; we were constantly thrown together at school and church.

I was forbidden from befriending Protestants or pagans or anyone whom Mama felt did not embody the qualities she required in my playmates. When I associated with an undesirable person, Mama would summon me to her room, her sanctuary, and subject me to an extensive lecture about "the company we keep." I remember an incident involving a girl who lived in our neighborhood. She was a Protestant and attended St. Paul's, the mixed-sex Anglican school in Nsukka. In people's eyes, it was bad enough that she was Protestant, but she was also attending a co-ed school. This girl had taken to stopping over at our house in the afternoons. Then Mama saw her leaving one day.

"What's that girl doing here?" she asked me directly.

"She came to find out something," I said, for lack of anything better to say. I knew I couldn't exactly say she came to make inquiries about homework or church activities.

"What could she be finding here?" Mama insisted. I stared down at the bare floor, saying nothing, knowing that I would be spending time kneeling down in Mama's room until she had time to lecture me, not only about lying, but on associating with people "with whom one has nothing in common."

I was never given a specific list of people or types of people to avoid, but after a while, I knew Protestants were high up on it. Mama often altered and embellished the list at her convenience, and often we were punished for associating with someone who'd been acceptable in the past. Except in cases where the father or mother were drunks or known to be lazy, Mama's list did not discriminate on the basis of economics, for she believed that one's successes came from God. She was more concerned about people's morality and how they lived their lives. If neighbors were always gathering at a certain family's doorstep to mediate fights between the man and his wife, we knew that their household was off limits. If the man was rumored to be a womanizer or the woman was known to have given birth to her first child in less than nine months of their church marriage, we stayed away. If the family had mannerisms or behaviors that could taint us in any way, we didn't associate with them. Mama probably decided that it had taken her long enough to get to where she was, and that she would not let others' indiscretions ruin her efforts.

On the day she caught the Protestant girl at our house, Mama simply asked, "Dympna, have you ever seen this girl's mother here?"

"No," I replied.

"Have you ever seen me visiting their house?"

"No, Ma," I answered, reading between the lines, as I was expected to do. If Mama did not find the family worthy of her friendship, we were to follow in her footsteps. What made her directives especially confusing was that Mama was the most benevolent person in our whole town and was known to treat everyone equally and with respect, at least in public. In fact, Mama's strictness about who we associated with did not apply to her. She was the first one to visit anyone in despair, to nurse a dying or sick person whom no one else would care for, to feed and clothe those who were not able to fend for themselves. I watched her, and it confused me no end, as she went on numerous housecalls to the same homes we were forbidden to enter. Sometimes she let me accompany her, and all I saw in her attitude toward these "off-limits" people was respect, not disdain or even pity. I never dared to ask questions, for maybe Mama would have told me her own rules did not apply to her. I learned early, without necessarily knowing why, that a good woman had to be discriminating in her associations, or one ran the risk of being dragged down to the level of her friends.

My approved friends and I became what were known throughout the Catholic tradition as flower girls, girls who on ceremonial occasions at the church would throw flowers at the Blessed Sacrament or statues of the Virgin. Being a flower girl was every little girl's dream, and many mothers tried, mostly without success, to buy one of the eight positions for their daughters.

Those ceremonies were the best part of my childhood. We were on display throughout the long processions for everyone to see. Our parents or the sisters made the lacy white dresses and white net veils we wore, along with white Mary Janes and stockings. The common belief was that flower girls unfailingly proceeded to greater things, becoming some important person's wife or holding an esteemed position in the community. That held true until the war came and destroyed everyone's dreams.

My sister, Martha, was chosen, but not as a flower girl. She was selected to be a guide for the flower girls during the only year of elementary school she spent in Mama's household. That was looked on favorably, and when I became old enough, after receiving first communion, Mama invested in a pair of white shoes and numerous white dresses of varying styles. She wanted me to be ready if I were called. I was a first draft; only one child was picked before me. Mama was ecstatic, but she guarded her joy and used muted tones when she told people about my accomplishments. Neighbors ran over when they heard, "Did we hear right? Dympna has been chosen to be a flower girl? God be praised."

On the Sunday of my debut, I almost suffocated from the attention; the flurry of activity around me was fit for a queen. My short-cropped hair, the school requirement, had to be straightened with a hot comb, which left numerous burns on my scalp. Mama herself bathed me, rubbing my ears for hidden dirt and scrubbing my skin with the tree-bark sponge that left me burning all over. My skin was doused with petroleum jelly and massaged till it had a definite glow. She rubbed colored powder on my face and outlined my eyebrows with a dark pencil and my eye lashes with *otanjere*, a powdery substance that got into my eyes and caused them to water. Finally, I was on stage with all of the town's eyes on me. I walked the dainty steps and turned on cue, throwing petals of flowers to the Blessed Sacrament, from the basket I carried.

"O Sacrament Most Holy; O Sacrament Divine;

All praise and all thanks given; Be every moment thine."

I recited the words with the other flower girls, neither understanding nor appreciating them. The day was important to everyone in my family. Although I myself was too young to fully grasp the implications, this day meant the opening of doors, a rare acceptance in our judgmental culture. It meant an acknowledgement, not only of my abilities but my family's as well. To Mama, it was the end of her isolation from society. Although we lived in the house that Mama built, and her clothing business was booming, she was just a woman, a widow, no one to be taken seriously. My honor became her redemption and people began to look at her with a new respect. She was, after all, the mother of a flower girl.

Did Mama Love Us?

One question about my life that I've grappled with is why my mother did the things she did when we were growing up. Why did she become the stern disciplinarian, the driven ambitious business woman, and the unrelenting teacher of morals and values? How did a shy, reluctant thirteen-year-old bride, who herself was imposed upon and who never once expressed her own will until her master's death, turn into the domineering mother who dictated our lives?

There's absolutely no doubt in my mind. Mama was motivated by one thing alone: love for her children. That love alone dictated the way she chose to lead her life. With that love as her guide, Mama was determined that we have a more secure life than she did, and she offered that life in the best way she knew how.

Many women of Mama's generation and circumstance would have taken other options after their husband's deaths. Many more options were available to an Ibo widow with seven children than Mama allowed herself. Easiest was to leave her husband's home after the mandatory grieving period and return alone to her village. Her husband's family would take care of her children, though not in the way that she would have preferred. At home, she would have been bombarded by marriage proposals and could have remarried, maybe not as a first or only wife, but a woman of her proven fertility would not have had problems finding another husband. Mama was only twenty-seven years old and had many more years of childbearing in front of her. She would have been able to fill another man's house with children. This was the path that most widows took then, because a single woman raising children was simply too arduous.

What about her responsibilities to her children? What responsibilities? Mama could have thrown back. As a woman, she had no claim to the children she bore. Had they been so inclined, her in-laws could have refused her access to those children after her master died, and she would have had no recourse. Mama had no responsibilities to us after our father died; she had fulfilled her marital obligations by bearing us.

Mama could have also taken lovers, men who would have helped her, through their gifts and money, with raising the children. These men would have spoken for her, represented her in instances where only a male presence was permitted, or stood up for her children. But Mama shunned all that. She's remained faithful to the memory of my father for almost forty years.

Mama instead chose to devote the rest of her life to raising us. To do so effectively, she had to assume the roles of both mother and father. She was so engrossed with providing the necessities and discipline, not only for us but also all the less fortunate relatives who lived with us, that she had no energy or time left to be warm or nurturing, even when we were children. Mama was so determined to succeed in her role as "father" that she sometimes was unable to be our mother.

But Mama was not totally devoid of warmth. When I was sick and stayed home from school, Mama also stayed home to sit by me as I lay in her bed. I can still picture her tears of fear, especially when the high fevers that came with our malaria made me delirious. I especially remember one fever that hovered stubbornly around 104 for days, and how she held my scalding body in her arms throughout that period. She patiently spooned broth into my mouth and held my middle when I vomited everything. She sponged my head through the nights, never once resting, although she must have been exhausted.

I also recall the horror in Mama's face one evening when I stepped on a broken bottle and cut my right foot badly. I ran home with the piece of bottle still stuck in my foot, looking for a place to hide because I knew I would have to explain how I got hurt. Someone saw the trail of blood and followed it to where I huddled in a corner, gradually turning gray from the loss of blood. Mama was alerted and she ran to me, rushing me into her room where she began to treat my extensive wound. She tugged at the piece of bottle, gasping as each tug brought on a new surge of blood, until she pulled it safely out. It was only after I was completely bandaged and had received a tetanus shot that Mama faced me squarely. I remember sitting in bed, my right foot elevated, when Mama, her tears still flowing, struck me repeatedly, uttering, "You evil child, you really want to kill me, don't you? You're determined to take my life; what did I ever do to you?" I don't remember the punches and slaps I received as particularly painful; what I remember was Mama's obvious pain at what had almost become of me. It was the closest she came to admitting that my death, and by implication any of her children's deaths, would devastate her.

Mama was extremely proud of our accomplishments. While she never admitted it during my childhood, I could sense the immense satisfaction she derived from the awards I received at school and her joy each time I was selected to represent the school or the town at any academic competition. She never once opened her mouth to say "You did a great job," or "I'm proud of you." I knew Mama delighted in my accomplishments not because of anything she said to me but what she said to others. Once she compared me with my brother John, whom I thought was the most brilliant person in the world. On another occasion, I overheard the concerns she shared with a friend about my unfeminine tendencies. "She's as smart as a boy," she stated, her voice reflecting a mixture of pride and sadness.

If Mama never praised me, it had nothing to do with her personally. My mother, like other women of her generation, avoided any reference to her own or her daughters' bodies. Most of her comments about my clothing or looks were disapproving: "Don't wear that dress anymore," or "That style is more appropriate for someone older." Mama never once told me that I was pretty or ugly. If she felt I deserved a compliment, she paid it indirectly. For instance, if my hair looked exceptionally full or well groomed for an occasion, Mama would comment, "I wonder what happened to your hair. It's not like any other person's in our family." I would have been shocked if Mama discussed her feelings openly. It would have been out of character. But underneath it all, I knew that she cared deeply for us.

Ibos believe that good fortune—children, success and wealth—has little to do with particular individuals. *Ifesinachi* (all things come from God) is the accepted explanation for life. Good fortune can easily come and go; Ibos have an abundant supply of anecdotes to support that, so one is generally careful about taking credit for anything that happens. If one congratulated a mother for her son's award, she would answer, "*Osi chukwu na aka* (It's in God's hands)." Likewise, if someone was convicted for armed robbery and another commiserated with his mother, her answer would be identical, "*O chukwu ka odi na aka* (it's all in God's hands)." In other words, no one is responsible for anything, neither their successes nor their failures.

If all the children of one family are doing poorly in school or life, their mother walks with her shoulders drooping, expecting condolences from neighbors. If anyone suspects that the reason for their failure stems from lack of parental discipline, it is never voiced. Instead, people whisper and caution would-be critics that, "The same can happen to any of us, but for the grace of God."

Mama could not therefore admit or lead me to believe that I had anything to do with my successes. In fact, in the past few years, my mother has taken to using an endearment for me, *Nwa Chinemelu* (literally, the child that God always looks out for). If I inform her of triumph, she says, "Haven't I always said that God looks out for you specially?" Besides, Ibos are characteristically undemonstrative of their love and affection, and our vocabulary is severely limited in that regard. Mama is a woman of her time and culture.

All my life, I've felt that Mama needed to be compensated for giving her own life to us, for not abandoning us when her master died, for sticking with us against all odds. It was this feeling of her immense sacrifice that kept me motivated through my childhood. I was obsessed with making her proud, with never failing her. I wanted Mama to look at me and say to herself, "It was worth the sacrifice; it all paid off." I did not want her to feel disappointed in me or in any of us, and it was this thought that also compelled me to make the crucial decision to marry Charles. My underlying belief was that Mama had done so much for us, how could I not give her the only thing she asked of me, if it was in my power, which it clearly was. I've no doubt that my choices, especially regarding my marriage, might have been different had I not felt this compulsion to reward Mama for her sacrifices.

As a child, I wondered constantly, "Why can't Mama be like other mothers? Why is she so difficult?" I thought then, in my child's mind, that I had the worst of lives, and no one's suffering could compare with mine. But even as I bemoaned my existence, and definitely when I was older and understood her more, I knew that there was no doubt that Mama did what she did to save us, especially me, from the same fate that had befallen her. "I don't want you to feel as helpless as I did when Master died. I don't want any of my children to suffer the way I have all my life," she told me repeatedly, warning me of what awaited me if I failed to get enough training to support myself and the children I'd surely bear.

I now know why I felt that Mama sent me conflicting messages about myself throughout my early years. She was quite unsure about how to raise me. Mama admitted with much pain, in my hearing, when I was barely old enough to understand, that she felt that of all her children, John and I were "cut from the same piece of cloth" and were destined for greatness. Once again, like most of Mama's major revelations, there had been no provocations or preamble. Mama was merely acknowledging her own ambivalence where I was concerned. She had not experienced anything of the sort in raising my older sisters.

This revelation took place in Mama's market stall, in the afternoon hours between school and the catechism classes I had to take. I stopped off at the market, which was a mile in the opposite direction from our home, so my measurements could be taken for the special lacy white dress I needed for my first Holy Communion. I don't remember why I had to make the trip to the market stall, rather than, as was Mama's custom, being measured at home. Now, as an adult, I can think up any number of explanations for that special trip, but the most logical is that I was several months away from my seventh birthday and was about to receive the sacrament of the Holy Eucharist. No one else that anyone in our town knew had ever received communion that early in life. Mama, therefore, wanted to use that occasion to show off her smart child.

I arrived at the marketplace, in the company of others, to the cheering of other women whose stalls were close to Mama's. I was pinched and poked and hugged in the hot stickiness and dust rising from the dirt floors. Later, Mama brought out the best of her white laces and I was draped with one scratchy material after another. It was in the aftermath of the commotion that Mama's confession was made. I remember being under the cutting table when I heard Mama compare me with John, my demi-God eldest brother, whom Mama thought was perfect in every way, a brother that I had seen three times in my whole life and who would later be my savior. I almost burst with joyful excitement, for although I was a child, I felt greatly honored to be named in the same breath as John. I still continued to listen intently, for I sensed Mama was not finished with her analogy.

"She certainly is smart. How many children receive communion at her age?" someone said to her.

"But it is not right for all that brain to be wasted on a girl when her twin could have had it," Mama sighed, her pain apparent. "I really don't know what to do with her. If only she had been a boy, none of this would be happening."

"Don't worry, there'll be plenty of wifely thoughts to keep her occupied in the years ahead. She'll settle down," a neighbor consoled her.

"I wish she had been a boy," Mama whispered before she turned her thoughts to something else. For years, I heard that almost inaudible whisper play over and over in my head as I struggled to define my place in life.

Mama felt that a more appropriate destiny for me had to be less embracing of Western education and culture than John's. Although she wanted me to be educated, she felt that my knowledge should be obtained within the boundaries of Ibo-ness. As always, the most important consideration was that I was an Ibo girl, and Mama knew what was best for me. She simply knew that my intelligence would deliver more difficulty than any reward I could ever reap from it.

The Fear of Becoming an Old Maid—at Age Eight

Among other tactics, Mama tried to scare me into accepting the expectations of Ibo womanhood by showing me women who never married and how little they were valued in our society. Anytime, anywhere, Mama would launch into a lecture.

"Did you see that lady who just walked past us? She has never married," she whispered, her lips pursed, like one reporting a grievous crime that another had committed. "Poor thing, what kind of life is that for a woman? It is every woman's worst nightmare. You see, my child, it is what we must guard against to make sure it does not happen to any of you."

"But why did it happen to her? What did she do wrong?"

"She supposedly laughed at a suitor, right in his face. No matter how 'little' a man is, you treat him like a king; let this be a lesson to you."

According to Mama, the woman, named Carol, was proposed to by a man she considered below her. She had no education and an average family background, but she felt she was entitled to better, someone who was literate and could make enough money to live in a self-contained flat (not in a house full of other tenants who rented rooms and shared kitchens and bathrooms). Her ambition was not that unusual, for women married higher than themselves. It was rare that a woman married someone lower than she, either in education or economic status. If this happened, the woman was viewed as having settled for a marriage, probably because no one in her acceptable range had asked her. She was deemed, in effect, to have bought the marriage. The man, on the other hand, was whispered about. "He lives off a woman; shame on him!"

Mama told me Carol had the misfortune of being selected by a man who was, of all things, a washerman for an expatriate family that lived in the area of Nsukka that we still refer to as *ugwu ndi ocha* (white man's hill), or if we were in good company, "European Quarters." A washerman is the lowest of the low as far as professions for men go. The man spends his every waking moment immersed up to his elbows in other people's dirty clothes, including his master's wife's underwear.

Carol's washerman was a small man, shorter than Carol, who was less than five feet five inches. He was also charcoal black, the kind of black that almost seemed blue, and the only features visible on his face were his teeth and the white part of his eyes. His arms, from the elbow down to the finger nails, had changed color over the years, to a grayish tone. Many in our town believed it had to do with the potency of the white man's detergent.

On Sundays, his day off, the washerman paraded the town in his starched khaki shorts and thin cotton white polo, believing himself really important, even though no one else agreed. "Run and hide, children! There goes that thing. We don't want him noticing you," mothers called to their daughters when they saw him passing by their homes on Sundays. They kept marriageable daughters out of his way, for they felt his proposing to them would be like a bad omen, one that could follow their daughters for the rest of their lives.

As fate would have it, he chose Carol as the subject of his first proposal. Then fourteen, Carol was the most attractive of all the girls who'd recently come of age. It was inevitable that when the washerman consulted people about which girls to propose to, Carol's name was on top of the list. He came calling at Carol's house on a Sunday afternoon, in the company of two others. His khakis seemed to have received an extra coat of starch and stood rigidly around his scrawny legs. He arrived uninvited and unannounced, quite natural in our culture. The prospective groom allowed his entourage, as is still the custom, to speak on his behalf, but only after the spokesperson had laid a bottle of schnapps (the drink of choice for ceremonies) on the bare floor of Carol's parents' sitting area of their two rooms.

"We're here, sir, because you have something that we've seen and like. We've heard only good things about your daughter, and we seek your permission for our brother to be considered as a suitor to her."

Carol's father didn't know which of the men sought his daughter's hand until the washerman stood up and bowed respectfully before his intended father-in-law.

"Oh?" Only a gasp managed to escape the man's throat, and he was lost about what to do. It is generally agreed that Carol's father bungled that incident, for had he had a better grasp of the situation, his daughter would have been spared the hardships that befell her, all as a result of that afternoon. He lived the rest of his life (only three more years) regretting his one moment of unguardedness. But if one looked at it from Carol's parents' perspective, it was understandable, considering the pressure under which they were operating. Carol was their first daughter, the first of eight children, six of whom were girls. They looked on Carol's impending marriage as the family's salvation. They raised her well, well enough to attract the kind of suitors who'd elevate their family to a higher level and open better doors to Carol's other sisters. Also, as the father of only two sons and a man of very modest means, the bride price paid on Carol's head would go a long way toward providing economic security for the family. The washerman could not be the kind of man they hoped for their daughter, and had Carol's father had an inkling that he would be put in that dreadful situation, he would have rehearsed and been better composed. He would have dismissed him with the usual excuse, "There's someone we're considering at the moment," or a more outright lie, "Carol's mother and I wish our daughter to go on with her education." Instead, he called to his daughter to greet the visitors, a step that's not usually taken until a suitor's second visit.

The visitors viewed this unusual turn of events as evidence that their host was receptive to their proposal, and when Carol, dazzling in her form-fitting receiving dress, made her appearance, the wowed washerman stood up and announced, "Your father has so graciously allowed us to call on you, and God willing, you'll be my wife in no time."

"What's this man talking about, Papa?" young Carol cried, not as much in surprise as in disgust, her feelings written all over her face. The heavy silence confirmed her fears and she began to cry, saying things that she's regretted since.

"I would rather be dead and buried! I'd much prefer any life than to be married to this sorry thing of a man," she blurted before her father, or her mother, who endured the whole episode listening through the crack of the door, could stop her. Then she exited, stumbling in the temporary blindness of her tears, from the men's presence. They departed soon after without uttering another word. Carol's father sat in stunned silence. "What have I done to my child?" he cried finally when his wife approached him.

"Why us?" she cried back. "Why do we have such bad luck? Our first daughter, her first proposal? We're doomed. Why us?" Her worst fears were realized, for a few days past the incident, it was known all over town that Carol *na aro di* (was choosy about husbands) and that a suitor better be sure he was up to par or "he'll be laughed out of her father's home" like the washerman. Even the other mothers who kept their daughters out of the washerman's way joined in the condemnation of Carol's family.

The term that Carol came to be associated with, *iro di*, is charged with cultural tension. The question that an outsider is likely to ask is: shouldn't a girl like Carol, even in her limited circumstances, select the man whom she deems most suitable for her needs, from the suitors that seek her hand? The answer is yes, a woman has some leeway, as long as it's done with minimal disgrace to the men not chosen. So while no one really expected Carol to accept the washerman's proposal, she should never have scorned him or caused him to feel any less than a man. Carol's downfall was immediate and long lasting. When she passed Mama and me on the street that time, she was in her late twenties, and wore a gown (a mark of her spinsterhood) rather than the traditional cloth wrappers that a woman her age should have worn.

Even today, not only at home but among us transplanted Ibos living in America, the phrase *iro di* is commonly used to explain a woman's unmarried state. Ibos have little patience for choosiness about a husband, reserving serious anger for women who succumb to it. Such a woman is making a subconscious statement—that she deems herself better than men. She, in fact, treats men like men treat women. If such a woman fails to marry eventually, no one feels sympathy for her; she's considered to have brought it upon herself. No one wants to introduce such a girl to an available man, for "Who knows what faults she'll find with him?" She's likely to find most suitors lacking in one or more areas. She may state that he would be perfect "if he had grown an additional three inches," or that "It's the way his eyes follow you," any excuse to push the man aside.

Mama warned all of us—not only her biological daughters, but the tens of cousins, nieces, and goddaughters who lived in our household—to beware of the temptations to look at men as less than men, and treat them as market ware.

Mama's first godchild, Rose, who lived in our household during a major part of my childhood, is another example of what happens to choosy women. In her prime, she was deemed to have had the best of prospects: parentage, looks, skills, everything that raises the premium on Ibo girls. Her body was all curves and she had the voluptuousness that Ibos admire greatly; *Arunwa* (a body full of children) was an endearment for such beauties. Rose had a yellow complexion so light that people rumored there was more to her story than met the eye, but Mama told us not to mind such gossip, for she knew Rose's mother, whose skin was even fairer than her daughter's. Rose was already a student nurse and taking a midwifery course at the hospital where I was born by the time I was old enough to understand the situation.

I remember the stream of men that came to our house and were received in Mama's parlor, and how eager they seemed to make their intentions known to Rose, each one hoping to be selected. Many times, Rose refused to emerge from the room where she hid. "Tell them I'm not here!" she shrieked to the children who were sent to call her, not caring whether the men heard or not. Many of them did hear her clearly and quickly made their excuses and left. But they kept coming, for by then, Mama was highly esteemed and people said, "We're doing it for Mama Edoga."

Mama of course was troubled by the way things were going, but she was so intent on marrying off her first godchild that she decided to save Rose for her nephew-in-law Isaac, who at that time was returning to Nigeria after years of studies in England. Isaac, the first child of Papa's brother Crescent, had been sent abroad by my father, who died in his absence. He had received a degree in civil engineering and was coming home with more job prospects than anyone had ever seen. Mama honestly believed the two would be a good match: Isaac's newly acquired European taste and Rose's good looks would be very suited to the high life of the "senior service." Once Mama's decision was made, everyone who came for Rose was told that she was spoken for and that she was waiting for her betrothed's return. For his part, Isaac agreed wholeheartedly. "If Mama chose her, she's perfect." Even Rose seemed excited by the prospect, and other girls teased her about her pending high life.

Isaac came to visit Mama and meet his intended two days after his return, and in the chaotic celebration that resulted, Mama happened upon Rose lurking in the backyard, not hanging by Isaac's every word as everyone expected her to be doing at the time.

"Why aren't you in the parlor with the others?" Mama asked.

"I'd rather be out here," she replied.

"I want you in there. Go in and talk to the others," Mama ordered and began to walk away when she heard Rose's comment.

"I don't like him, Mama."

"What did you say?" Mama stared at her favorite godchild with her mouth hanging open.

"I didn't know he wears glasses. He has four eyes," Rose announced with the same seriousness that one would report that a suitor was blind or lame. Mama simply walked away from her, leaving her to her own self-destructive instincts. She did not last much longer in our household. "She has other things in mind," Mama explained about Rose's unattainable expectations, "things that cannot be accommodated in this household."

Rose never married; no one approached her after the Isaac debacle. People said of her, "If she refused the engineer with all his prospects, what makes you think she will not spit in your face?" No one cared to find out, and soon, a new crop of marriageable young girls came up. If any man noticed her and asked about approaching her, he was told, "Are you blind? Don't you see all the young girls all over town? Why do you seek one that's past her time?"

"Don't let what happened to Rose happen to you," Mama warned anyone who would listen. More often than not, the comment was directed at me, for she felt that I was headed along the same self-destructive path for insisting that I be completely educated before I settled for any man. "Make hay while the sun shines. A woman's time passes, and before you know it, all these men will be gone forever. Look at Rose if you don't believe me." I never really doubted her; I had seen with my own eyes what became of women who thought themselves too good for regular men.

Rose became the symbol in our household for much more than *iro di*. Mama used her as an example for everything that could go wrong in a woman's life. Whether we discussed the plight of unmarried Ibo women, women's professions, women's illnesses, or even women's walks, Mama pointed at Rose who, at the time I returned home from America in 1980, lived only a block away from Mama's house in a crowded yard, full of other families with children. Everything that could go wrong did go wrong with Rose. After it became evident that Rose was no longer marriageable, she poured herself into her work and seemed truly committed to helping her patients, but her torments followed her. She rotated between the pediatric and obstetrics services in the local hospital, and although she was the best nurse there, patients treated her with disdain once they learned, for someone was sure to tell them, that Rose wasn't married.

Rumors have it that Rose's breaking point came one day when she walked into the pediatric ward and heard a group of children singing a song, used to chide unmarried working women. Rose was upset, she said, only because they were children she cared for and nursed back to health.

Rose handled herself with as much dignity as was possible under the circumstances and retreated to the nurses' room, where she sobbed uncontrollably. Not many people consoled her, for everyone felt it was her fault that she ended up where she did. Then she began to complain that her colleagues were sabotaging her work and undermining her relationships with patients. People found her lurking by the doors, eavesdropping. Sometimes, she barged in on their private conversations, always with an accusation that the people were talking about her.

Things went from bad to worse and Rose became unbearable to work with. Finally she was fired from the job she loved. She drifted to a government out-patient health center, which was not nearly as prestigious as the Catholic hospital. The pitiful pay meant giving up even the most basic necessities.

I remember asking Mama why the Ibo culture is so hard on unmarried women, especially those who are believed to have contributed to their husbandlessness.

"Because a woman is created to be under a man," Mama answered. "If she isn't, then something's wrong. It's just not natural."

"But what if it's not her fault, and nobody asks for her hand?"

"No girl with a decent background passes through life without her share of proposals. It's what you do with the proposals that matter."

I lived in fear, irrational though it was, that I would be the unlucky one in my family, the only daughter condemned to be like Mama's godchild Rose, doomed to misery no matter how successful I was.

Suitors Start to Show Up

Mama never permitted me to get too far away from the issue of marriage. She made everyone live with it, day after day, and she was a master at inventing creative new ways of presenting the same old subject. As much as this issue dominated our lives, Mama also assured me that she wouldn't want me to marry too early, or to settle for a man before she felt I was adequately prepared to handle the rigors of wifehood. I began to get marriage proposals before I was ten. I was no exception. Ibos see nothing unusual about families trying to secure a girl from good stock for their son early in the girl's life, before others begin to notice her. If anyone asks the prospective groom's family why the rush, the family simply asks in return, "You think we're the only ones with an eye for pretty things?"

But Mama kept every one of my suitors at bay. Most times I was not even told about them. If I suspected and wondered aloud, Mama retorted, "If you ask for and are given a dog's head, what will you do with its jaw?" This question always put me in my place and ended whatever interest I had in the subject. A child was not supposed to ask questions of adults, for adults provided the child with whatever information they felt was necessary.

My first known suitor was Emma (Emmanuel). His persistence caused me no end of embarrassment in my childhood. I now wonder what would have become of me had I been given to him then or had he been around when I as old enough to seriously consider proposals from suitors. It was a fortuitous combination of circumstances and my family background that I emerged from his attentions unscathed, for Emma could have severely damaged my prospects. I could have been labeled used property, not for any fault of mine, but because someone, a much older man, had chosen me as his intended with or without my consent.

When I close my eyes, I can still see Emma clearly. I remember he was exceedingly tall, at least from my perspective then. His legs were so long that while he lived, I never grew to the top of them. He had an oval face that was accentuated by parting his short hair in the center of his head. He was a printer by trade, and he owned his own printing press.

Emma became enamored of me on the day he moved into my mother's house as a tenant. On that fateful day, Emma asked one of my older cousins living in our house to fetch him a bucket of water from the public tap less than a block from our house. The way the story is remembered, my cousin said no.

This is the first unlikely detail. Ibo children never refuse an adult. The second unlikely detail is that I then approached Emma, scolded my cousin, and immediately offered to meet his every need. Though the scenario is dubious, the result was important: everyone, except Mama (though her resolve near the end was almost worn down), believed that Emma and I were fated to be linked together.

I walked the distance to the public tap, waited in the long line, carried the bucket of water home, and set it in the public bathroom before telling him his bath was ready. I was seven years old. Emma was thirty-two and already betrothed to a girl in his village, a little detail he hid from my family. But that incident convinced him that I was destined to be his bride, whether or not I chose to cooperate. People began to refer to me as *Nwunye Emma* (Emma's Wife).

The hardest thing about having Emma as a suitor was that he lived in our household. I saw him when I woke up and when I went to sleep, and there was no getting away from him. Worst of all, he insisted on calling me "My Queen."

I'm now sure that some of my problems with Emma's pursuit of me were of my own making and may have resulted in part from my confusion about Mama's sexuality. Emma was, although I didn't realize it then, closer in age to Mama than to any of us. At the very most, there may have been only a few years separating them. All I recall is my irritation at him, but I could not articulate the cause of my discontent. Could I have felt that he desired my mother and had not even known it, or worse yet, redirected it at me because that was so much more acceptable and fruitful? I now wonder.

But Emma treated Mama more like his mother than a potential paramour and hung on her every word. I was particularly bothered by the fact that he insisted on sitting close to Mama at all times, especially at meal and prayer times, so close that he often rested his head on her shoulder (as if his own head was too heavy for him to carry). Still, there was nothing to suggest that he felt anything improper for Mama or that Mama even saw anything wrong with what he was doing. But his close proximity irked me beyond words. In those years, I harbored evil thoughts about him even though I wasn't sure why. If I had had a chance or the nerve to say it, I would have told him to get as far away as possible from my mother and me.

My relationship with Emma reflects the helplessness, I felt about my life (as all Ibo girls do). I had absolutely no control over the course of its development. He insisted and Mama permitted that he be part of everything I did. He came to school open houses and award cere-monies, for I always won prizes; he hired tutors (with or without con-sulting Mama) to supplement my school work; he showered me with gifts, and Mama, who taught us not to allow ourselves to be swayed by material things, never felt it necessary to stop or even caution him. He was allowed free reign over me, while his mere presence tormented me. Yet, no one saw fit to discourage this suffocating relationship. I was to be cordial to him at all times and smile at him in the presence of others. My feelings didn't matter; they were never even considered. I was a female and a child, after all.

Emma bought me expensive things which, I must admit with some shame, I greedily accepted, while at the same time I spurned him on every other level. He bought me my very first real doll. The "dolls" I had before Emma's did not resemble human babies. The arms and legs were not distinct from the body, and I had no way of dressing or undressing them. As I grew older and needed an outlet for my budding maternal urges, I resorted to creating dolls from shrubs. I broke off a stick with branches that could serve as arms and legs. I spent my after-noons sewing dresses from Mama's scraps for these stick babies, which I took to bed and pretended to feed. Then, one afternoon, I saw a doll brought into school by a student whose father was a professor at the University of Nigeria and had just returned from his sabbatical in England with a European doll for his daughter. When I first set eyes on it, I longed to own it in a way that I had never wanted anything before. The doll called me to it, and I could not resist touching it or cradling it; it was as if we were meant for each other. I began to plot how to acquire the doll. After thinking up and rejecting several schemes, it dawned on me that I could exploit Emma for this purpose. I marched straight to him when I returned from school.

"I want you to get me a doll," I ordered, without as much as a "good afternoon" to him. But Emma did not seem to notice my impoliteness, for he jumped at the chance to please me.

"A doll? Did you say a doll? What type? Where can it be bought?"

I described it to him, and for the next few weeks, I rationed my smiles to him, giving him just enough to string him along, but not one more than was necessary. He reported to me intermittently on the state of the search and incurred my wrath when he seemed to want to give up.

"I've asked traders to help me search for this doll that you described, but no one has seen anything like it. Maybe you've not told me every-thing I need to know," he told me one morning.

"Maybe you're not looking in the right places," I snapped, clicked my tongue, and began to walk away. He was the only adult I recall ever being rude to, and only when no one else was present. He tolerated it and never reported me.

"Please don't be upset, my queen; I'll do everything in my power to get this doll for you." A few days later, he met me with an ear-to-ear grin as I climbed the front steps of our house. "It will be here soon; I found someone who sent for it. They could only find it in England," he announced. I allowed myself to smile at him.

My doll arrived on a Saturday. Emma told me on Friday night that he had to go to Onitsha, a good ninety miles away, to bring it home. I barely slept that night. So great was my anticipation, my desire, even my love for this object that I dared not close my eyes all night long, for fear that it wouldn't be true anymore. In my adult life, I can remember very few occasions when I've felt nearly as excited about anything.

I rushed through my chores and church obligations early and then waited for my doll's arrival. I hid from Emma when he returned, and when no one else was around, I snuck into his room to behold my doll. She was exactly as I'd imagined her. I held her tightly, close to my chest, as I would with my children after they were born, and I stood in my 'intended's' room, swaying with her in my arms. A wave of con-tentment washed over me. I can remember feeling similar sentiments when my first son was born. I was so happy that had my life ended then, I would have been content to go.

She (I didn't keep her long enough to even give her a name) was 18 inches long and white skinned, with straw-colored hair and royal blue eyes. Her flawless rubber skin felt so soft and warm against mine, and when I moved her, her long-lashed blue eyes blinked at me. The best part was her intricately detailed red pinafore dress and white blouse. What seemed like yards of lace were sewn under the skirt of the red dress, serving as her slip. She even had a pair of plain nylon white panties with lace trim and matching socks, complete with black patent leather shoes.

"You like her! I'm so happy you like her," Emma said, coming into the room.

"Thank you," I told him, feeling genuinely grateful.

"Look what Emma gave me!" I announced to Mama when she returned, my outstretched arms cradling the doll. She was just as fascinated with it as everyone else; nobody had seen such an object before. She checked the dress closely and then handed it back to me, sans comment. Everyone else's reaction, however, turned me against the doll.

"Emma has given Dympu a baby," someone said soon after I took my doll to the backyard. At first, no one paid much attention to the detractor, because they were more interested in my doll. But when the novelty began to wear off, and probably because I didn't allow anyone near enough to hold it, the other children teased me mercilessly.

Nwunye Emma (Emma's Wife) took over my name temporarily and they called my doll *Nwa Emma* (Emma's Child). I tried to bear it, for I desperately loved my doll, but each day brought more torment. Rumor spread outside of our home and friends asked me if I had become betrothed to Emma.

"But how could he buy you something like that if he's not your husband?" they asked if I denied the allegations. I decided then to get rid of the doll, and to this date I don't remember what I did with it.

Emma continued his relentless pursuit of me. With each day that passed, Mama seemed closer to accepting Emma as my spouse. He bought me gifts that were not appropriate for a child my age. I gave the creams and perfumes to my oldest sister, but Mama insisted that I keep and wear the dresses and shoes. He gave me pocket money for extras and snacks, things that I never knew I wanted until I began to get them. Emma bought me a Parker fountain pen for my tenth birthday. I clearly didn't know its worth or appreciate it, or I simply didn't care and was more intent on driving Emma away, for I lost the pen less than a week after I received it. Emma was livid when he found out. "How can you be so careless, Dympna?" he shouted, earning my momentary respect for standing up to me and using my full name. For a moment I hoped he might leave me alone and start to focus his attention on one more deserving of his attention, but Emma quickly recovered his composure and apologized profusely. I was besieged with Emma's letters when I went away to live at school around my eleventh birthday. They all started the same way: "My Dear Queen." He poured out his heart on paper. He was a thirty-five-year-old, writing love letters to a child. But because he had announced his intentions for me and they were quite honorable, no one found fault with his actions. He was the first to arrive on Visitor's Day and the last to leave, even though I left him in the lounge by himself unless he came with other members of my family. I can now say that no one else has loved me as intensely and as completely as he. Had he been required to do so, Emma would have gladly laid down his life for me. Still, I hated him.

He followed us to Aku when the war drove us from Nsukka, moving into the family compound where Mama had spent her year of grieving. That was unusual, for others who lived with Mama in Nsukka went to their hometowns. But Emma couldn't bear to be separated from us. Mama worried for him. "Emma, surely you know your mother and your other relatives will be concerned about you. They may think you perished in Nsukka." Mama urged him to visit home, reassure his family, and then return to us. He tried to resist, but no one I know can resist Mama's wishes when she sets her mind to it.

"But what if we're cut off from each other? What if I never return to you? Can't I just stay and find a way to send a message to them?" he begged, telling of his premonitions that if he left, he would never see us again.

"Have faith, Emma. By the grace of God, we'll all survive this war," Mama admonished.

"But with me gone, D's attention may be drawn to someone else. Will you help me guard her? Will you watch her for me, for when I return?" Armed with Mama's promise, Emma readied to leave. He asked to speak to me the night before, and having no way out, I followed him a few feet away from the front yard where we stood under the orange trees at the entrance. I stood awkwardly, uncomfortable, for I knew everyone watched our every move.

Emma explained why he had to leave me and promised to return soon. He handed me some pound notes, which, had I been a less calculating person, I should have refused. I was as abrupt and cold with him on that last day as I was in all the days that I knew him. I couldn't wait to be rid of him. And when I saw him walking away from our lives the next morning, I was filled with relief. I felt immense joy and freedom from him.

Then we got news that he had been conscripted, and everyone, to my chagrin, was talking about brave Emma. I thought, how could they have forgotten his softness so quickly? But mine was a lone opinion; the war made a hero of him. Then he was gone. He disappeared during a reconnaissance training of Biafran recruits in Onitsha. He never returned from the exercise, and his body was never found, thus, he was never buried. It was just like Emma to torment me even in death, for everyone told me it was possible he didn't die. He could have simply run away, waiting for the time he could reclaim me.

Mama was inconsolable and wailed when news got to us.

"God certainly takes the best ones early," Mama moaned. "Emma never hurt anyone. He had a child's heart. Why him?" Others echoed Mama's sentiments, praising him in death, mourning him like one of their own sons. "Dympu, you must feel terrible, for you were his favorite person in the whole world." Mama sought to console me for grief that I did not feel. "You'll feel better with time."

I've been told that I cried when Emma died. If I did, I either faked the tears or they were for my guilt that I never had one pleasant thought about him or word for him through all the years I knew him. Or maybe it was pure relief that he was permanently out of my life. I still wonder how I could have cried when I felt no pain, when all I remember feeling was that I was free of him, forever.

I remember my exhilaration, the sense of freedom that I felt that he was gone, and then my shame and guilt that I felt happy that someone had died.

Emma was only one suitor gone. When things returned to the way they'd been before the war, plenty of others took his place. Most followed the traditional route and came calling at our house on Sunday afternoons between lunch and evening benedictions. Mama was not deemed important enough to receive these suitors; a male presence was required. During those years, my brothers Anthony and Christopher or even my twin sat through the sessions with Mama responding to a prospective groom's request to be allowed to "get to know Dympna." But my brothers' response was memorized and rehearsed beforehand. It was almost identical for all the visitors. "My family wishes that Dympna finish school before deciding on all other matters. We don't want to delay your own plans, and it wouldn't be fair to ask you to wait for her." My suitors often left feeling disappointed, but not angry with me or my family.

Defining My Criteria for a Husband

Even though I resented Emma in the extreme and considered all the other suitors little more than a nuisance, I always knew that I desired to marry and have children. In fact, there was a time when I had everything planned, from where my husband and I would live to the schools my children would attend. Long before I decided on the actual man I would share this life with, I'd formed a picture of my ideal mate.

The husband of my dream remained faceless for years. I never imagined myself as an adult unless as a wife and mother, and through my childhood and adolescence, my fictitious husband changed as I matured and redefined my needs. It took until I was finished with college in America to finally settle on the criteria that were necessary in my future husband. In light of the restrictive reality of Ibo society, it seems ludicrous that I felt my individual needs would even be considered in the final decision on whom I married. But I used my criteria to assess my serious suitors and to select my husband.

The stories about the hopeless existence of old maids that Mama supplied certainly contributed to my premature thoughts of marriage and fear that married life would pass me by and that I would wake up one day and find myself a version of Rose, an object of pity and ridicule. After my suitors had dispelled that fear, then I was consumed with anxiety that I would never carry and bear a child—even though my family, both on Mama's and my father's sides, was mostly blessed with women who got pregnant every time their husbands looked at them.

I now know that I did not crave a husband per se. Rather, I wanted to have children for as long as I can remember. But even as naive as I was about the reproductive process, I understood the necessity of having a husband to accomplish this goal. A husband was a necessary condition to my real-life ambitions. Had I grown up in a different society, where single parenting and pre-marital sex were permissible, I might have explored bearing children outside of a marriage.

When I was a child, my maternal proclivities pulled me to households with newborn infants. If the family lived in Mama's yard, I would practically move in with them. At those times, my longing to have one of my own was most intense. Everyone who knew my family when I was growing up knew of my urges. There were plenty of opportunities to expend my maternal feelings. Scores of cousins passed through our home, some temporarily, others on a permanent basis. I was often assigned the task of bathing their babies or carrying them.

After the war started, the young family of one of our cousins fled from Lagos and moved into the family house in Aku. Their two daughters, then six and two, became my children. My feelings for those children, although there were only five years between me and the six-year-old, rivaled then what I feel today for my own children. There were no schools or churches or activities to occupy our pre-war days, so I revelled in my motherhood of Nonye (two) and Chinyere (six). I slept between them, my two arms providing pillows for their little heads, on the mats spread in the parlor of our family house.

I woke early to sweep the front yard of our home before I put the cooking pot on the wood stove to boil water for the children's baths. While the water warmed, I rushed through my own cold bath and dressed in whatever rags were available to us. I bathed my cousins, better than any adult would have; I oiled and dressed them in their Lagos fineries that were more suitable for parties than our rugged life during the war. I took it upon myself to wash their clothes. Often the public taps a mile away were not working, and I had to walk more than three rocky miles each way to a muddied stream to accomplish this task. So intense was my love for those sisters that I often gave them my own food and went without. When we all fled Aku about a month later, I continued my care of the children; I was assigned the special task of carrying the younger child piggyback-style whenever we had to go into hiding.

I wanted children desperately, and by extension, a husband. At first, when I was seven or eight and knew no differently, my dream husband had a job that would provide for me and my children in a yard full of other tenants. I envied the simple deprived lifestyles of the women whose families rented rooms from Mama. Their husbands, always identified by the names of their first born, held low-paying jobs with the local government, but were treated as lords at home. I remember their miserable existence, the men in their rubber sandals and khaki uniforms with sweat stains, but even then they were their wives' masters. In the mornings as we readied for school, the wives tried to outdo each other with their husbands' breakfast trays: fried plantains or *akara* and *akamu,* dishes that took up a woman's entire morning. It was only after their husbands left that the wives paid attention to their children or themselves. When lunchtime came, they slaved over their husbands' meals, to hold their interest, to guarantee that they returned home for it and didn't turn to the eating houses that were cropping up in large numbers. So content did they seem to me that I wanted their mundane existence to become mine.

As I became more exposed to other people from different parts of town, I began to see a different life, a life with more material things than I had been aware of. That view, made available to me by some children who lived on the University of Nigeria campus with their parents, began to redefine what I desired in a husband. Without even being aware of it, I started to measure a man's success by his income, academic achievements, and other accomplishments. By the time I was ten, I knew without doubt that I would not settle for a man who did not have enough training to easily afford my children what those professors' daughters had. I began to pity the women in Mama's yard.

Up until then, I was content with my life as it was. I felt neither better nor worse off than the hundreds of other families that lived in our area of town. In actuality, we were constantly told that we were better off than most families.

I envied many things about the university girls. Those children wore shoes to school and arrived by car, driven by either their parents or their parents' chauffeurs. They carried store-bought school bags, crafted from raffia dyed with bright colors, not like the simple calico cloth ones Mama sewed for me. Their school bags, with their long straps, hung from their shoulders and dangled on their hips. There was an air of superiority about them that my other friends and I lacked. They conversed about television programs (no one in a three-mile radius of our home owned a television). They brought in magazines of fancy resorts in places that I had only heard about in our geography lessons and they managed to create in me a desire for a life I hadn't known even existed.

I became close friends with Maria, one of the university children, although we had nothing in common. I never told her so, but Maria's life contributed more than any other friend toward setting the minimum standards that my future spouse had to meet and motivating me to achieve.

It started the first day I visited her home after we had known each other for about a year. I drove home with her in the back of her father's red Peugeot 404, the very first time I had a car seat to myself. On the few previous occasions I'd been in a car, I always sat in someone's lap. There was never enough sitting space for everyone, so the adults got the seats, while the children either stood or doubled up on adult laps. I was so enthralled with being in a car that I didn't notice or mind the cramped accommodations and stale air. I found a car's movement so soothing that I invariably fell asleep before I got to where we were headed.

When Maria's father's driver pulled into their circular driveway, I was dumbstruck by the opulence of the house before me. When the door opened, my lower jaw dropped and must have stayed that way through a good part of my visit. I had never seen such elegance and rich decor. I remember standing at the foot of a grand staircase, trying to take in the spread with my then eight-year-old eyes.

Maria's house became my standard for measuring success, and our house became shabby in comparison, even though I knew it was considered elegant by everyone in our town. In spite of my young age, I recognized the difference in our economic status, and much to my shame, I preferred hers; everything about her life seemed heavenly, so enviable, so perfect.

Of course, Mama put it all in perspective for me. "If you like that life, you'll have to study hard, do well in school, and marry well." I set my mind to attaining that kind of life early, and I knew that I needed a successful husband to help me reach that goal.

But as much I craved wealth, I wanted more in the man I would marry. If wealth was all I wanted in a man and marriage, I would have accepted any of the proposals I got from older, well-established men who proposed at different stages in my life.

One was an engineer from our hometown, who was believed to have acquired his wealth in dubious deals with the government. Swearing to make me his wife, he frequented our house, often coming as many as three times a day. He believed, he told friends, that I could be swayed by all his luxuries—his fleet of cars (he came in a different one every time), his fancy clothes, his jeweled rings. He was the first man I ever saw wearing a ring with stones. I knew that this man would provide me all the luxuries I wanted in life. But rather than being smitten by the gifts he brought to me, I was angered by them. I thought him arrogant and braggy, qualities that I could not live with. The decision was not mine, of course, but fortunately Mama did not like him and helped dissuade him.

"Dympna wants to be educated," I remember Mama telling him on one of his visits.

"For what? Why do you encourage her to waste her time reading books that will not help her?" he asked, a puzzled frown on his face.

"She's smart enough, and she can be independent if she needs to be," Mama replied.

"How much could she possibly make in a year as a teacher or a nurse? I could give more to her every month as pocket money. I'll make sure she has everything that money can buy." Neither Mama nor I were convinced by his exaggerations, and when he stopped pestering me, I did not miss his presence or his gifts one bit.

It is fair to say that Mama was never influenced by money when it came to marriage proposals. She valued economic security, but that came a distant third to the suitor's character and his family background. She said to me several times, "Long after the money is gone, you'll still have to live with the man." She equated a man's wealth with a woman's looks: both are precarious and could vanish overnight. She counseled hundreds of families that neither should ever become the main issue in the selection of a spouse. "Look at the man inside and his family, especially his father. If you like the father, you'll like the son."

The Training Girls

It was for wisdom such as this that when Mama decided the time was right to revitalize her girls-in-training business, she was overwhelmed with candidates. She had the room and needed the money, and she believed strongly in preparing girls for their future. She started slowly, as soon as she moved into her house, but throughout most of my childhood, up until the beginning of the war, we had at least fifteen to twenty teenage girls living with us.

Mama ran it like a formal school with rigid schedules, and she was the girls' headmistress, teacher, advisor, counselor, and surrogate mother. The average stay for each girl was two years, during which she acquired life skills, including sewing, knitting, cooking, housekeeping, and child care. This training was critical to the girls for many reasons. First, it gave them an edge over non-trained eligible females. Second, it gave them skills to fall back on, in case the kind of tragedy that befell Mama struck them. And third, at that time in the late 1950s and early 1960s, most young girls were still not educated or prepared for any skills, the assumption being that they would marry and have children. And there was nothing more for them to know. That assumption remained true for life in the agricultural setting of Ibo villages. But as the population became less rural and men depended less on farming and more on menial government jobs, they needed wives who could understand the rigors of township life, who could keep a rented room in habitable condition and raise children outside of the extended-family set-ups to which they were accustomed. The girls needed to be taught skills with which they could support their families or at least supplement their husbands' income, should the need arise.

At first the girls slept on mats spread on the concrete floor of the parlor. Their suitcases were stored in the room adjoining Mama's, where cousin Mary's bed was and which doubled as our workroom. They spent the day at the market, and when they returned, they sat outside around the kitchen, fixing dinner and cleaning up afterwards. They actually only came into the house to go to sleep. A few years later, Mama made several additions to the compound, including a seven-room rental house, a two-room storage house with an attached kitchen, and a three-room house specially designated for her trainees. The girls slept in those rooms, although still on mats, even well after Mama could afford to put beds there.

Mama believed that hardship builds character, and she was afraid that the girls, most of whom had never slept on beds before, would become spoiled and demand that their husbands provide beds for them also.

Their schedules were so rigorous that anyone who passed through Mama's training was tested beyond limits and was thus guaranteed to make a successful marriage. They rose soon after Mama's self-imposed rising time of four in the morning and half of them proceeded with their morning prayers while the other half readied for morning mass with Mama. Later, they performed their morning functions, and then lined up for their prescribed cold baths before dressing for the market. Mama's girls wore uniforms. In fact, they had a number of uniforms for the market, home, and Sundays. Mama wanted her girls different from all the others in training schools around town.

They trekked the four miles, carrying the heavy boxes of material and sewing machines on their heads. At the market, they took turns cutting, tacking, threading, sewing or hemming the materials or what-ever other duties Mama assigned, and had to be always ready to account for their day's activity.

I was treated like a younger version of Mama's girls, and was included in all of their activities, regardless of whatever other obliga-tions I had to meet at school. Mama insisted that I be part of her lessons, especially if the subject matter dealt with issues that she thought would be beneficial to me in the long run. Ironically, partly because of their presence, I never mastered the art of sewing or knit-ting, and I learned to cook much later than most Ibo girls. The trainees were so eager to practice their sewing and knitting that they always took over and completed my domestic science projects, which earned me high marks but left me unskilled in some very important areas. I cannot hem a dress, although Mama and both my sisters are great seamstresses; I've never knitted a stitch in my life or crocheted or mastered the art of darning torn clothes. I never cooked a pot of soup from beginning to end until I was married. What Mama did not know is that although she insisted that I learn the arts of womanhood, I was never allowed the opportunity to complete most aspects of it. The trainees either hovered over me or became impatient with my methodical by-the-book approach to cooking and shooed me out of the kitchen. I credit my sister-in-law, Delia, with teaching me how to cook. It is the height of irony that it was she, who educated me in the fine points of feminism, who also provided me with the tools necessary to become a good traditional wife.

Off to Boarding School

In 1966, Ogbonna and I were ten, in our last year of primary school, and aggressively pursuing admission into prestigious secondary schools (grades seven through twelve). At that time, the Nigerian education system followed the British pattern, and the five-year secondary school-program was conducted in boarding schools.

In those days, only a fraction of children continued their education past the sixth grade. Most girls either got married or became apprentices in domestic science centers like Mama's to learn what was deemed important. For most boys, it was a matter of economics. Few parents could afford the high fees charged by the schools, especially in view of the fact that the average Christian Ibo family had seven children. The cost of tuition, room, and board for one child each term (each school year had three terms) was more than a typical high school graduate earned in three months. In addition, the school required that parents equip their children with a long list of supplies, including a twin-sized bed (of a prescribed standard), linen, several sets of uniforms, and at least three pairs of shoes—items that most parents could hardly afford in their own homes.

Even given the reduced number of students who could afford to continue beyond primary school, few applicants survived the rigorous entrance-examination process. First, each application had to pass an exhaustive screening. The candidate's next step was a three-hour written exam in math, English and social studies. The last step, the oral interview, was the most grueling. Each child sat before a panel of six adults who threw questions from every side. Many children left the interview sessions in tears.

It was even harder for Ogbonna and me to secure a position in a reputable secondary school in 1967 because of the looming political crisis, which had forced hundreds of thousands of Ibos to flee their residence in other parts of Nigeria. It meant that at least ten times the usual number of children competed for each open spot in the few secondary schools in our area. I remember the long months of reviewing, drilling, and memorizing the facts and figures that we would be tested on.

Where we did our secondary education was important. It had to be owned and operated by the Catholic church, be within a few hours drive of Nsukka, and be nationally recognized as an academically reputable institution. It was so important that a woman could not be trusted to make such a large decision. Even though Mama made sure that plans for our secondary schooling were made well in advance, she had to seek and receive the blessing of our Uncle Cyril, Papa Li. I recall the night that Mama invited him to "discuss the options." She had just returned from the market, at a time when Papa Li was usually not around. My uncle's routine was to return home briefly from his sporadic employment as a mason with the Works Department and eat his lunch, then change from his khaki uniform to less constrictive attire and proceed to a nearby bar. The "bar" was an establishment that only existed at night in the front yard of a disreputable widow's house. Men sat in a circle on backless wooden benches and were served palm wine by the unmarried girls who worked for the widow. Despite the apparent discomfort, the men congregated religiously each evening as if their lives depended on the hours they shared together. Papa Li and his drinking buddies saw nothing wrong with their drinking and did not seem perturbed by the fact that everyone, including their own children, saw them.

So Papa Li was already slightly drunk and visibly aggravated that Mama had insisted that he leave his drinking group to come home and listen to her plans for her children. I knew even then that his "anger" was faked; it was important to him that "these women remember" he was still a man. He never once turned down a request by Mama to be present at a meeting or at a session to negotiate any of her land deals. They had an efficient quid-pro-quo arrangement: Mama provided the housing, food, and everything else his family needed, and he made himself available at every occasion that his male presence was required.

"Hurry up, I have only a few moments before I need to leave," he called as Mama changed from her market clothes to the more comfortable ones she wore at home. Mama deliberately took her time, infuriating him. When she emerged, she said, "We need to decide which schools to send applications to for the children. The schools are equally good, although we must consider other things." I later learned that Mama was often deliberate in her vagueness. While she stuck to the letter of tradition, she was not eager to have serious decisions made by a man who could not walk a straight line.

"Do what you think is the right thing," Papa Li muttered as he swaggered away to continue his drinking.

I sailed through the exams and was admitted to my first choice of schools, Queen of the Rosary in Nsukka, an all-girls convent school operated by the Irish Holy Rosary sisters who lived in an adjoining noviciate. Ogbonna got into an equally reputable all-boys Catholic school, St. Patrick's, in Obollo-Eke, a little town north of Nsukka.

As was the rule, we had to live in the boarding school with everyone else. But because of our age, Mama had paid more attention to our safety than academics in selecting what schools we attended. Although I was admitted into every school I applied to, she insisted that I attend Queen of the Rosary where my sister Virginia was a senior and for which Mama supplied all the food. She saw me at least twice a week during her normal business transactions. Mama felt that I needed my older sister's watchful eyes around the clock. Ogbo's school was twenty-five miles from Nsukka and was also on Mama's supply list. Most importantly, Li (Uncle Cyril's son) was a fourth-year student at St. Patrick's, and Mama trusted that he would guarantee Ogbo's protection.

As planned, we made preparations for my move into boarding school in January 1967, right after New Year's. Mama took Ogbonna and me to Onitsha where she bought each of us a six-spring bed, mattress, and two suitcases. I was also outfitted with shoes, Sunday dresses, and my first store-bought underwear. (Prior to Onitsha, Mama made all of my underwear). We touched bales of white material before she selected the ones from which my uniforms would be sewn. I watched as Mama chose ribbons and laces to trim the white slips and nightdresses that I needed.

I could not wait to live away from home. I thought it would be an extended sleep-over, and I would roam, unrestricted, with my friends who were all attending the same school. But secondary school was nothing like I expected, and by the end of the first week, I was ready to go back home to Mama. If I'd thought of my earlier years as restrictive and controlled, they were footloose and carefree compared to boarding school. What I remember most is the sound of bells ringing to herd us to our places, plus rules and rules and more rules, the breaking of which resulted in severe punishments.

We lived in long, narrow rooms, housing about thirty girls each, with beds lined on opposite walls. At most, we were each allowed a few feet of personal space. We woke at five o'clock in the morning to the jarring bell and ran (we were forbidden to walk), carrying our buckets of cold water, to the communal bathroooms. It always took me minutes to muster the courage to throw the cold water (mandatory) on my naked body, and I would stand in one corner of the room, cowering, shielding my body from water splashed from all sides by as many as twenty-five other girls. But it wasn't just the cold water that intimidated me. It was also the openness and lack of privacy in our bathrooms, the display of girls' bodies in varying degrees of shape and size in the dimly lit space. Most mornings, I only managed to wash my face, arms, and legs before mass.

After the hour-long mass, we ate breakfast and then did our morning chores. The actual school day lasted from eight o'clock in the morning till two in the afternoon, during which we were taught subjects ranging from science to music, from Latin to economics. After school, we had lunch, took an hour-long siesta, and returned to our classrooms for afternoon prep. Then there was one hour for organized play or club activities, followed by evening prayers and dinner. Then we headed back to the classrooms for night prep which lasted until nine o'clock. Finally, we retired to our dormitories, only to kneel by our beds for another hour's worth of prayers, after which the generators that supplied our electricity were turned off. Our lives were planned down to the minute, and the regimen had to be followed strictly, almost as if we were not trusted to do the right things by ourselves.

Then, around one o'clock on a blazingly hot Wednesday afternoon in March 1967, everything changed. Just before our last lesson of the day, a large group of students from the University of Nigeria at Nsukka interrupted our hectic lives. We heard their voices before we saw them and ran out of our classrooms into the long corridors, straining to see our invaders through the glass windows. In spite of our prefects' orders to return to the classrooms, we stayed in the corridor, waiting, probably sensing that what was about to happen would change our lives forever. The students marched through the school gate, and up the unpaved path to our main building. My heart pounded as if it would jump out of my chest as the university radicals guided us to the assembly field, where they addressed us. Within an hour, we too were swaying to the revolutionary songs they taught us.

> We shall not...we shall not be moved
> We shall not...we shall not be moved
> Just like a tree that's planted by the water
> We shall not be moved.

The leaders of the group had announced that no foreigners could participate in that afternoon's activities, so our school authorities watched from a distance. They must have felt helpless to protect us from what we were being drawn into. And they were right, because after that day, our lives raced rapidly into a state of chaos. School became rowdy. Our university mentors interrupted our classes whenever they wanted and even had us march into town, to chant our defiant slogans and wave our hands in support of the voices that were demanding that Ibos break away from Nigeria.

Part III
The Nigerian-Biafran War

Our Worlds Came Tumbling Down

I refer to "the war" as if everyone lived it, because to this day, it continues to define me. Images from this brutal period are permanently etched in my mind's eye, images that become sharper with time and still haunt me in horrendous nightmares. I cannot talk for very long about my life without the Nigerian-Biafran war coming up. It started in July 1967 and ended in January 1970, thirty long months of fear, hunger, torture, and death that still torment me even twenty-four years later.

The war came at a time when Mama finally had a good handle on life. She had completed the backyard house with all the additions, and all the rooms were rented. She'd also built another huge house, strategically located near a small motor park. The ten-room house had two stores in front; she sold provisions from one of them. Her clothing business was booming and her market stall kept expanding. No fewer than twenty trainees lived under Mama's tutelage; hundreds of others were turned down. Mama had also branched into other areas and had secured the lucrative contracts for food supply to the half dozen Catholic secondary schools in the area. In terms of business, things couldn't have been better.

On a personal front, Mama had finally allowed herself to be persuaded to discard the mourner's black clothing she had worn since her master died. While her clothing remained conservative, Mama seemed more human and less intimidating in regular garments. She was more confident and radiated self-assurance in her speech and dealings. People pointed her out in the crowd. "That is no ordinary woman," they said. "She's evidence that hard work pays off." The entire town had begun to refer to her as Mama, not Mama John or Nwunye Honorable. Mama, still in her thirties, had become the town's mother. Even women who were older than she called her Mama Nwunye Edoga (Mama, the wife of Edoga). People came from far to seek her counsel on every issue.

Her children were doing exceptionally well in school. John was completing his bachelor's degree at Columbia University in New York that year and had gained admission to some of the most prestigious medical schools in America: Harvard, Yale, Columbia. We were confident he was headed for glory.

Anthony, who'd been moved from home to home, from bad guardian to worse guardian, had finally settled into secondary school and was in his last year. He had just taken entrance examinations to study engineering in one of three Nigerian universities and would have started in 1968.

Virginia's education had not been hampered by her servitude under cousin Cecilia, and by 1967, she was also in her final year of secondary school and was the school's senior prefect (student body president). Virginia had applied to both teachers' colleges and nursing schools. Most immediate in Mama's and everyone's eyes was marriage, so Virgy was expected to begin serious consideration of the numerous marriage proposals she was receiving, with an aim toward getting married soon after.

Anthony's twin, Christopher, had, after receiving the reluctant permission of Mama and paternal uncles, chosen years earlier not to attend secondary school. He was not a particularly good student and struggled through primary school. Mama would have preferred that he continue, but was realistic enough to accept that he was not cut out for academics. He was apprenticed to a trader in Onitsha, where he spent three years learning the retail business. The provisions store that Mama had opened was in his name and at the time the war started, he stood poised to make his mark in business.

Martha had lived with Aunt Monica until she was a sixth grader and was ready to take her entrance examination to get into secondary school. At that point she returned home to Nsukka to live with us. I still remember the first day I met her; she arrived in a taxi with her guardian. She spoke only Hausa and barely discernible English, while we spoke Ibo and very little English. Used to being an only child, Martha did not want to communicate with anyone. She cried for my aunt to take her back home, and she threatened to run away when her "Mom" left her with us.

For days, she locked herself in a room we used for storage of bulk foods and sang Hausa songs, which no one understood. Sometimes, we heard her stamping feet and saw her, through the peephole and cracks in the mud wall, dancing vigorously as if she had hundreds of spectators.

Martha provided a lot of entertainment for us in those days and we watched her every move. I don't recall if I knew then that she was my sister, but the many years between us and her absence in my early years had created a wedge that we could not overcome until after the war.

Meanwhile, she was also the prettiest of Mama's daughters and grew very tall in her teen years: long-legged, slim-waisted, and graceful. She inherited Mama's yellow complexion and her jet-black hair. Martha walked as if the world belonged to her. Her stride was measured, calculated; wherever she went, eyes turned and followed her.

"Whose daughter is that? Who gave birth to that pretty angel?" strangers asked of her. Before the Nigerian-Biafran war, Mama was concerned that no one would seek Martha's hand; she thought that Martha's beauty would cause men to think her arrogant. Once when we visited Aku for the holidays and lingered in the market square, we overheard someone say about Martha, "That one is sure to stay with her family for the rest of her life, for who would dare approach her? What man could be as tall, as handsome, as graceful and assured as she seems to be? What a pity that her beauty would be the thing that ruins her!"

But Mama and the strangers were wrong. Suitors almost ran us out of the house with their persistence for Martha's hand. Men came from all over Ibo land to inquire about the swan-necked beauty who was also of good parentage. In spite of Mama's warnings, Martha cut her eyes at the suitors and clicked her tongue in disgust. Mama would wring her hands and sometimes cry, but she never used the strict tones with Martha that she did with me. I suppose Mama was guilt-laden about giving Martha away and, as a result, often let her abide by her own conscience. The other reality was that having spent her crucial childhood years with Yorubas and Hausas, Martha never learned the finer points in the code of behavior that governs Ibo womanhood.

By 1967, the year the war started, Martha was sixteen and in her third year of secondary school at Queen of the Rosary College in Onitsha, a convent school similar to the one Virginia was attending, and Mama was telling her numerous suitors that she wanted Martha to finish school before choosing a husband.

"What a difference ten years make!" people commented about the turnabout in Mama's life. There were no similiarities between the withdrawn, teary, newly widowed woman of years past and the person Mama had become.

Then the war came. Overnight she lost everything: her homes, sewing businesses, supply contracts, stores, and children's education. One day we owned a large compound, the next, all we had were the clothes on our backs. We woke up and all of Mama's hard-earned efforts were lost, her dreams gone; she had nothing to show for ten back-breaking years.

Maybe we should have anticipated the war, for there was ample evidence that it was inevitable. Possibly, had we done so, we would have been better able to prepare for it. But how does one prepare for something that's as unpredictable and disassembling as a civil war?

How could we have readied for something that was not like any known experience, with no point of reference? Our kind of war only became popular recently, in arenas like Bosnia and Rwanda. Before us, I don't think the world could have imagined such atrocities perpetrated on one group of human beings by other groups. The level of our devastation and suffering was beyond words, and our mere survival was by the grace of God.

The Nigerian-Biafran war was long in the making. It resulted from tribal politics and inexcusably bad government. When Nigeria got its independence from Britain in October 1960, the country was divided into four regions, representing the dominant tribes and language groups: North, Hausas and Fulanis; East, Ibos; West, Yorubas; Mid-West, a number of small minority groups.

The north is larger than the three southern regions combined and its populace, Hausas and Fulanis, are mostly Muslim. Their culture, language, and lifestyle are much like those of the Arab world. Partly because of geography (the area that was Northern Nigeria is land-locked), but mostly because of their religion, the northerners had very little contact with the Western world before the Nigerian crisis started. They were generally less educated, but, ironically, they were more politically astute than anyone had given them credit for. They used their large numbers to elect their tribesmen to lead the country.

The Yorubas in the west, by their geography alone (Lagos, Nigeria's main port and capital, is in Yoruba land), had tremendous economic power. Like the Ibos, they were becoming increasingly frustrated by their lack of political power, which they assumed should have come with economic control. The Yorubas practice the three dominant religions, Islam, Christianity, and paganism, in equal numbers.

The eastern Ibos were the most embracing of Western culture and were comprised of the largest number of Christians. With their formal education, they occupied key positions in the civil service and wielded a lot of bureaucratic power. Ibos are the most outgoing of Nigeria's peoples and even early in Nigeria's history, they refused to allow regional boundaries to dictate the scope of their lives. By the beginning of the civil strife, as many Ibos lived outside the boundaries of Eastern Nigeria as lived within them. While the Hausas/Fulanis had the numbers and the Yorubas had their money, Ibos had nothing more than ingenuity and hard work. Consequently, they were in the forefront of the fight for Nigeria's independence and, had it not been for tribal politics, would have taken over power from the British.

In the six years between civil war and independence, Nigerian politics was fraught with tension: riots, massacres, mini-wars, corruption, and outright usurping of power by whoever had the rowdiest and most daring group of followers.

The crisis worsened in January 1966, a year before the actual war began. I remember the day we arrived in school and were told by our teacher that we had to memorize a new set of answers for the entrance examinations for which we had been preparing. Nigeria had changed its leadership overnight, our new rulers assuming power in a bloody military coup that wiped out Nigeria's political elite. The commander of Nigeria's army, an Ibo man, became the head of government. I don't remember feeling particularly concerned. I hadn't yet heard discussions at school or home that expressed worry about the political situation. Lagos and national leadership were abstract concepts and we could not imagine that whatever happened in the capital could change the price of rice or beans or affect the way we lived.

The story changed dramatically in the next six months. Ibos became the object of the Northerners' anger for the simple reason that an Ibo man held the reins of the country. A well-planned pogrom targeting Ibos was launched by Hausas and Fulanis; Yorubas and other tribes across Nigeria also took part. Ibos who lived outside of Ibo land were slaughtered without cause; women were raped and even children were not spared. We were told that the plan was to wipe the Ibo race from the face of the Earth.

So threatened, Ibos living outside the east abandoned their livelihood and property and fled home. Millions of people were confined to a geographical region and physical infrastructure that could barely hold a fraction of that population. The refugee problem almost overwhelmed us; our school classrooms were so full that children sat on the bare floor and overflowed onto the window sills. Even the holiest sanctuaries at church became makeshift shelters. Families littered the streets with their sleeping mats and possessions. It was like nothing that anyone in our town had ever seen. But we continued our lives, or so we thought.

The leader of the eastern region buckled under pressure from Ibos and declared Biafra's secession from Nigeria in May 1967. Thus, I learned that I no longer pledged allegiance to Nigeria. My new homeland was called Biafra. Nigeria, the country we were taught to love and sworn to give our lives for, had become the enemy.

The Nigerian-Biafran war started on a Thursday. We woke up on Saturday to abject chaos. Our principal and other foreign-born teachers were whisked away in the darkness of night, and we were on our own, with no one to tell us what to do. My sister, Virginia, the senior prefect, took charge, but nothing she said or did could allay our fears. Nothing could camouflage the distinct rifle and mortar sounds. Nothing could lift the gloom that settled on our lives. Early on Sunday morning, Virginia gave up and announced that students who wanted to leave could. We all did. Mercifully, our school was only five miles away from the town of Nsukka and we didn't have too long to trek. We were home before lunch.

At home the next night, as we said our prayers, Felix Ugwu-Oju, who later became my father-in-law, arrived to inform Mama that Nsukka had already fallen to the enemy soldiers. We had to flee immediately; there was no time to pack a thing. It was the only time I remember Mama allowing our night prayers to be interrupted, and we left straight from where we knelt. There was no last-minute look around; even the money Mama brought home from the market that day was left behind, tucked under a pillow on her bed. Our dinner was left hot in the pots. I don't believe that the fires were put out, or that the electric lights we used sparingly were turned off as we went out, through the verandah, down the steps to our abyss.

We could never have foreseen what the war would entail. As we left our home that night, we honestly believed that we would return in a matter of hours or days when things calmed down. We didn't return for thirty months.

Our tranquil little town was different than I had ever seen before (or after) that night. Thousands of people milled around, going in circles, heading nowhere. Everyone seemed as confused about what to do as the person beside him, and I remember wondering, "Where did all these people come from and where are they all going?" Had there been food and music, the gathering would have had a celebratory feel to it, like a carnival almost, as men and women, weighed down by the treasured possessions they carried on their heads, mingled in the craziness. Some even remembered to call out greetings to faces they recognized. Others shouted out the names of family members from whom they'd become separated.

"Papa Ike, Papa Ike, where are you?"

"Adanna! Has anyone see my little girl?"

"Somebody please help me find my only son!"

Cries for assistance permeated the crowd, but no one ran to anyone's aid that night; everyone was intent on survival. Hundreds of people were left behind in the chaos. Because the flight was at night, many children were already asleep and many men hadn't returned for the day. There was no opportunity to run back home, even to retrieve a sleeping child.

We stayed in the market square for several minutes before we got on a back road and walked the seventeen miles to our hometown, Aku. When we arrived at the family compound, where Mama had spent her grieving period, we found that all the Edogas, several generations of them, had to share the cramped accommodations. There were more than fifty of us, and no one earned an income anymore. We survived those first weeks of the war only on the mercy of friends and Aku villagers who brought us enough yams, cassava, and rice to provide one main meal each day. I remember the hunger pangs and churnings of our empty stomachs, but much later in the war, we began to look back to those first days at Aku as the good old days, before life itself lost its meaning.

But food was secondary to a bigger worry: the fate of my siblings. Ogbonna, Martha, and Anthony had not returned before we fled and every story we heard pointed to hopelessness. Ogbonna's and Li's school was closer to the northern border of Biafra than Nsukka, and the enemy had to have gotten there before they got to us. "Ogbonna! Where are you? Lord, where is my little husband?" Mama cried aloud. We learned that enemy soldiers had invaded school dormitories at night, roused and lined up disoriented school boys, and shot them in the back. We were also told of how boys younger than Ogbonna were ordered to dig mass graves and were shot and buried in the holes. Every new story was more grim than the one before it. We kept vigil, praying to occupy ourselves.

On our fifth day at Aku, Ogbo and Li walked into our compound. It was a miracle that either of them survived their ordeal, for most of their schoolmates did not. They had woken to gunfire and had started running. It was pure coincidence that they connected later and traced their steps to us.

Anthony's and Martha's schools were in areas that had not been captured yet, but Mama still worried that they would be misled by Biafra's radio announcements, which denied that the enemy had taken over any part of Biafra, and head home to Nsukka.

Fortunately, they returned to Aku instead, soon after Ogbo's return. With her children in relative safety, Mama turned her mind elsewhere.

She and I reacted differently to the first few weeks of the war. I relished my freedom from the restrictions of school and other obligations that dictated pre-war life. I was willing to endure the hunger, the deprivations, in exchange for the long lazy days. The fact that I had to wash my only outfit at night to wear it the next morning and that I had no shoes to wear (I was wearing flip flops when we left Nsukka, and the flimsy plastic soles did not survive the trek to Aku) did not diminish the pleasure I derived from my lack of responsibility.

Mama, on the other hand, returned to the teary desolate woman I knew in my early years. At first, she held out hope that we would return to Nsukka in a matter of days, but as days became weeks, her face became long and drawn and her eyes permanently red and swollen. I can still see her pained face, the constant shaking of her head, and the rosary beads in her hand as she sat on a bench in the verandah, her back supported by the wall. She barely spoke to anyone, except during our night prayers, which she extended by another hour. "Lord Jesus, please intervene on our behalf; save us; bring us home," she implored night after night; for my part, I prayed that the war would continue indefinitely, and the Lord seemed to favor me. Mama hardly slept, and many nights when we passed by the verandah on our way to the outhouse, Mama sat in the darkness alone, quiet, except for her muted sobs.

About two months after the war started, the Biafran government decided that schools would reopen and our lives would go on, regardless of the obvious inconveniences. Those of us whose schools were in areas already captured and occupied by the enemy were reposted. I was assigned to a school in Emekukwu, hundreds of miles away from our home and every family we knew, but Mama was determined that I go. Readying for our return to school gave her something worthy to do. It was not easy, but in spite of our meager possessions, Mama borrowed to purchase everything listed on our prospectus—the uniforms, bed sheets, blankets—a tall order for our deprived state.

We rode to Enugu on the bed of a lorry, the only transport that traveled from Aku; then we took a bus to Owerri and squeezed into a crowded mini-bus to Emekukwu. We arrived at the school, and for the first few days, it was like there was no war in progress. We maintained a rigid schedule, only interrupted by the frequent air-raid sirens, but we seemed well on our way to returning to normal life.

Then, exactly a week after we returned, our dormitory was bombed. I remember the night as if it just happened; at times, even the most microscopic detail becomes vivid and tormenting. It occurred well after our bedtime, so we were all in bed. We had our relief-supplied dinner and were lying around the dormitory, telling stories, gossiping. Then our prefect urged us to kneel for night prayers. It was while we knelt that we were besieged. I remember the sudden brightness as a jet swooped down and the deafening noise of the explosions, the called-out prayers and cries for our mothers, the heat, and then the nothingness.

I don't know how or why I survived. Most of the girls in my dorm that night perished. I was only injured. When I recovered, we returned to Aku, my schooling temporarily forgotten. Mama helped me deal with the loss and the guilt that overwhelmed me. "How can we question God's will? Only He knows why these things happen." My youth took over, and in a short while I allowed myself to move on. We had so many miseries of our own that we didn't have room for anyone else's miseries.

My experience was not at all unusual. Ours was not the only school targeted that night. My friends were not the only children killed in the carnage. If Mama mentioned to anyone what I had been through, she was likely to be told, "Thank God she's alive; so and so's daughter was not so lucky." Or they would tell of their own woes, and there wasn't anyone who didn't know someone who'd died or didn't have a war story to tell. We counted our blessings and kept praying.

A month later, Aku fell to the Nigerian soldiers and our lives plummeted to a lower level, a level we had not known existed. We lived like animals, feral animals with no predictable schedules. For the next 28 months until the war ended, our every move was dictated by enemy soldiers. Constantly on the run, we often did not go to sleep where we woke up. Fleeing from Aku was similar to our departure from Nsukka and all the other departures that followed. There was no warning. We were readying to go to the market to buy dinner when the deafening mortar bombs and shells began to land, practically on our homes. It was terrifying, for there was no telling where the next shell would strike. After watching several neighbors' homes explode, we took off, although none of us knew what our destination would be. Each of us carried items from our Aku home: mats, cooking pots, buckets, practically everything we had that could be moved. We walked in the direction that the crowd was going, not stopping until nightfall.

The fifty-plus people in our entourage took refuge in a deserted six-by-eight-foot farmhouse, a thatched-roof shack open on all sides. It was no more than a makeshift shelter where farmers took their midday breaks from the sun. The shack was bare, and after minutes of hand wringing, a mat was spread on the floor where only Mama and the youngest children in our entourage stayed; the rest of us made our beds in the yam farm, on mounds of wet soil, vulnerable to the elements. But our bodies were exhausted from the anxiety and ached from the long walk, and most of us fell asleep in no time, despite the discomfort of our "beds." We barely noticed the wet grass we lay in or our empty complaining stomachs.

That night, sometime before daybreak, it began to rain heavily, and because there was no room in our shelter, most of us shivered from the soaking cold as we huddled under tree branches. When the rain abated, we scrambled for food, harvesting roots that were nowhere near ready, but anything was preferable to the hunger. In the days that followed, we built three mud-walled straw-roof shacks, where we lived until the soldiers drove us out six weeks later.

Mama remained semi-conscious until it began to set in that our condition was as good as it was going to be during that war. We had shelter, food, and barely drinkable water; most of our needs were met, even if in the most crude way.

Outhouses did not exist in those parts, and in a matter of time, we let go of our inhibitions and learned, along with everyone else, to squat in the bushes, often only a few feet from our shacks. Our toilet paper was fresh leaves gathered as we needed them. Our water supply came from a spring originating in one of the hills that surrounded the farm, which often dried up in the dry season. It was only luck that we did not all die from bacterial infections, for right by the spring were mounds of excrement and other wastes. We also bathed in that spring and washed our clothes there.

Initially, most of us became ill, and since there was no way of diagnosing our illnesses, it was assumed that we had malaria, a common tropical ailment. Our malaise lingered, and Mama became troubled enough to suggest that we move from the area further into the interior of Biafra, near the center of government. But there were several reasons why the move that Mama was suggesting was not viable. We heard, from the transistor radio we managed to save from Aku, of all the atrocities going on in inner Biafra. The entire six million refugees were cramped in a geographical area that could barely hold thousands and with that came diseases and, worst of all, hunger. The farms (where we were) were the only food supply for the whole eastern region prior to the war, and because the enemy held the main roads that connected the farms to Biafra, there was no way of sending the food to areas where it was needed.

We heard reports of a newly diagnosed illness, *kwashiorkor* (malnutrition), which was claiming the lives of Biafran children by the thousands each day. In fact, when the war ended and everything was tallied, it was discovered that more people died from starvation than from the bountiful bullets and bombs. In addition, Biafra's air raids had gotten worse than during my stay at school. Bombs fell on hospital wards, churches, and marketplaces. We were somewhat shielded by the rough, uncharted terrain of our hiding place, and while we were occasionally subjected to bomb scares, they were infrequent and did not pose the threat that they did in inner Biafra.

But while we weren't starving, our lifestyle was one of utter deprivation. We lacked even the most basic necessities, like a change of clothes, shoes, and medicine. We resorted to native doctors and their herbs which, more times than not, harmed us more than helped us. Oke, a cousin of mine who was a final-year engineering student at the university when the war began, died from a disease that could have been treated very easily. I remember his vacant stare at the end, and how he called to Mama to soothe his cramping stomach. When he got worse, he begged for death. "Mama, let me go; the pain is too much to bear." Oke cried like a child, protesting all attempts to save his life.

His death was ironic, for he lived with us out of fear that he would be conscripted into the Biafran Army and killed at the front. Sadly, death found him even where he hid, surrounded by all who loved him. I was by no means a stranger to death, but Oke's was my first close encounter. I stood watching as he breathed his last. I helped as his body was bathed, oiled and dressed, then wrapped in a raffia mat. We were all too devastated to console each other, but after his death, many others in our entourage died also. It became so common, so ordinary, that I no longer felt the loss that I did when Oke died.

Then my uncle Crescent, Papa's older brother, was shot and killed by enemy soldiers. His death affected us deeply not only because of the extent of his involvement in our lives, but also because of the traditional implications of how he died. He was the uncle who had provided Mama's refuge in her year of mourning and was in fact the first father I knew. When we were children, we returned to Aku at least once a year, and it was Uncle Crescent who provided for us during those times. When war came and we returned to Aku, he received us, albeit grudgingly. But when Aku fell to the enemy, *Nna Anyi* (Our Father) refused to flee with us. Though we begged him to come with us, he said that all his life, he'd been taught that "a man's home is his sanctuary, and no real man flees from his home." He refused to listen to reason, believing that the soldiers would only bother those who interfered with their way of doing things. He assured us that he would keep safe and sent his wife with us.

A few weeks later, our aunt was unable to stay away from her husband and returned to him. According to our aunt, they stayed out of harm's way, rising early to hide in the nearby bushes and only returning when it was dark. But the soldiers started going from house to house, and supposedly when they came to the Edoga home, they saw a bookcase filled with books in all fields, and concluded that members of our family held important posts in Biafra and were threats to Nigeria. They loaded all their evidence onto a truck and sat in the verandah, awaiting my uncle's return. He walked into their deadly trap. When they saw him, they fired many rounds of ammunition into an unarmed, helpless, illiterate old man who had never read a book in his life. His crime? Harboring instruments of knowledge in his home. It was senseless. Nothing about my uncle suggested he knew anything about Biafra. He was wrinkly and bent and walked with a cane, and in all the time I knew him, he never wore clothing. All that covered his body was a man's wrapper, which he knotted at one side of his hip, just enough material to cover his manhood and buttocks. While he lay dying, the soldiers stripped him of even that, leaving his manhood uncovered.

That was how his wife found him. I can't even imagine how she must have felt, not only to see her husband dead, but to see him so exposed. In the darkness, she ran through the whole town looking for someone to help her bury him. The only person she could find was an old lady who was at death's door; this woman had witnessed the murder and told us the horrendous story. Auntie worked furiously through the night. She dug up dirt from the yam farm nearby and dumped it on her husband where he lay. She said she couldn't leave him unburied to be devoured by vultures. She did the only thing she could have done. But, by the time she made her way back to us at the farms, she was a raving lunatic who no longer knew who she was.

People talked of how her madness resulted from seeing her husband uncovered, and then having to bury him. No woman before her had ever buried a corpse. It was simply never done. Women waited for men to do it no matter how long it took, even during wars, even at the risk of the body never being buried. Our aunt had done the unthinkable, the villagers proclaimed; she forgot she was a woman, and her impulsive act doomed her. She never recovered, and she quickly followed her husband to her maker, her experience too grim to bear. Even in war, even in desperate situations, women were to remember that they were only women.

Papa Li, our uncle Cyril, also died suddenly during the war, and we had no way of really determining what caused his death, although there's an unvoiced understanding that it had to do with his liver.

We'd gone in different directions after fleeing Aku, when our day-to-day survival was no longer guaranteed. Mama had suggested that our two families separate to better guarantee that someone would survive to tell the stories of the war. I also suspect that Mama's motivation may have been economic: since we could barely feed ourselves, she did not want to split the little food she scrounged with another family.

Then we returned from working in the farm one evening and found Li sitting by our hut. He broke into a sing-song crying when he saw us and we knew his father had died. Everyone began to wail, but I stood stunned, dry-eyed and unsure of what I felt. Mama wailed even louder than Mama Li, whose farm we trekked to that night. She thrashed her body on the floor, crying over and over, "All our men are gone; who'll take care of us," although she knew that Papa Li hardly took care of himself, let alone anyone else. It was only when we returned to Nsukka that I realized how much he had meant to us. The house seemed strangely empty without him, and our nights less dramatic and comical. We could no longer wait up for him, eagerly counting on his drunken stagger and incoherent speech. We also had no other male that we could call Papa, no other man to provide much needed counsel. Ours became a house full of women.

We fled again and again, until January 1968 when we settled at the farm where we stayed the rest of the war. We'd been constantly on the move for seven months, never knowing where we would spend the night. We lost all elements of civilization; the only proof we had of a once-decent life was Mama's rosary and prayer books, plus a framed photograph of her master, the only item she had saved from Nsukka. But even when we thought we had hit rock bottom, things got worse and we believed that we had reached the end of our lives.

Living in that farm community, I learned the Ibo tradition at close range; there was no escaping it. Ours was the only family among hundreds that professed Christianity. My siblings and I were the only children who had ever attended school or ridden in cars or been in a house with electricity. We stepped back in time to a way of life that I had only observed from afar. We lived and breathed that life now; our hut was surrounded by many others, and often we were dragged into traditional pagan practices against our will. And if we had thought that women in our experience were mistreated, we suddenly realized how lucky we really were.

The women we encountered in the farms did not have nearly as many rights or as much opportunity as we did. Most of them were in polygamous marriages, content as second, third, fourth, or even fifth wives to their husbands. They began bearing children, at least from our perspective, too early in life. Their husbands treated them as replaceable items, with no regard—unless of course the woman was the favored wife, a status that a man accorded at his whim. Not a day passed that we did not hear the screams of a woman being beaten by her husband. At first, we were drawn to every domestic situation, watching with fascination as men slapped, kicked, and whipped their errant wives in front of a crowd that would often egg them on. Very few women fought back or offered any resistance to protect themselves; the few who did were wrestled to the ground and held by observers so their husbands could beat them even more.

I remember a particular incident involving the first wife of a man who had three additional wives. Everyone in the farm recognized that the man was derelict in his responsibilities to his children with her. He often neglected to give her a portion of his yam farm where she could plant vegetables and deliberately bypassed her hut when he shared food with his other wives. She confronted him after months of pleading and appealing to the elders to intervene, and when he began to beat her, she grabbed his legs and brought him to the ground.

What an uproar that created. "A woman, a man's wife, pushed him to the ground! What an abomination!" Men and women alike spat at her when they passed her in the square where she was condemned to sit. Her pleas fell on deaf ears, until she fulfilled a series of cleansing rituals prescribed by the elders. The first ritual involved her being led around the whole camp, from hut to hut, farm to farm, one patch of land to another. At each stop she said, "I accept that I am no better than the excrement on the ground." She progressed from there to sacrificing a goat to appease the gods. Finally the community deemed her worthy once again to inhabit her husband's household. No one ever addressed the initial issue, and she never brought it up again.

In trying to be as inconspicuous as possible, we had to become part of that culture, at least enough not to condemn it publicly.

One of Mama's lasting scars from the Nigerian-Biafran war came from the paganism she was forced to practice. Mama had been born into paganism, so although she was converted and baptized at age five, she knew paganism firsthand, and her mother and siblings remained pagans. (Mama herself baptized her mother as she lay dying.) We were the only Christians in the farm community where we'd hid. The villagers insisted that our family take an oath in the presence of their totem. They expressed their concern over our betraying their hidden location to the enemy soldiers, who would bring disorder to their tranquil lives. Mama refused, outrightly at first, explaining that what we were being asked to do was against our religion. But the elders of the farm stood firm, giving us little option. "You can either do what we ask or pack up your children and leave our farm," they responded to Mama's protests.

"But we'll go to hell if we do what you ask us to do," Mama reasoned.

"You'll have no refuge if you don't do it," they barked. Faced with such a choice, Mama finally agreed, but it was a decision that continues to haunt her to this day. She led us all to the front of the shrine, where we faced their totem, ready to repeat whatever words they called to us. Unknown to them, however, Mama hid a Bible under an extra wrapper she carried, and she placed her hand on this bible when she recited her oath of loyalty to the new community. Still, she cried for days after that experience. "I betrayed my God; I chose material things over my soul." We let her mourn; there was no convincing her that she did what had to be done, that the alternative was to have chosen certain death. Certainly, not even God would have demanded that of us.

What Are They Doing to That Girl?

I witnessed my first female circumcision soon after we settled in the farm community. We were still becoming acquainted with the traditional pagan way of life. The war forced us to live the tradition in close range, and there was no avoiding some of the practices, for even the most intimate of all acts was public, on display.

Ibos, especially those living in the rawness of tradition undiluted by Western influence or Christianity, spent their lives as much as possible in open view. Everyone knew everything about everyone else, including when one's neighbors went to the bathroom. "Why not?" they would ask if one wondered about the lack of privacy. Their philosophy stemmed from the notion that an upright person has nothing to hide. Someone who had a habit of closing his doors or being secretive about his activities was believed to be acting suspiciously.

Until I saw an eight-day-old infant girl's circumcision in the planting season of 1968, I had not been aware of the procedure. At Nsukka before the war, Mama Li and the other women in Mama's compound bore their children at the hospital, and because of the high rate of infant mortality, newborns were several weeks old before they were brought home. Whatever procedures they required had already been administered.

The child whose clitorectomy I witnessed was born to a woman whose husband was distantly related to Mama, and who offered his farmhouse to us before we were able to build our own. The baby was her tenth live birth, though the other nine hadn't lived past infancy. Umebe (Let the Deaths End) was the first baby born in the farm after we moved there. We were ecstatic over it, but it seemed we were alone in our feelings. No one else, not even the woman's husband, met us even halfway in our excitement. It was Mama who cooked the peppery broth for the new mother, made sure that she was bathed, and reminded her to take the precautions which new mothers have to take. If Mama was too busy to wash Umebe in her first few days, no one else did; the little girl seemed almost to belong to us. I learned, much later, that there was a logic to the lukewarm reception of this new baby. The villagers had lived through many births of this woman and had watched the infants whom they so carefully tended die for no explained reason. By this time they'd given up any hope that any babies she bore would be any different. But when Umebe survived to her eighth day, impending death or not, the new infant had to go through the ritualistic entrance into the community, a practice that is performed to this day on both male and female Ibo babies.

Umebe's circumcision was performed early in the morning, before the sun's rays could be felt. The ceremony was at the square, where most events occurred, and no invitations were necessary to anyone who wanted to observe. The Edogas were the only nonparticipants in attendance, probably because the procedure was so routine that only outsiders like us would have been drawn to it. An older woman cradled the naked baby, with her head lodged in the crook of the woman's arm, as if to shield the infant's eyes from an impending horror. A second individual held the baby's legs apart, exposing her diminutive female parts. I watched intently, both in fascination and abhorrence.

In all my life, I had never seen a female's privates so graphically displayed. In fact, I had never observed a female part, except cursorily on naked village girls, but even then, the girls were always moving and I barely glimpsed the outside frontal skin. But there was Umebe, spread-eagled before the male native doctor, who took an extraordinarily long time observing her private parts. I cringed when he touched her with his grime-covered hands, but no one else was troubled by his activities. He probed, prodded, and even peered deep into the little baby before returning to his goat-skinned medicine bag from which he produced a tarnished razor blade with old blood crusted on its sides. I froze with fear, my own insides churning in revulsion, threatening to exclude me from the procedure I felt so compelled to observe.

The actual operation lasted but a second, and it was too fast for me to see what happened, but as long as I live I will never forget Umebe's horror-filled voice. It was like nothing I have ever heard before or after. Her spasmic body and her heart-wrenching cries did not seem to move the women who held her or the medicine man; his dirty finger, now reddened by Umebe's blood, searched the sore genitals while he uttered words I couldn't understand then, but which became clear after I observed the procedure on subsequent occasions. "We must leave none of that behind; all of it must go." I looked away when he once again retrieved his instrument and inched closer to the wailing infant whose body still writhed in pain. The women present were strange in their calmness. Not one cry of sympathy was uttered for the distressed child. They were placid and matter-of-fact.

Only after the medicine man left did the older woman begin to soothe the infant. "It will be all right, child. You're only passing through where every woman before you has travelled. Someday, you'll be thankful for this ritual. If you live long enough, this will not compare with the pain of childbirth. It's our lot as women."

As the child was returned to her mother, her blood left a distinct trail in the dusty ground, from the square to her mother's hut. No one made an effort to stop the bleeding; it almost seemed like a mark of pride, something to be celebrated. The baby's persistent screams continued unabated, and not even her mother's nipple, forced into her mouth, soothed her. "She'll stop crying after she's urinated; the pain will be less then," the women explained as they left, instructing Umebe's mother to apply palm oil to the wound until it healed.

My entire system went into shock. It was several hours until I garnered enough strength to elicit an explanation of the event from Mama. "Mama, what were they doing to that girl?" I asked, mindful that I was venturing into areas I should not have.

"Why, you saw as much of what happened as I." Mama would not, I knew, willingly participate in a discussion about a female's body, even an infant's. But I was touched enough by what I saw not to give up easily, so I persisted.

"Why did they do that to the child's body?" Again, I made no direct reference to the part of the body that was affected, and in her non-specific, non-descriptive terms, Mama disclosed the meaning of the ritual of female circumcision.

"They were circumcising her," she offered.

"Is this done to all babies, boy and girls?"

"Most," Mama was beginning to sound irritated at the inquisition.

"Was this done to all of us?"

"All your brothers were. Of all the females in this household, you alone were not circumcised," Mama started.

"Thank goodness!" I yelped, unaware of the implications, but feeling relieved that I was not subjected to the torture I witnessed that day. Mama grabbed my arm as I rose to leave her side.

"You're never to tell anyone that you were not circumcised! It could affect your chances to marry," Mama cautioned, her tone revealing the seriousness of our discussion.

"But Mama, it looked terribly painful. How could it be of any help to me or anyone?" I asked, confused.

"What can I tell you except what I was told, that it is the tradition and was started by our forefathers a long time before anyone we know was born. It is not our place to refuse it or argue against it or even wonder why it's done."

"Why was it *not* done to me?" I asked, suddenly concerned that I was somehow deficient in my womanhood because I was spared the gruesome surgery.

"You were born in the hospital where such things were not practiced. When we returned from the hospital, you were over a month old, and I was grieving for your father. We just never got around to it."

Mama then explained the common belief that women who were not circumcised were less sought after when the time came for marriage, although she did not know why. "Maybe it has to do with child bearing."

Now that I'm more aware of clitorectomy, I do not find it unusual that Mama, like others in her generation, would not understand why it was practiced. People simply did not question tradition, and if they did, they were given a simple answer. "It's the way our fathers taught us to do it; who are we to question their wisdom?" Besides, those of us raised Catholic dared not ask questions that directly involved a body part, especially a sex organ.

On another occasion, I asked Mama why it was important for me not to reveal that I had not been circumcised. We were stooping side by side besides the parallel rows of the soil mounds of our yam farm, weeding. She looked up and stared at me for a second, then she rose, took my hand, and started walking in the direction of the shack that shaded us during our breaks.

"Do you remember Mama Antonia, the woman who lived by us in Nsukka?"

"Yes, Ma," I answered quickly. Everyone knew the woman with four grown but unmarried daughters. She was the laughing stock of the town, although no one had ever told me what she did to deserve such scorn.

"Do you remember what is unusual about her situation?"

"Her daughters are unmarried although they're of age."

"Do you know why her daughters are not married?"

"No, Ma," I answered truthfully.

"It's because they're not circumcised," she whispered, looking around to make sure no one else was about to hear her.

"Why were they not circumcised?"

"I don't know anything except what I've heard in stories," Mama admitted before recounting the ordeal of Mama Antonia, whose first born daughter had bled to death when she was only ten days old, two horrible days after she was circumcised. The child had not been held down adequately and had jerked her body just as the razor blade made contact. Her blood flowed like water, the stories tell, and everyone wondered how such a tiny creature could have so much blood. Everything was done to save her—every remedy contained in the confines of a traditional medicine man's bag. Her bleeding, like her crying, went unabated for two straight days, and they only stopped when she was dead. Mama Antonia was inconsolable, and swore as her child was buried that she would not subject another of her children to that torture.

"It's just an accident. That's how her God wanted her," friends and neighbors told her.

"Look at you. It was done to you. Did it kill you?" others reminded her.

"I will not bury another child," she vowed, but no one took her words seriously. Everyone dismissed her blasphemy as arising from her grief. Thus, the neighbors were shocked when she refused to present her next child, another girl, to the elders on the baby's eighth day of life. When her mother who was visiting reminded her of her duty, she replied, "I lost one child; I don't want to lose another." When she began to feel barraged from all sides, she took her daughter and quietly stole away, not returning until she was many months old. She did the same with the next daughter, and by the time her other two came, no one bothered her.

Her decision returned to haunt her, however. When the first daughter was old enough to marry, the story, which she probably hoped had been forgotten, surfaced and loomed over their lives. Her well-behaved, swan-necked daughters watched as suitors passed them by, seeking the hands of less desirable girls. If suitors from distant lands asked why such pretty girls were unspoken for, the full story was eventually whispered to them. They left as fast as they came, leaving Mama Antonia with her uncircumcised daughters.

As strange as it sounds, until I was a student in America, I never once heard that there was a relationship between female circumcision and a woman's sexuality, or that the procedure would diminish a woman's sexual desire. I had, like my mother, accepted that it was just one of those numerous customs that was part of our existence. In fact, until just a few years ago, I didn't completely believe Western claims that clitorectomies were a conspiracy to keep women docile sexual partners. I knew a few "promiscuous" circumcised girls as I grew up.

In addition, after I finished my education and returned to Nigeria in 1980, I served in the National Youth Service Corp with a group of girls from Calabar, an area in southeastern Nigeria.

These girls, all in their early twenties, had just graduated from the university. They shared a common experience, a phenomenon that continues to this date. In the period between leaving the university (May) and joining the service (August), they participated in the "fattening room," a coming-of-age ritual that initiates girls from that region to womanhood. This ceremony is usually held when girls are much younger, but for my friends, it was delayed to accommodate their lengthy educations. As part of the ritual, they submitted themselves to the elders of their community to be "womanized," a process that involved some cutting of their private parts. What I found most interesting was that most of these girls had sexual relationships prior to the clitorectomies, yet they were just as willing as pre-pubescent girls to pass through this ritual, believing it would complete their womanhood. None spoke of the horrors (mutilation, infection, pain during sex) with which I've come to associate the surgery. None described or even alluded to a decreased sexual pleasure. None felt anger or resentment toward the perpetrators. If they felt anything, it was fulfillment and relief.

Recently, however, I met a young Ibo woman, Onyinye, who has resided in the United States with her husband for years. Onyinye said her quest started many years after she moved to the United States and read women's magazines and heard claims on TV talk shows, such as "Oprah," that women are entitled to pleasure during sex. At first, she didn't believe it; she couldn't even imagine such a thing. In the more than ten years she'd been married, she never once found sexual intercourse enjoyable. Instead, she claims that she's had to bite down on her lips to keep from crying out in pain. What's more, she had no reason to believe that her lack of desire was not normal. It was as it should be, as she was taught not only at home but at school: sex was to create children, and she had no reason to expect more out of it. Consequently, she dreaded sex, and only acquiesced when her husband insisted on claiming his marital rights. But after digging deeper, searching in mainstream and trade journals, she found it was true. Women not only received pleasure from sex, but many achieved ecstasy.

Armed with this information, Onyinye dared to take her quest a step further when her mother visited by asking the older woman directly if she (Onyinye) were circumcised.

"Today's girls!" her mother spat. "Nothing is taboo anymore. In my time I would not have dared to ask my mother a question like that."

"Mama, I just need to know whether I was circumcised or not," Onyinye asserted.

"And what would you do with that information if you had it?" Onyinye's persistence angered her mother, who neither confirmed nor denied her daughter's suspicions.

Later, Onyinye complained, "It was like I had no right to know what had been done to me," adding that she was still resentful about "what was taken from me and my own mother's lack of empathy."

Today, I often find myself caught in the middle of this clitorectomy debate. On one hand, while I do not support its continuing practice in many African nations, I decry the Western media's depiction of it as driven by African men's desire to deprive its female population of all sexual pleasure. That could not be further from the truth. From all indications, diminished sexual pleasure for women could not have been the initial intention of our forefathers. It may have been to them a surprising, albeit welcome, result.

I've been told that it may have started as a guarantee of equal treatment to women. Men have their foreskin removed; why shouldn't women? I also learned that female circumcision may be closely linked to the fact that women did not wear clothes then. They walked around naked, and even their most intimate parts were exposed to all who looked. The "cutting off" was to limit the bulk, to give a more graceful appearance to that area, to distinguish the males from females.

On the other hand, there's no confusion in my mind that that was then, when they didn't wear clothes and didn't know any better. Now that we know the effects—the health risks and deprivation of sexual pleasures—there's no reason for the continuing practice of clitorectomies anywhere in the world.

To Save Their Honor

The war raged all around us, even though we had fled so deep into uncharted territory that we thought we'd arrived at the end of the world. Our refuge was a place that was not accessible by any transport, not even a bicycle. So remote was our hiding place that there were hardly any trails; the nearest paved roads were seven miles away. When we built our two-room hut with a verandah, we were certain that we had found a permanent refuge until the war ended, but we were wrong.

Soldiers traced our paths to the farm, and those around us. They came in the middle of the night, when people were less able to escape. We did not believe the first set of stories that came from besieged farms; we thought they were fabricated, like a horror story.

The survivors told us of being suddenly woken from their sleep by bursts of gunfire and explosions. Men and women were rounded up by soldiers who had barricaded all routes of escape beforehand. The men, women, and children who survived the first assault were separated according to their age. The very old men and women who seemed in the last stages of their lives were let go first, followed by the very young children. Initially children below puberty were let go with the old. Most times, however, the cut-off age for boys was five; for girls it was the onset of signs of womanhood. The men who were left behind were lined up, and right before their wives, mothers, and children, shot in the back.

With their work done, the soldiers rewarded themselves with the women, whom they bound and dragged to camp, where they were shared. The few women who escaped told gory tales of rape and mutilation, of being ravaged by troops of men, at times by more than one man at a time. Not too many women survived the ordeal. Most bled to death or died from massive infections; others were so maimed that they never walked again. But the fate that awaited the women survivors was worse than anything the soldiers could have done to them. The married ones could not return to their husbands; they had defiled the soil by their "infidelities." I listened to their accounts with my mouth open.

"But surely you don't blame them for what happened to them! They were taken against their will, unwilling victims at the hands of soldiers," I wailed.

"It really does not matter," someone explained. "They have violated the laws of the land." These doomed women were paraded through the community, accused of infidelity, the worst of crimes. They went through a cleansing ritual, entailing sacrificing chickens and goats to appease the gods, to seek forgiveness and reacceptance into the community. I was told that even if the women's pleas were accepted, they were nonetheless stigmatized for the rest of their lives, and their children and children's children were stained by it.

Years later, some of it all began to make sense to me. I then understood why a number of the abducted women chose to die running rather than be taken by the soldiers.

For an unmarried girl, the fate was worse than death. So for us and families like ours whose teenage daughters were unmarried and in hiding, it was probably the single worst worry we had. After we settled in the farm, my two sisters (and even I, to some extent) were the objects of much ridicule from farmers and their wives, who came from miles away to behold these old unmarried maids. It was a circus with Virginia and Martha as the main attraction. "What a pity! No men sought their hands?" someone always asked Mama.

"They are going to school and will marry when they finish," one of us always explained.

"Who would marry them now? What man would invest his money in a woman who is past her prime? All the children are gone, wasted in monthly flows." But as upset as their comments made Mama, she understood their views completely. None of the women we encountered in the farms had ever seen the inside of a school building. They'd all been taught that they had no use for extra knowledge. Their grooming was directed at their fulfillment—marriage and children. We were, therefore, all alone in the difficulty of protecting my sisters' honor; no other family near our farm had unmarried daughters of age. We could only look to distant farms to find families that shared our agony, families much like mine who during peacetime, were raising their children as Christians and sending their daughters to school.

We learned firsthand what could happen to an unmarried girl who was abducted. Two of our cousins were taken by soldiers within weeks of each other, and when one of them escaped and returned, she was treated like someone with leprosy. Her whole family was forced from the farm; she was tainted and no one wanted anything to do with her or those around her. Marriage was out of the question, and previous suitors shunned her. Her mother fled with her daughter to an unknown location, where no one had heard their story, hoping for a fresh start. But the story followed them, and my cousin was tormented wherever she went.

Mama went into a panic about what to do with my sisters, Martha and Virginia, sixteen and eighteen years old respectively, especially after our own farm was ambushed by enemy soldiers. We were lucky, thanks to a family friend, a man whose wife had been trained by Mama, who visited our hut just as we were settling to sleep and warned Mama to take her children and hide. He knew that our farm would be under siege that night and passed the information to Mama. She roused all of us, and in the quiet of the night we stole away. We could not alert others because our informer had warned against that, and Mama did not want to antagonize him. We walked as far away as possible before we laid down our mats and settled in for the night. We were awakened by the sounds of gunfire and the traces of bullets that whizzed past us. We crawled aimlessly in our confusion. The night magnified the sound of gunfire, and the bullets seemed aimed at us, although later we discovered they were fired indiscriminately.

The next day, we discovered the gruesome aftermath of the raid. Bodies were strewn all over, and we stepped over body parts to get back to the site of our own hut, which had been burned down. Almost every young woman was taken by the soldiers, and Mama decided then and there that she had to save my sisters, before the unthinkable had happened. Her first step was to keep them permanently hidden in the bushes; they could no longer come "home." Almost overnight, a hut was constructed for them and everything they owned in the world was carried there in an old pillowcase. Mama worked furiously, passing messages to relatives and friends throughout the region, letting it be known that her daughters were on the market for husbands. The urgency in her tone signaled that she was willing to settle for lesser suitors for my sisters; there was no time to be selective.

But even given our limited options, Mama was adamant about certain criteria necessary in the men my sisters ultimately married. They had to be practicing Catholics and unwavering in their faith. The men had to have been gainfully employed before the war started as well as upright members of their communities. Even in the middle of a brutal civil war, with danger all around and life at its cheapest, the response was overwhelming. Suitors or their representatives lined up in front of our hut to seek my sisters' hands. Neither of my sisters were present as each suitor made his plea. Most of the pre-war protocols were bypassed; nevertheless, they laid the cola nuts and palm wine they brought before stating the reason for their visit.

Everyone was given a routine response delivered by Christopher or Anthony. "It was not our wish to marry these girls off before they finished school. But these horrible times call for drastic measures. We will, however, convey your interests to the girl in question and send a message back to you as soon as we can."

Mama settled for a husband for Martha before one for Virginia. Most of the suitors did not specify which of the girls they sought. They had an "either-of-the-above" attitude, which left it up to Mama to decide which daughter the men seemed best suited for.

Emma Egbe, Martha's betrothed, was a university student who belonged to a family not known to us before. Everyone testified to his impeccable character and intelligence, good traits in a marriageable man, but not necessarily what Mama had hoped for in her first son-in-law. He lacked fire, spirit; he would do well, provide adequately for my sister and the children she bore, but he lacked oomph, a presence Mama felt was needed in a major in-law. Still, Martha's face lit up with pleasure when she was informed of her future husband while Virginia's drooped in disappointment. Martha chatted endlessly, asking question after question, "Is he handsome? Is he as tall as Papa Li? How does he walk?" She was unstoppable, and understandably so; at last she could exit from her hiding place and join another family, her real family. At last she would begin to fulfill the destiny for which she was created. She had been chosen by a man to be his wife.

Martha, however, remained in seclusion until her *igba nmanya* ceremony, when her husband's family paid a price on her head. The agreed-upon amount was four hundred and eighty-six pounds, a hefty sum for that period. Mama had instructed our male relatives who negotiated for the bride price that she did not wish it paid until the war ended, a wise tactical move on her part. Mama's stated reason at the time was because John was not present, and she did not want to be saddled with the immense task of safeguarding such a heavy sum of money. The real reason, however, was that the Biafran currency had lost all of its value, and five hundred pounds was not enough to feed a family for a month. Mama, using her business sense, was willing to take the risk that the war would not end and that the currency would be worth even less in time.

For the day of Martha's emergence and her transfer over to her in-laws, Mama made Martha a blouse and two wrappers out of prints she had managed to purchase from traders who dealt on the black market. Clothing material, like most essentials, was not available during the war, and only traders who crossed enemy lines possessed those rare treasures. Martha was radiant in her fineries as she worked the crowd that witnessed her traditional marriage. Everyone commented on her elegance in the way she walked, cocked her head to one side, smiled, and curtsied; she towered over the females gathered and was taller than some of the men. Her yellow skin, in contrast with the dark print, seemed even lighter, and everyone agreed that getting her married was the only option. There was too much at stake, too much to be lost if she was abducted by soldiers.

Martha's marriage was a bittersweet experience for everyone in our family. I watched, as if dazed, throughout the ceremony. As much as we tried to put a positive spin to it, the overpowering sentiments were gloom and helplessness. Even at the age of twelve, I knew that it wasn't happening the way it was supposed to. Martha should not have had to settle in marriage. She was the first of Mama's daughters to be married, and the prettiest. It should not have been done hastily, under cover, with lookouts watching all the entrances from tree tops, at a time chosen carefully to guarantee that the enemy soldiers were far away. Not even music had been allowed to herald Martha's transition to womanhood. "We can't call attention to ourselves," Mama had cautioned.

As the event wound down, Martha was invited to the center of the ring and handed a gourd of palm wine. She searched the faces of the crowd until she found her betrothed. She knelt in front of him with her head bowed in submission. Then, she held out the glass of wine to him, a sign to all present that she was in full support of the proceedings and that she willingly accepted her new role in life. When he took the glass from her, the crowd exploded with joy. "It is as it should be," a woman's voice rang out in the wedding chorus. "She's fulfilled at last."

We huddled as Martha departed with her in-laws. On her head, she carried an empty jar, the container that had held the palm wine. The practice of the bride carrying the empty jar is symbolic of her lowly position, and no matter how old or enlightened a bride is, she's expected to place that jar on her head, even if only for a brief moment, before turning it over to someone else. Martha gladly carried her jar and fell into line several steps behind her new husband, again and as always as it was supposed to be.

With Martha gone, I was designated to take her place in the shelter with my sister Virginia. Mercifully for Virginia, it was not long before Mama agreed to a proposal for Virgy's hand by a man who was not even there, but whose family spoke on his behalf. Unlike Martha's case, we knew this family well, and it was not as hard a decision as Martha's had been. There was no way of knowing if my new brother-in-law, who lived inside Biafra, was even aware of the developments, let alone in support of them. But it wouldn't have mattered anyway, for Ibo men and women rarely selected their own life partners. So we forged ahead with all the plans as if the groom himself were present. Her husband-to-be was an executive with Biafra's only broadcasting service and a likable bubbly young man, although he had very little education to fall back on, which Mama pointed out as she enumerated his qualities to my sister in her hideout.

"But as you know, no one knows how much longer we have before these soldiers find all of us. We can't keep turning suitors away. We need to settle on someone soon and he seems to be the best one so far," Mama explained. She did not, however, voice her concern that the more time she allowed to lapse between the two girls' marriages, the more people would notice the oddity that Virginia, the older sister, was getting married later than her younger sister. They could begin to spread ugly rumors about the reverse in the usual order of things.

As in Martha's case, Virgy emerged for her *igba nmanya* ceremony. Her bride price was pegged at five hundred pounds; Mama had insisted that she fetch a higher sum than Martha, for Virgy was not only more advanced in her education, but also more skilled at housekeeping and the general requirements of Ibo womanhood. Her glass of palm wine was given to her husband's older brother, who accepted on his brother's behalf, and when she left with them that night, we cried inconsolably.

Our family had been reduced drastically: to Mama, Anthony, Christopher, Ogbonna, and me. Even the cousins who'd always filled our household were gone—the girls married and the boys recruited into the army. We stayed up all night, Mama's sobs and sing-song crying lasting the entire vigil. "All I have is gone; my daughters are gone as I know they should, but why this way? Is this what I labored for all my life?" She would have grieved for a longer period had the situation allowed it, but the very next day, the day following Virginia's marriage, our family faced its biggest crisis yet.

Mama, seated in the middle, a few days before John (on Mama's right) departed for the U.S. in 1963. I'm at John's side. Virginia is on Mama's left; Ogbonna (my twin) is on Virgy's left. Christopher stands behind Virgy and Mama, Martha is in the middle, and Anthony is behind John and me.

My grandmother, Ogbu, who gave her daughter, Mama, to the Catholic mission to save her from being a group wife.

Mama, standing, third from left, in the year she stopped wearing her black mourning clothes. To her left is her brother's second wife. Seated (from left): Onugu Ugwu, Mama's only biological brother's first wife (she's barren); Mama Mgbada (Bene), Mama's sister (also without child); Grandmother; Nwa Ani and Olanya, Mama's sisters; and the woman grandmother married for her dead husband. On the floor (far right): Mary, the unlucky one, who helped raise us.

Five generations of strong Ibo women: My grandmother; her oldest daughter, Nwa Ani; Nwa Ani's oldest daughter, Josephine; Josephine's oldest daughter, Franca; and Franca's oldest daughter, Ify. Nwa Ani is Mary's mother.

Mama's master, my father, Honorable
Bernard Oyigbo Edoga.

Mama Helena in her youth.

The bleak days of our infancy. From left: Cousin Veronica, holding me, Christopher, Virginia, Anthony, Martha, Cousin Theresa, holding Ogbo.

Martha (center), following her surgeries, after she was placed with our Aunt Monica. On her left is Monica's husband. The other child is his niece.

Aunt Monica, Martha's guardian.

The early 1960s. Mama is second from left. My future mother-in-law is seated at right. The photograph was taken on the outing of the baby held by her mother, second from right.

Visiting relatives. I'm on the floor, far right; Ogbo is fourth from the right. Martha is standing at left; Virginia sits first from the left, next to Cousin Cecilia, who raised her. Cousin Eddie stands on the right.

At a send-off party from high school, a few months before I left for the United States.

A few months after the war ended in 1970. We had just returned to school. Far right: Virginia (whose husband permitted her to return to complete her high school education); Miriam; me; Franca; Rose. Miriam, Franca, and Rose are our cousins.

The Ugwu-Ojus in 1972. From right: Theresa; Charles; Mrs. Ugwu-Oju. Lower row: Obinna; K.C. (toddler); Mr. Ugwu-Oju; Emeka (standing in back); Priscilla (right of Papa); Rita (between Papa and Priscilla); Justina.

Emma, my first known suitor, who tormented my childhood.

Charles in his first year of medical school.

Outing ceremony for Martha's first child, Ogochukwu Chinelo Egbe. Mama is seated center, holding the baby; to her left is Martha's husband, Emmanuel Egbe; Martha is seated left.

Three generations on the outing of Martha's first.
Left to right: Martha, Mama, baby Ogochukwu.

My send-off party. I'm seated front center. Mama's house is in the background.
Li is top right.

My departure. Mama sits on my right; Mama Li sits on my left.
Martha stands at left.

The day I left for the U.S.

Martha (1974) with her daughter Ogochukwu and her infant son Chiedozie.

Virginia (1976) with her daughter Uzoamaka and her infant son Obiora.

The day Ogbonna left for the U.S., July 1977. He's in the middle with the bag hanging from his neck. Mama Helena is second from left in the black blouse. Mama is fifth from right, second from Ogbo's left. Mama Li is on Mama's left. My future mother-in-law is second from right. Stooping, from right: Virginia, her daughter Uzoamaka, and Anthony.

Grandmother, seated on Mama's right, and her children and some grandchildren and great-grandchildren, 1970. Neither Ogbo nor I was present for this photograph.

Mama (second row, sixth from right), surrounded by one of the many women's groups she leads. My mother-in-law is seated two seats to the right of Mama. Mama's house is in the background.

Mama, second from left, with church leaders, in her capacity as the president of the Christian Women's Organization.

Mama in 1978 when she visited the U.S.

During Mama's 1978 visit. Lower level: me, Miata, Che, Sherifa. Upper: Ogbo, Mama, John, Delia.

My college years in America, at Briarcliff and Syracuse.

Sherifa and me at the center of Morristown,
New Jersey, summer 1981.

Summer 1981. From left: me holding Sherifa; Ifeoma; Virginia; Chinyere (a cousin);
Che; Ogbo at back.

December 1981, on my wedding day, with Sherifa Omade Edoga, my maid of honor.

John walks me down the aisle on my wedding day.

The bride and groom with our parents. From left: John, my mother-in-law, Charles, me, Mama, my father-in-law.

The inlaws: Mama and my mother-in-law.

Following my wedding, at Aku, Delia and I do a traditional dance.

In December 1981, a few days after my wedding, Delia poses with other wives, women married to men from our village.

Delia and Papa's brother, Papa Thadeus, on my wedding day. He died in 1992.

My twin and me in 1982. I was six months pregnant with my first child.

January 1983. Delia holds her godchild, named after her — the child who made me a mother — Delia Virginia Nneka Ugwu-Oju.

Mama and her granddaughter, Delia, at seven months.

Immediately following the burial of Grandmother in December 1983. Sitting from left: Martha, cousin Mary, Mama, cousin Justina, Emeli (Mama's brother's second wife). Standing is Felix, Mama's brother's son. The beads are a sign of their bereavement.

After the death of Aunt Alice, Papa's only sister. Seated from left: Mama Li; Marcel, our cousin who doubled as Papa's valet and driver; Mama; Christopher, Marcel's brother; and Aunt Maria. Standing from left: Lizzy, Christopher's wife; Vicky, Marcel's wife; Bene, Aunt Alice's daughter; and Aunt Alice's other daughter, Arua.

Pregnant with Chuka — I had him less than a week after the picture was taken.

"My life is now complete." My prize child, Chuka, the day after he was born.

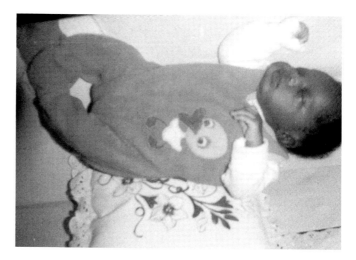

Mama and Delia, then four years old, when Mama visited in 1987.

From left: Anthony, John, me, and Ogbonna in 1990.

Martha, today, a mother of seven, grand-mother of two.

On Delia's first holy communion, with me, 1990.

Ogochukwu's wedding (Martha's first daughter). Mama stands next to the bride.

At Rositta's wedding (Li's sister). Felicia (Anthony's wife) is at left; third from left is Sherifa. John is behind Rositta and me. Ogbo stands between Charles and Delia. My children are in front.

John and Delia, Summer 1992.

Sherifa's graduation from Stanford University, June 1992. From left: me, Delia, Sherifa, John, Miata.

At Ogbo's wedding. From left: me, Ogbo, Elizabeth (Ogbo's wife), and Charles.

Charles and me in December 1994.

My children: Delia, Obi, and Chuka, summer 1993.

Sherifa Omade Edoga: John's first child, Mama's first grandchild, my maid of honor, my son Obi's godmother, my best friend. Sherifa died on March 12, 1994.

The day started quietly. We had not been awakened by gunshots, as was normal. We rose and proceeded to the farms to weed and do our other chores, fully expecting to return by day's end. But near lunchtime, before our only meal of the day, we heard the distinct sound of the alarm: enemy soldiers were upon us. The five of us dove in different directions because there had been no previous discussion about where to head. I remember stumbling and falling and being caught in the prickly thorns of a yam bush, but my primary concern was making it to the safety of the forest and I ran as if pursued by demons.

I don't remember much more of that day except that after dark, when we returned to the farm to assess our losses, my brothers Christopher and Anthony were gone. We assumed that they were delayed by imagined obstacles and waited, our eyes searching the terrain, but all in vain. We even searched the faces of that day's carnage. That gruesome exercise, thankfully, yielded nothing, but we were still no closer to solving the mystery of their disappearance. No one had seen or heard anything; they simply vanished as if they had never existed, leaving no trace. We returned to the farm, the place we last saw them, and kept watch.

Mama prayed through the long night, and by daybreak, her voice was completely gone. "God help me, where are my children? Who has taken them? Lord, don't abandon me in my time of need. Help find my children, your lost sheep. Lord, you told us to ask and we shall be given…" There was no stopping her, and I had never seen such fire in Mama's eyes or heard such desperation in her voice as that day. She paced our confined space like a woman gone mad, barely noticing Ogbonna and me where we crouched, crying. We waited for daybreak as if a new dawn would provide the answers that we sought, but it came and passed with no sign of them still.

The worst was not knowing what had happened to them in the endless possibilities of wartime. They could have been shot dead as they fled the soldiers; knowing my nineteen-year-old brothers, I felt that they would not allow themselves to be captured and tortured and would probably have chosen a quicker exit. Even as we waited for them to return, we all feared that their bodies were lying in some bush, undiscovered except by wild animals. They also could have drowned in one of the numerous rivers that flowed in that area. This was unlikely because the boys swam well and it would've been unusual for both of them to get into rough waters, if at all, at the same time. As we narrowed our options, we contemplated the worst, that they could

have been abducted and held by the enemy soldiers. The first nightfall met us still at the farm waiting for my brothers to return and so did
the second nightfall, and the third. Each day that passed diminished
that possibility, and when all hope was lost, we returned to our routine, trying to follow as normal a schedule as possible. But how normal
could our lives have been? I remember a darkness settling over us, a
gloom that didn't lift till the end of the war.

Then, as if we didn't have enough worry and grief, we received
heartbreaking news from Tailor's wife, who had visited Nsukka on a
black-market trading expedition. Tailor's family had, over the years,
maintained close contact with our family. They fled to Aku when the
war started and moved to the farms, although their exact location was
ten miles away from ours. Mama and Tailor's wife stayed up all night
as our guest described the scene in our town.

"Horrible! You would not recognize the place if you saw it."

"Everything's gone?" Mama asked, her voice quivering.

"Almost everything," the other woman confirmed. From where I
listened, I knew Mama was dying to find out about her house, but did
not want to ask directly, so she skirted the issue. But the other woman
brought it up herself. "My sister, nothing was spared, not even your
own house," Tailor's wife delivered Mama's death sentence.

"My house is gone," Mama mumbled. Then she said nothing for at
least another hour, although Tailor's wife continued to ramble on
about the burnt houses and dead bodies she observed during her visit.
I watched Mama closely, for I knew how pained she had to be at that
moment. Everything that meant anything to her had now been taken
from her—her daughters, her sons, and now her house. There was
nothing left, and even if this godforsaken war ever ended, there was
nothing to live for anymore. Our last hope was gone from our lives.
We now existed only from moment to moment, too afraid to reach at
all into the future.

It was at least four months before we discovered that Anthony and
Christopher were not dead as we had feared. Martha's husband, who
was a high-ranking officer in the Biafran army, informed us as that as
my brothers fled from enemy soldiers that day, they ran right into a
conscription ambush set up by the Biafran Organization of Freedom
Fighters, a guerrilla unit that operated mostly in enemy-occupied
regions. But by that time, we were so mired in our hopelessness that
the news barely cheered us up. Out of the hundred people who'd
arrived at Aku the night we fled Nsukka, our family had dwindled to

Mama, Ogbo, and me. We stuck to each other like glue, and although it was never voiced, an undercurrent of fear paralyzed us. Unless we had to run from the constant barrage of gunfire, we hardly got up. We performed only the most basic tasks that were necessary for our survival; otherwise, we did nothing. We mostly lay on the mat inside the latest hut. Sometimes we spread the mat outside and sat with our backs against the wall.

We did everything together, including going to the nearby bushes to ease ourselves. None of us could get out of the other's sight at any time. On our good days, we made it to the yam farm where we weeded or harvested vegetables or beans for meals that we never prepared. I don't recall eating a meal during that long stretch of time.

Though I was only twelve years old, I noticed that something was terribly wrong with Mama. It was much more than simple grief for her lost sons and house. She stayed up nights talking to herself, at times about things that were completely disconnected. Most often, however, Mama spoke about her house. "It's gone, all my suffering, all my efforts, gone." Occasionally, she seemed transported to a time when the house was still being built, and she would urge the workers to speed up construction. Sometimes, she began to sing out loud, as if she were a member of an invisible choir. Or she would talk to phantoms, holding up both sides of the conversation. She had become haggardly thin and her once renowned yellow skin had sallowed to a sickly gray. Her eyes had sunk into their deepset sockets. Her hair was matted and covered with dirt, and I couldn't remember when she or any of us had last taken a bath. It was as if we saw nothing, not even ourselves.

Then Mama became truly ill, with a fever and chills that caused her body to shiver and her teeth to chatter. Like most illnesses, it was treated as malaria, which usually lasted a few days and disappeared as abruptly as it began. Because there was no medicine anywhere, I went to the native doctor to prepare some herbs for Mama. But nothing worked; in fact, Mama seemed to get progressively worse. She reached a point where she could no longer sit up, not even to use the old bucket I found for her. Mama—my proud, compulsively clean Mama—did whatever she needed to do all over herself, right on the pallet where she lay.

At first other women helped me lift Mama and clean her, but soon they found excuses whenever I asked for their help. Then they stopped coming by our hut altogether, and I began to notice that sometimes several days passed in which we didn't see anyone. One night, I feared that Mama had reached her end and ran to our closest neighbor to solicit her aid. She had been particularly helpful in the past, so I did not hesitate one bit when I barged into the hut where she slept with her children.

"Please come help us. Mama is worse," I pleaded with her.

"Please leave. There's nothing that any of us can do for your mother. Only she knows what she did wrong."

The woman's reply made no sense to me then, and I continued to plead for her help for several more minutes before I ran to another neighbor. But everywhere I went, I received the same treatment. No one came to assist me in my desperation, and after I returned and found Mama calmer, I began to wonder the meaning of their words. What did Mama do to deserve that kind of treatment from anyone?

What I learned the next day was as scary as it was baffling, and revealed to me even more blatantly how precarious a woman's life is. I was told by our closest neighbor that a woman who becomes untreatably ill or dies for any reason other than old age is believed to have offended the gods in some way. The same theory, predictably, is not applied to men; only women are judged by these strict standards—in life, sickness, and death.

Mama was supposedly guilty of crimes against our tradition and she would not get better until she confessed. The most grievous of the crimes against women is *iladi* (adultery), a transgression so loosely defined that a woman can be deemed guilty of it if she shares a seat with a man who's not her husband. The laws governing *iladi* change from area to area and even from hamlet to hamlet. For example, a married woman from one village was not to have a conversation with a man other than a husband or blood relative, while in other villages a married woman was allowed male contact as long as it didn't take place in her marital home or husband's village. Women remained at the mercy of men who interpreted these laws as they saw fit, often to suit their own purposes. These practices still hold in my hometown of Aku to this day.

A girl I went to school with died of cancer a few years ago. Upon her death, it was decided that she had committed adultery with an unnamed man, and she was refused burial in her husband's village in spite of the fact that she gave birth to three sons who are natives of the village. She had to be returned to her father's home for burial, the worst treatment ever accorded a woman's corpse. The burden of proof lies on the woman or her family at all times. All that's needed is the suspicion, which at times is planted by individuals who stand to gain from the woman's family being discredited.

Another possible transgression is *izuori* (thievery), which though not as serious as adultery merited the same treatment. A third, *ikwa-puihe*, arises when a woman is believed to have given gifts to her relatives without the express permission of her husband.

It was under such a cloud of suspicion and ostracizing that my twin and I watched Mama deteriorate to the point where we were certain she would die. We took turns guarding her, talking to her even when we were no longer sure she could hear us. We mostly cried during that stretch, for no matter what we did, she lay limp, completely drained of energy and the will to live. One night, Ogbo fell asleep during his watch and we both woke to Mama's barely audible but persistent voice, calling out our names. We moved close and watched as she labored to talk to us.

"I want to tell you goodbye." We both began to wail, drowning her voice. Although it took great effort on her part, she shook her head vigorously, indicating that our behavior was inappropriate.

"I want you to promise me that you'll take care of each other, always."

"Please don't talk like that, Mama," one of us said.

"Just promise," she ordered, and we both whispered our pledges before she drifted off again.

I have never felt as scared and probably will never again experience the depth of pain that I felt during Mama's illness. All through my life, she was constant. Her constancy, I believe, was what made the big difference in our lives, especially for Ogbo and me, who never knew our father. As I lay as close to her as I could, grabbing onto her as if my own life depended on it, my mind wandered over our past years. Every scene, every frame captured in my mind's eye, had Mama in it: Mama in her mourning black; Mama as she inspected her house; Mama as she battled Papa Li; Mama as she lowered her voice, her lips pursed and her index finger wagging at me where I knelt; Mama beaming with pride at our last awards ceremony at school, right after I passed the national examinations with Distinction; Mama at her market stall surrounded by her trainees; Mama's tears cascading down her face right after we fled our home. The pictures were endless and tormented me mercilessly. There was no doubt in my mind. If Mama died, I too would die.

My mind rewound and played back memories of her hard life. Why would God take her now? Didn't she at least deserve some happiness in life? What could she have done to merit the relentless tragedy after tragedy, from her birth to the period she lay dying? Why had God never allowed her even one day of happiness? I concluded then that if Mama died, I would stop believing in God for whatever brief period I outlasted her. Maybe, I thought in my delirium, the elders in Mama's village had been right all along. Maybe Mama did not deserve any more than the position of a group wife, for which they had designated her. Maybe it's all my grandmother's fault for trying to rewrite the course of Mama's life. Why didn't she let Mama stay where they wanted her? Perhaps, even if only briefly, she might have experienced a little joy.

What would become of Ogbonna and me? Without the complications of the war, some relative would have certainly taken us into his home. But in our current situation, our fate was anybody's guess. At age twelve, I felt quite capable of taking care of myself physically, but I wasn't sure that I could manage to go on without my mother. My two sisters were quite settled in their marital homes. Virginia had already joined her husband in the interior of Biafra, and while Martha remained in our general vicinity, we had not heard or seen much of her since she left. She did not have control of her own fate anymore.

Mama slept nonstop for two days, and her breathing was so shallow that at times we could not see the lifting and falling of her chest. We had just about given up hope when she began to stir and gradually awaken. For the next few days, we vacillated between fear that she was taking her last breath and elation that she was getting better. I was vastly encouraged when Mama asked for something to eat, which she hadn't done in weeks. I hastily prepared a broth and spooned it into her mouth until she indicated by shaking her head that she did not want any more. As amazing as it seemed to us, Mama recovered from that illness, although she never fully regained her strength till the war ended.

But as fate would have it, before she was fully able to walk, our farm was again invaded by enemy soldiers. It is a day that I will never forget for I feared not only for Mama but for myself. Ogbo and I had gone to the farm that morning to harvest our dinner, leaving Mama on her pallet, fully intending to return before she got up. We had just gotten to the farm when the alarm sounded—enemy soldiers were in the vicinity.

The farm community had devised its own security system to minimize the casualties. Men took turns, perched on tree tops in different positions around the farm, keeping watch of entries and entrances into our area. When they saw large movements of people, they alerted residents by pre-arranged codes that everyone but intruders would understand. On that fateful day, Ogbo and I were busy gathering fresh green beans when we heard the horn sound; we rose, unsure that we had heard right. It came again, louder and more clearly. We made out the words, "*Okuko chiri umuya gbana na egbe na evu okuko abia; ha shiri ne* (Hens, take your chicks and flee, for there are many hawks hovering)."

We took off toward our home, running as if chased, thinking of nothing but Mama's safety. The crowds that we bumped into in our haste urged us to turn around and run the other way. "Better only she than you all perish!" But no, not even the distinct sounds of gunfire deterred me. The closer I got to the huts, the louder the cackling gunshots became and fewer people I met. But I ran on, spurred by a strange mixture of fear and of revulsion at what could happen to Mama. I was not willing to take any chances.

The possibilities seemed endless. I imagined the soldiers finding her where she lay helpless, her limbs still atrophied from her protracted illness. Could they tell at first that she was ill? Or would they pounce on her and take their liberties before gathering the women to take back to camp? Would they become angered by her "faked" illness and exact their revenge in some way? Would they shoot her, then set the thatched hut on fire? I continued to run, willing my body to keep pace with my mind. Somewhere before the entrance to our settlement, I noticed that Ogbonna was no longer running beside me, but even then I didn't slow down.

As I passed the first row of huts, I was suddenly confronted by thick dark billowing smoke. Instant darkness engulfed me, and for a brief moment, I was not sure of where I was. I fell on my knees and began to crawl, trying to move as far away from the smoke as possible, but it was everywhere. The soldiers had set fire to most of the huts, which burned unchecked. It was a popular tactic of theirs, for the fires always drove out whoever was hiding indoors, netting them a catch.

Still I continued to move in the direction of our hut. My mission now was even more urgent; I would not let Mama burn to death. The surrounding huts were aflame, and it was just a matter of time before a flying speck ignited ours. In the thick smoke, it was nearly impossible to distinguish the huts from each other, but ours alone had a verandah. Suddenly, I heard Mama's voice, calling to me, guiding me to where she lay. In the complete darkness of the room, she recognized the touch of my hands, and without speaking a word, we began to work together to save our lives.

I suppose I half-carried and half-dragged her outside, but in all honesty, I still don't know how it was possible. I was small for my age, and before that day, my twin and I combined could barely help Mama rise from her mat. I must have possessed supernatural strength to lift her. Mama and I crawled furiously; we did not speak for fear the soldiers would hear us, but headed toward a cluster of trees which had provided us shade on many afternoons past. The underbrush would shield us from the enemy's view and the tree branches and leaves would keep away the flying specks from the raging fires that consumed the huts. Mama collapsed as soon as we reached our hiding place, but I stayed alert, watching all directions for any sign of advancing soldiers. I also rubbed Mama's body, which had begun to shiver with cold, to warm her and keep her teeth from chattering and giving us away.

We remained in our position until we were found late that afternoon by farmers who had returned to salvage whatever they could from their burnt huts. No hut in the farm community was spared that day. All that was left as evidence of our lives were the charred remains of mud walls. But we were the lucky ones, we later found out. Dozens of families suffered the loss of their sons and daughters, while ours, dwindled as it had become, stayed intact, miraculously untouched by that major assault. Even neighbors who had previously shunned Mama acted more charitably, maybe because Mama showed signs of recovery or simply because of the devastation of that day's events. The larger men took turns carrying Mama, piggy-back style, to a clearing which became our new settlement.

From that day until the war ended, we did not last longer than a week at any location. Instead, we moved from one clearing to another in the bushes, each deeper in the woods than the one before it. We no longer bothered to construct homes or makeshift roofs over our heads. We merely laid our mats in the grass or on dirt mounds. No one cared. It was what life had become. In the mornings, our faces, legs, and arms were covered by fresh welts and rashes from insect bites—our battle scars, we began to call them.

Mama did get better, and soon was able to walk around without support. As she regained her strength, she once again assumed the reins of her family, shepherding us through the woods to less threatened areas, staying awake most nights to keep watch if there were any suspicions of pending raids, cautioning me to straighten my legs when

I sat and to always remember that prospective husbands were every-where—being herself, being Mama as I always knew her.

As strange as it sounds, life went on, almost as if the barrages of gunfire were normal, and the mortars and shells that occasionally dropped on our hiding places were routine. All through the war, even when our homes were in the bushes, men continued to search for possible wives and women bore babies. There was no pause in this most important duty in a woman's life.

My Near Marriage

War or no war, hut or no hut, I continued to live, grow older, and develop, and be the object of attention from single men and their families. I'd been shielded somewhat from marriage expectations by my sisters' presence. Next to their women's bodies, I looked like the child I was. Also, sisters are usually married in order of their ages. It would have been an aberration had I been deluged with proposals while my sisters were still available. But after Virginia's and Martha's departures with their husbands, I stepped up into the spotlight. Suddenly, I began to feel like a grown woman which, in the eyes of many, I was. I was twelve years old.

With my sisters gone, there was no reason not to seriously entertain marriage proposals. After all, Mama was as much afraid for me as she was for my sisters: I could be abducted and (she never voiced the word) raped; her preferred euphemism was "ruined for life." Also, most of the farm girls my age were settled in their marriages and having children. Proposals came from farmers and traders, none of whom Mama felt were qualified for reasons of religion and their status in the community. "Even if this war never ends," Mama muttered after yet another unqualified suitor, "we can't forget who we are." The suitors came at all times, even while we were evading enemy raids inside the bushes and hiding places. People had begun to take the bombs in stride and to proceed with their lives, and though Mama and I were reluctant to participate in the wartime marriage games, we were dragged along.

For as long as we could, before my breasts began to sprout and my hips to curve, we told all suitors that "Dympna's still too young." Then, it was easy to camouflage my gender with my twin's clothing and by cropping my hair almost bald like a boy. Only when it was no longer possible to hide my womanhood, she began to seriously weigh marriage proposals for me, even though she claimed that every one of them threatened to break her heart.

"I had really hoped that you'd become somebody important. How could you not, with your brains? But this war has ruined all our hopes," she sobbed.

There was nothing to suggest that it would end in the near future, or that life as we knew it would ever return. Finally, after two years of having our lives turned upside down, Mama felt it necessary to stir me toward adapting to our war realities. The possibilities of marriage loomed larger as each day passed.

I was also aware, however, that Mama wanted to hold on to me for as long as she could. She felt I was too young to be a wife and mother and she couldn't bear to part with another of her children so soon. She battled the conflict she felt between keeping me with her and the fate I would suffer if I were abducted by soldiers.

Sometime in 1969, just before turning thirteen, I began to itch to get married. Every girl I knew was married, and I was envious of them. Most were younger than I. I watched the girls on the day their bride prices were paid and they were given to their husbands in exchange. The young girls all had a smile that extended from ear to ear, a new grace in the swinging of their arms and their stride, and even a new sense of self, as if they had been transported to a higher plane, a level certainly superior to the one I was on. Only I remained unmarried, and suffered the snickering and taunting of much younger girls and boys, who called me *mkpogu* (old maid). I dared not join the hip-grinding dancing that characterized the *igba nmanya* ceremonies, fully aware that the attention would shift to me and my husbandlessness. In desperation, I almost accepted a proposal from a farmer, a man who had no education and would not have offered me anything more than I had in the depths of our desolate war existence, a man who was unlikely to have honored his word that he would not marry a second or third wife.

When an old family friend sought my hand for his only son, Mama finally, reluctantly, agreed. The father was a successful trader and his son was still in high school after several failed attempts to pass the General Certificate of Examinations (a test that every high school senior must pass to graduate). He would never have qualified under normal circumstances, but again, Mama felt we were in no position to be selective. I remember that my proposal came not from my intended, but his father. I had returned from the farm and was dirty and streaked with sweat, but that had no effect on him; as soon as he had Mama's permission, he asked me if I would marry into his family. Well rehearsed as always, I shrugged, adding coyly, "If that's God's plan for me."

The next time my intended father-in-law came, he presented us with a bottle of schnapps, evidence that some understanding had been reached by the parties. Because Mama was the only adult relative pre-sent, she could not open the bottle without violating the traditional customs. In fact, she went to great lengths to protect it whenever we fled from enemy soldiers. She wrapped it with rags to ensure that it was not accidentally broken.

Although I received many love letters from my intended, I never set eyes on him, for he was an officer in the Biafran Army and did not come home all the time we were courting. But it was not meant to be. The war ended and we returned to Nsukka, moving away from the life that had dictated marriage at that time. When I went back to school and my convent life, marriage suddenly no longer presented the appeal that it had. I became once again a pre-pubescent child; cou-pling was the farthest thing from my mind. I sought my freedom from the agreement reached over a bottle of spirits, but knowing our culture and how binding marital agreements could be, I took the easy way out. I lied. I told Mama that I wanted to become a nun, to live my adult life in the convent. She either believed me or also regretted the mar-riage, for she promptly informed my would-be-husband's family and returned the unopened bottle of schnapps to them.

My Shame

The war ended suddenly, without warning. It had been over for a few days before those of us in the farms found out about it. I remember the end of the war as distinctly as I remember the beginning of it.

It was in early morning and I was at the market to trade tubers of yam for condiments like salt. Mama had sent me along with other women from our farm, convinced that I would be safe with them. The journey was several hours long, so we traveled there in the evening and slept in the open space of the market—all women, huddled and relying only on each other for protection. We traded our goods early the next morning, before it was light enough for air raids, and were ready to head home when we were surrounded by Biafran freedom fighters. They were in retreat and in various stages of undress, having shed their uniforms to conceal their identities. We watched as most women in our group were stripped of their wrappers. Grabbing clothing from men and women to appear like civilians, one of the soldiers told us he heard that the war had ended and that we had lost. Biafra had surrendered.

"No, that can't be!" I cried out. How could we just surrender? Didn't we all vow to fight till the last man? I refused to believe it, but in a matter of minutes, the news was all over the market. Someone even had a radio, which broadcast Biafra's unconditional-surrender announcement in English and then Ibo. Anger slowly crept up on me. By the time we got home, it was almost choking me. I had never before and have never since been as bitter as I was that day. When I finally began to cry, I didn't know if I could put an end to the tears. "Why? Why? Why?" was all I could manage. Later, my anger took form and I knew who and what my tears were for.

I cried for the years that I lost—for the child whose girlhood was interrupted and for the young woman who was emerging. I cried for Mama, her still sickly self—her house, her energy, her pride. I cried for my friends who died in the school air raid. I cried for my uncle who was shot and stripped, for his wife who went mad, for Papa Li, Oke and all the others who'd died—died, it seemed, now that Biafra had lost, in vain. Why was it all for naught, I wondered, but no one had any answers.

Days later, the skies seemed brighter and our prospects better. At least we could go to bed and expect to sleep through the night; that alone seemed to make our defeat more bearable. Then we began to make plans to return to Nsukka.

We hid for two weeks more, and when it seemed safe enough, we trekked the thirty-odd miles to Nsukka. It was a two-day journey. We moved in a caravan with other refugees who, like us, were returning to the life they once lived. None of us knew what awaited us at Nsukka, but we were confident that whatever it was would be less severe than what we had suffered in the past three years.

"Nothing could be worse than the war itself," we thought, but we were wrong. Even as we journeyed back to "normal life," the war still confronted us. At every checkpoint, victorious Nigerian soldiers searched our ragged bundles and our bodies; their hands lingered on the women and they took liberties, but we were so concerned with surviving that everyone pretended not to notice. Many women were held back "for further searches," but the rest of us continued, relieved to be spared. At each stop, Mama held on to me, the wrap she wore around her shoulders extending to envelop me, shielding me from the soldiers' hawk eyes.

When we entered Nsukka, we were stunned by the devastation. Nothing could have prepared us for the shock of seeing our town plundered and stripped of its soul. Nothing was recognizable. It was one burnt-down house after another, zinc and other debris strewn all over the place. Dead bodies, some mummified, others still fresh, littered the streets. The stench of destruction was almost unbearable. Everyone we met seemed like us, wandering like lost sheep, uncertain about what awaited us and terrified to find out. Mama's tears began to flow unchecked as we got closer to our house, but I noticed a quickening in her stride.

We returned home from the war to nothing. All that was left of Mama's businesses, her houses, her sewing shops and equipment, was an empty shell. Contrary to the story told to us by Tailor's wife that Mama's house had been destroyed, it was still standing when we returned. It stood all alone. All others around it had been razed by mortar shells.

We were more shocked to see our house standing in the midst of the ruins, than we would've been to see it down. It was as if it alone had been singled out, spared for some reason, left alone to tell the stories of its survival. Mama broke into a trot, and I struggled after her. She stopped by the steps leading up to the verandah and stared up through the main entrance of the home she fought so bravely to build.

The door was ajar, beckoning, almost daring us to enter. The structure of the house seemed intact. We moved cautiously, staying together the first few minutes. We expected someone to jump out from a corner in any minute and arrest us or hurt us, so we remained in a state of heightened tension as we inspected the parlor, Mama's room, and the other rooms. All the doors were ajar. Nothing remained—no furniture, no clothing, not even a picture left hanging.

But the house was not completely bare. As we made our way through it, we were surprised and repulsed by what we found. One of the back rooms had been used as a toilet, and heap after heap of excrement, in different stages of decomposition, stared us in the face. We fled from that room, feeling defiled and contaminated. The house was filled with tons of debris, so much garbage that it had to have been brought and dumped inside. We set down our ragged baggage and began to clean the house. As we cleaned up, we hoped to find mementos, old photographs or keepsakes, but none of what was left in our house belonged to us. We were so charged that we didn't even mind walking a mile to the only source of water for Nsukka. We quickly found ourselves joined in the work by other families who, without asking, started to live with us until they could make other arrangements. On our part, we felt too lucky to object.

I believe Mama also felt guilty, for she could not explain why her house, of all the others, was spared. In private, she confided to us that she believed the wall, the boundary built by the Okafors to demarcate our two properties, had in fact saved hers, for the Okafors' residence was leveled. Not even burnt-out walls remained; it was as if someone had used a bulldozer to reduce it to rubble.

Staying ahead of the bullets in the war was the easy part; staying alive after the war and beginning life anew proved almost insurmountable. The war continued to rage inside of us and outside of us. We, Ibos, were "the vanquished," and could be stopped and interrogated without cause at any time and any place. Soldiers barged into homes at all hours. If anyone complained, he was told he was lucky that he wasn't shot dead. We lived under a self-imposed curfew that often extended many days at a stretch.

We returned from the war without a dime. In the thirty months since the war began, the Nigerian government, the victors, had changed the currency, rendering whatever money we had useless. In addition, we had fled Nsukka without any documents, so that even if we could, we had no way of claiming the money in our bank accounts from before the war. We had no choice but to join thousands of other families in international relief food lines, holding our pans and sacks before us, hoping to eat enough to survive.

That occupied our every waking moment. Often we had to be at the relief centers before cock's crow, but were not attended to till late in the afternoon. We'd become beggars, pushing and shoving, fighting for our places in line. At times, Mama sent one of us to wait, but because only those present were allocated the food, the more of us there, the more ration we received that day. It became a trap, for we could not do anything else. Each day that we did not go meant we had nothing to eat, but each day that we went meant the whole day was wasted there.

Mama even contemplated returning to the farm, to a place where we'd actually controlled our lives and ate food we'd grown. But as she was reminded constantly, at least she was lucky. She still had a house, which was more than most people had.

Then, one day, while we waited in line for our daily ration, a man who had known my father and had attended teacher's college with him recognized Mama. According to Mama, this man became our savior, for at the end of their conversation, he gave Mama two pounds, a hefty sum by all accounts. And again, as Mama claims, that whatever she had resulted from my father.

With the two pounds as her capital, Mama was given a new lease on life. She started business afresh as she did after her year of mourning, in the food business, making and selling *akara*. This time, however, I was the hawker. Each night, Mama and I chopped, soaked and washed the beans. We rose early, often before three in the morning. I ground the beans using grinding stones, then we packed up and went to the motor park where we set up our stall. Travelers stopped in for breakfast, and when all the transport had left, I carried the remainders in a tray set on my head to the army hospital where I sold them off. If I finished on time, we made it to the relief center to join the lines, so that all our gain from the ·akara trade was reinvested in the business.

At home, we slept on raffia mats, which we rolled away in the mornings. The relief centers handed each of us a set of used clothing. We had no shoes, but neither did anyone else. And that was how we lived in the tumultuous aftermath of the war.

Around that time my body rebelled and came of age. In the first weeks of the post-war era, I began to menstruate. This milestone in my life caused me immense shame because I had very little understanding of how a woman's body functioned. A shroud of secrecy surrounded even the most natural processes in a woman's existence. Before I saw my first period, all I had heard of a woman's menstrual cycle was from a female cousin who told me that "the curse" only happened to women who did bad things.

"Like lying?" I had wondered. I was probably ten years old at the time.

"No, you know, like doing bad things with boys," she explained, managing to convince me that only bad girls need worry about it. "It's God's way of punishing them."

My cousin's revelations created havoc in my already confused world. I searched every woman I came in contact with for signs of "the curse." No one ever explained to me what happens to women; no one ever told me of the changes in our bodies, so I never thought those things would happen to me.

I remember the most minor details of the day my period started. I was in the kitchen, a separate shack (still without a roof, which had disappeared while we were gone), stooped in front of the fire, stacking more wood to speed up dinner. I remember feeling a little warmth between my legs, and later, a wetness. I ran into the windowless unlit bathroom. When I pulled down the fraying cotton drawers Mama had sewn from leftover material, I could make out a large dark stain. My heart sank. "It can't be true. This can't be happening to me. I haven't done anything." I stood in the darkness of that bathroom for what seemed like hours, until I realized that my long absence might seem suspicious, so I pulled my panties back up and rushed back to the kitchen. I sat on a log stool, feeling the dark substance ooze out of me.

Later, I took a bucket of water to that dark bathroom. I refused to take a lamp with me. My sin and shame matched the dark room. I washed myself, crying silently, wondering when I did the forbidden deed and with whom.

I barely slept that night, my mind wandering through the activities in which I had been involved the past few weeks.

I wondered if one of my numerous cousins who lived with us and slept in the same room with us had done something to me. I examined the minute details of every contact I had with boys. I remembered that I had helped a male cousin with his homework, and that our bodies had touched when he moved closer to view the passage I was reading. Was that it? I wondered.

I rose early the next morning and sneaked into Mama's room when she was in the bathroom. I held up a hand-held mirror, the only mirror in the entire house, dreading what I would see. At first, I kept my eyes tightly shut, but I got braver, opened them slightly, and was shocked by what I saw. Nothing was different. My face was still as round as the moon. No signs of my curse showed on my face.

I wish that had been the end of my misery, but it was just the beginning. By the end of that day, Mama and I had almost lost our lives.

Mama's Ultimate Sacrifice

Of all the lessons I learned about Ibo womanhood, the most important, at least as far as Mama was concerned, is sacrifice. A woman
has to be willing to forfeit her person, her life, for her family. A woman
who learns this early has a good start on happiness, because a woman
can only be truly happy if everyone around her—her husband and
children—is happy.

"What does a woman need to be happy for?"

"Did she say happy?"

"What is happy anyway?"

I've heard these phrases uttered by Ibo women more times than I
can remember. They reinforce the belief that a woman is not entitled
to happiness for her own sake. Her satisfaction, fulfillment, joy are the
inevitable result of marriage, where she knows her place.

Throughout my childhood, Mama demonstrated over and over the
importance of self-sacrifice. She reminded us constantly that without
the sacrifice of her own personal desires, she could not have been the
parent she was to us. I felt confident that if Mama needed to, she
would willingly give her life for any one of us.

The day after the onset of my womanhood, Mama and I were put in
a situation that brought this issue right to the forefront. If I had harbored any doubts about my mother's devotion, when that situation
came to an end, I had none left. I was in awe of her, her selflessness
and ability to give of herself totally. She demonstrated that evening
everything she had taught me to believe.

I was still in a daze, contemplating how to deal with the curse, when
Mama announced that she and I would journey to Aku to visit her sister who, we were told, was ill. In the postwar confusion, public transport between Nsukka and Aku was sporadic at best, and Mama sought
the help of my cousin Isaac, who was then the chief engineer of the
state government.

Mama, my cousin Isaac, and I were being driven to Aku from
Nsukka by Isaac's government-assigned driver when we were accosted
by soldiers. Mama and Isaac were seated in the passenger side of the
cab of an open-bed truck while I rode alone, in the bed of the truck

along the narrow unpaved road, overgrown with trees. When we approached a checkpoint, we thought it would be routine—that the armed soldiers would, at most, conduct a body search and send us on our way—but we were wrong. As the driver, Isaac and Mama were ordered off the vehicle, I watched a large group of armed soldiers barricade the road. Suddenly, soldiers were everywhere: soldiers hitting the windshield with the barrels of their guns until it shattered; soldiers shaking the truck, as if they expected some hidden object to fall from it, soldiers climbing into the car, ripping apart the dashboard, plundering the clearly marked government vehicle, soldiers hitting the driver, then my cousin Isaac, then—my God—my mother. Mama took a blow to the side of her face, and I saw her falter, then fall on the sandy road. It was madness if I ever saw it. I froze in fear, voiceless, seeing my mother's and cousin's faces covered with blood. And then someone looked up and saw me cowering in one corner of the truck's bed, my teeth chattering and my eyes bulging.

What seemed like a dozen men leapt onto the truck to grab me. One lifted me and threw me over the side to the eagerly waiting hands of his colleagues. A cheer rose. "A juicy tomato! A fresh girl!" They jeered as I was tossed from man to man to man. They touched every nook of my body, and for a minute, I knew terror.

My mind raced faster than light, seeking a way out of the situation, but none was near. From the corner of my eye, I saw Mama being dragged away from me. What a struggle she must have put up, clawing the soldiers to get back to my side, but she was no match for six burly men who hit her repeatedly until she could no longer lift her arms. I heard her screaming in a voice full of fear, as I had never heard before. All I could make out was "Please don't hurt her! Take me instead!"

When I finally landed on my feet, I saw myself surrounded by no less than thirty tongue-hanging, leering soldiers.

"I go first," one said.

"I'm second," another declared.

Others jockeyed for position, lining up for the prize. The apparent leader stepped up to me and pulled the neckline of my dress. The frayed fabric yielded, the tear running the length of the bodice. My budding breasts, never before touched or seen by anyone, were exposed. My eyes closed in humiliation, and my bare arms crossed over my chest, but the lead soldier commanded that I drop my arms. He tore the dress off my shoulders, and it crumpled around my ankles. I stood as naked as the day I was born, except for scanty underpants and a soaked rag between my legs. I prayed for a quick death while the men drooled and planned how to make that event memorable.

It's all so strange, how we focus on one thing, and believe it to be so overwhelming. Then something even more significant happens and the first thing is completely forgotten. An hour earlier the "curse" had threatened to "destroy" me, and now, I was struggling for my life.

I suddenly became aware of my nakedness. Forbidden from placing arms across my chest, I moved them to my pubis and began to scream. Mama says that when she heard my scream from where she was still being beaten, she thought the worst had happened. "It's over; they may as well kill me now," she muttered, and started a fresh struggle. I, on the other hand, continued to scream relentlessly, like one possessed. My lead tormentor circled me, then reached for my panties. The tempo of my screams increased as I struggled, refusing to move my hands. He overpowered me and in one pull, the panties ripped and the blood-soaked rag dropped a few inches from my feet.

I stared at it, probably more out of shame than anything else; my secret was out in the open, my sins public. The sudden quietness confirmed my greatest fear: the soldiers had noticed also. They stood as if transfixed, their eyes wide, staring at the rag as if it were a grenade, already smoking and about to go off.

"What's this? An unclean woman!" the leader shouted, his voice full of his disgust. He hit me repeatedly in the face, cursing in both his native Hausa and broken English. From his tirade, I gathered that I was a spoil-sport; I had ruined all their plans for that night and had to pay for it. Mercifully, no one else joined him or even cheered his actions. It was an eerie silence; even I couldn't utter a sound.

"Whore! Harlot! You deserve to die," he spat while he pounded me until he wore himself out. When he stopped, I looked up. I saw that the men who surrounded me had quietly walked away, and that my abuser was slowly following them. I felt Mama's presence even before I saw her, but I remained standing, my body fully exposed. I made no attempt to cover my body or hide the blood that trickled down my legs. I felt a strange mixture of shame and fear—fear of what Mama would do to me.

Mama walked up to me and put her arms around me, her swollen eyes shedding as many tears as mine. I know now that Mama cried for me, for my shame and her inability to protect me or lessen the pain I felt. She covered me with the top layer of her wrapper, and half carried me to the truck.

After the driver helped Mama lift me up, he started the engine, which mercifully responded. Cousin Isaac, whose eyes had swollen shut, stumbled into his seat. Mama clambered onto the back with me, my full weight resting on her shoulders. She rocked me even as our bodies shook when the truck went in and out of potholes. Between her sobs, she managed a few words. "It will be all right. You'll be fine soon."

The strangest part of this incident is that no one, neither Mama nor I, alluded to my period. I'm quite sure Mama saw the bloodied rag and noticed the bloodstains on her wrapper when we got to our destination. She must have sensed my need to protect my pride and did not pry.

The events of that day remain a secret between Mama and me; not even my sisters are aware of how close I came to losing that which I most treasured. To this day, one thing continues to trouble me about the incident. I wonder what transpired between the soldiers and Mama when they led her out of my view. I dare not even speculate, and I lack the courage to probe farther, afraid that my worst fears will be confirmed.

Back to School

At first, it seemed nearly impossible that I could return to school and continue my education. Mama could not afford the steep school fees for me, my twin, and Anthony (Virginia and Martha now were their husbands' responsibilities), plus feed the scores of cousins, including all of Papa Li's children, who had become Mama's full responsibility.

Also, it simply did not make great economic sense to send a girl to school. With the war barely over, parents were not able to recoup the great expenses spent on their daughters via the bride price. Most were glad to be rid of them before the still-marauding soldiers got them.

I watched Mama labor under the weight of the tough choice she had to make. Many nights I watched her count her money over and over, almost as if she expected to find more than she did the previous time. When she tired of that, she took to her rosary and prayed the rest of the night. On the day we were supposed to report for registration, I went through my market routine with her. As I readied to take the remaining *akara* to the hospital, she stopped me.

"Run home, get ready, and hurry to Queen's so you'll still make the sign-up," she said.

"Mama," I started, not really sure of what I would say. It was only then that I realized how anxious I had been over the issue, and how much I had prayed for the decision that Mama had just made. I remember that my eyes clouded with tears and that I had an incredible longing to wrap myself around Mama and hold her, but instead, I hugged myself tightly while I rocked on my feet.

"You're already late. Hurry," Mama said, waving me off. I ran the five miles to Queen of the Holy Rosary, the all-girl secondary school at which I had spent one term just before the war started. It was a disheveled bunch that assembled, very different from every memory we had of convent students. We were dressed in tattered clothing, and only a few wore shoes. The rest of us looked like we belonged on a farm somewhere, digging up yams instead of sitting in a classroom. Our school had been a soldier's camp during the war, but while the

building structure had been saved, nothing else was the same. The soldiers had defecated in the dormitories, even beside their own sleeping
areas; it defied all reason.

But slowly, I returned to school life. I had to cover the ten-mile
round trip from home to save the boarding fees; that was the only way
Mama could afford tuition for all of us. To me, it did not matter. I was
just happy to be in school once again. I reveled in the pleasures I found
in little things, like being able to read, gossip, throw net balls, be a
child. No matter how hard I tried, I could not fill the void of the time
lost. Still, I went at my second chance with a determination that I
didn't know I had. I was content to rise with Mama, set up the *akara*
stall and begin selling before dashing home for a bath and running to
school. I don't know how I did it, but I succeeded. By the end of the
first term in June, I was again performing at the top of my class. I
moved into the boarding school when school reopened in September
and stayed there until I graduated three years later.

Everything had changed. As a condition of our surrender, we relin-
quished all rights to self-determination. The states took over our education system. We were no longer affiliated with the convents, and
nuns no longer ran the school. Religion, the controlling element in
our pre-war system, was no longer allowed in our schools, and attendance at masses became optional. The strict discipline imposed by the
nuns was lifted, and we were like cattle without herdsmen. There were
very few rules, and they were easy to bend.

Soldiers had free access to the dorms and their occupants. Lured by
their money and the trinkets they promised, our girls flocked to them.
Mothers shook their heads but were powerless to stop their daughters
from flinging themselves at the soldiers. The temptation was overwhelming: girls, including those younger than me, flaunted their loot,
the short mini-dresses and shiny fake jewelry they acquired. Beside
them, I looked drab in my relief leftovers.

I was tempted to go on one of the excursions with my friends, but
something always held me back. When I visited home during the
weekends, Mama scrutinized me closely, probably looking for signs
that I had become an "army girl." Once, I made the mistake of going
home dressed in an outfit I had borrowed from one of my friends. It
was a red mini-skirt with a white ribbed tank top. I must have been
quite a sight—the little clothing barely covering my still-forming
woman's body—for as soon as I stepped into the house, Mama led me
by my ear to her room.

"Where did you get that?" she asked as she simultaneously pushed and punched me. From where I huddled against the wall with my arms shielding my face, I saw the rage in Mama's eyes.

"Who gave you those rags?" she screeched, lunging at me.

"I borrowed them from a friend," I stuttered, completely taken aback by Mama's outburst.

"What's wrong with your own clothes?"

"Nothing," I lied, when I should have told her I hated looking like a maid all the time, that my rags were torn, patched all over, and fit poorly, that everyone recognized them for the handouts that they were, and that when I wore them I felt like nothing. I should have told Mama that my borrowed outfit made me feel special and that I didn't have to hide when anyone looked in my direction. Instead, I told Mama how sorry I was to have caused her pain and that I would never again repeat what I did.

When she let me out of her room, I was without the outfit; I was dressed in one of my own, a dress even drabber than the ones I took to school with me. I cried by myself that day, probably the first time I ever did. In the past, my tears had been for attention, for someone to notice and soothe the pain. That night, I felt all alone. No one understood me, and there was no one I could explain myself to.

"You need to be patient, Dympna," Mama woke me from sleep that night and told me. "Yes, often it seems that everyone has it better than you. Your friends have lots of new clothes. They have shoes. They have it all, and you have nothing, except castoffs. I know how that can make you feel, but you must be patient."

"Yes, Ma," I said, hoping the conversation would end before she remembered something else I did wrong.

"The good things in life are infinite; that is my promise to you. If you work hard, all these things will still be available when you can afford them. Don't reap your fruits before they're ripe."

Of course, I continued to want things I knew I couldn't have, but at least I held on to Mama's promise that hard work would give me things she couldn't. Many, many years later, when I had every material possession that I could possibly want, she reminded me of the promise she made to me that bleak miserable night.

Part IV
Coming to America

My Husband Is Selected

As the state of affairs in Nsukka and Mama's compound slowly struggled back to normal from the worst upheaval it had ever seen, Mama's attentions naturally returned to the topic nearest to her heart: my betrothal. I suspect she recognized that my "desire" to be a nun was a mere ruse to extricate myself from the wartime proposal we'd accepted, and I also suspect that she was relieved and grateful that she could return the fateful bottle of schnapps and cancel the deal—even though her reason was a lie. In her heart of hearts, Mama knew that I was destined to marry Charles Ugwu-Oju.

The Ugwu-Ojus and Edogas go a long way back. Both his parents, like mine, were born and raised in Aku. His father, like mine, graduated from St. Charles Teacher's College, although my father was several years ahead of his. Charles' immediate younger sister, Priscilla, was in all my classes through elementary and high school, and we were the best of friends. She later married my first cousin, Eddie, Uncle Crescent's youngest son. When we were growing up, Charles' father was the equivalent of a mayor in Nsukka and wielded a lot of power. According to Mama, the reason she did not hesitate to give her "most prized possession" to them was because of the father's integrity. "If the son has one-tenth of his father's integrity," she reasoned, "I'll have nothing to worry about."

After my father's death and Mama's resettlement in Nsukka, Felix Ugwu-Oju became a sort of "husband" to Mama. The relationship, of course, was not sexual. Indeed, the fact that Mr. Ugwu-Oju did not take advantage of her vulnerability further endeared him to Mama. Unlike the motions she went through with Papa Li, Mama sought Mr. Ugwu-Oju's opinion on every matter of importance, ranging from schools to business to marriage. He also accompanied her to negotiate and sign land deals and other contracts. Because of his influential position, my future father-in-law also helped Mama secure government contracts, but only, as the two of them insisted, through proper channels.

My future mother-in-law, for her part, never showed any resentment toward Mama for her husband's involvement with her. "How many women do you think would sit by while their husbands went running to a widow every single time she called?" Mama insists that quality in Mrs. Ugwu-Oju convinced her that I was theirs for the asking. What Mama's statement neglects to say is that my mother-in-law's opinion on the subject never mattered and that her husband was within his rights as a man. But to this day, Mama tells anyone who'll listen that my future parents-in-law's good nature was only the icing on the cake. Even if they were the worst people on Earth, she would have found it impossible to say no to them when they asked that I be betrothed to their son.

Charles was not a stranger. When people ask me how long I knew my husband before we married, I tell them I've known him for as long as I've known myself. One of my earliest memories was of riding in his father's blue Volkswagon and of being bathed by his mother at her house. Charles' parents' home was a second home to us as we grew up; his father is my twin brother's godfather, and since my twin and I were close, we spent a great deal of time with them. I remember Mr. Ugwu-Oju's presence at our awards ceremonies at school. I now believe he was there as much for us as he was for his own children. He came to the ceremonies in a car loaded with presents which he shared with all of us, his children included, in equal parts. Charles was present during most of our childhood, for he was only a class higher than I was in school, although he went to the boy's school with my twin brother.

Their house, the largest building that I ever saw before the war, was strategically perched on a hill that could be seen from all over town. What I remember most about the house was sitting on the roof balcony from which I could see the whole town. That left a big impression on me as a child. The house was not more than a five-minute walk from my mother's house, so we went back and forth on numerous errands throughout the day. My sister Martha, after she returned to our household, was classmates with one of Charles' sisters; the two went away to the same boarding school and were friends. So intertwined were our lives that what developed was inevitable.

Once, for a period of about six months, Charles lived with us. It was all explained neatly at the time, and though it's unlikely, I occasionally wonder if it was not part of the grand plan. According to the stories told by both Mama and the Ugwu-Ojus, Charles' father was going abroad for a course and his mother was pregnant and could not be relied on to ensure that his heir's education continued uninterrupted. Charles moved in with us during his father's absence. He and I became friends even then, when cross-gender closeness was discouraged. Strangely, we slept together on a mat spread on the floor of Mama's room. My twin and I slept on that mat in Mama's room until we went away to school, so it was natural that Charles be asked to share our "bed," located at a place where Mama could keep a watchful eye over us. I remember him then as a brilliant boy who kept me captivated by his knack for solving math problems and explaining scientific concepts that I couldn't make sense out of.

Why was I the one chosen to seal the two families' friendship? It was very simple. Charles is his father's first son—the heir, the most valued of his children, at least at that time in the Ibo experience. My two sisters were older than Charles, and Ibo men *never* marry women older than they. I was both the only daughter left and the one with the most promise. I can't claim to know when the two families decided to pair us up. It's unclear whether they even discussed it or just assumed and silently understood. My mother refuses to be pegged to a time frame, and when I insist that she tell me when an understanding was reached between the parties, she uses the dog-head question in response: "If you ask for a dog's head, what will you do with its jaw?"

It is quite possible that the agreement was reached when Charles and I were children. But my own best guess is that it couldn't have been before the war ended because Emma was a fixture during most of my childhood and Mama did promise me to someone else at the end of the war. There's nothing to suggest that Charles knew of or was part of the maneuverings that went on until the two of us began to communicate directly.

Marriage as a Group Effort

Marriage among Ibos is a community venture, so a married woman is referred to by her husband's entire clan as *Nwunye Anyi* (Our Wife). The woman is married to the entire community of men, women, and children. She treats them all as she would her husband, and any one of them has a right to rebuke her, punish her, even influence her relationship with her actual husband. A married woman wields more power in her father's village than she does in her husband's. In the village of her birth, she's a *nwada* (daughter of the land), and she joins the group of *umuada* (daughters of the land). As a group, the *umuada* of any Ibo village is a power to be reckoned with, often more powerful than most male groups. They are primarily entrusted with maintaining social order and ensuring that men and women, husbands and wives, stay within their prescribed roles. *Umuada* could find that their "brother" was mistreating his wife and send a warning to him to cease and desist or incur their wrath. They could equally send a wife (who's also a *nwada* but only in her father's village) packing if they felt she was mistreating her husband. But the same *nwada* who leads the females in her father's village would crawl on her hands and knees before the *umuada* of her husband's village. A woman's daughter, by implication, can throw her own mother out of her father's home. The daughter is a *nwada* in her father's home, but the mother is merely a wife.

So marriage extends beyond the immediate and extended family. In my case, Mama wanted to ensure that mistakes made with my sisters would not be repeated. The decisions on who they married were made quickly without a long bond tying their husbands' families to ours. Virginia married a man from Umundikwu, a small village in Aku, the same village where one of Mama's sisters was married. Mama's sister, Benedette or *Mama Ngbada* (Mama That Lives Down the Hill), never had a child and was miserable in her husband's household. Everyone in our family believed that it was due to the evil thoughts of the villagers. Mama swore that no one she knew would marry an Umundikwu man or woman again, for *obi taru ha nmiri* (their hearts are dry).

But given the war and our limited options, Mama had to agree on an Umundikwu man for my oldest sister. Even as she did, she ranted and raved about every misstep his family took. If they haggled over the bride price longer than Mama felt was acceptable, she muttered under her breath, "Didn't I say how hard-hearted they were? It's just because of this war or I would not let them near my child, not after what they did to my sister."

Charles' family represented stability, Christianity, hard work, intelligence, power, and wealth. Mama kept reminding me that a good family was crucial, "not for the good times, but for when things go wrong."

Mama pointed out several people I knew as examples of bad families, clans that did nothing when circumstances began to turn sour. She reminded me of a woman we referred to as *Mama Ikechukwu* who lived in Nsukka and died just before I left for the United States. According to stories, Mama Ikechukwu and her husband lived in Lagos during the ten years of their marriage, until his sudden death in 1967, just before the war started. After her husband was buried, Mama Ikechukwu's "bad" in-laws demanded that she give an account of her husband's wealth. She swore to them that she knew nothing of her husband's dealings and that his pay as a police sergeant was often not enough for the family's upkeep. They didn't believe her and took revenge against her. Her four children were given to relatives, and she was ordered to leave and return to her own village. No one in her husband's village had spoken against what everyone knew to be a grave injustice. Mama Ikechukwu never beheld any of her four children again.

Mama was determined to make the best of my situation, and not just for my benefit but for everything our family could gain from it. Marriages were often made for political reasons, for uniting two powerful families. In spite of my father's early death and the hardships my family endured afterwards, there was not a better family in everyone's opinion than ours. The number of suitors and marriage proposals I received is evidence of that.

Ibos value a good name more than wealth, and many remember my father as a man of generosity and strong conviction. They talked about my father's strictness and discipline, implying that his children inherited some of his mettle. My mother, in spite of her precarious beginnings, ingrained herself in everyone's consciousness as the enduring wife, the symbol of both piety and motherhood. The few who remembered chose to ignore the circumstances of her childhood or her parentage. She had been redeemed through her husband; she was *Nwunye Honorable* and that was the identity they assigned her. Every family with an eligible child sought to be connected with ours, and the most available avenue was through marriage.

Faced with the barrage of suitors who expressed interest in me , Mama wished she had more daughters with which she could create long-lasting loyalties. She tried to extend proposals meant for me to my cousins. Most times, because the suitors were unwilling to offend Mama, they went along with whomever she suggested, often believing that even a remotely distant Edoga was better than none. Sometimes, however, the suitors balked and extricated themselves, especially if there were issues in the particular girl's background that even the Edoga name could not cover.

Had the Nigeria-Biafra war never been fought, Mama would have had three opportunities to obtain what she wanted: Virginia, Martha and me. But the war came and stripped her of two of them, leaving me alone to build the alliance she desired. My future in-laws had a tall order to meet: they had to make up for Mama's failed chances.

The Ugwu-Ojus had pressures that originated from me, as well as Mama, concerning their first son's marriage. They settled on me soon after I was born, and they never wavered. They were pleased with my physical and academic development; nothing out of the ordinary happened along the way. There were a few nervous moments involving how tall I would grow. My two sisters grew to be five-nine, "too tall for boys." Members of Charles' family, on the other hand, are on the short side; he's five-seven. I remained smallish, shorter than normal, through adolescence, but then I had a growth spurt, and everyone held their breath, hoping I wouldn't grow as tall as my sisters. That would have been disastrous, for I would have towered over him. I wasn't aware of it then, but they held novenas and offered gifts to the poor; God must have heard their prayers for I stopped growing short of five-six.

Finally, my future parents-in-law believed that if Charles made a good marriage, so would his three brothers. The first son's is the most crucial, because it is to him that the responsibilities of the household fall after his father is gone. It is he who guarantees that the family succeeds. My mother-in-law confided in me that they couldn't trust their future to anyone other than someone they had known all her life, someone like me. "You will hold our family together, like your mother did your father's family."

The first official pronouncement of my future in-laws' intentions was made in December 1973, when I was 17 and had just graduated from high school. My oldest brother John was visiting home from New York, where he was doing his surgical residency at Roosevelt Hospital. I was not privy to the exchange until years after it happened.

On the Sunday before John's planned departure, the Ugwu-Ojus paid him a visit befitting of a dignitary. If I had been more aware, I would have suspected that it was more than a visit, for they came laden with gifts traditionally recognized as those made to one's in-laws. All eight of their children at that time (my future mother-in-law was pregnant with her ninth), dressed in finery, graced the occasion. A live goat, three large hens, a fifty-kilogram bag of rice, twelve tubers of yam, more smoked fish and dried meat than I had ever seen, plus other condiments were laid out on the floor of the verandah and presented to John as gifts.

Later, according to John, my future parents-in-law, Mama, and John engaged in a somewhat secretive discussion about Charles and me. Felix Ugwu-Oju, an acclaimed orator, presented his case so convincingly that even John was wowed by it. "We're here to ask you, since you're Dympna's father by our tradition, to permit us to continue to hope that if it is the Lord's will, that Charles and Dympna will be married in the future."

John says that in his American way of looking at things then, he was not aware that a request had been made of him, or that he was expected to provide an answer. He continued to listen for more but nothing more was said. An uncomfortable silence ensued until Mama nudged him. John spoke, saying that he had known the Ugwu-Ojus well and that Mr. Ugwu-Oju had been very generous with him, but he felt thrown back in time and forced to address an issue that wasn't his in the first place.

"Thanks for your interest in my sister, but the little I've seen of Dympna suggests that she still has far to go in her education. Let's postpone this discussion until a time when she's ready to think about marriage, and even then, it should be her decision, not mine."

"We're not asking that anything be finalized right away, for our son is only in his first year of a pre-med program. We only seek an understanding between us, so we can all have peace of mind, knowing that their union is guaranteed," Charles' father said. But John, in his new American liberalism and convictions, refused to yield.

"Nothing can be guaranteed without the approval of the two involved. I cannot in good conscience commit my sister to a relationship that she may not sanction. Everything just has to wait until she's ready."

Which is when Mama intervened. Her first son, her "husband," was taking the discussion in a direction that she did not wish it to go. It was she, after all, who encouraged the Ugwu-Ojus to make the presentation while John was there; it was Mama who thought that with John's seal of approval, I would go along. John's answer took her completely by surprise and she sought a quick way to contain the damage that was being done.

"John has been gone a long time and is quite rusty in our ways; please forgive his impulsiveness."

The Ugwu-Ojus chuckled, which eased some of the tension.

"John," Mama turned her full attention to her first living son, her eyes begging, pleading for his support, as she'd done when he was a child. "There's nothing wrong with what Charles' parents are asking. They're not asking that your sister be handed over to them today. They desire as much as we do that she be well educated, for that would benefit them as much as us. The ultimate decision, of course, would be Dympna's and Charles'."

Put that way, John found little objection to it, and nodded his head in agreement. A bottle of schnapps, which sat on a small table in the center of the room, was opened and poured into four glasses that appeared instantly. Unknown to Charles and me, his parents, my mother, and my titular father drank to our life together. On that Sunday afternoon in December 1973, our fate was sealed. They convinced John that it would be better if neither Charles nor I was made aware of the discussion. My official father-in-law-to-be insisted, "It could distract them from their studies, which should be foremost in their lives now."

John now says that the exchange that afternoon made up his mind about me. It reminded him of the inequitable traditions in our culture. If he desired a better life for me, it would not be attained if I were left to pursue my higher education in Nigeria. He felt that I would be married off in the church before I completed my education "just to secure the relationship," and that I would be compelled to begin to bear children "just to consummate the deal." He decided then and there that he would not leave me in Nigeria. When he returned to America, he would prepare to bring me over. But he dared not bring that issue up with Mama for fear that she'd discourage him.

I stayed in the dark about my impending marriage, while John enlightened Mama about his plans for my education. He wasted no time in processing my papers after he went back to New York. Mama was reluctant to let me go. She used one argument after another. "She's too young and naive about a lot of things," she responded to John's initial letter on the subject of my education abroad. John reminded her that at my age, she herself was married and had four children. Then she raised the issue of my future. "She'll be too old when she returns."

"Too old for what?" inquired John, who continued with his plans.

I knew that Mama was uncomfortable with the path my brother wanted my life to take, and her discomfort, for a reason I didn't know then, pleased me immensely. When she seemed to stall the processing of the papers from her side, I wrote my brother for his intervention, and he came to my rescue. When it was evident to Mama that I would go to America with or without her support, she began to reveal the real reasons for her hesitation. It was during one of these conversations, one that I remember distinctly, that she told me about my impending marriage for the first time, though she did not reveal the identity of my intended.

If I close my eyes, I can almost see everything that happened in this exchange. I was readying for bed about a month before I left for America. Dressed in my virginal-white, puffed-sleeve, gathered-at-the-bust cotton nightgown that we had to wear in the dormitory at school, I was standing in the same room once inhabited by Emma, my first serious suitor, and by Mama's godchild Rose, the one who never married. Since finishing high school, Ogbonna and I shared that room with whoever visited our household. But Ogbonna was not home when Mama made the revelation.

She started with a number of conditions about my time in the United States, to which I had to agree. I committed to return as soon as I completed my degree and to keep myself chaste while I lived away from her. It was her third condition that threw me. Mama simply said, "I would feel better if you were spoken for before you leave."

"Spoken for?" I understood exactly what she was referring to, but I feigned ignorance, speaking like a person to whom the language of Ibo marriage was alien. But Mama was the one asking a favor of me, and the dog-head riddle would not have sufficed at that time.

"Yes, betrothed," she clarified, adding that although many families had sought my hand, she was interested in one family in particular.

"Who is it?" I asked her then, my eyes locking with hers in a rare challenge of wills.

"The particular young man in question isn't as important as what agreeing to his proposal would represent," she said, trying to evade the subject.

"Mama, how can I agree to a proposal without knowing who the man is?" I knew that I was out of line, but something kept me going.

"Do you trust me?"

"Yes, Mama."

"Have I ever steered you wrong?"

"No."

"Why then would I mislead you now? Why would I settle for someone who isn't the best possible choice for you?"

I said nothing, for I'd already said more than I should. She begged me to trust her and to give my consent to the union. Mama could certainly have proceeded with or without my consent had she had John's approval. However, she felt that since John was opposed, she needed me not only to agree, but also to help convince my brother that I approved of the plan.

"It could do no harm," she said, her eyes begging me. When she thought I was nearly convinced, she progressed, "We can say yes to them now, and everything else can wait until you return. This way, your suitor will wait for you. He won't propose to another girl until you return."

I agreed to consider it, but in the meantime, I dashed off an SOS to John to intervene.

I pondered the implications of whatever decision I made on the matter. Both entailed immense risks, but if I were really my mother's daughter, the Ibo girl I was raised to be, I would take the safer course and agree to the arrangement. If nothing out of the ordinary happened, I would be guaranteed a husband whenever I returned from America, spared the fate of an old maid. On the other hand, my intuition cautioned me to hold out, to delay my agreement. Who knew how I would be a few years later. "What if something changes and I don't like him when I come back or he doesn't like me?" I asked Mama over and over.

My brother's letter settled the issue. It arrived via express one afternoon in Mama's absence. I suspected it contained the news I awaited and felt relieved, but also panicked that she would be angry with me. I waited for her return, knowing that she would ask me to read the letter for her as I had others before. It took me a second to skim the letter; I'd already decided that I would temper the harsh words that my brother John would surely use in it. In place of John's "If you don't stop harassing Dympna about marriage, you'll alienate her and possibly lose her forever," I said, "Leave Dympna alone; I do not want her married until she's done with her education. I want to make sure she has a choice about what she does in her life."

Still, Mama felt I had betrayed her. She switched tactics, and for the rest of my stay with her (two weeks), she resorted to telling me more stories about unmarried Ibo women. She had dozens of them, each a variation on the same theme: Ibo women who wait too long invite a life of misery.

Miss Thomas

Have I told you about Miss Nwa Thomas?" Mama asked the day after John's letter arrived.

"No," I replied, aware that Mama wanted to tell me the story again even though I'd heard it a hundred times. Before she started, I knew how she would tell it, certain points embellished and others diminished, all in the hope that I would learn my lesson before it was too late. No one in Aku who wasn't deaf hadn't heard about Miss Nwa Thomas. She was a local legend, though her notoriety didn't stem from the work she did with the schools or educating rural women. She was known and will probably always be remembered for "educating herself out of a husband."

I'd been familiar with Miss Nwa Thomas' story since my childhood. Her name came up a number of times every week in different conversations in our house. There was no knowing when someone would refer to her. It could be about anything. Sometimes when I was younger, the frequent reference to "Miss" confused me for she didn't seem to be relevant to the discussion in progress.

"Did you know that St. Cyprian's Teacher's College Women's Netball team won against Holy Rosary?" someone might mention.

"Great for Nsukka! Are they now the state champions?" another responded.

"Who knows?"

"Didn't Miss Nwa Thomas attend Holy Rosary Teacher's College?" Someone else asked, though everyone knew by then where she was educated.

"Poor Miss," another commented, and all attention focused on everyone's favorite subject. By the time the analysis was over, one wondered if Miss had somehow brought the ill luck on her alma mater or if the school was to blame for her husbandlessness.

Many times, Mama used the Miss Nwa Thomas story to make her points more clearly to parents who brought their daughters to seek her counsel on the variety of complexities involving the issue of marriage versus a woman's education. In one particular case, Janet, the daughter in question, was guilty of having "too much brain." Against advice, she had applied to numerous institutions of higher learning and had the misfortune of being accepted into all of them. Her parents felt marriage should come first.

"Mama, I want to be a teacher before I marry," Janet said.

"Education is valuable, but marriage is even more valuable to a woman. A woman with all that knowledge and no husband would be an example of what Jesus talked about in the Bible. 'What would it benefit a man to gain all the wealth in the world and lose his soul?' Ask yourself the question, what would it benefit you to have all the education in the world but end up with no husband? You have a rare chance to have both; don't let this ship leave without you.

"You may not know it, but many women with your background and experience wish they had a chance to change the blunders they made in their own lives. I know one in particular whose situation is very similar to yours. She's Miss Nwa Thomas, the principal of the largest school in the Aku district. She's probably the best principal they've ever had, but do you think anyone knows it? What does everybody think about when they look at her? They think of how sad it is that she's not married. People feel sorry for her—what a life it must be for poor Miss. It is a similar fate that your wise parents are trying to protect you from; your parents would never lead you astray."

Janet's tears began to flow somewhere in the middle of Mama's lesson and continued even as they left. Not quite two weeks later, Janet's mother returned to our house to thank Mama for "making her come to her senses." Janet agreed to an engagement to a man who promised her that after they married and had a few children, she could "get whatever degrees" she desired. But first things first.

I knew what was coming when Mama mentioned Miss Nwa Thomas, and I waited patiently. Miss Nwa Thomas' childhood was very similar to mine in many ways. People made comparisons of us, but caught themselves before any conclusions on our similiarities were drawn, as if being compared to Miss Nwa Thomas meant that my life would be doomed just like hers. Miss was brilliant in ways that girls were not supposed to be. Her father, Thomas, had no education but aggressively sought it for his children, his five sons and one daughter. Miss was the first of the brood and her father's pride.

Thomas had not intended to educate his daughter, for women of her generation did not go to school. (She's about my mother's age. Mama, who went as far as the second grade, only had that opportunity because she lived in the convent and the nuns did not know what else to do with her. People marvel that Mama can sign her name, for most in her age group cannot.) When Miss Nwa Thomas' brothers were ready to go to school, her father could not stand to see the tears and the sadness in his young daughter's eyes when she watched her brothers go where she had been forbidden to go. He relented and readied her to go with them, but "only for one year." One year turned to two, then three. At the beginning of each school year, the doting father called the apple of his eye for a talk. "I'll let you go just one more year, but you have to promise that you will not beg to go next year."

"I promise!" the excited little girl cried. But at the end of each year, the little girl came back with the same request.

"Nna (Father), can I go one more year? I'm almost perfect at adding and subtracting, and all I need is one year."

"You swore you wouldn't do this again. Besides, what do you need adding and subtracting for? How can that help you be a good wife and bear healthy sons like your mother?"

"Do you want me to have to beg my children to add up my money or to read and write my letters for me like you and my mother do? Please, my teacher says it could do no harm."

But how wrong her teacher was, for all agree that her education cost her the one thing in life that she needed, her marriage and children. All because her father, who should have known better, could not say no to his daughter and kept agreeing to one more year.

Both father and daughter reached a point of no return, for the longer she stayed in school, the harder it was to stop her. She loved school and excelled in her work, beating all the boys in most subjects. She seemed undaunted by the fact that she was the only girl in the whole school and pursued her learning like one entitled to it, as if her life depended on whatever she could grasp from the classroom.

Well-meaning neighbors and friends tried to reason with Thomas. "This has gone too far; have you lost your mind? Don't you see what this will do to her? Stop this craziness and find her a husband."

"How can I say no to something that gives her so much joy?" he explained, knowing even as he uttered those words that he was damaging his child's future. Thomas decided that when she finished the six years of elementary school, he would stop her. But Miss had so impressed the school's priests that they lined up scholarships for many more years of education, and her father felt it was out of his hands. Villagers love to talk about the man who started out to indulge his child but ended up dooming her. They caution indulgent parents to beware of harming their children. "Why not let her cry? Does she shed blood when she cries? Crying doesn't hurt anyone, or will you be like Thomas who was so intent that his daughter not cry that he ruined her?"

It's said that in spite of Miss' unusual pursuits, she received her share of suitors, especially when she was still in elementary school. The suitors and their families reasoned that she was born of a mother who gave birth to five healthy sons and that even with her displaced priorities, she would make a good wife. Miss, who had her father wrapped around her little finger, convinced him that she wanted to wait. "Wait for what?" a wiser father would have asked. She gave one excuse after another to men who lined the entrance to her father's hut. The higher she went in her education, the fewer suitors showed up. The more daring of the men came when she was already in Teachers' College, but Miss told them, "I want to wait until I finish."

But by the time she was finished, the suitors were gone and Miss was considered way past her prime. "Look around you," anyone who expressed interest in her was told. "Every girl in her age group has children of marriageable age already. Why settle for an old hen when there're plenty of chicks to select?" My estimate is that Miss Nwa Thomas could not have been much more than twenty at that time.

She finished Teacher's College and was assigned a post in the school she had attended. She was the first female teacher anyone had ever seen or heard of. Children lined up to watch her, some following her around the school as if she were an aberration. When she taught, they snickered. If she punished someone, the child said in her hearing, "You can beat me all you want; it will not help you get a husband." If she spoke loudly to her class, the older boys answered back, "Talk like a woman. Which man will marry you if you insist on raising your voice?" On her assigned assembly days, she could hear a familiar tune hummed in the background. She tried to ignore it, for she knew that saying something would only make the situation worse.

"*Miss kwusi nkuzi nunye anyi di* (Miss stop teaching and find us a husband)."

"*Miss Ojili pillow melu nwa ya* (Miss who uses a pillow for her child)."

But the story does not end there. When she felt herself ready, Miss proceeded with her own plans to marry. She hatched elaborate plans to catch a husband. She used her charms, of which everyone acknowledges she had plenty. She showed them her earnings, implying that she would not be financially dependent. She supposedly almost nabbed a man who was not from our area and had not heard her story. She excited his taste buds with the intricate menus she learned in her cookery classes (Ibos believe that the fastest way to a man's heart is through his stomach). He proposed marriage and our whole town was abuzz with excitement. Her father felt vindicated and was finally able to hold his head up when he walked down the street.

But his pleasure was short-lived. The man's family's routine search turned up plenty, the most damaging of which was her extended education and her refusal to be committed to one man. "She's too old," they concluded. "Not too many children are left in her."

Thus ended Miss' hope, and no one since then has offered, except for rumors here and there that several widowers with young children approached her, to help "raise the children." The last I heard, Miss is retired from teaching. She raised her brothers' families and spent her unused maternal urges and earnings on them. She even owns a small brick house, which she built for her retirement. When she walks by, people sigh in pity for her wasted life. "All this, the house, the fineries, all wasted, for nothing. Tell me, just tell me what she's gained from all that book knowledge? A lifetime of suffering and she has no child of her own to warm her heart."

Mama, concluding the story for the hundred and first time, added for my benefit, "You do know, my child, that no man wants to be married to a woman who thinks she's too smart. Please don't let what happened to Miss Nwa Thomas happen to you."

Holding My Ground

That I didn't buckle under the immense pressure put on me to accept betrothal in the weeks before I left Nigeria for the United States testifies to my strong will. Many times I almost yielded, just so I could have some peace. The onslaught was non-stop, and there was nowhere to hide. From the moment I woke in the morning to the minute I fell asleep at night, Mama's refrain played over and over in my mind. "Don't let what happened to Miss Nwa Thomas happen to you." "A woman's time passes; make hay while the sun shines."

There was no way of escaping her, for she decided that she would stay home with me for the remainder of my time in Nigeria. She woke extra early to make sure I was up and ready to accompany her to morning mass. We didn't speak during the three-mile walk in the pre-dawn darkness because Mama believed that our first words each day should be to God. As tormenting as the silence was to me, I almost welcomed the respite; the half hour that it took us to get to church was the only period of the day when I was not bombarded with Mama's warnings about what would befall me if I continued to insist on finishing school before anything else.

In the informal setting of morning mass, I sat next to Mama, though during Sunday masses, I had to sit in a different section, for the pews in the front were reserved for known dedicated worshipers like Mama. Afterwards, I followed Mama outside to the front of the parish house where worshipers gathered to exchange news.

"Mama Theresa is ill, but her husband will not permit her to go to the hospital."

"Justina gave birth to a boy at last."

It was all small talk, deliberately about light topics, too early in the day for serious business.

Eventually, the crowd turned to the subject of my departure to America. Although there had been no announcements and the masses and parties would come later, news spread like wildfire that the youngest of the Edoga girls was headed where no other female of our area had ever gone.

"You didn't inform us you're sending your daughter to America. Did you ask enough about the place?" The men and women directed their conversation to Mama, and I stood by awaiting my cue. It would have been too forward of me to offer any explanations, but I would have been thought rude had I seemed completely disinterested. I stood awkwardly in my limbo, like a child, although I was a grown woman.

"You know my son lives there. He's the one who sends for her," Mama explained.

"But Nwunye Honorable, a girl's life is very different from a boy's. What is she going to do there anyway? She finished high school—what else does she need?"

"It's out of my hands. Her brother wants her there. She'll be gone only a few years and she'll return before you know it," Mama put up a courageous defense for something with which she had vehemently disagreed. But, as she taught me, in public a family must appear united.

"She's your daughter, but if you ask me, I'd not send even an enemy's daughter to America. Didn't you hear what happened to the son of a friend of the catechist who lived in America? Mind you, he's a man, but if the story they're telling is true, imagine what will become of this girl here."

I rolled my eyes, but discreetly so none of the women saw me. I knew the story of the catechist's friend's son, which had been circulating for years and only survived because our people tend to believe everything they're told about foreign cultures. I knew it was fictitious and that the boy didn't vanish to the moon as was claimed.

"Young lady, we hear men have been lining up in front of your mother's house. Make sure we are offered some drinks [accepting and consummating a marriage deal] before you leave. Take it from us, that step will save your mother a lot of heartache."

"If it's God's will," I answered as I had been groomed to respond to a lot of things.

"Make sure she doesn't leave without a firm deal in your hands. She'll not look as fresh and pretty in a few years," someone called as we dispersed.

"You see what problems this is creating? You heard all those women. Do you think they're telling you lies?" Mama started in as soon as we were out of the group's hearing.

"No, Ma."

"Then why won't you listen to anything anyone tells you? I don't know why you're set on destroying our whole family."

"Mama, I'm only doing what John wants me to do," I snapped, my patience stretched to the limit.

"Then we don't have to tell John. It will just be between you and me. Just agree to this proposal, and everything else will wait." Her voice had softened, and she took my hand and covered it with both of hers, squeezing it, almost sapping my resistance. I said nothing then, and we walked the rest of the way in silence.

Each day that passed brought more proposals. My imminent departure made the matter urgent. The men sat in Mama's parlor, and since Mama stayed home throughout the period, she sat in on all the proposals. Most were hastily put together, and the men came calling with one or two relatives, not with a large entourage as was befitting a girl of my background. Each suitor brought a bottle of schnapps and cola nuts, and when their intentions became known, Mama forbade them to speak until one of my brothers was in the room.

Each went the same. "We've always had an eye on your daughter, and we would have waited for our brother here to be better situated, but we have to act in haste before she leaves. Please don't hold our skimpiness against us. It's all due to the suddenness of this," the leader spoke, his eyes never directed at me throughout the presentation.

I never said a word during the sessions, for my input was not required. In fact, my presence was not necessary, but Mama felt that the matter would be concluded faster if I stayed in the room during the exchanges. One of my brothers or uncles would give our agreed-upon response and a cue to the visitors to leave. Even by a conservative estimate, we received no less than fifteen proposals in that two-week period. My head was spinning from them all, and I almost ruined everything at a party held on my behalf two days before I left. All it took was a single impulsive act on my part and everything, all that Mama had worked for all my life, almost came crashing down.

My party was formal, more so than most events I had attended in our little town. Mama spared nothing. Engraved invitations, a glossy white postcard with black lettering, were sent to a hundred people, including several of my suitors. They read simply, "The Edoga family cordially invites you to a send-off party for their daughter Dympna, who departs for the U.S. for further studies."

It started at five in the afternoon and ended around nine. Only the unmarried men and women, numbering about forty, stayed in the tent in the front yard, the designated arena for the party. Others sat or stood in clusters in Mama's parlor and in the back courtyard. Every speech echoed the advice that I had been bombarded with: "Education without fulfillment leads you nowhere." When we began to dance, I found myself in an awkward situation. As the honoree, I had to "open the dance floor" with a dance, and not alone either: with anyone, except a relative, that I chose. Whoever I picked for the dance would be designated, by default, my intended.

The slow dancing music had been pre-selected and I had to dance to Peter, Paul, and Mary's song "Leaving on a Jet Plane" with a yet undesignated love. My eyes roved the crowded tent for someone to choose.

It would be fair to state that I wasn't exactly devoid of feelings and that I had at certain points in my teen years fancied certain gentlemen. However, because of my strict upbringing, I had no way of expressing my feelings without violating the traditional Ibo code of conduct. At that particular time, there was in fact a man in my heart. The thought of him kept me awake many nights and, had he asked before the party and received Mama's approval, I would have seriously contemplated becoming betrothed before I left. The young man in question was from a large and powerful family in our town, and I really wasn't sure whether I desired his family or him. Even then, I was realistic about whom or what I settled for, and I knew that this man would not be good for me in many ways. Simply put, he was dull. He'd struggled with school throughout. At the time I was leaving, he still had not passed entrance examinations to any universities.

Maybe I thought that I had only one day left in Nsukka and everyone would forget by the time I came back, but I made up my mind to choose the object of my desire. I walked up to him and asked, in a clear voice that was heard in every corner of our tent, "Would you dance with me?" With that question alone, I created more problems that I could have ever imagined.

He turned red in the face, but quickly recovered and walked me to the dance floor. I allowed him to envelop me completely, his flowing *agbada* wrapping me, almost sealing me to him. For a moment, nothing else existed but us; I could feel the tension, the heavy breath of anticipation of whatever would unfold later.

> *So kiss me and smile for me;*
> *Tell me that you'll wait for me;*
> *Hold me like you'll never let me go;*
> *I'm leaving on a jet plane;*
> *I don't know when I'll be back again;*
> *Oh baby, I hate to go.*

I sang along, my newly coiffed head on his shoulders. I was told that my eyes were closed, that my face had a look of contentment, and that I seemed at peace. Ever since then, I've told myself that it had to do with the music and my confused state of mind, but for those three minutes I clung to him as if my life depended on it.

How was I to know, I told Mama, that people would see it the way they did?

"Have you been asleep all your life? How can you claim not to know the kind of effect this would have?"

By the time we finished the dance, we were paired. He left his seat and moved up to the dais where I was sitting. There was no getting away from it. In everyone's minds, we were betrothed. His arm was draped possessively over my chair, and his body formed a barrier around me. Everyone else who asked to dance with me sought his permission, which he gave at his discretion. I fumed but dared not say or do anything; it was all of my own making.

Right there and then, even as the music continued to blast, he proposed to me. What a difference a few hours make! Had his proposal come before the dance and his clinging dominance, I would have been thrilled by it. But when it came, I did all I could to restrain myself from saying something that could seal my doom. I could barely hear him over the music, but I distinctly made out his words, "Can we be engaged before you leave?"

I said nothing for a few moments, while I contemplated how to deliver the message so he wouldn't misunderstand whatever I told him. It was one of the few times during that period when I wished Mama was close by. She always knew what to say, where to pause and how to anticipate and smooth problem areas.

"But I'm leaving in two days," I managed to say, my face looking sad, like one whose greatest pleasure was being denied.

"All I need to know is that you're interested. The rest can wait till you return," he was more persistent that I thought he would be, and I decided to be firmer.

"I would rather wait till I return," I said and rose from my seat to join a group of friends. I stayed out of his way the rest of the party and by the time the night ended, I thought the incident was over. I was wrong.

Early the next morning, the eve of my departure, my dance partner, along with his mother, father, and older brother, waited for Mama's and my return from morning mass. I knew something was wrong when I saw the live goat, tied by a leash to the guava tree by the steps to

Mama's verandah. On the floor of the verandah were six huge tubers of yam, two white cocks, a bowl of cola nuts, a gallon of palm oil, a large basin of rice—more food than our household used in two weeks.

They wasted no time after the customary greetings, which on that morning weren't so customary. His mother referred to me the entire time as *Nwunye Nwam* (My Son's Wife) and refused to relinquish my hands, which she held in hers. Because of the time of day, all the men had already gone to work; not even my twin was around. So Mama called a cousin who lived with us to be witness to the exchange. Any male presence was better than none at all.

"You know why we're here. Let's not waste words. Our son came home last night and said there would be no peace in our house until we secure what he wants most in his life. He wants your daughter's hand. We realize there's no time left, but your word that she'll agree to an engagement would be enough for us," his father said. While the man spoke, I sensed Mama's eyes on me; when we made eye contact, her eyes sought an explanation. I shrugged, pretending that I was just as surprised as she was.

"Thank you very much for this honor," she said simply. It was indeed an honor that this family, with its influence and wealth, made such a gesture. I'm almost sure, although Mama disagrees, that had Mama not committed herself to Charles' family, she would have agreed to this proposal. But Mama would never back away from an agreement, no matter how much sweeter the deals were that came later.

"There's too little time left to do anything; she leaves tomorrow. God willing, she'll return in a few years and we can continue this," Mama said.

"We're only asking for your permission to nurture the relationship. They can keep in touch until she returns, but we need to know that it's with your blessing," the father insisted.

"I will not stop Dympna from corresponding with whomever she chooses as long as the family's position is clear. Her brother John forbids us from entertaining an engagement until she's done with her studies. That's how he wishes it and I have no option but to abide by it."

After they'd gone, Mama immediately ordered that I not write letters to any man without her prior knowledge. "You have to make sure you don't say the wrong things." She explained how difficult it would be for all of us if it seemed that we were stringing suitors along.

On the night before I left home, a group of women, whom I now believe were hand-picked by Mama, gathered in our parlor to advise me on what was really important in life. There were no surprises, but I had to sit through the same lecture from more than a dozen women.

"All this will get you nowhere, our daughter. A husband is a woman's glory."

Mama thanked them on our behalf and I went to bed the last time for the next six years under Mama's care.

A mix of conflicting emotions kept me awake that night. I was leaving everything I knew and a mother who, in spite of her dominance, had never strayed from my life. I would be thousands of miles away, the first time that I had been farther than fifty miles from her. I wondered if the move was the best thing for me, but again, my opinion on that matter did not matter, for whether it was to marry or pursue higher education, I was expected to go along. No one asked me what I wanted to do in any case, and had I been asked, my answer would have been simple. "Whatever you decide will be fine with me," I would have said with the ease with which I say the same if someone offers me a choice of ice cream. I knew, as both Mama and John knew, that I could have handled either option superbly. Mama had more than prepared me to be an excellent wife to an Ibo man, and the schools that I'd gone to had provided me more than I needed to tackle a university education.

I was going to America to live with a brother I barely knew, his wife, Delia, whom I had never met, and their two young daughters, one of whom I had never met. I had no way of knowing what to expect from them or what they expected of me. Mama and I cried so hard at the Enugu airport that other travelers wondered if I were leaving to die. Mama clutched me as my plane was called, her face pressed to mine and our tears mixing, and whispered over and over, "Never forget who you are, my child."

For a fleeting moment, probably because I was overcome by emotion, I wished that I was not going to America and that I was safely cradled in Mama's arms. But there was no way of reversing courses: I was bound to a life and future that Mama could not have imagined and that my grandmother did not even know existed. I was the first girl in the whole region who had ever gone abroad to pursue an education. Others before me had migrated to a foreign country to join a husband and start a family. None had ever gone for the reason that my family gave: to better my life. Better a woman's life, everyone wondered, for what purpose?

Culture Shock

I arrived on American soil on a hot humid afternoon in August 1974 during a sanitation strike. My first impression of New York, and America, was that it stank, and my first instinct was to get back on the British Airways plane that brought me and head right back home.

It was, and has remained, my greatest letdown, and it has forever affected the way I look at things. I now view everything with a hint of skepticism; nothing is taken at face value anymore.

I thought my high school geography classes had prepared me for everything there was to know about North America. As soon as my brother John hinted that he wanted me educated in America, I voraciously read whatever information I could get my hands on, wanting to avoid surprises once I got there. I purchased *Time*, *Newsweek* and other expensive imported magazines to learn about life in America, to make my transition smoother. But nothing that I read could have girded me for the real thing.

I was first struck by the chaos at the airport, the sheer number of people who drifted around and circled the new arrivals, pestering them. It was so unlike what I had expected of America—streets paved with gold—that if I had not read the signs and filled out the immigration forms myself, I would have thought that our plane had been diverted to a Third World country with worse conditions than the one I had just left. As I waited for my sister-in-law Delia to pick me up from the airport, I was approached by individuals who seemed to be demanding money.

"Miss, do you have any spare change?"

"Can you loan me a quarter?"

I thought to myself, "Surely, this cannot be America. How could there be beggars in America?"

But at least those people were standing and could speak! As Delia and I walked to the car, we had to step over unwashed bodies of grown men and women, whose stench and tattered clothing were worse than I had ever seen, even during our war. I held my breath, believing that I was probably caught in a nightmare and that I would wake up and find myself in the real New York.

But it only got worse as we drove from Queens to Manhattan, and I sat in the front passenger seat, silent, in shock, as Delia chattered on. The sidewalks and edges of streets were littered with heaps of garbage, and rows and rows of aluminium garbage cans met my every glance. The hot sticky air smelled horrible, but we could not roll up the windows because the car had no air conditioning.

When my sister-in-law pulled up in front of their Riverside Drive apartment complex, I saw a dreary stone building that needed a paint job and a great deal of cleaning. I had never been inside a building that was more than two stories high, or inside rooms that were completely surrounded by others, without windows, without some connection to the outside. I spent the first few minutes wandering the spacious apartment, searching for reassurance, for something of the America that I had read about and had been captivated by. Nothing was as my books had promised; it all seemed a lie, a big terrible lie.

On the streets of New York, on the crowded sidewalks of Washington Heights, my first neighborhood in America, I felt all alone. I had never in my life seen so many people all at once, yet I'd never felt more lonely. Every night as I cried myself to sleep, I had to remind myself that coming to America was something I'd been excited about, the experience of a lifetme. I even began to miss Mama's constantly admonishing voice.

The first few times I ventured over to Broadway and 162nd Street, I saw so many different kinds of people, of all races: some blacker than me, others so light that I needed my sister-in-law's discerning eye to tell that they were in fact black. I was most fascinated by whites, some so pale that it seemed they were ghosts. I was enthralled by the length of their hair and had to resist the impulse to feel the billowy tresses that flowed behind the passersby. I had known a handful of Europeans when I was growing up, but I don't recall being close enough to have noticed the varieties of the color of their eyes or hair. There were others whose shades placed them somewhere in between white and black, and in my limited experience, I had no way of classifying them.

Imagine my shock on those first few outings in New York. I looked into every face that passed and didn't recognize a single one. No one recognized me either or gave any indication that they even saw me. I craved a smile, a look in my direction, a touch, anything that would acknowledge my existence, but none came. Men, women, children walked briskly by, as if they were pursued by an invisible demon. They seemed to be deliberately avoiding contact with each other, saying not a word to anyone. Many times I called, "Good morning," to people who passed me, but I got only puzzled stares.

I never expected that degree of coldness in Americans. I didn't think it was possible that people could be so unconcerned about other people. I felt so completely isolated that I wanted to return to Nigeria. In fact, the only reason I didn't return was the shame I would bring on my family. Neighbors, especially those who had warned against sending me to America, were bound to snicker, "Has she completed the degree already, or was it too hard for her?" I couldn't live with disgracing my family, so I bore my loneliness. I daydreamed every spare moment I had, of years later when I would be done with my schooling, return home, hold an important position with the government, and make Mama and everyone proud of me. That was what kept me going, the belief that the rewards would far outweigh the distress I felt early on in America.

The incongruity of it all was numbing, because I had never felt alone before. I'd been surrounded by people who expressed concern for me whether at home or on the street. I was raised to acknowledge everyone who walked by me. If the person was older, I had to call out a greeting, bowing in the process with a smile fixed on my face. If passersby were younger than I, I was supposed to acknowledge their greetings of me, and to remind them of their transgression if they did not salute me. Everyone knew me or my family and I had never been in a social situation where at least half the people didn't know who I was.

Often, in the throng of bustling New Yorkers, I found myself thinking, "If anything happened to me right here, would anyone care? Would anyone even know who I am or where I belonged?" I felt utterly insignificant, a nobody. I thought about how Mama could never understand the world I had entered. Hadn't she always cautioned against bad behavior outside of the home, "Someone is bound to know who you are and you'll bring shame to the family."

"How wrong you are, Mama; I could commit a horrible offense and no one would know whose daughter I am." I kept my mind busy by talking to myself.

I had a constant yearning for home, for a glimpse of Mama's parlor, for the leisurely way things were done there, especially since I found New Yorkers to be more in a hurry than any other group of people I met, before or since. I moved slower than most people I encountered in New York, and they did not hesitate to show their impatience. Many times, I was bumped into from behind or shoved aside during their constant rush.

Even the clocks seemed to move faster than the ones we had in Nigeria. Most mornings by the time I got out of bed, I found out it was already closer to noon than daybreak. I had always been an early riser and was used to waking up at five in the morning to attend mass, but in my first weeks in America, I never woke before ten. As if that wasn't bad enough, before I was able to accomplish anything, it was already time to go to bed.

Nothing was simple. Everything required an enormous effort, even the most straight forward tasks. And I was the smartest girl in my class! I'd studied a lot of English, but I found it nearly impossible to understand Americans. They spoke too fast and swallowed half of the words, leaving me scrambling for the real meaning. Also, I thought I spoke good English, but no one could understand me either. Conversation was impossible with Americans. Between their "Huhs," "what did you say?" and "could you repeat that just one more time," I decided that it was less strenuous to keep to myself. I felt like a child, a big, awkward, stumbling child, who had to learn everything from scratch.

Delia was seven months pregnant and studying for the law school entrance examinations the summer I arrived, but in spite of her busy schedule, she guided me through the maze of New York City and taught me how to survive in America. I can't imagine what she expected of me or what she perceived her obligations toward me to be, but from my arrival, she let me know that she was in charge and that she was determined to make a success out of me. She drilled me in simple everyday things that ordinary Americans take for granted. I must have provided some entertainment for her, if not frustration, for each day revealed a new area that I needed to learn.

Before I came to America, I had never held or dialed a telephone. I had seen one, but in our small town, telephones were more for decoration than anything else since most phones never worked. I had only heard a phone ringing on television, never in real life. The day after I arrived, Delia told me to call Malcolm-King College, an extension of Fordham and Marymount where I first enrolled, to arrange a time for my placement tests.

"How do I get there?" I asked instinctively. My experience was that one either shouted messages across compound walls or walked over to where we wanted our messages delivered.

"I'll take you there for your test," she responded, misunderstanding my inquiry. But in my mind, everything was settled. Delia would take me when I needed to go. I began to walk away, but she called me back.

"Aren't you going to make the appointment?"

"Won't you take me anymore?" I was beginning to get confused.

"Yes, for the test, but first you need to make an appointment. You can't just walk in without an appointment," she spoke slowly, as if she wasn't sure I was understanding what she was saying.

"But how can I make the appointment if I don't go there?" I was rapidly coming to the conclusion that my sister-in-law was not able to understand me.

"Use the t-e-l-e-p-h-o-n-e," she ordered and lifted the receiver of the rotary phone hanging on the kitchen wall and placed it squarely in the palm of my hands.

I stared at the telephone for several minutes before replacing it in its cradle. I simply did not know how to use the thing, and I don't remember if it was fear or shame that kept me from admitting it to Delia. I remained standing beside the phone, as if my mere proximity would facilitate the task that I had before me.

"Don't you know how to use the telephone?" Delia startled me. I was so distracted by my predicament that I had not seen her return to the kitchen. I stared at her, consumed by my humiliation, like someone who was caught in an inappropriate act. When she locked her eyes with mine, I shook my head no.

"You mean you've never used a phone before?" Delia's eyes widened in surprise.

"No." Nor had I ever turned a television on or off, because the televisions I had watched in Nigeria did not belong to us; we had to go to other people's homes to watch special programs, usually religious ones, mandated by the church. I had never cooked on a gas stove or used a toaster, blender, or vacuum cleaner.

She watched me as if in shock, as one would an alien from another planet, and in the course of that day, Delia discovered that her eighteen-year-old sister-in-law had been exposed to less technology than a typical eighteen-month-old American child. She had to take a step back in time to teach me the things I needed to know in order to function.

Delia confided later than nothing she'd read about Africa had prepared her for what she saw in me. She said it was like having another child, except that I was toilet trained (or so she hoped). "How does this work?" "What's this called?" I was a bigger pest, I'm sure, than my two nieces combined. So she started the arduous task of Americanizing me, even employing the help of my young nieces, Sherifa and Tita, then four and two years old, respectively. Sherifa bailed me out of a potential catastrophe on one of those early days. She walked into the kitchen and saw me attempting to squeeze two slices of bread, complete with tuna in between, into one slot of the toaster.

"That's not how, Dympna," my four-year-old niece warned. Then Delia came in and explained how it worked. It was not that I hadn't watched Delia do it before; she had made me a tuna sandwich a day earlier, and I remembered seeing her use the toaster. I just didn't know that the bread was toasted first.

Delia also taught me personal-hygiene basics. I was never sloppy in my grooming, but there were areas that we did not pay attention to at home. For instance, the use of deodorants was a relatively new concept in Nigeria, believed to be more suitable for "high-life" women than for regular, marriageable, everyday girls like me. In fact, I recall that the few girls in my dorm who used deodorants were ridiculed for using ointments under their arms to charm attractive men to their side. It was a complete reorientation. I was overhauled in a matter of a week or two. And I hadn't started school yet.

My straight-to-the-point, in-your-face sister-in-law also created a lot of confusion in important areas of my life. Often, it wasn't what she said as much as how she said it, how lightly she treated earth-moving issues. Sex, for example. In our very first serious discussion, Delia gave me a glimpse of America's "do-your-own-thing" attitude toward sex. She asked me outright what contraception I used.

"None," I answered quickly, believing that the "contraception" was another grooming "contraption" that I needed.

"You mean you do it without contraception?" Something in her reaction alerted me to the fact that the word could have a completely different meaning than I was aware of.

"What does 'contraception' mean?" I threw back at her.

"Birth control," she stated. Again, I was left in a lurch. I knew what the words "birth" and "control" meant separately, but placed together, I didn't know what to make of them.

"I don't know what birth control means," I admitted.

"What protection do you use when you have sex?" Her voice showed her patience had been strained by what she thought was game playing on my part.

"Sex?" Even repeating the word after her proved difficult. I had probably never uttered the word aloud before that day.

"Don't tell me that you've never had sex," Delia continued and there was nothing in her demeanor to suggest that she could be joking.

"Never!" I stated emphatically, feeling suddenly like she had accused me of a major crime. I shook my head in shock, my entire body hollering in protest: *Doesn't Delia know that I'm not married? How could she ask me such a question? How could an unmarried person be having sex?* I think my shock was worsened by her casualness about the whole subject, as if it were an everyday topic. *Doesn't she know how serious the matter is?* The more I thought about it, the more indignant I became. *What kind of person does she think I am in the first place? How could she raise such an issue with me?*

In later conversations, I learned that Delia had just assumed that an eighteen-year-old girl would have had sexual experiences and she was simply interested in getting me the protection that she thought I would need. But I went to bed that night convinced that Mama may have been right about America and that I had to be on guard to remain free of its influences.

John the Standard

And then there was John. As Mama was for me the epitome of Ibo womanhood, and Delia the epitome of American womanhood, John was the ultimate male. I could not believe that any one individual could possess as many superior qualities as were evident in John, but he absolutely did. He embodied all my criteria for measuring the man that I would marry.

When I arrived in the United States, John was a third-year surgical resident at Roosevelt Hospital in New York City. He and Delia had been married for six years. Together, they had two girls, Sherifa and Tita (Miata), and were awaiting the birth of their son, Che.

I did not set eyes on my brother for days after my arrival. He was on a swing shift, one that lasted more than seventy-two hours. I was naturally excited on the day Delia told me my brother was returning home, and I expected that he would be treated, at least in his home, like the important man that he was. I waited for my sister-in-law to fix John an elaborate dinner fit for a king, or at least to go through some motions toward that end. But I saw nothing, absolutely nothing that would suggest that the master of the household was returning after a long absence. I waited patiently, but grew restless as his arrival time neared, so I approached Delia.

"What are we going to prepare for my brother's dinner?"

"Nothing, he can scrounge up some leftovers. I believe there's enough in the refrigerator for him," she said and returned her attention to what she was doing.

Nothing? Leftovers? Scrounge? I could not believe what I heard.

What kind of woman is this that cares so little for her hard-working husband? My brother, my titular father, scavenge for food? Doesn't she realize he's the man? The head of his household? Questions raced through my head, but I was one who always knew my place in every situation, so I said nothing and retreated to my room. Surely, I told myself, John will explode when he returns. He will be angry and refuse to eat for the next several days. He'll really put Delia in her place and assert his position as the master. Thus I reassured myself that the situation would be taken care of.

Is it any wonder that I was gravely troubled when, after the hugs and kisses with his wife and children, John went into the kitchen, just as his wife had ordered, and prepared a plate for himself? I didn't once hear him ask where his meal was. My brother, the man in the house, went into the kitchen to find his own dinner.

I went into shock. Everything I was taught about manhood was crumbling before my eyes, and I wasn't sure my pounding Ibo heart could handle it. I'd been told all my life that a man never *ever* goes into the kitchen, but there was my idol, my hero, doing exactly that. The strangest thing was that he did not seem perturbed by it.

Those first few days were filled with the most amazing discoveries about my brother's life. On my first Saturday in New York, I asked my sister-in-law to show me how to use the various housecleaning contraptions so I could tidy up the apartment. She responded, "Don't worry about it, Dympna; your brother will take care of it when he comes home."

Again I cringed. Surely this woman must know that housework is not a man's province, that it would be insulting to ask John to clean after he worked nonstop for days. But again, John wasn't troubled by the insults hurled at him. In fact, he seemed eager to change from his work clothes to his housecleaning attire and became engrossed in his duties. He enjoyed the dusting, polishing, even mopping the floors. It irked me no end. I wondered, is John not a man or is this what America has done to him? I knew with certainty that my mother would have a stroke if she found out, so I guarded the secret of John's degrading situation, keeping it well hidden until other members of our family started coming from Nigeria.

Ibos have a name for a man who behaved like John, who was ruled by his wife. We call him "a woman's wrapper," depicting that the husband was so wrapped around his wife that he had absolutely no control over the situation. It was too sudden for me to go from the absolute subjugation of women in my culture to John's marriage, in which his wife seemed to have more power than her husband. I watched silently, although everything I'd ever learned rebelled against what I was witnessing.

To my chagrin those first few months, John cooked dinner more often than Delia. Their situation seemed natural to them and their American friends. It took months and probably years for me to become accustomed to John's unorthodox marriage. It took a major change in my own attitudes about men and women and gender roles.

Years of studying the classics and philosophy, along with exposure to everyday Americans, helped open my eyes, and I gradually became desensitized to cross-gender roles. Finally, I understood and accepted John's attitude towards his wife, children, and housework. Only a man who felt sure of himself could do what he was doing. He extended himself at work and at home, all to make life easier on others. It didn't matter what outsiders thought, as long as he made those closest to him happy.

So completely won over was I that, in 1977 when my twin brother joined us in America and in 1978 when Mama first visited, I was the one who put John's domesticity into perspective for them.

In America, I learned so much about John that he became the standard against which other men were measured. My brother is the most brilliant individual I know. He has a long list of academic successes behind him, and not a person who's met him hasn't been impressed by him. John has a quick wit and fits into every situation easily, without strain. He gives selflessly; it was this generosity that brought not only me over to the U.S. but four additional members of our family.

John is as articulate as he is intelligent and could debate a Supreme Court judge on any legal issue. His brilliance came in handy in the first year of my American education when he rescued me from grave blunders in my papers. He writes better than I although I'm the journalist; he argues the points of law more poignantly than my sister-in-law, who's a lawyer. The best part of my brother was the way he treated his wife and children. His devotion to them knew no bounds; he spared nothing where they were concerned.

John and I have completely different relationships with our mother. He viewed himself as her protector, her provider. Whereas with me, Mama dictated, and I followed. Although there are not quite eleven years between us, John viewed me more as a daughter than a sister. How often I've thought of the great burden that John, ten years old when my father died, had to shoulder: a mother and six siblings to support and worry over when he was little more than a child himself.

My oldest brother went to the College of Immaculate Conception, the top boys' secondary school in Eastern Nigeria, run by Jesuit priests. His fees were paid with the funds provided by the House of Assembly, but Mama still had to finance his other necessities, and it was a struggle to raise the pocket money he needed. But John never spent his money. He always managed to wear his undersized sneakers or old white shirts one more term. Mama loved to compare the rest of us to him, especially in my secondary-school days when I seemed to want endlessly.

"When John was in school," Mama would begin, "he went without food," I completed in my head.

According to Mama, at the end of each term, John returned his pocket money, intact. "But you were supposed to use it to buy things for yourself," Mama said she told him constantly, often with tears in her eyes.

"They feed me three times a day. How could I buy myself extras when you and the children are suffering so?" young John argued then. If Mama refused to accept the money from him, he used it to buy study aids for his siblings and would urge them to study hard to make Mama proud.

John, at age ten, became the man of the household. But his commitment to the role went beyond the bounds of tradition. He advised Mama on her major decisions and counseled his brothers and sisters, who were then spread out in relatives' homes. Virginia and Anthony lived in Enugu where John attended school, and as stories have it, John visited them to make sure they were paying enough attention to their schoolwork and not functioning merely as servants to their guardians. During one visit to Anthony, who lived with cousin Isaac and his wife, John found Anthony unable to speak, his jaw dislocated, shifted a couple of millimeters. Anthony was in excrutiating pain, but neither cousin Isaac nor his wife noticed. John took one look at Anthony and marched over to his guardians for an explanation.

"Why should I care what's wrong with Anthony?" Isaac's wife asked. Isaac offered no explanation; he simply didn't consider Anthony's affliction important enough. Although it was already dark, John took his brother, only two years his junior, and marched out of his older cousin's home. Without money for a public bus, the two boys walked four miles to the General Hospital.

John remembers that long walk as one of the turning points in his life. He said he was acutely aware of his brother's severe pain and was desperate to find him some help. The doctor who treated Anthony explained that it was a simple procedure, but that if not treated promptly or properly it could lead to a permanent speech impairment. John decided then and there, without waiting for Mama's imput, that Anthony would no longer live with Isaac and his wife. He put him on the bus to Nsukka, back to Mama, to whom he explained the situation in a carefully worded letter.

Mama tells other stories of John's heroics, especially his academic achievements. At the time he went to school in Nigeria, Nigeria's high school certificate examinations were formulated and graded in England. Students had to be proficient in several areas of study, including humanities, math, sciences, and social sciences. When John took his examinations, he achieved not only the highest possible score, but also the best result Nigeria had ever seen. I was too young to have any recollection of the impact of that accomplishment, but John's triumph translated into accolades for Mama. People wrote her from all over the country, seeking information on her exceptional son. She says that people began to view her differently, that it might have started the turn-about in her own existence. People believed that although Mama did not play a direct role in her son's education, it was the leadership that she provided that helped direct him to success.

Mama remembers when John announced to her that he would be a doctor. It was during the year that she lived at Aku, grieving for her husband. He crept onto her mat, as he did frequently, and asked her pointedly if she knew what Papa had died of. Mama didn't know; I don't know if she simply didn't ask or just felt that knowing would not change her life one bit.

"I'm going to be a doctor," he told her, "so if you should ever become ill, I'll cure you." Over the years, he defined his motivation as being driven by an urge to take care of his family, meaning not only his own wife and children, but also his brothers, sisters, aunts and uncles.

When John was offered a scholarship by U.S. International Aid to be educated in America, there was no doubt that he should accept it. It was the realization of his dream, one that he had since his father died.

Mama's plan was that John would go to the United States, obtain his undergraduate degree, and attend medical school. Somewhere in the course of his education, Mama was supposed to complete traditional ceremonies for marriage on a local girl who would become John's wife. John would visit sometime between completion of his undergraduate program and medical school to claim his wife and take her with him to the U.S. John would return to Nigeria when he was done with his medical training and either accept a consultant's position with one of the Teaching Hospitals or start his own clinic and hospital. Mama was already looking forward to the day when she would be known as "Mama Doctor." She would have considered it the greatest honor in the world to be identified by her son's achievements.

Both he and Mama proceeded with their plans. John attended
Columbia University and won awards for his superior academic
achievements. Mama screened and narrowed down the list of girls
from which a wife would be chosen. By 1967, the year that John graduated from Columbia University, Mama had settled on Tessy, not for
her beauty, although she was quite breathtaking, but for her family
connections. Both Tessy and her family accepted, and the first steps in
the traditional marriage ceremonies were taken. But then the
Nigerian-Biafran War erupted just as John was completing his degree
program.

For three years, there was no way of keeping in touch with John,
for all communication with the outside world ended. Every night
during our prayers, Mama devoted long minutes praying that God
would keep John safe for us and would grant him the courage to deal
with whatever became of us. When we reached the lowest point of
that war, when we believed we would perish either from the slaughtering of innocent civilians, the indiscriminate bombings, or the starvation, Mama was thankful to God that at least John would be
spared. "He will marry and bear children and your father's name will
not be forgotten."

Occasionally, when we learned of relief organizations that could
smuggle out letters to relatives abroad, we wrote to John, lying to him
that we were all right and telling him not to worry about us. John
never received any of the letters. He said that the longer the war
lasted, the more he lost hope that we were still alive. He himself tried
valiantly to reach us, but there was no organized way of transporting
messages to relatives, and after a while he no longer knew what to
believe. On his good days, he held out hope, but on other days, and he
had many of them, he believed us dead. He convinced himself that we
could not have survived the onslaught of the enemy and tried to move
on with his life. He started medical school at Columbia College of
Physicians and Surgeons and on the completion of his first year, he got
married.

Delia was then a PhD student at St. John's University and was
teaching Afro-American History. Delia was born and raised in
Panama (her family immigrated to the U.S. when she was ten) and
grew up with the same value and familial systems as an Ibo. She
understood John, more than any American-born woman could have.
Delia says that John seemed tortured her first years with him. He
would awaken suddenly at night and begin to cry, his sobs wracking his

body. She did not understand his nightmares until she knew us. John would cry in a ten-year-old's voice; he moaned of his shame at failing his father and for not helping his mother, as he had promised many years before. "I'm sorry, Mama," he would utter over and over, and Delia said at those times she often asked herself what she'd gotten into. But she held onto him, providing the strength that he needed to recover, and encouraged him to write us letters, almost convincing him that we were receiving them. We did receive one such letter; it came at the tail end of the war after having been in transit for more than nine months.

John and Delia met at a wedding reception held at the Columbia University social hall. It was a Nigerian wedding. John was sitting with his closest friend when Delia walked into the hall with a friend. Something happened to John, a combination of elation and suffocation, all at the same time. When he recovered his breath, he turned to his friend and announced, "You see that lady there in the yellow dress? She's my wife."

John's friend, who was as Ibo as John, laughed, believing John to have temporarily lost his senses. "That's not how wives are chosen," he said. "Besides, there're plenty of Ibo refugee girls to choose a wife from when the time comes."

But John persisted, and when the band struck the first dance note, he walked up to Delia and asked her to dance. While they danced, before he even told her his name or found out hers, John asked Delia to marry him. She laughed at him.

"Listen, you don't even know my name or who I am. Is this how they do things where you come from?" she said to rebuff him.

"The minute you walked in, I knew you would become my wife, and whether we do it today or in a year, that's the way it's going to be." When Delia refused and became angered by his insistence, he told her, "I bet you one hundred dollars that by the end of the week, you'll be begging me to marry you."

Delia says she laughed so loud that her voice was heard all over the room. She yelled at his retreating back, "How cocky! If this African thinks I'm a tribal woman who can be forced into marriage, he has something else coming."

She went home believing the incident to be over, but in the few days that followed, John pursued her with everything he had. He telephoned so many times she threatened to call the police. He inundated her with flowers that he could barely afford. Delia says it was just a case of John wearing down her resolve. She agreed to meet him for dinner on Wednesday and again on Thursday. And then it hit her, suddenly, and she felt that she couldn't survive another hour or day without him.

"There's something about your brother, something that I still can't describe," she says of their first few days together. Still, she wanted to outlast the week and beat him at his game. She fought her over-whelming desire to claim him: just two more days, she told herself, two more days and then you can tell him. But fear of losing him took over. "What if he decides to look elsewhere after the week is up?" It was a chance she didn't want to take. On Friday, a day shy of a week's an-niversary of their meeting, they went to a movie and dinner. During the course of that meal, Delia battled with her emotions. Many times she felt she had complete control, but otherwise, she was overcome with her fears.

"Edozie? (Delia prefers John's Ibo name; she once told me that the name John sounds too colonial and she couldn't imagine herself being married to a John.) Do you still want to marry me?" she blurted out. She said she couldn't wait another second; she had to say it then, to ensure that he would be hers forever.

"Not until you pay up your hundred dollars," John responded, and he made her pay him in cash. He says that from the time he set eyes on Delia, he knew she was meant for him. It was so strong that he didn't even think of Mama or the objections she might have to the union; he just felt himself pulled with such a force that he could not resist it. John and Delia met in June 1968 and were married a month later, in the heat of the Nigerian-Biafran War.

We found out about Delia on an airless afternoon while we sat in the shade of a tree, fanning ourselves with our crudely made raffia fans. Someone arrived (I don't remember who), causing a commotion and disrupting our lethargic routine. Our household buzzed with rare excitement. Our visitor had come from the interior of Biafra, the seat of government, and it had been so long we last heard anything believable about Biafra. We had since learned not to trust radio announcements, for each side exaggerated its victories and the other's losses. Mama made room on her side on the mat for the person and soon, the children were shooed away, so the adults could talk. From afar, I heard Mama gasp, then groan, as if she were in immense pain. I ran to her, and the first thing I saw upon reaching her side were three color photographs dropped in her lap. A closer examination revealed that the pictures were of John, elegant in a gray tuxedo, holding on tightly to a "white" woman who was dressed in a white wedding gown. (We all thought my sister-in-law Delia was white because of her very fair complexion. Besides, as far as Ibos are concerned, even the blackest Black American is "white." The term describes the European culture more than it does an individual's ethnic or racial background.)

It was obvious to everyone what the pictures meant. John had gotten married without asking for Mama's permission or blessing. The pictures were all Mama saw or felt she needed to see, for moments later, she was thrashing about on the bare muddied ground and crying more pitifully than I had ever seen.

"John Mu, John Mu, what did I do to deserve this treatment? What did I ever deny you? Why have you broken my heart so?" The adults around tried to restrain her, to stop her from hurting herself, but she was inconsolable.

"Haven't I suffered enough in my life?" she asked no one in particular. "Why has John done this to me? How could he be thinking of marriage when he doesn't even know if we're still alive? He no longer cares if we're dead."

My twin and I, her only biological children still living with her, joined in the crying and our tears flowed unchecked. Later, when all the neighbors who gathered had left, Mama thrust the letter at me, indicating without speaking that I should read it.

I remember holding up the photographs and being mesmerized by them. I thought, somewhere in this world life goes on as usual. People actually wake in the morning and retire at their normal bedtimes in their own beds. John and Delia seemed worlds away from us, and I was not sure how to feel. John was always my hero, and I knew that any marriage would cause some alienation on his part. I was old enough to understand that a non-Ibo could never appreciate our intricately woven lives and might in fact resent it. I wondered if John would forget us gradually and then disown us completely, and I caught myself crying again, but this time for myself, not because of Mama.

John's letter addressed his concerns about our safety more than it did his marriage. It was a masterpiece of appeasement. Knowing Mama well, he had to craft it in a way that made the marriage seem like something she had planned. I now know that the first few paragraphs of the letter, which dealt with his concerns about our safety, were deliberately designed to disarm Mama. He almost created an impression that his marriage, and by extension his wife, came second to us and our needs. *Even as I write this letter to tell you of my marriage, I'm filled with fear that you will never read these lines. I can't continue to go on with my life until I find out what's become of you.* He wrote about the letters he'd previously written and how anxious he'd become about our safety. *Delia and I got married on July 20, 1968, and all through the ceremony I kept saying to myself, 'Mama should have been here. She's given me so much.' I even felt worse because I didn't know with certainty that you are all right.*

Then John addressed the timing of his marriage, the area that most troubled Mama. She'd wondered how John could have been occupied with finding a wife when he had no clue about his mother's and siblings' whereabouts. John simply turned the table on Mama and presented his marriage as something that she had envisioned for him. *When I met Delia, I knew that she was the kind of wife you would have picked out for me. She's hardworking, humble, warm, and very intelligent. She already has a master's degree.*

You always talked about keeping our father's name alive, not only in our deeds and hard work, but by ensuring that his blood line continues. Everything I've read about the war points to how hopeless the situation is, and as much as I hold on, I must ensure that Papa's name continues. Delia is more than a wife to me. She's filled the void created by you all.

Mama cried through that night and on and off for the next few days. She walked around the farm with droopy shoulders, like one who was in mourning for someone beloved. If anyone asked who she mourned, she burst into a fresh sob, muttering, "My oldest son, John."

"Your son died?" Many asked her.

"No, he married a white woman," she retorted.

"Count your blessings; at least he's still alive."

It took a while, until Sherifa was born and John made his first visit home three years after the war ended, for Mama to accept that John was married. Then she began to worry about the traditional implications of the fact that no bride price had been paid on Delia's head.

"We have to do something about it," she wrote to John a few years afterwards. "We must ensure that the children belong to us. How can you claim she's your wife if she's living with you free of charge?"

There were several reasons why John's marriage to a "white" woman would present immense problems to Mama and our entire family. We had some exposure, albeit limited, to certain families, mostly from the university, consisting of Ibo men and their European or American wives. Many of these mixed couples sent their children to the same school I attended. I'll be the first to admit that our objection to these families was based mostly on fear of the unknown, rather than any tangible evidence of their wrongdoing. But when I was a child, I relished the opportunities to torment the "half-castes," the products of these "unnatural" unions. My friends and I would tease them about their mothers' sickly paleness and laugh uncontrollably when our victims turned beet red.

On Parents' Days or other occasions that brought these parents to our school, I joined a group of other children who trailed the steps of foreign-born mothers and mimic their walk and speech. We pushed our pelvises forward to simulate their flat backsides and walked on tip toes to imitate the effect of their high-heeled shoes. Even our mothers were convinced that they were not completely human, but were creatures that fit somewhere between ghosts and dying people. We spent many hours discussing their sorry state—the hair that sprouted like weeds, the nose that grew forward instead of broadening, and the eyes. I was terrified by their strange-colored cat eyes and always wondered if they could see. When they talked, their nasal accents made it seem as if most white people spoke through their noses.

No one, not even Mama, could explain what might possess a full-blooded Ibo man to choose one of these pitiful individuals as a spouse. On the few occasions when I saw the foreign women dressed in the Ibo print wrappers and lace blouses, they looked like masquerades, the entertaining variety that came out only on Christmas.

They were unsuited to our way of life. These white women did not seem to treat their husbands like real men. Whenever we met them in church, it was always the man who carried the babies, never the woman. Instead, she always walked several steps ahead of her husband while he struggled with whatever she'd left behind.

The worst that we witnessed occurred at the marketplace. Our markets were like open-air flea markets with thousands of stalls, all run by market women who tug at or call to passersby to try their wares. The floors were not paved. During the rainy season, they turned into slippery puddles of mud. We had no shopping baskets or carts, and every shopper lugged purchases in her own basket, preferably on her head since that freed the arms for assessing the goods and for haggling. No Ibo man of any standing would ever step into the market, unless he were heading specifically to areas where large household items like electronics or furniture were sold. Normal Ibo men did not venture into the women's section, for it wasn't a man's place to haggle over peppers or greens or palm oil. Even bachelors avoided the market-places, and instead gave their lists to female relatives or other women who lived in their yards. This is not to say that there were no exceptions, but only certain types of men, those who mistrusted their wives or women in general, and wanted to ensure that their money was going where they designated, ventured into the market. Everyone recognized these men, and they were preceded by whispers and cajoling by the market women.

Everybody knew that a marketplace was no place for a man, everybody except the university men with their expatriate wives. They always came on Saturdays, the only days that the men were off from work. I'm sure the men came for very practical reasons, but in our way of looking at things, we were convinced that their presence was a mark of their subservience in the marriage. They carried the baskets and did the bantering over the prices of the items for their wives, who spoke little, if any, Ibo. It was a pitiful sight, for the market women seemed to enjoy the Saturday drama. If the couple stopped by a stall to check out the items, the stall owner would call out to the others, "Ha abiago (They've come)," fully aware that the man understood her, which would cause a crowd of women to form a tight circle around the Ibo husband and his foreign wife, staring at them, mimicking the woman if she said anything.

A majority of the foreign wives we knew smoked cigarettes. They did so openly at public gatherings without regard to what anyone thought. They were always enclosed within a cloud of smoke, which meant that most people stayed far away from them. It was hardly a way to endear them to the locals, who believed that prostitutes were the only kind of women who smoked. It must have been a combination of things, including cigarette smoke, but our people swore that these women had a foul smell that overpowered anyone within a few feet. We had seen nothing good in these women. And now my brother, Mama's oldest son, had chosen one to be his bride.

Our other serious concern regarding John's marriage was that as straightforward as selecting an Ibo wife seems on the surface, the process involves numerous subtle intricacies. The search process involves digging into the woman's background to determine that she's free-born. In other words, that her *family's* ancestry can be traced for generations, and that there's no known slavery of any kind involving anyone in her family. It is still very much taboo for a free-born Ibo man to marry a woman of questionable ancestry and vice versa. Such an individual is called an *osu* (slave), an owned person.

The *osu* practice, a rigid caste system that separates a group of people only on the basis of their birth, is probably the ugliest part of the Ibo culture. It is worse than racism, for it is sanctioned by every establishment in our society, and though everyone agrees this unfair practice needs to be discarded, not many people are eager to break the cycle and befriend or marry an *osu*. Occasionally, one or two families would slip through the cracks and no one would know until someone proposed marriage. But it is always found out, and then the prospective bridegroom is treated worse than a leper.

Our family had a somewhat close relationship with a woman who was an *osu,* and the only reason it did not impact adversely us was because Mama was held in such high regard. This woman's daughter, Ngozi, was my friend, and she took a fancy to my twin brother and visited our home every day. Mama became concerned that Ogbonna could be reciprocating the girl's amorous desires. She called my twin and me into her room when the household had retired for the night and expressed her fears. She also laid down the rules: the girl was to stop visiting, she was no longer welcome in our house, and it was up to me to explain the situation to my friend.

"Mama, she's been my friend all along. What did she do wrong?"

"It's not her. I don't like this particular tradition, but it was in practice since before my time and will still probably be after yours. All I know is that my child will not be sacrificed."

"We're Christians. Haven't you always taught us to accept everyone?"

"Yes. Haven't I allowed you to be friends with her? But this is different, and I don't want Ogbonna involved."

This incident occurred after John's marriage, when I was already well versed in the ways of our Ibo caste system. My knowledge of Ibo history is somewhat limited, but the *osu* system predates the trans-Atlantic slave trade. Since our traditional practices have stagnated for centuries, the system remains intact. *Osus* marry other *osus*, for there's no way to hide one's ancestry. Many have tried to, but all have failed.

We had another *osu* acquaintance, a tragic fellow who held a university degree, occupied a good position, and was quite capable of succeeding in a less intolerant environment. He tried without success to marry a girl he'd liked all his life. Not only was he rejected, he was booed out of town. The girl's family went to his home to warn him to keep away from their daughter and not taint her image. Then, according to what he told others, co-workers at his job at the university began to leave derogatory notes and dead lizards on his desk. One of the notes warned him to keep to his place or face the consequences. Someone broke into his flat and destroyed his television set and other valuables. He was heckled, even by children, as he walked to and from work each day. His co-tenants complained of stench around his apartment, and when the landlord broke his door down, his bloated corpse was hanging from a rope connected to a hook that had been provided for a ceiling fan. I felt immense guilt at his death, for I knew him well enough to have said at least one consoling word to him during his ordeal, but never did. I felt helpless and everyone I had spoken to expressed the same feelings: "We can't change tradition." This particular tradition deprived a bright young man of his life. This was in 1984.

In John's case, Mama never voiced that concern, but I knew that it troubled her immensely. She asked the question in many ways in the letters she wrote to her son: "Are you sure you checked her background thoroughly?" If John had married a known *osu*, it would have affected the rest of us, especially in making marriages. Who would want to become in-laws with people who have relatives with questionable pasts? It was that simple. Ibos are ambivalent about marriage to foreigners because there's no way of reliably verifying their ancestry. This is particularly troublesome in relationships with African-Americans who, many Ibos argue, fall into the *osu* caste. "Their ancestors were sold into slavery, weren't they?"

John's wife Delia was born in Panama and her ancestry is a medley of Indian, European and African heritage. Her family lived in Panama for as long as they can remember and were respectable members of society. The news of her daughter-in-law's background brought Mama immense joy. John didn't just marry anybody; his wife had a good family name and was deserving of her son. She volunteered the information about Delia's family to anyone who was likely to snicker about John's wife.

"John tells us his wife's family is the ruling family in their town," she would say, which was always more than enough to quell anyone's curiosity. Ibos know that only free-born citizens rule wherever they are, and that not-quite-true claim erased whatever doubts our friends harbored about John's wife's ancestry.

Had John not been Mama's first-born son and my father's heir, his marriage to a non-Ibo would have been of very little consequence. Of course Ibos prefer that all their sons marry women hand-picked by them, but the requirement is stricter for first sons than for the others. To begin with, first sons are trustees of the family's name and position;

consequently, their marriages must be to women who completely understand the culture and are willing to uphold it. In John's particular case, our father's early death forced him into a larger role, much sooner than would ordinarily have been expected. It was taken for granted that if John became successful, he would take care of all of us. We assumed that when he returned to Nigeria after his training, he would install Mama in a larger home and take charge of her life, assuming her debts and erasing even the smallest worries. This was his traditional duty as the first son. Mama's major concern after John's marriage was that John would not meet his responsibilities to her and the rest of us, not necessarily because he didn't want to but because his bride, with her own different culture, might not understand that John's first loyalty was to his mother, not his wife.

But the remarkable thing about John is his sense of responsibility. He never once neglected his mother or his siblings. Delia says that it took her several months of marriage to understand and accept his definition of his "immediate family," because it was much more expansive than the way she defined it. She discovered that his immediate family included his mother, his brothers and sisters, and numerous aunts, uncles, and cousins who were dependent on him.

John visited Nigeria as soon as he could after the war ended, and then proceeded with his plans for our education. Three years after I was brought over, my twin came, and Anthony arrived soon after. Our cousins Rositta and Chinyere were also brought over in 1981. With each of us, John and Delia were responsible for tuition, room and board, and all the other fees associated with our maintenance. They never once complained of the burden, although it was a heavy load for them. I know that without their intervention in my life, I would have ended up differently—my scope would have been more limited and my perspective much more narrow.

Convent Convenience

John and Delia provided me the basic necessities for survival in America. But as my first weeks extended into months, they realized that New York City was *too* much America for me to survive on my own and that a less intimidating setting would provide an easier transition to the life I was determined to live. I applied to colleges in Westchester County in New York State, all of them women's colleges. America or not, I sought an environment that was at least familiar, a life I understood—I settled for an imitation convent.

Briarcliff promised to meet all my needs. It was extremely small (about four hundred students), and students received so much attention it would almost be like living with Mama. Every dorm had a "mother"—an elderly spinster who used her unspent maternal love on the students. These dorm mothers provided the girls everything, from extra blankets when they were cold to a hug or a sympathetic ear.

True enough, when I got to Briarcliff in the fall of 1975, my whole experience of America changed. I lived in the dorm with girls my age, who, though they had different orientations and concerns, drew me out of my lonely funk. Before I knew it, I was so immersed in college life—classes, perfecting my English, and Friday night mixers with cadets from West Point, undergraduates from Yale, and other neighboring co-eds—that I hardly remembered to miss home. My friendship with my suite-mates was as immediate as it was at the convent school at Nsukka. The relationships that I formed at Briarcliff went beyond the bounds of college; my friends were quite generous and invited me to their homes during the holidays, and we've stayed close to this day.

On the down side, my classmates at Briarcliff exhibited an unusual level of ignorance where Africa was concerned, and many of their questions were not only insensitive but downright humiliating.

"Don't you people go around naked in Africa? You must be really uncomfortable in your clothes."

"How does it feel to be in real clothes?"

"How did you all manage to sleep on tree tops without falling?"

Even some of the professors were no better. One actually commented after he ascertained I was from Nigeria, "Aren't you lucky to be here, with that ugly communist takeover of your emperor's power!"

"Emperor?" I wondered. What in the world is he referring to?

Others merely told me, "It's so sad to see all those starving kids in your country on television." What starving kids? Well, maybe during the Nigerian-Biafran war, which had ended several years before.

I quickly discovered that even the most intelligent Americans did not know the first thing about Africa. Their most common mistake was viewing Africa as a country or even a city instead of a continent, and erroneously believing that everyone knew everyone else there. With time, I was able to laugh at their gross inaccuracies and even give them a dose of their own medicine. Idi-Amin's reign of terror, for example, took place in Uganda, a country in East Africa more than a thousand miles away from Nigeria. But my American inquisitors thought it was the next town over.

"What a terror, that bully Idi-Amin, what he's doing to your people," I was told more times than I can recall. I accepted the concept of "my people," for I accepted all Africans as my brothers and sisters. But if only they had stopped there.

"Do you know him? I hope you're not related to him," others sympathized.

After explaining several times the geographical relation between Uganda and Nigeria, I decided to join them at their own game. With the help of one of my professors, I came up with responses to the most common questions about Africa. To Idi-Amin, I responded, "Yes, he's my uncle, from the bad side of the family, of course. Too bad, your own uncle, Anastasia Somoza, isn't doing much better!"

"What are you talking about?" My poor American acquaintances became so confused.

To questions about sleeping on tree tops, I answered, "But of course, if that's what you're raised with, you get used to it."

"But what about the children; how do they get up there?" my inquisitors would seek further clarification.

"Oh, they used elevators," I responded with a straight face.

"Ah, of course," they responded, probably thinking that anything was possible in Africa.

Unfortunately, I can't say that the situation has gotten any better, and although more than twenty years have passed since my first arrival to the United States, I find the questions no more enlightened than before.

Professions for Women

Though I'd settled down to a livable and even enjoyable routine at Briarcliff, my mind was still filled with doubts about everything during my first year in the United States—doubts about America and Americans, doubts about Ibos and marriage and Mama, and most of all, doubts about where on Earth I belonged. But one thing I did not have any doubt about was my chosen field.

Mama says that for as long as she can remember, I had an answer when someone asked what I would be when I grew up. This supposedly goes all the way back to when I first learned to talk. Most children in my community answered that they would be whatever God desired for them, and little girls did not forget to add their wish to be married and have many healthy children. But I was ready to tell anyone who asked, "I want to be somebody."

"You already are somebody," they said in reply.

"I want to be somebody important," I clarified as I got older.

"Important doing what?" I was further challenged.

I don't remember how old I was when I knew exactly what it was I wanted to do. But at some point, I began saying, "I want to be a writer."

Everyone who knew me was aware of this dream. My teachers, both in primary and secondary schools, heard it so many times that when I ran into them in my adulthood, they teased me about my writing aspirations. Yet, as I completed my final year in high school and began taking entrance examinations to universities, I was challenged about my choice, which was deemed an unwomanly profession.

I applied to the University of Nigeria while John was processing my papers to come to the United States. I sought to be admitted into the B.A. program in journalism. My first confrontation occurred with our form mistress, to whom I had brought the application for her signature.

"You need to choose another major," she demanded, insisting that that was a condition for her signature.

"I want to study journalism," I told her.

"It is not a profession for women—at least, not for women who respect themselves," she answered, her voice raised to show her irritation with me.

"But it's what I want to do," I persisted, trailing behind her after she had begun to walk away from me.

"Then get someone else to sign it for you," she hissed, which ended my audience with her.

"Have you given this a lot of thought, Dympna?" another female teacher asked. "A woman cannot be in a profession that puts her in the limelight. It's too forward. No man would want a wife who's public property." This teacher explained the rigors of marriage versus the unpredictable hours of a journalist's schedule. "You must decide what's important to you: your career or your life."

Still, I held my ground, asking teacher after teacher to be my recommender, hoping that someone would validate my right to enter a career of my own choosing.

"Major in education. Everyone knows women are natural-born teachers, and a school schedule allows you the flexibility you'll need for your family," my math teacher told me.

"Who told you a woman can be a journalist?" the principal asked me. "What's wrong with becoming a teacher, or a nurse, or settling into something that your future husband can live with? Why do you insist on something that will ruin you?"

"Because I've chosen to be a writer, and majoring in journalism will bring me closer to that goal," I explained.

"Then major in English. You can still be a writer, but without the labels that can destroy your life. Besides, if your writing profession does not work, you could become a teacher," my principal reasoned.

I debated the wisdom of including Mama in the career-choice argument. I felt that as much as Mama would claim that the issues were over her head, she had perfect instincts for what was right and wrong. But I wondered if this fresh problem would not create more doubts in her mind concerning the wisdom of continuing my education. If she felt that my career choice threatened my chances of real fulfillment, I was afraid she would pull the plug immediately.

I was irked by how much attention I was receiving from every corner of the community. Women and men alike stopped me in the streets to whisper a word of caution in my ears. Girls my age, those graduating school with me, flaunted their new status as newly engaged wives and spared me no details of their elaborate wedding plans.

I only went to Mama as a last resort, because I was not sure what else to do about the approaching deadline for the application. Mama feigned ignorance when I confronted her and, as is her custom, threw her hands up in the air. "You know, Dympna, that I don't know the difference. I never had more than two years in school." So I explained the problem in detail, describing the differences between the professions that had been recommended to me.

"If you go into this thing that you like, does that mean you have to be on television for everyone to see, like that lady who spends all her time clapping her hands and singing as if there's nothing better for her to do?" I could not help but laugh at Mama's reference to the hostess of a children's program whose face was widely recognizable. In our way of looking at things, nothing could be worse than the life she led: she was not only an old maid, she also had the misfortune of having to entertain other people's children, as if life were making a mockery of her.

"I don't want to be on television. I want to write," I asserted.

"I don't know the difference, but everyone cannot be wrong about this. They're trying to save you from a mistake that could ruin your life."

Finally, I buckled under the onslaught and chose not to "ruin my life." No one whom I told of my desires to be a journalist supported me; instead, they all reminded me of my womanhood and how that should determine whatever I did. I carefully erased Journalism and printed "English" in its place under "Field of Study." As it turned out, the whole controversy was irrelevant, since I went to college in America, not Nigeria.

At Briarcliff, nobody tried to dictate what my major should be for any reason other than what I wanted to do. And by then, I was so totally immersed in the liberal arts curriculum that my declaration of a major no longer mattered. Besides, I was already set on continuing my education beyond a four-year college degree, so I knew there'd be ample chance to focus on what I really wanted. I earned my first degree in English, with a minor in magazine journalism, and when I enrolled for my master's program, I was already four years in America and had lost some of Mama's hold on me. Without an ounce of guilty conscience, I applied to Syracuse University's master's program in journalism.

Four years of exposure to American journalism, especially Barbara Walters and other female reporters and writers, demonstrated over and over to me that gender was not the issue in their job performance. My decision to do my post-graduate work in journalism was a definitive statement of who and what I had become. I had shed most of the timidity that I came with and was as eager as my American peers to follow my own dreams. There was no imperative, cultural or maternal, to compromise. In fact, I don't recall even informing Mama of my intended course of study.

The Undoing of Mama's Handiwork

My education was by no means limited to what I learned in undergraduate or graduate school. Delia continued to undo what Mama had spent a lifetime putting into place.

My sister-in-law became for me the symbol of American woman-hood: fearless, determined, and aggressive. She taught me independence in my thinking and actions: that I, and I alone, should dictate what I wanted to do with my life. Delia invalidated almost everything Mama taught me about womanhood; to her, it was about speaking up for oneself, looking everyone straight in the eye, and following one's heart. I'm quite sure that without Delia's guidance, my American experience would not have been as rich and encompassing as it was. She became my primary educator, pushing me way beyond the bounds of academia.

Delia introduced me to writings of radical African Americans, especially the women's perspective, areas that my extensive education in predominantly white colleges had not touched. I studied Maya Angelou, Angela Davis, and others; Delia selected the books I read with as much care as she would her young daughters'. We moved from slavery to the Civil War to the reconstruction, from the civil rights movement to the women's movement. From there, I was guided to biographies of most American presidents as well as of other influential leaders, both national and international. I felt so deficient in knowl-edge, so unprepared for the world I was thrown into, that I read as fast as Delia could push the books my way. I had to write a summary of each book I read and present it to Delia before I could go on to another one.

Delia also opened my eyes to a part of life I never knew existed. She introduced me to Black America. On the day of my placement test as an incoming freshman at Malcolm-King College extension, as Delia drove me to the campus at 125th Street, we passed hordes of black people—men, women and children of all sizes and shades. In spite of my extensive study of America, I was surprised by the large number of blacks we saw.

"There are many, many Africans here in New York," I observed in a matter-of-fact way.

"They're not Africans, they're Americans," Delia replied, sounding indignant.

"But they look like Africans; where did they all come from?"

Delia looked at me as if I were an alien creature. "How can you not be aware of America's blacks?" she uttered in what I took to be disgust for my ignorance. How could any African not be aware of the existence of American blacks? The truth is that, my education about America notwithstanding, I believed (and I'm sure no one saw fit to contradict my erroneous assumptions) that all blacks, all descendants of American eighteenth-century slaves, were resettled in Liberia, Newfoundland, and the Caribbean countries. I was not aware that there were any blacks left in America; there was nothing in the textbooks—no pictures, no clues—that could have led me to that understanding.

Everything I thought I knew of America contradicted what I was seeing on the streets of New York. The history and geography texts had treated slavery as a historical issue; blacks were not mentioned or pictured in the books I had read in Nigeria. In addition, we were caught in our own civil war during America's civil rights movement, and much to my shame, I had never heard the name of Martin Luther King, Jr., or of other leaders of the black community until I came to America. I was not aware of the millions of Americans who have a common ancestry with me; I was completely oblivious to terms like racism. My ignorance stared me in the face, and there in the car with my sister-in-law, I had nowhere to hide.

Without Delia, the black experience would have remained remote and abstract. She brought it home for me. Before she embarked on her law career, she'd been a teacher of African-American history, a subject she knew inside and out. She herself had marched in Washington, D.C., on the day of Martin Luther King's "I Have a Dream" speech, and she already possessed most of the resources I needed to understand what it means to be black in America.

It took a while before it would all come together for me, and it was several years before I could begin to identify myself as a black person. It's strange but true. I must have felt some affinity with the blacks I saw on my first outing and subsequently, but there was nothing about their speech, their walk, the whining about "the system," the drunks who swaggered even in the mornings as I walked to school, with which I could identify. I saw American blacks from a distance, and with or without my sister-in-law's lessons, I was at a loss to find what I could really embrace. I thought racism was a figment of their collective imagination, and I never hesitated to point out to the few black girls at Briarcliff with me that "racism only exists in people's minds." I just didn't believe it.

I was probably one of ten blacks attending Briarcliff. I felt that I was treated as well as anyone else. I mixed well with the other students. In fact, I chose to live with white students and we became fast friends. I saw no difference in our lives. I got as many A's as my white friends. I simply did not see how my black skin had anything to do with my life.

On the other hand, I noticed that the other black students flocked together, as if separating from each other, even for one minute, would diminish their identity. They breathed, talked, walked their blackness and would not allow anyone who was different to come close to them. They dismissed me as not being one of them. "She acts white," they explained to those who asked why I was excluded from their group. If any of them received an undesirable grade, it was easily explained. "The professor hates blacks."

I argued with Yolanda, the leader of the black group, about why she missed more than half of the class meetings of an international relations course she took with me. "What difference would it make? The professor would still find a way to fail me," she said resignedly.

"How come he doesn't fail me?" I challenged her.

"Because you're African; you talk different. You don't rub them the wrong way."

"But I'm just as black," I threw back at her.

"You just don't understand," she said and walked away. As hard as I tried, I simply couldn't understand that mindset. How could they be so defeatist? How could they give up before trying? There was no room for self-pity where I was raised. No circumstance was deemed too hard to overcome, even when all doors were slamming in one's face. Even during the war, when our huts were razed to the ground and we had no more than the rags on our backs, we continued our struggle to survive; we had no time to point fingers at our persecutors. Hadn't I personally gone through worse adversities than any of them could possibly imagine? Hadn't I passed through a war and survived hunger, danger, and deprivation? Hadn't my own mother gone through worse, traded like an animal and passed from hand to hand until no one wanted her? Hadn't she also picked up the pieces when her husband died and left her with seven children? What could they have suffered that could be worse than I had? But as Yolanda told me, I simply didn't understand, and she was right. I couldn't then. It took many more years of living in America before I could see the debilitating effects of racism.

I discovered my blackness at Syracuse, well into my fifth year in America. Suddenly, in something of a blinding revelation, I saw myself as a black person for the very first time. Of course, I'd known I wasn't white, but I did not see myself as black either. It was as though I believed I belonged in a no-color zone. I don't know how that could have happened, except to attribute it to growing up in Nigeria, where black people were in the majority. I probably could not make the transition to being a member of a minority.

At Syracuse, there were many more black students and professors than at Briarcliff, but the only other black woman in the journalism masters program was forced to drop out because she could not maintain the required B average. So I alone was left to answer sometimes irritating or embarrassing questions about blacks. My colleagues, at times, boxed me into a stereotype that even after five years in the country was hard for me to comprehend.

The turning point took place at a lunch meeting I arranged to do a special feature article on students from countries with political instabilities. My partner in the assignment (Janelle, a white woman), two black Ethiopian students we were interviewing, and I were seated around a table at the College Center cafeteria, when another student in our program stopped by. "Janelle, you're outnumbered. There's only one of you to three blacks," he chuckled, before moving on.

My first reaction was that he had it wrong. "What in the world does he mean?" There were *two* black girls at the table, plus Janelle and me. "Who's the third black girl?"

Then it hit me. It felt like someone dropped a ton of bricks on my chest and knocked the wind out of me. For a few seconds, I was out of breath, was suffocating to death. "It's *me* he's talking about. I am the third black girl. I'm black, I'm black," I said over and over to myself, repeating what should have been obvious to me years ago. I don't remember much else of that meeting other than my sudden awareness of the color of my skin. And from that moment on, I began to see myself in a different light: as a black person in America. For the first time, I was aware of what others saw when they looked at me.

Armed with my new awareness, I no longer dismissed blacks' complaints of racism as groundless whining. I reinvestigated the plight of blacks, using Syracuse as my new laboratory. I truly began to understand how crippled they'd become as a result of institutionalized and internalized racism. I reviewed everything I came across for its black-white implications. I stared in every face I saw, looking for signs that they looked at me differently. I scrutinized every gesture, action, conversation, every nuance of friends, professors, and even strangers on the streets, for racial undertones. If I wrote a check at a store and was asked for an ID, even though my rational self understood the need for the ID, my first reaction was, "Did he do this because I'm black? Would he ask a white person for an ID?"

My black awareness was also the driving force behind my decision after I completed my master's program not to aggressively pursue a job with mainstream media organizations, but instead to accept a position as the editor of the *Syracuse Gazette*, the only weekly black newspaper in the central New York area. The job paid poorly but allowed me the independence to make the newspaper whatever I desired. It was also an excellent opportunity to explore the dimensions of being black in America. Each week, I built the newspaper around a major issue that I felt concerned blacks: issues of teenage parenting, feminism, poverty, more. I spent hour after hour interviewing disenfranchised blacks: black matrons in rundown public tenements, young black men in county holding cells awaiting arraignment, black teenage mothers battling welfare and child protective agency officers, black women in no-win relationships with their men. I was completely immersed, up to my elbows in it. By the time I left the paper, I thought I knew everything I needed to know.

Strangely, my new black solidarity did not cross over to my social life. I never once felt that I could relate to American blacks as anything other than colleagues or friends. I never dated a black American man, although I contemplated doing so from time to time. They were as strange to me as were Hausas and Yorubas. I felt their world too far removed from mine. They simply would not know my worth and would treat me as they treated their own women. When I considered serious relationships, especially marriage, it was always with an Ibo man. That never changed.

Not Quite American, Not Quite Ibo

The same way that Delia heightened my awareness of black America, she also opened my eyes to women's struggle for equality. Delia made a feminist out of me—not a banner-waving radical, but a redefined woman. I credit my sister-in-law with awakening a part of me that I did not know existed and for educating me on why it was important that I knew my real worth as a woman.

When I arrived in New York, I was molded in Mama's image, exactly what my mother wanted me to be. I was constantly aware of my womanhood, and that dictated everything I did. I was raised to look down or away when people spoke to me. In fact, I did anything but look into their eyes. I kept my mouth shut until I was addressed directly, and even then, I barely spoke more words than were necessary to answer the question at hand. Delia confided that she was troubled by my "shyness" and felt that it would affect my performance in American classrooms. She set out to work immediately, determined to help me shed some of the timidity that would impede my progress.

"Look at me when you're speaking to me," Delia admonished at least ten times each day, and I would look up, but invariably cast my eyes to the floor before I even completed a sentence.

"Look straight at me!" she yelled impatiently, and I did, but again, for only a few seconds. Delia ordered me to stand in front a mirror at least three times each day and practice talking into my own eyes. The more I did it, the longer I held eye contact with my image and the less I had to be reminded by Delia to look up.

Each day that passed brought me closer to Delia's goals, and by the time school started, I felt confident enough so that I didn't avert my eyes every time the professors looked at me. Before I knew it, I was speaking to people who did not initiate the conversation. In less than two years of living in America, I was so emboldened that I began to express my thoughts on paper, in the Briarcliff College newspaper. That act was my declaration of independence from my mother and everything she wanted me to be. I sought the forefront and was noticed not only by my fellow students, but by teachers as well. I was appointed to serve on college committees, to oversee problem areas involving the college's relationship with foreign and minority students. I became editor of the *Cliff*, and I wrote essays on controversial subjects, such as abortion and South Africa, taking progressive positions in each instance.

I reread Shakespeare, paying particular attention to his female characters and a woman's place in the Elizabethan era. I took a course in the Bible as literature, which provided yet another perspective into the treatment of women. I read the works of Simone De Beauvoir, Gloria Steinem, and other feminist writers, and soon, before I was even aware of it, I was espousing feminism on almost every front. In the midst of American students, I was not unusual. But as an Ibo, I stood out like a Martian.

The stark reality of my new feminism struck me when I visited Nkiru, a friend from high school, in the apartment she shared with her sister and brother-in-law. I cringed as the Ibo men discussed "American women" and their aggressiveness. They concluded that they had nothing to worry about because they would only marry well-raised Ibo girls who knew their places, in America or not.

"There's nothing wrong with a woman fighting for her rights," I stated, and in the sudden silence of the room, my words boomed, unlike a woman's. All attention was directed at me. Nkiru reached out to cover my mouth with her hand, saying quickly, "Don't mind Dympna; she's kidding."

"I'm not," I managed through my friend's hand cupped over my mouth. "I mean what I just said. A woman has the right to speak up for herself."

"Does speaking up for herself include not cooking for her family and making the man do most of the house work?"

"If that's what works for her, why not?" I answered defiantly, pushing away my friend's attempts to protect me from harming myself.

"So tell us, Miss America," one of the men rose from his seat and walked to within inches of my face. "Are you going to insist on your husband sharing the housework when you marry, or should I say, if you marry?"

"There's no rule that says men cannot do housework. Personally, I'll not marry a man who cannot help around the house."

"Maybe you've been too long in America; it's time to touch base with Nigeria, get back in touch with home reality," another man said, and I chose not to respond. I knew I had grievously offended my friend, who would forever be accused of keeping radical feminist company. My outburst could even begin to cost her suitors, which she could ill afford. My apologies met with stern lectures from Nkiru's older sister. "You cannot forget where we're from, America or not. Our women are different; don't ever believe otherwise."

Home reality. The term haunted me during my last year in America. Home reality meant that I would give up my newfound freedom, not only in action, but in thoughts. Home reality meant I had to be constantly aware that I was a woman, no matter where I went. Home reality was a death sentence, a condemnation of my new self.

There were other incidents when I moved to Syracuse. I joined an association of Nigerian students, with whom I was permanently locked in a battle over what I told them was their mistreatment of women. I was particularly peeved when, at a party celebrating the anniversary of Nigeria's independence from Britain, it became apparent that the men had left all the cooking and cleaning to the women, without as much as asking. It was just taken for granted that we would do it. Mine was the only voice against the injustice; everyone else acted like what the men did was normal and my anger was the only abnormal incident of that day.

When my ranting continued, one of the women led me to the side of the meeting room and spoke in as stern a voice as she could muster. "Dympna, if you want to be part of this group, we expect you to know that when you come to our meetings, we do things the way we were taught at home. That's the whole purpose of it."

"But we're saying to the men it's all right for them to mistreat us," I told her.

"You've become too American for your own good," she said, leaving it up to me to be part of the organization or not. I struggled over the decision, knowing that walking away would be easier. But I also craved to be close to people with whom I closely identified, who talked about things I had fond memories of, who understood where I came from. Still, no one I met in that group of Nigerians accepted my new self. They spoke in unison against my Americanism. "Just remember that you will return home one day. Where will all this take you?"

I heard all the old criticisms. "Of all the majors in this world, how could you choose journalism?" On the occasions that my feature articles were published in Syracuse newspapers, I was met with coldness, not the congratulatory pats on the back that I felt I deserved. They complained about my clothing and friends. "Look at her skirt, and that blouse, how revealing. Good thing her mother isn't here to see her now," I heard the women say several times. They even needled me on my choice of residence, away from the area of Syracuse where most Nigerian families lived. When one of them asked me, I told her that I wanted to experience as much of America as I could, but later I heard that it was so I "could do whatever I wanted without fear of being seen."

I tried to relate to the women, but I couldn't. Most Ibo girls came to the United States to join their spouses, so I had very little in common with any of the wives and mothers. In the years that I was a student in America, virtually all the Nigerian women I met were married or close to it. My case was as unusual in America as it was in Nsukka. Ibo American women did not hesitate to tell me they felt I was crazy for even believing that men and women were equal.

"I don't know how a well-raised Ibo girl like you could think such nonsense," they would say before steering the conversation to an area they thought was much more important: my unmarried state. "What are you waiting for to get married?" some woman inevitably asked.

It was this limited association with Nigerians in America that provided me with home reality, a reminder of the world I would return to when I completed my education.

I don't exactly remember the point at which I decided to return to Nigeria, but I do remember that the firmness of my decision was as much a surprise to me as it was to everyone who knew me well.

"You're returning to Nigeria to stay?" my sister-in-law Delia had asked, literally open-mouthed. "Why? Why now? "Did something happen?"

"No, nothing happened. I just feel I should give it a try," I said, not quite sure myself what I was hoping to accomplish by returning to Nigeria.

"But you've changed so much, Dympna! It's not going to be easy," Delia told me, her voice filled with sadness.

I took my master's degree comprehensive examinations in August 1979, exactly five years after arriving. Right after the results were released, I began to make serious plans to return to Nigeria. Having accomplished my educational goals, there were no compelling reasons for me to stay in the United States any longer. I could have gone on to a PhD, or I could have stayed on at my job. I could have applied for better jobs. It's just that right then and there, I had an incredible need to leave the United States of America. The discovery of my blackness the previous year had precipitated a disenchantment with the country I had grown to love. The magic was over, and all the little things that had previously fascinated me, I now found tedious. I was no longer eager to gobble down every bit of news on the feminist movement or the Mideast peace plan, nor was I interested in American politics. "Just another opportunity for them to trample on black people," became my standard response to almost every situation.

When it became obvious that Senator Kennedy would challenge Jimmy Carter in the Democratic primaries, my friends from Briarcliff who had marveled at my insatiable appetite for information on American politics telephoned to discuss the issue with me. "Why should I care? It's not as if any of them is black or gives a damn about black people," I said, stunning my friends into silence. Likewise, during the news-anchor battle between Barbara Walters and Harry Reasoner on ABC, I merely shrugged my shoulders over an issue that would have previously had me charged and running. "Two overpaid, highly successful white people can certainly take care of themselves. It wouldn't change anything for blacks, would it?" No matter how hard I tried, I could not shake the lethargy that had settled into my life. I felt deceived, conned, taken for a long ride along a winding dusty road that led nowhere. "How could I have been so blind to the real America, to the plight of my black brothers and sisters?" I wondered. "Why is the whole world deceived about the real America?" In my then limited "black-and-white" way of seeing things, it made my decision to return to Nigeria, something that held no appeal to me when I got immersed in American life, much more logical and obvious. I could not see beyond it. I thought, "I'll return to a place where I won't be judged strictly on the color of my skin, where my life will have value."

Now I look back at that period in my life and judge myself childish and narrow-minded. How could I have overlooked Nigeria's faults, problems that are at best comparable to racism? I'd blocked the war out of my mind, which resulted not from racism but tribalism—prejudice, nevertheless. How could I have forgotten that even after five years abroad and a master's degree in journalism, in Nigeria I would be merely a woman?

Part V
A Husband is a
Woman's Glory

Love

By the time I was ready to return to Nigeria, I'd come to the conclusion that my brother John was the model for any man who would become my husband. I first announced it to my sister-in-law during one of our discussions on men.

"I want my future husband to be like John. He has to be sensitive, brilliant, and supportive," I declared.

"Those are great qualities, but you also have to love the man," she suggested.

"Not really," I said, meaning it.

My American friends are often appalled by my quick dismissal of love as an essential ingredient in marriage, but I believe that the importance of love in a marriage is often exaggerated. I've always known that when I was ready to get married, I would be ruled by my head rather than my heart or emotions.

Being ruled by one's heart is what "love" is all about, at least in its popular definitions. In fact, I decided to marry Charles before I ever felt love (by Western definition) for him. Love was never one of my requirements, for I decided years ago that liking a person is much more fulfilling than loving a person. In my view, "love" is fickle and short-lived, whereas "like" grows and lasts indefinitely. Besides, passion has no place in an Ibo marriage because it has been known to complicate things between a husband and wife. It blurs the strict lines that divide women from men and often causes more pain in the end than is necessary. It is deemed improper for a man to lust after his wife. People would say of such a man, "Why does he treat his own wife as if she were a common prostitute?" Besides, everyone knows that passion makes a man soft in the head, vulnerable, and easily manipulated by his wife, if she is so inclined. It is safer to spend one's passion on a nonbinding, fleeting relationship.

I lived my entire childhood believing that marriages result from necessity and a careful selection process, not any compelling urge to be coupled with a particular individual. My background is testimony that marriages without the complication of love do work well. They even work better than love-driven marriages. Hadn't my father married my mother without benefit of so-called love? Ibo marriages rarely fail, and if they do, it's usually for external factors concerning the woman, such as her inability to bear children (particularly males) or, her infidelity (rare) or mere appearances of it (more common). Other marriage-threatening issues are generally eliminated by the thorough search conducted at the beginning of the marriage negotiations. Divorce is never caused by incompatibility or lack of love. Both men and women bring high levels of energy and commitment to an Ibo marriage, enough to sustain the union and guarantee its success. Marriage is viewed as a life-long relationship, not something that can be undone on a whim.

Ibo marriages are also, for the most part, polygamous. The husband is allowed to marry and maintain as many wives as he can support. Most times, he houses, feeds, and clothes his wives and fathers their children. Where does formal love fit into this kind of relationship? The Ibo language, as a matter of fact, does not have an extensive vocabulary for love and lovemaking. Most Ibos, if they think themselves out of control and taken over by "love," resort to conversing in English or another language that allows them to express their thoughts. If they insist on speaking Ibo, they can not go much beyond the first statement, "*Afulum gi na anya*" (literally, "I see you with my eyes"). Over the years it has come to mean "I love you," but in the same sense for all kinds of love, between an individual and his God, his child, his mother, his spouse, his job, his home.

Love in the Ibo context is synonymous with duty. A man who provides abundantly for his household is said to love his family. If he buys a car for his wife, neighbors cheer about how much he loves her. If a man builds his aging mother a house, relatives applaud him, commenting on his love for his mother. On the other hand, a man who neglects his family is believed not to love them, even if he's passionate in his physical relationship with his spouse. Love is a "put-your-money-where-your-mouth-is" kind of thing. To love is to be willing to give, whether it be to your spouse, children, or parents.

Love also connotes sacrifice and selflessness, giving of yourself for the general good. In my particular circumstance, I agreed to Charles' proposal to marriage, not because I was under any illusion that I felt love (in the Western sense) toward him, but because I wanted to make my mother happy, to ensure that her later years were spent in relative peace and contentment. In the same way that my mother wanted to repay my in-laws with my hand in marriage for their support through many years, I felt that Mama deserved to be compensated for the sacrifices she had made for us. I didn't feel (even after years of battling her) that she was asking too much of me; it was within my power to grant her only wish of me, so I did, without much regret. I probably would have married Charles even if I didn't like him; I would have been content to live with my displeasure as long as Mama was happy. The question that I still ask myself is: has the marriage been beneficial to the general good? Has it created the bonds that our two families intended? The answer, yes, means that even had my relationship to Charles been unsuccessful, the marriage would not have been in vain.

As I grew up, the subject of love became the center of many discussions, not only in our classrooms but during our Saturday liturgy classes with the nuns and in private conversation with our friends. Often the books we read were selected for their messages, and after Shakespeare and other European tragedies, the underlying implication was that so-called love is irrational, dangerous, foolish, and destructive.

As I got older and my circle of friends widened, I was exposed to students who were either foreign born or whose parents had lived abroad extensively and were thus raised with a different set of values. These friends would profess their "love" of certain boys and engage in furious letter-writing campaigns and secret meetings with them. But the relationship always soured and failed, and my friends walked around with heavy hearts for a longer period than the so-called love affair had lasted. I experienced the tugging at the heart and blurry-eyed nonsense with a number of boys, but even then I was able to determine it was mere passion or lust. I remember the sense of losing control and the overwhelming urge to throw myself at the other person. But I never yielded, for I always knew that passion passes with time and that I would have nothing to show for it when it was over.

When I got to America, I saw that nearly everyone mistook passion and lust for love. During my undergraduate education at Briarcliff, all my American friends talked about was men and love. I watched them go in and out of relationships, swearing each time that they loved their partners. Every time, however, the results were the same. The men and women soon tired of each other, because there was nothing, other than fleeting passion, to keep the relationships going.

In the worst cases, the partners got married and the rate of divorce in America, especially compared to Nigeria, alarmed me. All those reasons convinced me that I was right, that love had no place in a good marriage.

I was besieged by marriage proposals throughout my stay in America. There were days that I received as many as three; other times several months passed without any. I even received proposals from two sets of brothers. I'm not sure if either was aware of the other's, but my instinct is that they must have known—a man does not propose until he's ascertained that the girl is acceptable to his family. In rare mischievous moments, I wondered if it would be proper to send my standard letter, "Thanks for your interest, but I can't yet," to both brothers in a single envelope. But I allowed my actions on the proposal matter to be guided by Mama's words to me, even though she was not there to reprimand me.

One letter, postmarked Arkansas, came from an Aku man who had lived in the United States for more than twenty years, and by the time he proposed, he was in his late forties and had completed a PhD in divinity studies. He wrote that he felt at last ready for a wife. He had visited home and was told of the Edoga girl who just left for America. He reported that everyone raved about my beauty, intelligence, and good manners, and that if I had my mother's qualities, he would have nothing to worry about. He wondered when I could visit him or give an okay to my mother to accept gifts from his family at home.

I sent him my form letter without even consulting Mama. His case was easy to handle. He disqualified outright. Yes, he was from Aku (a plus) and he held a PhD (good provider). But he was Protestant (unacceptable). My roommates at Briarcliff had fun with my marriage-proposal letters. They started keeping count, but there were so many they eventually lost interest.

When I attended Nigerian functions in New York City, the unmarried men crowded around me, testing me for my Ibo-ness. I usually received many proposals and rejected them all outright by insisting I wanted to marry only when I had attained my academic goals.

"How much longer do you have?" my suitors always asked.

"I wish I knew," I responded, trying to get rid of them.

If they persisted, I would dig deeper into their backgrounds. "Where are you from?" The men were often pleased that I seemed interested in them.

"Onitsha." "Awka." "Enugu." But no matter what answer they gave, I told them that I had decided long ago that I would marry only someone from my hometown, Aku. I knew there wasn't much chance of meeting someone that close. I never entertained any of the proposals made in America. I still had a little Ibo sense left. What kind of a man would propose to a girl he just met? Only a desperate one.

Charles proposed to me in the fall of 1977, right after I completed my undergraduate studies. When I got his letter, I was living again with my brother's family while I contemplated what direction my life should take. When I saw his name on the envelope, my heart started pounding in excitement. I knew that it would be a proposal and I felt flattered at his attention. But then I read the letter. The tone was of one who'd been coerced to propose to a girl he detested. I felt that as much as he wanted to fulfill a promise to his parents, he was determined that I derive no pleasure from his pains.

"My parents are pressuring me to get serious about a girl," he wrote, "and of all the girls on the list they gave me, you're the most suitable to be my wife."

"Who in the world does he think he is?" His lackluster approach irked me beyond words, and right then and there I decided I would not marry him if he were the last person on Earth. I informed Mama that I would send Charles my routine answer. That was her worst fear.

So she launched a letter-writing campaign. She recruited everyone who could write in English—my sisters, brothers, cousins, friends—to bombard me with letters in the hope of getting me to make a commitment.

"Dear Dympu," they all started, "we're wondering when we will hear the news. It's been so long since you left and every day that passes adds more years to your age. A woman's time passes; make hay while the sun shines." It was as if Mama had dictated one letter and everyone copied it. In her own letters, she was more specific. "The young man I spoke to you about is still interested and wishes to know your feelings on the subject. Don't disappoint me on this issue." Unfortunately for Mama, the more letters I received, the more irritated I became and the less accommodating I was willing to be.

When the effect she desired was not achieved, she changed tactics. She began to suggest to John, who had finished his surgical residency and had joined a successful practice, that she missed us all and wanted an opportunity to visit and meet the grandchildren she'd never seen. (Mama had not met Sherifa, John's older daughter who, because of a heart condition, could not travel to Nigeria, and Che, his son, born three months after I arrived.) I believe that Mama may have had more compelling reasons for her 1978 visit. After trying unsuccessfully to convince me through her letters and those of my family and friends, she came to ensure that I responded favorably to Charles' marriage proposal.

Mama arrived while I lived in Syracuse, engaged in my master's program at the Newhouse School of Public Communications, and since she stayed with John in Morristown, I was thus unavailable to her on a day-to-day basis. As much as I could, I visited, but our time together was so tormenting that I was glad to return to Syracuse and to my life. However, she would not leave until she extracted what she wanted from me, and stayed through Christmas. The three-week holiday almost destroyed my relationship with Mama, for that was the first time I stood up to her; I openly defied her and caused her much grief. She had come determined to obtain my promise that I would marry Charles, but I was equally unbending in my conviction that I had a right to marry whom I wanted, when I wanted. She cried silently, as I remember her from my early life. Her tears were more out of surprise than anger, that I, her daughter, could dictate what I wanted with my life instead of following the path that her life and my sisters' had gone. "Dympna, *obuzi kwa gi* (Is this still you)?" she responded to my insistence that I did not want to marry Charles. Mama simply could not understand that after five years in America, I felt entitled to some rights and self-determination.

I recall a conversation with Delia. I told her that I no longer bought into the concept of Ibo womanhood, that I would not go along with my mother's choice for my husband; I was more interested in my own happiness than hers. Delia urged caution: born and bred in Panama, she understood the complexities of a traditional upbringing. She insisted that there was room for compromise between Mama's and my positions. "Certainly, your mother wouldn't object to your marrying an Ibo man who lives here in the United States," she suggested, but only because she did not know my mother as I did. Mama believed that there was only one right position: the one she held.

Which is why Mama did not take the proposals from Ibos living in America seriously. "How do you know where they're coming from, what's in their background? I'll tell you this, if they have nothing to hide, they should marry a girl from their hometowns. You have to marry a man who knows your worth, a man who'll respect you not just for you alone but for your whole family. He'll not dare mistreat you, for fear of what your relatives would do."

"Mama, I know my worth and that's the only thing that's important. I don't expect a man to define my worth," I retorted, getting up to leave as I uttered the last sentence.

"Sit down, Dympna. If you weren't my daughter, I would question what kind of upbringing you had." Her eyes bore into me, and I knew the fight that was bound to ensue wasn't worth it, but I was not able to control myself.

"You raised me to be intelligent and to use my head."

"I've looked and looked for my daughter since I came, and I've not seen her yet. I see someone I don't recognize," she said, her tears beginning to flow.

"I'm your daughter, Mama. I just do not agree with everything you want me to do." Her tears made me feel guilty and I moved over to where she sat on the bed and knelt by her.

"If you were really my daughter, you would trust my judgment and accept whatever decisions I make on your behalf. Would I mislead you? Would I knowingly put you in a difficult situation?"

"What you want and what I need are very different. You raised me well; trust me to make the right decisions for myself."

"You can't ask for a better family than the one I've chosen. They've known you all your life, since you were born. They love you like one of their own. If anything happens, the family will protect you. They know your worth."

"I'll choose my own husband," I said, leaving the room before she could add something else.

On another occasion, Mama tried a softer approach. She had probably come to the realization that I was no longer intimidated by her and that I wasn't afraid of what she would do to me. It was in the middle of the night and I was sharing the room with her. I felt her unmistakable pat on my arm and I thought to myself, "Nothing has changed. She wakes me up in the middle of the night like she used to. This woman does not respect my rights." But I sat up straight, ready to listen to whatever she had to say.

"What do you want me to do in order for you to accept this proposal? Name whatever it is. Think of me if you will not think of yourself." I sensed the desperation in her voice, and had I been more awake, I would have ended that exchange right then, but I pushed on.

"Mama, surely no one will hold my refusal against you. Tell them when you get back that you tried your best and that I refused. I'm the one to blame, not you."

"I gave my word, Dympna. Don't you understand that I already told them that you'll be married to their son when you return. If we default on this, my word will mean nothing. I'll be finished. No one will listen to me anymore. Is that what you want?"

"What about me, Mama? What about what I want? How could you give your word that I'd marry anyone without my consent? Didn't you think I could refuse?" I was furious at her then and was temporarily blinded by my American liberation. I was as incapable of seeing the issue from an Ibo point of view as Mama was of seeing it from an American point of view. All I thought of was how she was stripping me of my individuality and right to self-determination, concepts that meant everything to me and nothing to her.

"Nobody got my consent when I married your father. Your sisters' consent was not sought when they married. Why should you be different?

"They've done so much for us, for you, Dympna. Where do you think you'd be without Charles' father's help? Do you think your brother would have gotten to where he is or would have been able to bring you over? We might never have made it without them. I believe giving you to them is the least I could do to show our gratitude."

I fumed deep inside. What was I? A gift? What was I worth? Same as a cow? Why me? Couldn't she have promised someone else? Why must I be the sacrificial lamb?

As she readied to return to Nigeria, she became more desperate in her demands. I almost buckled a few times, but I decided that Mama needed to accept and appreciate the change that I had gone through.

She cried whenever we were together and even tried blackmailing me.

"Well, Dympna, if I die, you'll know what killed me."

"Mama, you're not dying," I laughed out loud, so she saw how lightly I took it.

"What's there to live for? My youngest child insults me and looks at the top of my head (shows disrespect). I never thought this day would arrive, after all the sacrifices I made, especially for you." Mama knew I'd never been able to hold out against the sacrifice argument, but this time I was firm. I felt I was fighting for my life.

"I will always honor you and be grateful for everything you gave me, but I refuse to give my life in return," I concluded.

As I walked her to the gate at the airport, she made one last-ditch effort. "Your mother will be the laughingstock of our town. If you don't say yes, I'm finished." She held on to me in a tight embrace, refusing to release me, although I made efforts to be let go, as if Mama felt I needed some sense squeezed into me.

Then finally, I relented, but only a little. "I'll write you," I called to her, "I'll consider everything and give you my answer in a letter," I repeated, more to soothe her and give her something to go home with; even in my most radical days, I could not stand to see pain in my mother's eyes. While she did not get the commitment she desired, she could honestly report that I had not refused the proposal outright, because the letter would state my final position on the matter.

But Mama would not even wait for my letter; hers awaited my return to Syracuse. My roommate welcomed me with her express mail. It was written by my sister, Virginia, on the night Mama arrived at Enugu Airport, where my sister and her family lived. Mama passed the night with my sister and wrote the letter there. "I cried the entire plane ride home thinking of how you have broken my heart. What offenses have I committed against you, my child, that make you so hard-hearted against your own mother? Did I deny you anything that you needed? Did you ever want for anything? Was I not willing to sacrifice my own life to save yours? Why would you refuse the only thing I've ever asked you in your entire life? Is it too much to ask you to make your mother happy? To help her enrich a friendship she treasures? Even to save her from humiliation? I beg you once again, Dympna. Please say yes and I'll never ask you another thing in your life. Think of your blessed father in his grave; think of all of us, not just yourself."

My reply was intended to put an end to the debate. I gave it a lot of thought and restrained myself from using harsh language, for I had no way of predicting who would read the letter to her or how they would interpret my words. That fact was always a major concern to me, for I knew that I, on several occasions, had read Mama's letters to her as I saw fit. At times, I softened words and postponed reporting bad news to spare her, or at least to lessen the pain I knew the letter would cause.

"Mama, not a day goes by when I don't thank God that you're my mother and that you gave me the opportunities that have led to where I presently am. You raised me to be good and smart, to tell good from bad and to respect the truth at all times. You told me you did all this because you wanted us to have options that you did not have, so we wouldn't find ourselves in the same desperate situation you were in after our father's death. Mama, good or bad, you've raised a girl who, based on your teachings, feels she can choose her own husband. I want to have only myself to blame if anything goes wrong, but if you raised me well, why would you fear that I could choose anyone who is unsuitable for me? Trust in me to use everything you've taught me. With God's guidance, my choice will not be too different from yours. All we both want is my happiness."

To my utter amazement, she relented. To this day, I don't know what she told my in-laws or how she explained my position, but she stopped pestering me almost entirely about my marriage choices. The closest she came to mentioning it was in a letter about a cousin who was being too selective about who she married. "I told her that a woman's time passes, and that she ought to make hay while the sun shines," she wrote, knowing that I would know she was directing the comments to me as well.

Meanwhile, Charles wrote me sporadically, and he used each occasion to report on his progressing medical education. He discussed his plans without actually promising that there'd be room for me in them. I, for my part, replied to every letter he wrote. We matched each other in dryness and nonchalance. What our letters lacked in warmth, we made up with pages of mundane subjects that we each knew the other did not care about. In retrospect, it was as if we were in a game in which the winner was the one who seemed most indifferent. The issue of marriage was deliberately absent in our letters, and had we been warmer to each other, an observer might have concluded that we were just good friends. It was a torturous exercise for both of us, I'm sure. Charles wrote because his parents insisted. I wrote back because not doing so would break my mother's heart and cause friction between our families. It was hardly the making of a satisfying correspondence, let alone the beginnings of an epic courtship.

It's possible that subconsciously, I had in fact already decided to go with my mother's choice. I fielded countless proposals without considering a single one. I dismissed all eligible Ibo men in America with an impossible demand that they be from Aku. I never once entertained a thought of marrying a non-Ibo. And partly because I sensed it was time to marry, here I was, returning to Nigeria. I wrote to Mama and told her I was coming home.

Homeward Bound

Mama was overjoyed at the news of my return and hurriedly set up a schedule to make sure I did not back out of my plans. She warned against my initial intention to show up around Christmas 1979.

"No, there are too many people around Christmas, too many activities." What Mama was really saying was that the hectic Christmas season would detract from the triumphant return of her daughter, with people drawn in too many other directions. She wanted me back in January, during the doldrums that followed the holiday season, when people were more likely to seek out entertainment, to respond to invitations to receptions for an overly qualified female.

I'm sure that Mama carefully calculated my return to be after the departure of girls from the cities who routinely came home for Christmas, to minimize whatever competition would come from them. I was to shine alone. As the day of my departure from America approached, the number of her letters increased and their tone was more intense. One could almost hear Mama's heavy breathing as she detailed every miniscule moment, avoiding the one topic I knew weighed most heavily on her mind.

As much as I knew that my independence would be sacrificed, I had reached a point of no return and needed to go home. I felt both excitement and trepidation about what faced me. To look the part of a sophisticated American-educated journalist, I took the train to New York City from John and Delia's house in New Jersey, where I was spending my last weeks in America, and carefully shopped the clearance racks at Bloomingdales and Macy's. I was after a classy look, straight cut, nothing frilly or extremely feminine, nothing that would detract from my new identity. Delia's urgings prompted me to purchase a few dressy outfits, "just in case."

"You know you don't have to go back, Dympna," Delia told me after days of watching me labor under the weight of my decision.

"I know," I told her.

"Why then? You don't seem thrilled about it; why subject yourself to it?" she probed.

"I don't know why, but I thought I'd at least try it before giving up," I said, fighting back tears. At night all alone, I rewound and watched, reel by reel, my years in America. How frustrating it had been at first, how I had hated it and longed for home, but then Briarcliff changed everything. The outpouring of love and support, finding myself, blossoming, the careless happy times when I had managed to forget who I was or what awaited me. And then Syracuse, my highly pressured life, to excel in my classes, to show that as the only foreigner and only surviving black in the program, that I could do it just as well, if not better, than all the others.

Why did I have to discover my blackness in that crowded dining hall of the college center? Why did I have to ruin everything with the constant questioning, the continuous probing, to see what might or might not have been there? My film always got stuck at that period of disenchantment, my disappointment written all over my face. I knew that I couldn't continue to stay on in such a frame of mind. I needed a change of venue, an opportunity to reflect, a new perspective on the situation, none of which I could do in the suffocating confines of America.

I cried as I dragged my heavy baggage down the long walkways of JFK airport. John, Delia, and the children had said their goodbyes and were already on their way back home. My leaving had become a reality; there was no going back. It was ending where it had started only five and a half years before, which seemed more like a century. I was far from the starry-eyed, idealistic child who'd arrived to "God's own country"; I felt jaded, much older in more ways than the obvious. Had I used my head better, I would have realized that returning to Nigeria in that frame of mind was the worst step that I could have taken, that I needed to resolve my conflicts about my blackness within America.

Somewhere over the Atlantic Ocean, past midnight Eastern time, our plane crossed the Greenwich Meridian. Although a majority of the passengers were asleep, the pilot of the PanAm 747 announced, "Welcome to Africa," as we were suddenly surrounded by sunlight.

The beauty of it lies in its suddenness: one minute we were in darkness, and the next we were bathed by a glorious sunlight that stayed with us until we touched down in Liberia. I hung by the window and watched, mesmerized by nature's wonders. I also became suddenly charged with excitement, transformed by the light of the sun. It radiated such warmth, it was beckoning to me, reassuring me about my journey. My insides felt hollow and I hugged my middle tightly, just to catch my breath. "I'm going home! I'm really going home!" There was only one way to interpret the omen: God was blessing my decision to return.

And then suddenly, I was consumed by impatience. The plane seemed to be dragging, not up to full speed. I couldn't wait to get home, to see my sisters, my brothers, Mama, Mama's house; I could no longer sit still.

The Pan Am 747 left Liberia early and touched down in Lagos hours before the scheduled arrival. Mama had asked my cousin Ben to meet me at the Lagos airport, take me home with him for the night, and put me on the plane to Enugu the following day. However, Ben decided that I should continue home on the same day. He checked me onto a flight that was supposed to take off to Enugu and arrive there 45 minutes later. Then he left, believing that I would get home without a problem. He was wrong, terribly wrong in fact, and as Mama still reminds him, my life could have ended that day because he unilaterally chose to alter Mama's well-calculated plans.

I sat in that airport for six hours waiting for the flight to Enugu to take off. No announcements were made to excuse the delays; everyone sat leisurely, as if a six-hour unexplained flight delay was the most normal thing in the world. To complicate matters, I had no way of reaching Ben, who had no telephone in his home.

I waited anxiously, pacing the soiled carpeted floor of the waiting room, sipping warm Coca-Cola from the bottle (the airport had lost electric power days before and none of the refrigerators worked). The delay troubled very few other than me. Everyone took it in stride, and when I complained in my American-accented English to fellow travelers, they first stared at me in disbelief, as they would at one who wonders why a month-old baby does not walk yet. Then they asked me, "Where are you from?" I answered Nsukka, and they commented, "You've been gone a long time." My cream-colored linen suit (a graduation gift from John and Delia the previous year) was, by the time we finally boarded the Nigeria Airways flight to Enugu, closer to a deep brown than its original color.

Every minute that I stayed in Nigeria taught me something new. I found out that we were not required to wear seat belts even as the plane took off. The "buckle-your-seat-belt" signs came on, but everyone disregarded rules, and no one tried to enforce them. No one was assigned seat numbers, for there were no guarantees that you would get onto a flight for which you had a boarding pass.

Before our plane started its descent, a man whom I recognized from the Pan Am flight approached me and started a conversation that ended in a marriage proposal before our plane landed. He said he had noticed me and was interested in what I was doing and how come I was returning from America when most people were dying to get there. Then he revealed that he was coming home to get married.

"You're not married?" I blurted before I had time to think it out. He looked to be at least in his late forties and by my estimate, should have had college-aged children, within my age range.

"I'm sort of married," he said, shrugging his shoulders.

"Well, you're either married or not," I spoke unlike an Ibo woman, but I was out of practice. The man explained that he was married to an American woman. "But you know, it's not for real. She can never understand me, no matter how hard she tries."

"Are you still living with her?" I asked, more out of curiosity than anything else and because I wondered how he intended to manage two wives in the U.S.

"If I find someone I like, I'll set her up somewhere else until I'm free of the *akata*." (*Akata* is a derogatory term that Nigerians use to describe black Americans.)

This man became my savior that night, for by the time we disembarked at Enugu airport, he was so enthralled with me that he glued himself to my side. It was in the course of that discussion that he told me that he would want another opportunity to try and convince me to return to the United States and be married to him. My standard response, "We'll see," saved me that night, for when we collected our luggage, we both discovered that there was no one there to pick either one of us up. Mama was acting under the assumption that I was arriving at Enugu on an early-morning flight from Lagos and her plans were according to that schedule.

A deserted airport was nowhere for a young woman to be at nine-thirty at night. The airport taxi drivers hovered over me and my newly purchased luggage, dragging me in several different directions. "I'll take you wherever you're going," one announced, while another shouted, "I'll deliver you in one piece to your destination."

Nsukka is at least fifty miles from the Enugu airport. The logical step would have been to head to my sister Virginia's house, but my recollection of Virginia's address in Enugu was vague. My suitor must have noticed my confusion and ran to my side, acting quickly to dispel whatever notions the taxi drivers may have had of taking advantage of a lone girl in the middle of the night. He chartered two cars, had my luggage loaded, and directed the drivers to the area I described as my sister's neighborhood. Everyone was asleep by the time we made it to Virginia's house, and my knight asked me several times if I were sure she was my sister before he left for his own home.

Mama dispatched the dancing troupe and hundreds of friends and neighbors in rented buses to the airport before my scheduled arrival. Their every move was planned and rehearsed, down to what songs would be sung as I walked into the waiting room of the airport. She had arranged a reception fit for royalty, but it was not meant to be. Mama first stopped by Virginia's house so they could proceed to the airport together. Someone yelled that Mama was coming out of a car and I begged my sister to let me get to Mama first. My little surprise almost killed her and she started to cry.

"Is this you or your ghost?" she asked over and over. Minutes after she arrived, we were all on our knees thanking God for coming to my aid in the form of the suitor from New York. Another traveler, a young woman my age, never made it home from the airport; she'd been found strangled just the previous week. Although Mama was disappointed that her plans were ruined, she continued to tell the story of how I almost lost my life on the day I returned to Nigeria for months afterwards.

Upon arriving back in Nsukka, I learned that Thomas Wolfe's statement, "You can't go home again," is true. Of course, nothing was like I'd imagined it, and once again, I felt like a stranger, out of place and time and completely isolated by my feelings. Actually, my initial shock originated from discovering that nothing had changed. It was as if time had stood still, and I was the only one who'd moved forward into the future. Mama's house still looked the same as it always did. I walked into Mama's parlor and everything was exactly where it was before I left. The seat cushion covers were the only new items and I recognized the material that we had purchased together when Mama visited us in the United States. I could have sworn that even the door was open at the same angle it was on the day I left, almost six years earlier. I had thought maybe things would be different—that women would look at their husbands when they spoke to them, that neighbors would know not to touch me when they talked to me—but I was wrong.

I was surrounded, crowded by relatives who were genuinely happy to see me. "Is it true Americans are all over six feet tall? Do Americans really hop instead of walk?" I found myself answering one ignorant question after another. I started wishing that everyone would just leave me alone, so I could begin to figure out my new position in this old place. But there was no evidence that the throngs of people who followed me home from the airport had any plans of leaving, although it was close to midnight, and I had been traveling for more than 48 hours. Mama kept their drinks replenished and snack plates full, discouraging any early departures. No one was sensitive to my need to unwind even after I began to nod off, exhaustion getting the better of me.

I tried to facilitate the end of that long night by retreating into the room that had been prepared for me and changing into a cotton night dress, deliberately lingering long after I had completed dressing. But they would not let me be. Some of the women invaded the room, and one actually pulled me up from the bed where I was slumped so she could get a better look at the dress.

"Turn just so, no, a little to the left; Americans do know how to sew pretty things. This looks like you were born in it."

I played along even though I fumed as I did it, but even that was not enough for her. She dragged my barely clad body out to the parlor to the gawking "oohs" and "aahs" of all gathered.

"Doesn't she just look adorable? Like a newlywed bride?"

I was fully aware of the implications of their innuendos, but I was truly too exhausted to react either way.

I felt myself suffocating, entangled in weeds from which I couldn't extricate myself. I had never before felt such an overbearing, smothering weight from my family, friends and neighbors, who watched my every move as if I were a zoo animal. Maybe it was because until I left Nigeria, I had never felt the right to claim even my own person; my life had simply not been mine to live in the first place, and I had not known better. But having gotten used to the concept of self and individual space in the U.S., I didn't know how much I took it for granted until my return. After all, it had been years since I was last prodded, poked, and inspected like meat on a butcher's table. People were touching me without permission and there seemed to be a hand laid on a part of me at every instance. There was someone rubbing my shoulders, another massaging my arm, while yet another smoothed the wrinkles off my clothes. I longed for America, for my own space; I wished to be left alone, forgotten for a while by my adoring relatives, but there was no respite. And it was only my first day home.

During the days that followed, I was only able to function in an out-of-body capacity. I allowed myself to be led expressionless, zombie-like, and paraded in front of the thousands of callers who flooded our home. My face was fixed in a perpetual smile and my hands ached from all the shaking. The worst was that few people wanted to leave without making inquiries about America. Well-meaning aunts and uncles argued with each other over who would sit closest to me and about whose recommended suitors were introduced to me. I held on, surviving one long day at a time. The stifling harmattan heat did not ease my readjustment, and had it not been for the oscillating fan that followed me everywhere I went, I would have melted like the ice in the drinks I gulped down.

I was appalled at the state of my two sisters when I arrived home. Virginia was very pregnant with her fourth child and Martha had just given birth to her third. Neither of them had gotten much education and both lived at the mercies of their husbands. They and their children stayed at Mama's house during the first few days of my return, and I wished I could speak to them. Many times, I sat next to them, eager to hold a heart-to-heart conversation, like I used to enjoy with Delia, but all I could manage were a few bland, meaningless inquiries. "So what do the children like to eat for breakfast?" or "How exciting to bring a new life into the world." What I really wanted to ask was, "So how many more are you going to have before you decide to make something out of your life?" But that would not have been appropriate and my sisters would have been greatly upset. How long could I continue to live a lie, to wear the plastered smile, to feign interest in conversations that I detested?

I survived those first weeks by sheer will power and adrenaline, but then it was time to put to use all the training I'd obtained in America. People had all sorts of expectations, and many of them were disappointed that I insisted on doing things by the book, like they're done in America, instead of favoring the short-cut method that Nigerians are used to. Two days after I returned, I was invited to meet the governor of our state who was visiting Nsukka for a weekend.

"He'll like you," I was told over and over, "he'll love your American English."

What I later learned was that I was supposed to give myself to the governor, a known womanizer, so that I would get whatever I desired. Everyone was shocked that I was not willing to play. The American in me emerged and took over, and I gave my supposed enticers a lecture on self-respect. "It is not for these kind of games that I went to America. I want to be met on my terms, rewarded on my qualifications, not based on any other thing."

"But this is Nigeria; nobody gets what they deserve unless they play the game," my friends insisted. But I was adamant, and I refused to be bait for favor-seeking sycophants.

I made a lot of mistakes, and Mama was there to cover up and remind me later that I was in Nigeria, not America. They were not earth-shattering mistakes, but were noticeable enough to chase away future suitors if word got out. None of my trangressions were intentional, but as much as I tried to curtail myself, I couldn't help butting into men's conversations, especially if they were discussing international events or America. The first time, I cut off a man in mid-sentence.

"Get your facts right before you make such exaggerated claims," I told him after he told of a CIA plot to assassinate the Ayatollah Khomeini. The room suddenly grew silent, making me louder than I wanted to be. I deliberately looked away from Mama's gaze. Later, when the conversation resumed, Mama tapped my knees gently and walked into her room. I followed shortly, knowing that a long lecture awaited me.

The second confrontation occurred when I challenged my cousin, who compared his new wife to a goat he purchased from the market. I truly thought he was joking at first, but when he persisted, I felt I had to put an end to his cockiness. "You get as much respect as you give, mister; if your wife is a cow, then you're no better than a bull," I said to him.

"Dympna, a man has a right to treat his wife however he wants," Mama interjected.

"Not if he doesn't treat her right."

"He's still within his rights," she said. Later when we were alone, she admonished me, "Don't antagonize your cousin or he'll take it out on his wife when he gets home. I wish you would know when to talk and when not to."

I kept silent, knowing that my opinion would not matter.

"Everybody is watching you, and any little blunder could affect you for the rest of your life." I knew exactly what she was referring to: almighty marriage.

"What could anyone do to me now, Mama? I have my education, and in the worst possible case, I can support myself more than adequately." My patience was wearing thin from playing the dumb complacent female, a role that I hadn't played in a long time.

"You're back home, Dympna. We do things differently from the way Americans would. Try to remember that."

I tried to remember and, in the process, to relearn what being an Ibo girl was all about: the clothing, the walk, the gestures—all understated. I tuned my voice several octaves lower and mastered looking down at my lap where I rested my neatly folded hands. I was watching myself go through a transformation, a regrooming of sorts, a change that my true self did not want to go along with. I dared not interfere, because I lacked the courage or the will to put up the fight necessary. Thus, my real self slipped farther and farther into the background and rarely ever showed herself in public anymore. I allowed the reprogramming to proceed while everything I had become cried out in protest. But my minority self was drowned out by all the other voices. Finally, other people noticed.

"Now, you've really come home," they complimented me. "You're more like one of us now."

Charles Stakes His Claim

Charles came to visit me two days after I arrived. That he did not come the day after my return added to my irritation, but he came on his own terms, not as ordered by his parents. They, in fact, had demanded that he be on hand to welcome me at the airport, but he balked at the idea, primarily because he suspected that I would snub him. He told me weeks later that he had almost accepted that I would not marry him, but that he could not endure a public humiliation. So he waited, choosing to visit not the day after, when thousands of people came calling to view the "American girl," but one day later, when the crowd had ebbed somewhat. He brought his best friend, a young man who was still in medical school at the time, and they arrived in Charles' sister's new Japanese car.

When their presence was announced to me, I was resting in my room. I waited a few minutes, then rose slowly to stand in front of the mirror. I quickly glanced at my image, and not fully satisfied, I hurriedly applied electric-red lipstick and a fresh line of eyebrow liner. I fluffed my loosely rolled curls with a pik and doused myself with Charlie, my favorite perfume at that time. I took a long time deciding whether I should change from the creased Calvin Klein jeans (purposely worn with a white cotton T-shirt for the shock factor and to declare my independence) to an outfit that would be more acceptable to everyone. My rebellious spirit won, but in a conciliatory move, I smoothed the creases on the legs of the pants. I slipped my feet into the three-inch high-heel sandals that had been chosen for this occasion. Then I walked out of the room, strutting toward the parlor where my future waited.

I'm almost sure I heard a gasp from someone when I paused at the door to allow Charles full view in one take. I made my way to the only vacant seat, deliberately positioned where Charles awaited—Mama's attempt at casualness. He stood in awkward nervousness, unsure of what do or say. I did not avoid his eyes as I was taught to do, and my affrontery caused him immense discomfort; I noted his perspiring forehead with glee. One could cut the tension in that room with a knife; every available seat was taken, and not even any standing room was left. I took note of my mother's anxious stares and moved on to my aunts' and cousins' breathless anticipation. My sisters, Virginia and Martha, fidgeted in their standing space, their eyes focused on me.

"*Inatago* (Are you home)?" was all Charles could manage by way of breaking the ice. I could have had fun with that one, but it was a style of Ibo talk, stating the obvious.

"Uhm," I responded.

"*Ijekwelu ofuma* (Did the journey go well)?"

"Uhm," I answered the second time, aiming for a reaction that even I was not sure of.

"Dympna," Mama called from across the room, "Tell Charles of how we almost lost you, but for the grace of God." I glared at her, and when our eyes locked, hers pleaded with me, ultimately overpowering me. I started slowly, recounting every minor detail of my flight home, from the minute I boarded the plane at JFK Airport in New York to arriving at my sister's house. He interjected with exclamations of surprise, at times in places where I didn't think they belonged, but the room warmed up and everyone became involved in the drawn-out discussion of lack of safety at the airport. Then, having waited for some fireworks that didn't explode and weren't likely to, the crowd began to drift out of the parlor. Eventually, only Mama and two older aunts remained in the room with us, but they too were either engaged in or faking a private conversation, leaving Charles an opportunity to make personal talk. But he didn't; we talked about every subject but the issue that brought him to our house. He never once alluded to his marriage proposal or my refusal to commit to an engagement. We discussed international issues, the recently imposed economic sanctions on Moscow by the American government, Ted Kennedy's attempt to unseat an incumbent president from his own party, everything but us. I was surprised and impressed by his knowledge of international affairs, which were my own passion too. Charles was as versed in these topics as I was and his opinions agreed with my liberal viewpoints. He subscribed to both *Newsweek* and *Time* and listened to the Voice of America every night.

Right after Charles drove off, Mama pulled me to one side and whispered in my ear, "Give it time, I beg you. Don't make any decisions yet." I agreed to her request, for I did not sense any urgency. Left by myself to make my own decisions, I could, I knew, choose Charles or someone else that Mama approved of. I wanted it to be my choice, on my terms, wrong man or not.

Alone again, I began to ponder the strange situation that Charles and I were both in. He felt immense loyalty to his parents and would go ahead with a marriage, if for nothing else but to please them. I also was consumed by the wish to repay my mother for her years of sacrifice in raising us.

Many would argue that such a condition was the beginning of a good marriage. We were both parent-loving and respecting adults who would give the marriage everything in us. But I wanted more, more than my sisters had with their husbands, and more than Mama had with my father. It wasn't love or passion that I desired. I wanted to be respected, to be valued, to be viewed as a prize by whoever married me; I didn't want to go to Charles or any man who would not work hard for my acquisition. I felt that the man I married had to earn me, and Charles was not working hard enough yet.

That's when I realized that I felt a kinship with Charles I never felt with any of my suitors before or after him. After his initial nervousness, we felt comfortable with each other. We knew all the same people; all my relatives knew him and related well with him. It almost felt like many years before, when we were children and unencumbered by all the expectations. I knew then as I do now that I would never deliberately cause him pain or humiliate him in front of others. I waited for inspiration while continuing to entertain other suitors who came, some unannounced, to capture the fancy of the girl from America.

Subtlety was never one of my mother's strong points. In spite of our declared truce and my promise to give Charles a chance, Mama would not let a minute go by without saying or doing something that violated the terms of our cease fire. "Dympu, did you see the goat the Ugwu-Ojus brought for your reception?" Or "Wasn't it nice of Charles to come all the way from Aba to visit you?" She gave me no respite. When Mama tired, one of her surrogates continued to pester me with bits of information about the Ugwu-Ojus and their vast estate.

The next day was the reception to honor my accomplishments. Charles was not present, but his parents and the rest of his family came, bearing gifts and resplendent in their fineries. It was an all-day celebration, starting with mass, offered for me at St. Theresa's church where I received my first communion and confirmation. The Ugwu-Ojus provided a chauffeured Peugeot 504 for my use and when I arrived at the church, they lined up with the more important of our friends, waiting to present me to the monsignor who celebrated mass.

I allowed myself to be led and followed, afraid that any little protest on my part would cause Mama pain. My future parents-in-law, who sat in the front pew with us, came along with Mama and me when we presented the offerings. After mass, the family surrounded me, limiting others' access. Their message to the entire congregation was clear: keep away, she's spoken for, she's ours. At home, I sat on the dais with my prospective in-laws surrounding me; there was no escaping Mama's intricate web.

Charles' father, the chairperson of the occasion, several times stated his hope that in the not-so-distant future I would become his daughter. I sat as if in a daze, listening to the endless list of speakers echo each other. The message was a replay of the speeches I sat through before I left for America—that my education meant nothing without a marriage. I wondered if things would ever change in our culture. I wondered what could have possessed me to think I'd fit back in after years of living in America.

A male friend of mine, who was a few years older and completing his PhD at the University of Nigeria, walked up to the dais to chat with me. I embraced him with all my might, believing that at last, someone would speak a different theme. When he asked to be permitted to speak, I encouraged him, but his presentation did nothing to relieve my isolation. "Dympna has earned a B.A. and an M.S.; as much as we know that she's capable of earning a PhD, we would rather she earned an MRS first."

He was loudly cheered and fondly patted on the back. I'm sure that the crowd hoped for an announcement of an impending marriage, but of course none was made. By evening, only a handful of people were left and they congregated in Mama's parlor to listen to stories about America. Then the talk drifted to my unmarried state. My cousin Anthony, a successful engineer with Shell Oil, was deeply troubled by the fact that I was still unspoken for and he wanted to remedy the situation. He was aware that we were too closely related to propose to me himself, but the more he listened to the speakers, the more determined he was to find a husband for me. Anthony told me that he had a few friends who were still unmarried, whom he felt he could talk into proposing to me. He was overly apologetic about his friends' shortfalls, for holding jobs with salaries that wouldn't provide the kind of life Anthony felt I was entitled to. I listened with my mouth open, shocked that I might be viewed by everyone, including my relatives, as being in a desperate strait. When I recovered, I laughed so hard I almost fell on the floor. But I was the only one laughing. Everyone else looked at me as they would at someone demented, as if I had cracked under pressure. Later I began to wonder, did I look desperate? Were they all feeling sorry for me? How could I possibly survive their onslaught alone?

Of course, I also had other immediate and serious issues to consider. I first had to serve a year in a mandated national program in which every university graduate participates. The goal of this program is to foster national unity, because participants are posted in states other than their own. Though I considered this duty an imposition and a nuisance, in the last week of January 1980, I took a trip to Lagos, Nigeria's capital city, where the National Youth Service Corps Headquarters were located.

My trip to Lagos, once again, confirmed my worst fears about being a woman in Nigeria. I had been warned beforehand that things were done differently in Nigeria. First, I was told I couldn't stay in a hotel for the three-day stay because no reputable women stayed in hotel rooms by themselves. "Please don't bring shame to our family," Mama pleaded. Instead, I had to lodge more than an hour's drive out of my way at an aunt's home. Next, I had to bribe every worker at the National Youth Service Corps secretariat to perform even the most basic clerical duty for me. I also had to fend off the overt advances of lecherous bureaucrats to get my papers signed and my assignment posted. My Lagos experience reminded me that most Nigerian men viewed women in only one way, as sexual objects, and this harassment would follow me no matter who I was. Even when I became highly esteemed in my work as the sole female professor of mass communications and was invited to present papers at numerous conferences, men of all levels and kinds expected me to "still be a woman" in the very traditional sense of it. This continued even after I was married and had children. I was constantly reminded that if I wanted to get ahead in life, I had to play the game of using my body; that's simply the Nigerian way.

Finally, with the help of relatives who had the right contacts, I was assigned to Imo state where Charles just happened to be doing his internship at Aba General Hospital. To avoid a repeat of my Lagos experience, I sought and obtained a letter from the Chief Inspector of the National Youth Service Corps in my home state to the person in charge of the state I was posted to. The letter contained a code understood by all men: "She's the daughter of a friend." In other words, don't harass her and make sure she's looked after. The note worked, at least initially, and opened some closed doors in Owerri, the capital of Imo state, without giving away my body. I was given a choice of an appointment to one of three different corporations. Two of the corporations, *The Statesman,* a daily newspaper, and Imo Broadcasting Service (IBS), a radio station, were in Owerri. The third, the Nigerian Television Service (NTA), was located in Aba, where Charles was living at that time. While visiting the Aba location, I decided to drop in on Charles, at the apartment he shared with two other interns. It was the most impulsive thing I had ever done in my life, but I was almost compelled to do it, as if I had no control over my actions.

To make matters worse, Charles and his friends weren't aware that a female would be visiting. I arrived at about seven o'clock on a hot breezeless evening. There was no electric power at the time (in Nigeria, blackout periods are more frequent than times when the electricity is on), but it was still light enough not to require a candle or lantern.

Charles and his two flatmates were wearing wrappers, little more than loin cloths, barely covering their private parts. Their door was wide open, so there was no reason for me to knock or alert them of my entrance. I was met with a combination of shock and shame, causing a temporary paralysis in the three men, none of whom rose or even made any attempts to right themselves. And that's how I walked in on the man I would agree to marry before dawn of the next day.

When Charles recovered his composure, he excitedly introduced me to his roommates as his fiance, which, I'm sure, he did more to protect my image than his. It would have caused him some discomfort had I been less than an intended bride to him, especially given that I clearly intended to pass the night with him.

We retired to his bedroom soon after, and we talked about everything there was to talk about: past relationships, siblings, dreams. I discovered that we had a lot of interests in common, much beyond international politics. He said he believed that women, like men, should have the right of self-determination, and that if I consented to be his wife, he would not in any way oppose anything I chose to do with my life. Charles insisted that he was resolved to making me his wife and that he would not rest until he'd accomplished that goal. He swore it had nothing to do with his parents' wishes, that he had always desired me, right from our childhood.

Then on the very first night that he and I were left alone together in the same room and shared more than a few sentences in conversation, we became lovers. There was no awkwardness in our union. In fact, it was as natural as if we had known each other that way for years, as if we were meant to be together.

I learned that Charles would spare nothing to achieve his goal, for he asked me at least fifty times that night if I would marry him. I remember going from "No," to "Let me think about it," to "Maybe," and then to "Yes," all in the course of one night. By the time dawn broke, I told him that I was convinced that he would be the best man for me to marry, and that I would no longer consider marriage proposals from other men. I looked Charles in the eye and said that to him, knowing that I did not believe it. Even as I mouthed the words, clouds of uncertainty hovered over me, and they darkened my days frequently over the following months.

I left Charles' apartment three days later. Once alone and able to think independently, the seriousness, the finality, of my actions finally hit me. I had not only consented to sex with him, but I'd also told him he could speak to his parents about starting our traditional marriage and had promised him that I would tell Mama that I had made up my mind.

My first reaction was shock. How could I have gone from a position of vehement opposition to one of total submission in less than a week? (Some of my more articulate friends have told me that my acceptance of Charles was inevitable, because of the mounting pressure from Mama and all my relatives. I may, in fact, have taken the steps I took as a pre-emptive measure, a move to disarm the opposition, to prevent more of the onslaught I knew awaited me.)

Whatever the reasons that compelled me to do it, I had done it, and between January 1980 when I consented and March 1981 when Charles officially paid a price on my head, my mood swings were monumental. I vacillated between desperately wanting marriage with Charles and abhorrence that I was settling for him because it was the convenient thing to do. On my bad days, it felt like I'd dug my grave and practically buried myself in it, for all of a sudden, my education, enlightenment, exposure, and intellect all seemed to have been for naught. By my choice, I had declared my life no different from my mother's and my sisters'. How was it that I, the first woman in my area to be educated in America, could limit my options to no more than my uneducated mother and unenlightened sisters had?

On my good days, the positive aspects of the marriage that I had consented to seemed to outweigh the negatives. I kept reminding myself that Charles was good for me. *He knows my worth and would never take me for granted. He said he will let me be whatever I want to be. He'll provide adequately for me and however many children we have.* I talked to myself until I was almost convinced that I was doing the right thing.

What I remember feeling most during that period of emotional turbulence was that at least Mama would be pleased. In fact, it was only my sense of duty, my belief that individuals occasionally need to sacrifice their personal happiness for the general good, that held me to my promise to marry Charles. I was able to maintain my rationality. I was doing what I was doing for Mama, because she desired it and because it was the only thing to do.

It was also during that period that I compared my life with that of my mother's at the same age. At age twenty-three, I had the world at my feet. I was superbly educated and highly esteemed in my field. I had achieved goals beyond anyone's imagination. At the same age, Mama had been married to my father for nearly ten years and was the mother of five children. She was allowed only limited use of her self. Her daily activities were dictated by her master. My education alone allowed me the independence that Mama never had in her entire married life. In the worst-case scenario, I could leave an abusive husband and support myself and my children. Mama did not have the same options at that age. Most importantly, I made my choices because I wanted to make them. In other words, I could, had I chosen to, have refused marriage to Charles or any man in particular and lived my life as I wanted. I could have also chosen to return to the United States. No one could have stopped me, Ibo tradition or not.

Mama, on the other hand, was never asked if she wanted to marry my father; there had been no discussion about the issue, and he had in fact paid the bride price on her head before she was even made aware of the deal. She never had an opportunity to express her feelings on the matter. My scope went much beyond the boundaries of my Ibo womanhood. I knew, unlike Mama, that life did not begin and end in Nsukka, Aku, or Enugu, and that I could extend my reach much beyond those borders. I was privileged, and Mama had nothing. Yet, she made the choices to arm us to be self-sufficient. Comparing my life to Mama's, I was again reminded of my primary reason for marrying Charles: to reward her for her good work, her steadfastness, and the sacrifices she made on my behalf. I wanted to repay her.

I debated whether I should tell Mama. I wondered whether I should hold out for a better time, to extract as much as I could from her. But I changed my mind once I got home from the trip to Imo. I was suddenly overcome with a sense of guilt and remorse for even contemplating prolonging her agony. I said to myself, "Mama will derive immense joy from it, and I'll have some peace of mind meanwhile." I approached her after dinner one night after I'd returned from my stay in Aba, after all the aunts and friends who ate with us had retired to their own rooms. The parlor was dark, and the only light emanated from a candle sitting on the low table in the center of the room.

"Mama, I think I'll marry Charles," I said quietly. There was neither joy nor sadness in my voice. It was said in a tone of resignation, of acceptance, like I was telling her that she was stronger than I was.

"What did you say?" she jerked her body forward in her seat and focused all her attention on me.

"I'll marry Charles whenever you all want," I repeated, my voice still flat.

"You don't sound like it's what you want," she said as if she would have let me off the hook, even if I told her the truth about the way I really felt.

"But isn't that what you want me to do?" I started to get angry.

"You know that I want you to want to marry him, Dympna, but not to do me a favor."

"Maybe that's what I want. Maybe I want to marry him. You and his parents can decide when to start the traditional marriage ceremonies."

"I will not tell them of this conversation for several months yet. I need to be convinced it's what you want for yourself," Mama declared, telling me I should not say anything about it to anyone.

Mama pulled it off again, I thought. She managed to convince me, at the last minute, after I had committed myself to Charles in a way I dared not tell her, that I didn't have to marry Charles if I didn't feel like it. I couldn't believe it! I finally agree to marry Charles, which she'd been hounding me to do for years, and then she tells me to think it over for a few months! I tossed and turned in my bed, barely sleeping that night as I wondered if it was too late to convince Charles that I wanted a postponement on a final decision. But by the very next day, Mama had come to her senses.

"I'm happy for you, Dympna. You'll see how happy Charles will make you," she said to me as she walked into the house from church.

I said nothing.

"The Ugwu-Ojus will be overjoyed. Their first son will get married to their first choice. This will seal the bond between our two families. Your father would be very proud of you. I can't wait for the day that you finally become theirs." Mama had either forgotten the conversation we had the night before or she was pretending. This catapulted me onto yet another emotional roller coaster, and it took another day or two of reasoning with myself to reconcile to the marriage. At least I knew she was happy about my decision. I could not bear to break her heart.

Within a few weeks of telling Mama of my decision to marry Charles, the news of my engagement was all over Nsukka. Elders in our town congratulated me and held me up as an example to their own daughters. "Look at the Edoga girl. She's been to America, a place where very few have been, yet look at the way she carries herself. She's smart but you wouldn't know it from her humility. And you know the best of all, she's agreed to marry the Ugwu-Oju boy, just because that's what her mother wanted. I hope you all behave like that when your own time comes." If only they knew the roller coaster-sized turmoil that threatened to undo my resolve.

My mother-in-law used every opportunity there was to give me a gift. She held many dinners in my honor, and insisted on supplementing the two hundred *naira* (then three hundred dollars) a month I earned in the National Youth Service. She bought me wrappers and lace and gold bracelets and necklaces, which made Mama even more convinced that the entire family would accept me as completely as one of their own.

By mutual agreement, our traditional marriage was slated for March 1981, more than a year after I agreed to marry Charles and much later than Charles wanted it. But, his parents and Mama argued, the reasons why we should wait far outweighed the ones to pursue the marriage in a speedy fashion. Charles' immediate younger sister, Priscilla, was going through her own traditional marriage to my first cousin, the last son of Uncle Crescent, "Our father," who provided Mama shelter in the year she grieved for her husband. It almost seemed as if the two families were trading, exchanging daughters. Some even suggested that we forego the traditional negotiations over the bride prices, but that we view the two girls (Priscilla and me) as having equal value, to save time and money. Both sides rejected that position. No two girls were worth the same amount of money; everyone knew there were differences, and a girl's worth is determined by her individual bride

price. It was agreed that the two marriages should be separated so that
no confusion was created. Secondly, Charles still had a full year of
national service after his internship, and there was no telling where
he would be posted.

I continued to do my national service in Owerri, three hours by car
from Nsukka. I served at two locations, as a producer of documentaries
at a radio station and as a public relations officer at the secretariat of
the Youth Service Headquarters. I must admit that I had a ball that
year. It was my first opportunity to live with young Nigerians without
the strict, finger-wagging dominance of Mama or reverend sisters hovering over me.

At first we lived in hostels, all young people from different parts of
the country, with as diverse a background as could be found in a New
York City subway car. The experience was an eye opener, especially
when I discovered that my prejudices about Hausas and Yorubas were
based on half-truths and that I knew very little of the citizens of my
own country. After the initial skepticism, we became fast friends, all
of us, men and women alike. We were young and acted our ages, rel-
ishing every opportunity to be irresponsible. From the bugle horn that
roused us in the morning through the drills of our paramilitary training to the other activities throughout the day, it was one big party, and
I thoroughly enjoyed all the attention I was getting.

"The American girl," they called me, referring to my acquired
American accent and my mannerisms. Then it occurred to me what
separated the Youth Service experience from others that I had in
America. While I was close to my roommates at Briarcliff and partied
with them, there were usually no black men at the college mixers.
Even if there had been any, they would have preferred the fast-talking,
perfectly coiffed black American girls to the still starry-eyed African
student who couldn't manage more than a few dance steps without
tripping. I almost always sat through the noisy blasts of disco and rock
'n' roll alone.

My experience in Nigeria was the direct opposite. I was the center
of attention, and men lined up for an opportunity to dance with me. I
felt like a princess for the first time in my life, and had I not already
agreed to the marriage to Charles before I started my Youth Service, I
would have fallen for many other princes.

I came home for occasional weekends, opting to spend most of my
free time with Charles, who was rounding out his internship at Aba,
an hour away. Our physical relationship could only be described as

superb, flawless. But on the emotional and spiritual plane, it took a while for us to connect. I felt decades older than Charles. He tried hard to make me happy, but often, his ideas of pleasure were very far from mine. Also, in our private moments, he treated me like a goddess, but when we were in the company of others, he either ignored me, or if I became involved in a heated discussion on any issues, he reminded me that I was his wife and shouldn't embarrass him in public. He insisted on being the man of the relationship, and I was forced to play the role of the docile little woman, even though my rage nearly got the better of me several times.

After I was more than halfway through my national service, I commenced my search for permanent employment. I traveled to Lagos for interviews with Nigeria's major newspaper, *The Daily Times*, which offered me a job as the Senate correspondent. The editor of the newspaper was impressed not only by my academic credentials, but also my youth and charm, both of which he said would be assets in the position.

"Those senators would love you; they'll take you to their parties, and you'll have better scoops than other reporters."

I decided to tell him the truth about my impending marriage and that I would not be a willing participant in the senators' games.

"You can't speak of this engagement, ever. In fact, if you want to work with us, you'll postpone this marriage for at least three years. Your main attraction is your availability," he said angrily. I could not consider the job seriously after that.

I was offered a position with Nigerian Television Authority (NTA). "You're tailor-made for television," NTA male executives told me one after another, following the interview. After several months in Nigeria, I understood their language. Although the job seemed glamorous on the surface, I discovered that I would be assigned to the "Women's and Children's" department. Women couldn't be trusted to handle serious news stories. Besides, the position required regular appearance on television, exactly where Mama and my future husband did not want me.

I scrambled for a job that would be more palatable to me and my future husband, but even as I did it, I was fearful that my essence was being eroded gradually, and that very soon, I would have nothing left of myself that I could recognize.

As a last measure, I applied at the University of Nigeria for a lecturing position in mass communication. I would teach journalism to both undergraduate and graduate students on the campus at Nsukka. It was as if I had made a complete circle, returning to where it had all started. But working in Nsukka meant one thing: I would have to move in and live with Mama. I would have to abide by her rigid rules; I would have to be aware at all times of my Ibo womanhood. I could not exactly rent a flat by myself in Nsukka, although that would have provided the privacy and independence that I needed. Mama would never allow it, protesting vehemently and calling meetings to discuss the shame that I'd bring to the family. If I still refused to acquiesce, she would turn on the tears and refuse to stop crying until I bowed to her wishes. I could almost hear our neighbors asking, "Why would a young woman want to be alone unless she's living the kind of life her mother would be ashamed of?" The more benevolent ones would simply say, "Don't waste money on rent when your mother has room for you."

I also agonized over the university job because I simply didn't want to teach. I had gone into journalism for only one reason: my interest in the news and the process of gathering, writing, and publishing it. My courses were to prepare me for my eventual career as a working reporter. After all, one of my most serious rebellions as a teenager in high school was refusing to major in education. Thus, my decision to apply for and accept a teaching position was the beginning of the end of my rebelliousness and my American assertiveness.

It had taken less than a year to dismantle what I took six years to acquire. I was transformed into a person that I no longer recognized. I had turned into what everyone wanted me to become. I was fitting into the society I had chosen to return to; there was simply no other way. I tried to tell myself that I could write feature articles and sell them to magazines and that I had the best of both worlds. But I could barely get excited about it. Everyone else cheered, however, when I divulged that I had accepted the teaching position at the university. "Now you're talking," they told me. "This is more like a woman's job."

In December 1980, when I returned to Nsukka to begin my job at the university, I moved into the same room where Emma, my first suitor, and Rose, Mama's first godchild, had lived. My door was adjacent to Mama's and she could, when she wanted to, gaze directly into my room. She immediately set about to shape me. She wanted me to become involved in church activities, but I refused. She stayed angry with me for a few days and barely answered when I greeted her. Mama also wanted me to visit my parents-in-law regularly, especially on

Saturdays, "to help out with housework." Again, I refused, arguing that I did not want them to believe I would be a certain kind of wife when I had no intention of following up on it. Everyone in Nigeria had househelp, and my in-laws had more than their share.

"But you're going to be their wife. You need to show them that they're not making a mistake by marrying you," she insisted. Finally, one evening, I offered to help my mother-in-law with her laundry. She was very pleased by my dutifulness, but graciously turned me down. Thus my descent into traditional Ibo womanhood continued unabated. Worse, though I was full-grown and a professional, I wasn't married, so I was treated like a child.

My work at the university was exciting, which came as a pleasant surprise. The university environment was almost like living outside of the country. I was surrounded by eager students who were as curious about the subjects I taught as they were about my life in America. A majority of my colleagues were educated abroad, most in America, and a good number traveled frequently. We were therefore up to date on fashion, news, and everything happening abroad. I socialized with both men and women in the university; the rules were quite different from what they were less than a mile away in the main town. I was able to relax at the senior staff club where I registered as a member, although I knew Mama would have been incensed had she known that I was allowing myself to spend free time with men that were not relatives. My involvement took me back to my American days, but also created a duplicity in my life: one at home, in Mama's environment; the other at the university with a pervasive Western attitude.

That I was a woman did not bother my colleagues. Rather than seeing my womanhood as an impediment, they saw it as an asset, a unique perspective in a male-dominated culture. I was not expected to produce less or more than anyone else; I was treated as an equal in an academic environment. I turned into a celebrity of sorts and an expert on women's issues. During my tenure at the university, I became the most identifiable voice in the Nigerian media on the plight of women in the Nigeria media, a topic about which I wrote numerous articles and presented papers at conferences. Less than a few months after I began my job, working as a journalist no longer interested me. I truly felt more fulfilled as a teacher of journalism, molding future journalists. I felt I was touching lives directly, not just at a distance through the printed word.

The traditional pre-marriage ceremonies started in earnest in

December 1980, when Charles came home from Bauchi, where he was doing the mandatory national service as the medical director of a college health center. Despite the long-standing relationship between families, the marriage contract had to be undertaken as if we were complete strangers. The first step occurred a few days before Christmas, when my father-in-law sent a messenger to inform Mama that his family was sending an emissary to the Edoga house in Aku on an agreed date and time. Mama was not even required to be at that first meeting because she was a woman.

On the agreed day, Charles, along with his father, cousins, and uncles, a total of twelve men, arrived at our family house with a jar of palm wine, three cartons of beer, two crates of soft drinks, and one carton of stout. They were received by my male relatives, including my cousin Eddie, who had just been married to Charles' sister, Priscilla. The first meeting took place in the parlor of our family home, the same room in which Mama had lived her first year following my father's death. As is the tradition, my relatives offered them cola-nuts and drinking water, which they prayed over before accepting. Then my future father-in-law detailed why they had come.

"We're here to initiate a process which, God willing, will unite our two families even more than we are now bound. Last year, at this time, you came to us with a request similar to the one I now make (Eddie seeking Priscilla). We see something in your household that we want to possess, and it's our hope that you're amenable to the beginning of discussions on the subject." He spoke generally, as is the tradition in a marriage negotiation. Being concrete before he was requested to be would have been presumptuous of him.

"We don't know what you're referring to. What is it that we have that you want?" my uncle Aloy, our family spokesperson, asked, feigning ignorance of our open secret.

"If you insist, we're interested in your daughter, Dympna."

"Dympna? Our brilliant daughter? Our American girl? What makes you think you can afford her?" My uncle's questions were calculated to set the tone for the negotiations for the bride price. He wanted to inform them, without specifically stating it, that I would not come cheap, that they had to be willing to pay the steep price that was befitting of my status.

"We'd be crazy to claim that we can afford your daughter, but we were hoping that because of our long-term relationship, and in view of the fact that we virtually gave you our own daughter just last year, that you give us terms we can meet," my father-in-law stated.

"Well, we'll ask the young lady in question if she's interested in coming to your family. Then we'll send a message to you." My family accepted only the palm wine, the one perishable drink they brought. They insisted that my future in-laws return with the rest of the drinks after I consented to their continuing the discussion.

Mama and I were required to be at the second meeting, held again at Aku. Charles had returned to his post, but his father came with even more relatives and bearing more gifts. Mama and I waited in another room until we were called. My entry had been rehearsed a number of times. I was dressed simply in a straight-cut skirt and a silk T-shirt, and when I entered, I curtsied fully, first facing the side I was told my family would be seated on, and then a second time for my intended's side. I could hear the men chuckling; they made no attempt to hide their comments from me.

"You didn't tell us she's a full-grown woman. Isn't she too old for our son?" someone from Charles' side uttered.

From my side, I distinctly heard one of my cousins lavish praises on me. "Look, what beauty and grace. No one can afford her."

I was not offered a seat, so I stood in the open door, completely framed by it. Uncle Aloy cleared his throat, an indication to all present that he was about to begin the ceremonies.

"Dympna, the first question is for you because these people here say that they're interested in acquiring you for their son. We want to hear from your own lips whether or not you agree to become one of them. Do you authorize us to accept the drinks they bring for your hand?"

I acted as I had been coached to respond. I threw my hands to my face in faked embarrassment and a struggle for composure. Mama, my coach, stood directly behind the door that framed me, so no one else saw her. When she felt my pause was becoming too long, she signaled by a tug and mouthed, "Oya (It's time)."

"Yes, you should accept what they bring," I spoke in the most feminine voice I could muster and then curtsied before retreating from the room.

A loud cheer broke out, "Okwego! Okwego! (She's agreed! She's agreed!)" A two-hour celebration ensued. Both Mama and I were recruited to serve drinks and food to the men. Occasional songs broke out of the crowd, until my uncle, once again, cleared his throat, calling everyone's attention to the issue at hand. Having agreed to pursue their mutual interest, the next major obstacle was settling on a bride price that was mutually satisfactory. A date was set for the beginning of the negotiations, to allow my family to determine what was a fair value on my head, considering my unusual circumstances. My particular case was complex and very tricky, and the problems that could threaten the negotiations seemed, at the time, almost insurmountable.

A Woman's Worth

Everyone in my family, including John, knew that the most serious obstacle to my eventual marriage would be the inability of my prospective husband to pay my family what I was worth. As early as my second year in America when I had begun to master preparing American meals, John had predicted it. At the time, I thought he was joking when, after tasting whatever dish I'd cooked, he said "You realize your bride price has just gone up." By my fourth year in America, his statement had changed to, "You know, no man can afford you now; you may never get married."

As funny as it sounded, John spoke the absolute truth, because when it came down to the bottom line, neither the Ugwu-Ojus nor anyone, for that matter, could have paid my family what I was truly worth. The Edogas had two options in the Ibo way of doing things: they could insist on my actual worth and consequently render me unmarriageable; or they could discount a portion of my real price, put me on sale in a way, and marry me off. It was a risk either way, for whichever path they chose was sure to have long-term repercussions.

Simply put, a woman's *isi-afia* (literally, selling price—the same term used for items like oranges and yams in the market) is repayment to her family for their tangible and intangible investment in her through her childhood and young adulthood. It's a quid-pro-quo arrangement whereby the man gets the woman in exchange for a dowry. It is based on the concept that no one gets anything worthy for nothing and that a person gets what he pays for. Paying a bride price on a woman is not the same as buying the woman. Ibos distinguish the two different types of transactions. While a woman whose price has been paid belongs to her husband's family, she's not owned, as one would own a goat, for she or her family can refund the bride price and free her at any time.

Traditionally, a bride price is a system of assigning worth to a marrying woman. It allows both families to determine, in tangible terms, the value of the bride. This worth is determined by the woman's education (a recent phenomenon, for it was not until the sixties that Ibos began to enroll their daughters in school in large numbers), her job prospects and earning potential, any other benefit she brings to the marriage, and her fertility.

A woman in her thirties or late twenties is not likely to earn as high a price as a younger maiden, because it is believed that the older woman's fertility is already diminished and that her husband's family is taking a chance on her. Such a woman's family is usually so happy that their daughter is getting a chance at marriage that they do not haggle over the bride price. They're likely to accept whatever the groom's family offers. However, if the woman in her thirties is well educated and has good job prospects and high earning potential, her price will certainly be higher than that of a twenty-something woman with minimal education, who would be dependent on her husband for the rest of her life. Similarly, a child bride's price is low because her family has not invested in her in a substantial way.

A woman's worth is also affected by outside factors, such as how much was paid on the heads of other women of comparable education, age, and exposure. If, for instance, Mary, a twenty-three-year-old college graduate, earned $2,000 on her head in 1990, Janet, twenty-four and college educated, should earn at least that much in 1993. Janet's family would be shamed if they accepted less, because even her new in-laws would begin to wonder if they were acquiring damaged goods. It is generally accepted that a girl who's earned a university degree is worth more than one with only a high-school diploma, even if the latter has had numerous years of work experience.

Ibos insist on paying bride prices even in cases where the bride's family wishes to waive it. They insist because it protects both the bride and groom. As has been explained to me many times, a woman's bride price, especially if it's high, protects her from abuse in her marriage. A man who pays an exorbitant amount on a woman is less likely to lift his hand to strike her or to deny her the material things she needs. The popular thinking is, why would he damage an object for which he has paid so much? Why would anyone buy an expensive car, like a Mercedes Benz, only to deliberately shatter the windshield? On the contrary, the man will pamper his car, maintaining the service requirements, washing and polishing it so that it retains its value. He's more likely to neglect and even abuse the car if it cost him little or nothing, like a Volkswagen Bug. A man who abuses his wife is assumed to have paid a small *isi-afia*. Neighbors are likely to comment, "He wouldn't be doing this if she had cost him plenty. He would think twice about hitting her if he paid a hefty sum on her head." If a man abuses a wife that he paid an exorbitant amount on, he's called a fool, a bad businessman. "He's pouring money down the pit latrine."

The bride price protects the man even more than it protects the woman. Without a bride price, a man has no claim to his wife or even the children she bears him. She can leave their union, even if they're married under Western law. Her husband will be held to the Ibo standard and asked, "How can you expect to reap where you did not sow?"

There are other factors to consider when setting a bride price. For instance, if the girl is the first of many sisters in a family, it is crucial that a high price be paid on her head, since her sisters' worth is inadvertently determined by hers. Conversely, families are more likely not to insist on a high price for the last girl in a family, because by the time her value is negotiated, her family has already established its worth through the marriage of the older girls. It's a business decision: a shop owner who puts new merchandise on sale cannot then hope to raise the prices on the dregs after the choice objects are gone. To many women, one's bride price is evidence that your husband desires you so badly that he's willing to pay whatever your family demands to own you, no matter how high. It's confirmation that he would spare nothing for you, would jump through hoops to possess you. At gatherings, a woman who earned a high price is more likely to divulge how much she was worth to her husband than one who was a bargain.

In fact, an Ibo marriage is not valid until the man has paid a price on his bride's head. Occasionally, Ibos residing abroad may feel reluctant to make the journey to Nigeria to perform the traditional rites because of cost or time. But even if they decide to get married under church or civil rules, their families back home will not acknowledge the marriage until some money has been given to the girl's family. If the man's relatives are wise, they insist on performing some ceremonies, on leaving some money down, with the balance deferred until the man can return. Otherwise, the groom is viewed as the woman's lover, not her husband, and she could at any point in the marriage take her children and leave him. Traditionally, he has no claim to the woman or the children born before he pays the woman's *isi-afia*.

Parents warn every son to do "first things first" and pay the bride price on his intended's head before becoming amorous with her. They caution him against wasting his seed or creating unnecessary complications. If a prospective bride is already pregnant and that fact is known, her family may insist that the groom pay twice as much as he would have for the mother alone, for he's getting two people. In some

rare instances, a line would be inserted in the marriage contract stip-
ulating that any child born in less than nine months of the acceptance
of bride price would belong to the girl's family. That's usually a clue to
the groom's family that their prospective in-laws are aware that their
daughter is pregnant and that they should raise the stakes if they value
her and the child she carries.

Every institution, including the church, sanctions payment of the
bride price because of its stabilizing influence on the family. It is
believed that without it, marriages would be taken too lightly; men
would mistreat and discard their wives like used underwear, for they
could easily acquire new wives. In addition, a girl's parents would not
be rewarded or repaid for their investment in their daughter. Doing
away with the bride price could have reverberating repercussions, for
who knows how it would affect the relationship between parents and
their daughters, especially how much they invest in her education and
well being? Would they really, without the promise of a repayment at
the end, give her as much? Send her to school? View her as valuable?

I've never viewed bride prices negatively. In fact, I believe that it is
a worthy practice that should continue for as long as it meets the
intended purpose. I don't believe it is similar to slavery or trading in
humans, for it is done within the context of marriage. The woman and
her family are aware that her bride price can be refunded at any time
if she feels herself mistreated or undervalued.

Everyone in our town followed my traditional marriage proceedings with unprecedented interest. Most wagered bets on how much
value my family would place on my head and how far my in-laws
would be willing to go to secure my hand. In March 1981, when my
price was being haggled, I was a twenty-four-year-old college professor with the potential of earning a significant income in my produc-
tive years. I held a bachelor's degree from Briarcliff College, an ex-
clusive all-girls college which had cost my brother more than $8,000
a year in tuition alone, and a master's degree from the Newhouse
School of Public Communications at Syracuse University, with fees
and tuition totaling more than $15,000, plus other unqualified
know-how that I had acquired during my years in America. I was also
educated in convent schools through high school and was known to
have been of above average intelligence. I could cook both Ibo and
western foods; I felt as at home in the Western world as I did in a traditional Ibo environment. My name was widely recognizable, and
while that could become an impediment, it could also become an

immense asset to Charles, who was then planning to go into private practice. Furthermore, my most important asset was my name, my parentage, something that my in-laws couldn't find anywhere else. I would bring all of those tangibles and intangibles into a marriage, and they would all belong to Charles.

It was obvious that my bride price would be higher than had been paid on any other girl. Unfortunately, my family had no precedents to look to for guidelines. They agonized over how to come up with the right amount, without seeming either greedy or conciliatory. No matter what, they did not want to undervalue me. I was summoned to several meetings that were hurriedly arranged by my cousins and uncles and subjected to inquiries into the details of the cost of my American education and the *naira* equivalent of it. Mama wrote John asking how much should be charged for me, since every way they looked at it, their lowest price was at least twice as high as had ever been asked for any individual in our town's history.

John's reply came just in time, with only two days left before the scheduled *isi-afia* negotiations. John managed to save the situation, because our family had decided to set my price at 20,000 *naira*, then the equivalent of 30,000 American dollars. Even in the best of circumstances, Charles' beginning monthly salary as a surgical resident was not expected to exceed five hundred *naira*, which meant that he would have two options. His family could decide, and no one would have blamed them, to walk out of the negotiations and never return to the table. The alternative would be that they would offer whatever they could at the time and then work out an agreeable installment payment schedule over a reasonable period.

But John's letter made all that unnecessary and simplified the situation. As my titular father, John's words superseded all others, and the two families had to abide by his wishes. If John had demanded, for instance, that I not marry Charles, we would have done exactly as he wished, for even if I weren't willing to obey John's word, no one else in my family would have supported me. John's letter detailed how much I was worth. He enumerated not only the cost of my education, but the extra courses that I took: the swimming lessons, the driving school, gourmet cooking classes, the time and energy that was invested by both him and Delia in my life. He described the kind of life I led in America, the places I had been, the things I had seen which, in his opinion, rendered me "too costly to be afforded by any man." John then stressed that he did not want my prospective husband to pay a penny on my head. "Setting a monetary value would demean and diminish Dympna, for we could never hope to get what she's truly worth." He argued that "The noble thing to do would be to offer Dympna to her future husband in exchange for nothing. We would make a clear statement that my sister is too classy to be haggled over like a cheap piece of material."

"Think of it this way," John continued, trying to soothe the concerns of those in our family who would argue that his approach was wasteful and that all the money spent on me was going to naught. "If we subject our sister's future husband to a price he obviously can't afford, we would be asking for trouble. We would be condemning Dympna and her husband, plus whatever children she bears, to a poverty-ridden existence. They'll be so consumed with paying the debt that they'll have nothing left on which to live. I paid for her college education, but I look at that as investing in my sister to make her the best person she could possibly be, not as a means of increasing how much we can get from her husband."

I first read the letter to Mama, who seemed relieved by its contents. She invited other members of the family to listen to it, but as I read to the larger audience, several of them interrupted at numerous points, and I could sense their anger rising.

"Absolute nonsense! How ridiculous!" declared cousin Thaddeus.

"John has lost his mind," said cousin Eddie.

"He has forgotten what our culture is all about," screamed another cousin.

"How can he ask that we give away Dympna, our most prized possession, for nothing? All the money invested in her goes for nothing?" Not one single voice was raised in support of John's position; in fact, every voice argued why a hefty bride price should be set for me.

And then a very unusual thing happened: Mama interrupted the proceedings. As a woman, she had no part in setting my worth, even though she had nursed, nurtured, and provided for me until I was eighteen. A woman, even one who's earned the respect she commanded, was simply a woman. But Mama said that she felt things were getting out of hand and that she wanted to bring some order back to the meeting.

"I beg you, my husbands and children, to please find it in your hearts to honor John's wishes. He's been her father and he made her whatever she is today. Please don't go against his will in this matter," Mama implored the menfolk. Then she pulled her ace out of the hole and offered them an interpretation that they hadn't considered. She brought up an important issue in the distribution of the bride-price proceeds. It is usually split into two portions. The bulk of it, usually more than eighty percent, goes to the bride's father or surrogate. In my case, John would have received the lion's share. The rest of the money is divided equally to the *umunna* (the male kinfolk on her father's side). Mama asked them to separate the two shares, to set the price for the portion that went to my *umunna* and to waive the other part as John had requested. This suggestion generated more argument, but by the end of the meeting, my male relatives arrived at a consensus on how much the *umunna* should demand for themselves.

On the appointed date, our family spokesman stunned the large contingent from Charles' village with the news that the bride's older brother had ordered that he did not want any money paid for his sister. The news was greeted by Charles' delegation with as little enthusiasm as it was by mine.

"What? And have you hold this over our heads indefinitely? Absolutely not," announced a spokesperson for the in-laws.

"We insist on paying something. Or do you think we're so poor we can't afford your daughter?" another offered.

"Do you think we're ignorant of the tradition? We think you're trying to set us up, so our son has no control over your daughter and whatever offspring she has. We dealt fairly with you when we gave you our own daughter last year," one more added.

Uncle Aloy, Papa's only living brother and the spokesperson for my family, stood before the in-laws and explained the details of John's letter. He told them that they had to pay the *umunna* portion, for which they later began negotiations. I believe that John's position, and Mama's quick thinking, eased all our minds somewhat and the anticipated protracted haggling never took place. The *umunna* settled on the hefty sum of eight hundred *naira* (then $1,200), the highest sum paid to any set of bride's relatives anywhere. Even though the stakes were significantly lower, the two sides bantered back and forth, conferencing in between until they reached the agreed amount. Everyone, including me, was happy.

In a ritual, the leader of the in-laws counted the money out loud, one twenty *naira* note at a time, onto the dirt ground of the front yard. My relatives had to repeat the process, verifying that they had received the agreed-upon amount. Each of my male kinfolk, most of whom I did not know, became entitled on the basis of blood alone to a portion of that money. Right after the distant relatives departed, Charles' father, who had said very little during the proceedings, asked to speak to Mama and cousin Eddie. He pressed 1,000 *naira* ($1,500), rolled in a tight bundle, into Mama's hands. "Please don't refuse this. We won't have it any other way," he said, closing Mama's hand over the money. He explained that he was overwhelmed by our family's generosity, for he too realized that no amount of money would have been sufficient. Mama accepted the money graciously; I believe she understood what it symbolized to him. He would not have let it go as decided by the *umunna*; he could not allow his first son's wife to come into his household under the terms dictated by her own family. The money he gave to Mama, albeit a fraction of what would have been required of them, ensured that my fate was sealed, that I would be totally theirs without condition, for he knew that I could use the gross underpayment as a way out of the marriage.

A few weeks later came *nmanya Nne* (the bride's mother's wine), a recognition of the role the mother of the bride has played in her daughter's life. In cases where the bride's biological mother is dead or not resident in her father's home, a surrogate is designated, usually an aunt or another female who's served as a role model for the bride. It's usually an all-female affair. In my case, as were all the rites in my traditional marriage, the occasion was at Aku in the family compound. All the married females from Aku, both Mama's and my father's village, arrived resplendent in their most colorful print wrappers, blouses, and scarves. It was an array of bright blues, purples, reds, and yellows. They all arrived at the appointed time of four o'clock in the afternoon, and sat outside in the area of the front yard shaded by the orange trees. Mama and others had spent all morning scrubbing and polishing the wood furniture and sweeping the yards. Pots of *egusi* and *ogbono* soup simmered on the makeshift wood stoves outside of the cramped kitchen and their aroma added to the celebratory mood.

The women arrived in small groups, and each group's entry was proclaimed by their voices, raised in songs of praise of my father. "It is as it should be. Our great son's name will be heard at every corner of this town. His youngest daughter is going to the best family in this town." After the sumptuous meal and drinks, the women formed a circle in the middle of the seats and danced to drum and *ichaka* sounds. Their wedding songs could be heard all the way to the next village: "Our daughter is fulfilled at last; she's found happiness." The songs lasted till darkness forced them to leave for their homes. As each woman left, she was given a package of food, containing uncooked yam and rice and raw meat. The food is symbolic of a woman's transition from spinsterhood to married life; her essence has changed and she's supposed to be more focused, more domestic, as well as more particular about what foods she serves her husband.

We returned to Nsukka to ready for the grandest of the celebrations, the *igba nmanya* ceremony, the actual transfer of a woman's ownership from her birth family to her husband's.

You Belong to Us

My life as an Edoga ended on Saturday, March 28, 1981. I continued to use my maiden name and live in my mother's house until our church wedding on the following December 5. Technically, I was stretching the rules, for I had become Charles' wife by Ibo laws and tradition.

My *igba nmanya* ceremony (literally, the acceptance of drinks by the bride's family) was, understandably, a mixture of both Ibo and Western celebrations. Christianity has transformed the *igba nmanya* from the marriage ceremony to the engagement; the actual wedding takes place in the church. But to this day, the girl's rights are transferred to the husband's family whether the engagement is long or short. Following the *igba nmanya*, her activities, associations, and movements, including visits to her own father's compound, are dictated by her in-laws. If she becomes ill while visiting her parents' home, for instance, her own mother will not seek help for her without first contacting her husband's family. Her successes and failures belong to her new family, not her original one. From that day on, the bride can no longer visit her home without the express permission of her husband. If she does, she's deemed to have run away and will not be returned without elaborate ceremonies.

That day is the end of a girl's innocence as well. Even if she's still a child, her entire existence will be directed at fulfilling her marriage functions: procreation, and in the process, satisfying her husband. Even a child bride whose *igba nmanya* occurs early and who takes up residence in her in-laws' household in her childhood, is closely scrutinized for signs of her budding womanhood. The bride's young body is prodded, poked, and checked on a regular basis; every sign is analyzed, and husbands as well as mothers-in-law have been known to express disappointment that their investment isn't yielding any profits yet. The girl is told that the man's family did not pay a high price on her head only to wait for her indefinitely. In circumstances where her husband's family is anxious about offspring, the girl, although everyone recognizes she's too young, is forced into sexual activity with her husband, for it's also widely believed that early sexual activity speeds up a woman's development. Sometimes, families resort to native doctors to prescribe remedies or potions to broaden a young girl's hips or cause her breasts to sprout.

Even in the best of circumstances, the *igba nmanya* is usually a bittersweet ritual for the bride: she is attaining her lifelong dream of marriage, but at the same time is leaving behind everything familiar and moving to another village where, more likely than not, she'll be less valued. Her smiling painted face is always replaced by a teary smudged one as she's led out of her father's compound for the last time.

Days before my own *igba nmanya* event, my in-laws brought a truckload of food to our home. It is widely recognized that, although the guests will actually be coming to the bride's home, they are invited by the groom's family. It is therefore the groom's responsibility to feed everyone present. I remember the disappointment expressed by some of my aunts after the food was off-loaded, although to me it seemed like a mountain of food, certainly more than could be consumed by a village of people.

"Don't they know who they're marrying? How can they bring these measley yams and sickly looking goats as if our daughter is a nobody?"

"We have to say something to them now or they'll forever take us for granted."

Mama, composed as ever, scolded the aunts in the kind of tone she usually reserved for children. "I will not have any of you speaking ill of our in-laws, especially the Ugwu-Ojus. If the food is inadequate, I'll make it up. The guests will be coming for us, for our daughter, not for them."

"But that's not the tradition," someone yelled.

"It does not matter to me. I'll not ruin a lifelong relationship over food." That was the extent of the discussion, and the next day when my parents-in-law stopped over on their way home from morning mass, Mama and my aunts were tripping over themselves in praise of their generosity. "You brought enough food to feed a village for ten days!"

Every relative returned home to Aku for the ceremony. Mama got there two days prior to the occasion to make the preparations. I, on the other hand, stayed in Nsukka until the morning of the 28th. I wasn't needed for the preliminaries, and Charles wouldn't even be present for the ceremony. His father would speak for him.

I arrived at Aku around noon with three busloads of professors, students, and friends. Our buses had to stop at least half a mile away from our family compound, because the crowd spilled way beyond the canopies and chairs arranged in the expansive front yard. People were already making places for themselves past the orange trees that marked the end of our property in the neighbors' front yards. The sounds of traditional drums, as well as Western music favored by the younger crowd, could be heard blocks away. As my guests and I approached and were sighted, a loud cheer arose. "She's here! She's here!" The crowd surged toward me, and I was dragged half a block before I could regain my balance and composure. People clamored to touch me as they would a celebrity, shouting as they did. "She's finally moving in the right direction." "She's now truly fulfilled!"

The day was a whirlwind of activity. Two dance troupes, representing my hamlet and Charles', competed to outdo each other's dance steps. Guests "sprayed" (pasted) *naira* notes on the faces of the sweaty dancers, a sign of appreciation of the art. During the intermissions, my young students, dressed mostly in Western attire, swayed to Diana Ross's music blasting from rented commercial-size loudspeakers.

In a preliminary ritual, I was led by a group of women to the center of the yard. We shuffled to an African beat. Hundreds of men and women lined up to get a turn at embracing and "spraying" me with large notes, which one of my friends collected in a basket.

At the designated time, right after sundown, I was again returned to the center of the ring and handed a glass of palm wine. I had rehearsed the scene hundreds of times and knew what was expected of me. This was the high point of the ceremony and the crowd jockeyed for position, some standing on chairs to see. I stood still, looking at no one in particular, but concentrating on the task I was about to perform.

When the crowd quieted down, I walked slowly toward my in-laws. I stopped in front of my father-in-law. I curtsied, then knelt down in front of him on the mud floor. The crowd watched our every move, and although no one expected anything unusual to happen, one could hear a pin drop. My head still bowed in respect, I stretched out the glass to him. He accepted the drink, then handed it to someone in his entourage before rising and pulling me up on my feet.

The crowd exploded with excitement. "It's done! It's done!" "Thank goodness it's done!" That act of subservience marked the end of the ceremonies. I had, before the witnesses, accepted my lowly place as a woman.

During rehearsals, I had resisted that part of the ceremony, but Mama and others insisted. "You're not the first woman who's done it, and you won't be the last," Mama told me.

"But how many of those other women have my background? How can I demean myself in front of everyone?"

"A woman is a woman, no matter your background. Kneeling before your in-laws will not be the end of the world. Besides, they'll be insulted if you don't."

Once again, I ceded, and performed just as gracefully as any bride before me. No one could have guessed I had reservations about it. But right after I knelt down, I felt my head swelling with tears. I fought bravely to suppress them, but they overtook me, and flowed unchallenged down my face. I don't believe many people noticed, since it had darkened a bit. And even if someone had, it would have been dismissed as a new bride's jitters.

On the journey from my family's compound to Charles', I insisted on riding in one of the university buses, instead of with my father-in-law. I continued to cry during the ride to Charles' hamlet. I made a great effort to hide my tears, more for the benefit of my colleagues and friends who rode in the bus than for me. I was not sure how they would interpret my breakdown, and I didn't want my tear-stricken face to be what they remembered of that day. I told myself it was just an attack of nerves, and that the adrenaline was wearing thin. It was not as if I didn't know what I was getting into. I had been at Charles' parents' compound before and I knew his family almost as well as I knew mine. Yet, when the time came for me to become one of them, I was overcome by fear.

It was completely dark when we pulled up to their fenced home, where hundreds of others had gathered to view their new wife. We were greeted with music and cheers as we drove through the iron gates. My parents-in-law's home in Aku was one of two or three houses that had electricity. The entire fenced compound with its many buildings was lit by multi-colored blinking bulbs. The crowd that awaited me seemed just as large as the one I'd just said goodbye to, and I was expected to make the rounds, curtsying before the men and shaking hands with the women and even hugging some. Everyone felt the need to make a comment to me or about me. "She's just like her mother; may she bear many sons like her." "You're lucky our son found you worthy."

I kept silent, for I knew how to behave during a woman's *ije di* (marriage journey). She's watched more closely than a specimen under a microscope. She's scrutinized for her habits: how hurriedly she eats, how she sits. Does she bow low enough? Does she walk in a dignified manner? I've even heard that someone checks her up on her as she sleeps to determine if she snores or throws her legs about in an unbecoming manner. Any shortcoming could be considered grounds enough to send the girl home and terminate the marriage.

Young brides are cautioned not to do anything that could cause their in-laws to reject them. I was told to wake up earlier than anyone in the house and offer to sweep the compound and dust all the furniture in the house. I was told to start the fire in the wood stove and begin cooking breakfast before anyone else was awake. These were the chores of the youngest wife in the compound, and regardless of my background, I would be subjected to the same treatment. Fortunately, my in-laws thought better of me and vehemently opposed my participation in housework. Someone else laid out the water for my bath the next morning and cleaned up after me while my father-in-law rebuffed the villagers who arrived to ascertain whether I was performing my duties in the household.

Later that day, I returned to my own compound with a truckload of presents. It is customary for a large crowd of women to gather to view the gifts, which included a trunk of Georges and print material, some already cut and sewn into blouses and wrappers. Colorful scarves were carefully selected to match the outfits. Wrapped in cotton wool in a little box within the trunk was a set of gold trinkets, a necklace, earrings, and bracelets. The one-hundred-kilogram bag of rice, beans, and twenty tubers of yam, plus the unslaughtered goat and other already dried meats and fish were shared among all the women gathered. If we had followed the tradition strictly, I would have returned to my in-laws that day, but because we had previously agreed that I stay with Mama until the church wedding, I journeyed back to Nsukka late that Sunday and was back at work on Monday.

Life returned to normal, but I continued to battle myself. I allowed myself to be led through the traditional ceremonies and I watched, helplessly, as everyone marched toward my wedding day. I was informed the date had been set for August, and I went along. But then my brother John wrote that the earliest he and his family could make the trip was in December. The planners grudgingly yielded and continued in their elaborate plans.

Arranged Marriages

My American friends shudder when I tell them that my marriage was arranged. They question how I could have gone along with such a primitive custom, especially in light of my modern American education. Of course, I balked at the idea when Mama was pressuring me to accept Charles as my husband, but now that we've been married for nearly fourteen years, I am convinced it is the only way to ensure that a marriage is based on more substantive issues than lust or fleeting commonalities.

Arranged marriages continue to be preferred even today among Ibos both in and out of Nigeria. It is an honored tradition, recognized as a reliable way of securing a life partner, and this holds true for even the most enlightened Ibo men and women.

It is a rare occurrence for an Ibo girl, even living in the U.S. in the 1990s, to choose her own husband or initiate her own marriage ceremonies. She relies on recommendations from others for the reason that Ibo marriages are more for the families than for the young people involved. The hope is that if the man's family is good, then he's good stock. The man knows that if he mistreats her, his family's name is put to shame. It is that kind of thinking that has bound Ibo marriages for generations.

One of my closest friends, a physician, had never set eyes on her husband until after her traditional marriage ceremonies. He lived in the U.S. while she completed her medical education in Nigeria. When his family approached her, Josephine and her family agreed, based purely on trust that he was what his family represented. All she knew of him was from snapshots she'd seen and letters he'd written.

She left Nigeria to join him in America, not sure of what she'd find, yet unwavering in her determination to like him, to live with him, and to build a strong marriage.

Josephine says that if her betrothed had turned out to be grotesquely deformed, it would not have made a difference to her. She was already his wife and had been so for months before she met him. Like most Ibo women, she'd been told since she was a child that a husband is like a wrapped package. A bride never knows what she'll discover inside until she unwraps it.

In other words, a woman never knows a man's true nature until she's begun to live with him. Women who insist on marrying someone they already know are asked, "So what if you find he has a major fault three months into the marriage? Can anyone really vouch for any man? What if he puts on an act while he's courting you and only lets his true nature show much later, after he's already your husband?"

I've met hundreds of Ibo women living in the United States who married their husbands without even the benefit of photographs. More and more, Ibo men who live in America send money home to their parents to select wives and perform the traditional ceremonies on their heads. These girls join their husbands whenever they obtain the necessary traveling papers.

With the traditional marriage ceremonies completed in March, there were no more obstacles on my way to marital bliss. Charles completed his national service in July 1981 and started a surgical residency at the University of Nigeria Teaching Hospital in Enugu. He lived in Eddie and Priscilla's home, and we spent most weekends together.

I traveled to the United States that summer to visit with John's family and to buy my wedding dress. I remember those long and humid stretches when all Delia and I could do was lie on lawn chairs and watch the children play in the pool, as I explained how I'd practically come to terms with myself about my marriage. Though I was sorely tempted to pretend that I'd never left the United States and was still living my own life, I by then had accepted that I'd made my bed, and I was resolved to sleep in it. Delia and I dissected my life from every possible angle. She'd been the mother and sister that I'd needed, and now I tried to help her understand.

"But why did you do this?" she asked repeatedly of my marriage decision. "Why did you subject yourself to all this?"

"Mama would have died if I didn't," I said.

"What about you? What about what you wanted? Didn't that matter?"

"I couldn't let Mama down, not after all the sacrifices she made for all of us. I felt I owed her that much." I told her the truth as I saw it: That I did have warm feelings for Charles regardless, but that Mama was the primary reason why I followed through with that marriage. I told her that I consoled myself with the belief that Mama or no Mama, Charles and I would have found each other somehow.

"Can you be happy in this marriage, Dympna?"

I nodded yes; I was determined to be as successful in the marriage as I was in my career, and I had no doubt that it would turn out that way. I explained to Delia what happiness meant to me at that crucial point in my life. I told her that it would have little to do with a fiery passion of a physical nature. "I like Charles a great deal, and together we can have a good life." Delia shrugged and shook her head a lot during our conversations; she could not understand, no matter how many times I explained it. As far as she was concerned, I was ruining my life, "throwing a perfectly good future away," all to please my mother.

Meanwhile, however, we ransacked all the bridal shops, looking for the perfect wedding dress. I wanted something dramatic, a cord lace, see-through bodice, with an off-the-shoulders neckline, puffed sleeves that ended at the elbow, a tight-fitting drop waist, and a flowing train—a dress that, except for its length and color, could be worn to a nightclub, an outfit that everyone who attended the wedding would surely remember. My sister-in-law argued for a chiffon dress with an umpire bust, a high neckline, long sleeves with lace-trimmed cuffs—a pristine, almost virginal look. Used to deferring to others, I buckled and we purchased the chiffon gown, along with a simple lace-trimmed veil that did not take attention from the subtle elegance of the dress. We bought an eighteen-inch fake pearl strand and matching earrings. (On the day of my wedding, I wore my sister-in-law's real pearls, a birthday gift from my brother that year. As she slipped it around my neck, she whispered, "Listen, girl, this thing cost your brother a fortune; make sure you do not lose it.")

In September, I returned to Nigeria and my job and to make final wedding plans. Though I thought I knew everything there was to know about Ibo marriages, I was wrong. I had my baptism by fire as we ironed out the details of the wedding. Every decision I made concerning the ceremony first had to be approved by my parents-in-law. I was frustrated and flabbergasted by Charles' attitude as he played the dutiful, helpless son who had to seek his parents' approval for every minor decision.

"But Charles, why should they care who I select as a bridesmaid?" I cried in anger after I was ordered to strike the name of a cousin off the list.

"I'm their first son. This is the biggest event in their lives. Can't you just go along?" he retorted.

"But I'm the one who will be surrounded by all these bridesmaids, not them. It should be who I want, not they." But it wasn't who I wanted. I learned the hard way that big marriages like Charles' and mine were used to pay back political favors, form alliances, and to build partnerships. The list of their preferred bridesmaids included people I didn't know, but whose qualifications were their father's business or political affiliations.

"Ngozi's father is likely to be the next commissioner appointed in our state; he'll remember that we honored his daughter," my mother-in-law explained about yet another must-be-on-the-list attendant.

What little authority I had continued to ebb as my list of attendants turn into a collection of the daughters of a Who's Who in Nigeria's politics and business. But one thing I insisted on was that all my nieces and nephews who were old enough to be part of the wedding be included in the bridal train. My then eleven-year-old niece, Sherifa, John's oldest child and Mama's first grandchild, was my maid-of-honor in spite of protests about her age. It was one of the few times in my wedding that I firmly stood my ground.

The choice of key functionaries—the chairman, the esteemed members of the community who were deemed influential enough to be seated at the high table, the person who proposed the toast of the bride and groom, our sponsors—prompted agonizingly prolonged debates about who was most worthy or would prove to be the most minimal liability to the families. In one specific instance, we butted heads; I openly challenged my in-laws' quick dismissal of a couple I wanted to stand in as our sponsors. My mother-in-law started shaking her head the minute I spoke the name of the couple, who were both from Aku and had helped me a great deal when I was readying to leave for the United States.

"We don't want such persons involved in this wedding," she interrupted.

"They have been very supportive of me, and I want to use this opportunity to show my gratitude," I explained.

"There'll be plenty of opportunity to honor them. It doesn't have to be this time," my father-in-law added. "Why not? Why can't they do it?" My frustration began to show.

"Dympna, you're very young, and there are things about our people that you may not understand. Trust us when we tell you that another couple would serve you better, not only at the wedding but for years to come," my father-in-law insisted.

I nodded, mouthing the words, "I understand." But I didn't.

My mother got more specific explanations about the unsuitability of the rejected couple. "The wife is believed to be too aggressive and bosses her husband around; she behaves like a man, and she's made a woman's wrapper out of her husband."

It was as clear as a bell. My in-laws did not want to seem to sanction the behavior of an aggressive woman by according her a position of respect at their first son's wedding. Other women would take it as a sign that unwomanly behavior pays off and might start imitating her, and what a havoc that could create in our little world. I was also quite convinced that the larger message was directed at me. I was supposed to read between the lines and understand that I had to play the submissive female part or be shunned like my woman friend. Tired of the bickering, I shrugged and left the rest of the planning in their hands.

It was not as if I didn't have enough worries of my own with coordinating the bridal outfits. Another thing I'd insisted on was paying for my outfits, including the expense of my trip to the United States. Breaking the tradition of letting the man pay for everything that's connected with the wedding, I bought the dresses for all six of the bridesmaids and the six flower girls, plus all their accessories, and the six page boys' suits and accessories. My mother and sisters argued against my generosity. "It's their responsibility to pay for everything connected."

"I know, but then I won't have a choice of what outfits are worn," I argued.

"You're making a big mistake. People will think you're so anxious for the marriage that you're willing to pay for it," Mama said.

I said nothing, but went ahead with my own plans. I channeled my energies into the wedding and making it the center of my life.

I also raised eyebrows about Mama's wedding outfit. Traditionally, Charles was supposed to present Mama with money to purchase the outfit she would wear at the wedding. I did not wait for him; instead, I commissioned a woman who traded in imported material to find the best lace anywhere for my mother. Mama's wedding clothes cost me an entire month's salary, but since it was my very first outfit to her, I wanted her to treasure it. The trader found an exquisite green lace from which a blouse was made for Mama; the rest was cut and prepared for the two wrappers. We bought a matching chiffon scarf, shoes, and handbag. Mama told me that she would wear the gold necklace with matching earrings and bracelet that my father had given her many years before I was born. "So he'll be with us on that day."

John, Delia, and the kids arrived four days before the wedding and their presence kicked off the festivities, which continued until they left a week after the wedding. Throngs of friends, family, and curiosity seekers packed the narrow drive to Mama's house and almost barricaded the gates to the six-apartment complex Mama had just completed in a lot adjacent to her house, where John's family would stay. I was afraid that the pit latrines and communal bath stalls would be too harsh for my American-born nieces and nephew. The apartment, which Mama had built for the sole purpose of renting to the university, would provide them a modicum of their American way of life. I borrowed university furniture—beds, living and dining room pieces, kitchen appliances like a refrigerator and a gas cooker. We even managed to stock the refrigerator with some American staples from Kingsway, a supermarket that catered to the expatriate community. I was determined to make their visit as pleasant as possible.

As is the case in all Ibo weddings, my family was supposed to provide me with all the necessities of my new life. Because of my long list of successes and my family background, a lot more than the basics were required. Mama made plans early and seemed determined to have my *idu uno* (marital goods) be the talk of town. She saved the bride price that my father-in-law had insisted on paying on my head and she called a meeting of all my relatives and presented them with a list of items she wanted included in my *idu-uno* package. The unprecedented lavish package included a bedroom set—bed, his and her dressers, bedside tables, and vanity; a living-room set complete with tables; a dining-room set with six tables, a color television set, a Sony VCR; a complete kitchen set—gas cooker, refrigerator, freezer, pots and pans, and the compulsory *ikwe* (a rounded wooden structure used in pounding yam and other condiments). With Mama's quiet urging, cousins, uncles, and aunts selected items from the list. Everything was bought and displayed in my mother's backyard days before the wedding. Friends trooped to our house, lured by the stories they heard of how Mama had spared no expense for her daughter. They were not disappointed by what they saw. In fact, they left with their mouths gaping in wonder and, I'm sure, some envy, for no one could hope to match or even come close to the extravagance of my *idu-uno* loot.

The day before the wedding, Nsukka was teeming with visitors, relatives, friends, long-lost acquaintances from all over; crowds milled in and around Mama's and my in-laws' houses. The entire backyard had been converted to a kitchen and women in Mama's church groups cooked in shifts for the masses of people. It was as if the carnival had come to town, and our usual snail's pace was slowed further by the immense crowd.

My sister-in-law Delia watched in awe. "It really is true what they write about Africans, their community spirit. Who would have thought that our little Dympna's wedding would cause a whole town to grind to a halt?" She seemed fascinated by everything that was happening and trailed my mother or sisters with her camera positioned to capture every little detail.

I was mechanical in my perfection, remembering every little detail, everybody's role and place as we attended to last-minute details. Charles stayed in Enugu until two days before the wedding. On the eve of my wedding, we rehearsed for the procession and then sat down to dinner in Mama's parlor. In the middle of the meal, I broke down and started to bawl like a child. It wasn't anything that anyone said; it was not preceded by anything in particular. I just started to cry and couldn't stop. At the time, I blamed it on exhaustion, for I had been going for weeks without a break, but now I know better. It finally caught up to me, as speaker after speaker (Ibos never pass up an opportunity to make a speech) preached the virtue of patience in a marriage. And all of it was directed at me.

That, and the tone of finality in the way my relatives bid me farewell, as if I was leaving for a distant planet and not likely to be seen or heard from again, set me off. I couldn't remember my sendoff to America being as serious as this, and the amazing thing was that I was only traveling, at the most, a block to Charles' father's house! Charles and I were to live in Enugu, a mere forty miles away. I would continue my job at the university, which meant that I would see my mother at least two to three times each week. But I was getting married in the Ibo sense, and that meant the end of my life as an Edoga and the severing, real or imagined, of all ties with my own family. I had to abide by my husband's wishes from then on and if he ordered that I never again visit my own mother, I wouldn't dare disobey him.

There, in front of the bridal party and other close relatives, the weight of that burden seemed too much for me to bear. I looked across to where Mama sat, and I saw that she was crying, but very quietly, as is her fashion. There was no denying the pain that she labored under, but she struggled to compose herself, probably so I wouldn't become even more upset.

If I could have gotten out of the marriage without bringing shame to all involved, in that moment of my breakdown, I would have. But as I was helped to my feet by John and Delia, I scanned faces of people I hadn't seen in years, all gathered for my wedding to Charles. How would they feel if I announced suddenly that I wouldn't be marrying Charles after all? Would my mother ever be able to hold up her head in town again? No. It was the kind of humiliation that I could not inflict on my family. It was the same reason that I had agreed to marry Charles in the first place.

So what changed that night? Nothing, other than the stark reality of my decision, my choice to play the good daughter rather than assert myself and insist on my independence—Ibo girl or not.

And as I leaned on Delia for support, I knew beyond a shadow of a doubt, as I had suspected all along, that I would not be treated any differently from any other Ibo wife. Our family ties and my education would not earn me any more respect or better status than a girl married straight out of elementary school. I would become Charles' wife, and that would become the extent of my identity from then on. I had chosen an Ibo marriage. And all the implications of it, the full force of it, hit me square in the tear ducts.

My brother John's fast thinking saved what could have been a disastrous situation. He quickly led me out of the packed room, announcing to the attendees, "It's normal. Bride's jitters." Delia followed, and they led me to their apartment, where John asked me if I wished the ceremonies called off. The seriousness in his voice shocked me, and at first I said nothing.

"Dympna, are you having any doubts about this marriage?" he repeated.

"Edozie, every bride carries on like this. It *is* normal," Delia explained, but her eyes revealed her concern.

"You know you don't have to go ahead with this if you have second thoughts," John added. My response was a fresh outburst of sobs, which shook my whole body. I made a futile attempt to tell John that I didn't want the wedding called off. From the corner of my eye, I saw John and Delia conferring furiously and then John was standing over me, holding a glass of water and two tablets of Valium. He coaxed the sedatives into me between sobs.

They sat with me in the bedroom while I continued to cry, until I slowly drifted into a restless sleep that lasted barely an hour. I awoke to music blasting from the several locations where bachelor's parties were being held for Charles. Lying there, feigning sleep, I decided that I knew what I was doing and that I would go through with it; there was no turning back.

When it quieted down and our small town slept, I sat up with my back resting on the wall, while I stared outside, watching the full moon through the louvers of the window. I pondered its mystery and wondered if Charles was going through the same torment that stole my sleep. I was still awake when the moon sunk and the sun gradually rose, its yellow harshness jarring me to the realities that dawned before my eyes. But I was ready.

Between sunrise and light, I knelt on the bare cement floor of the room in John's apartment, my knees smarting from the grains of sand trapped under them. Mine was a fervent prayer, in almost a fever pitch, and I prayed for happiness in the marriage. That was all—just plain simple happiness. I also sought God's protection for the thousands of people who'd be traveling to and from the wedding. It must have been a combination of the prayers, the residue of the previous night's drugs, and my total resignation that brought about my tranquility. My anxiety fled me, my questions and gnawing doubts deserted me, and all I was left with was calm.

No one who had witnessed my emotional outburst of the previous night would have recognized me the morning of my wedding. I wore my biggest smile as I made the rounds in Mama's house, greeting the hundreds of guests who had arrived early and soliciting their well wishes. Aunts and female cousins circled me in a shower of love. I lifted my arms when instructed and tilted my head to the right or left as commanded; for the first time in my life, I permitted myself to be fussed over. I did not need to lift a finger as I was readied for the most important day of my life.

Even Mama reminding me that I was but a woman could not dampen my spirits.

Then it was time to leave for church. What a spontaneous commotion when I stepped out of the front door! For a brief moment, I understood how Princess Diana must have felt. Hundreds were waiting anxiously to catch a glimpse of the bride before the long ride to the church. Hundreds of others lined the streets, waving frantically as the bridal cars, all white Mercedes Benzes (on loan from colleagues at the university), drove by. We arrived at the church to an even larger and more enthusiastic crowd.

To Love and to Hold

I was completely in control of my emotions when John marched me into the church. The pews were so crowded that guests already lined the side aisles. The congregation rose at the beginning of the entrance hymn. It must have been the sound of their rising, or the way everyone turned in my direction as if I were visiting royalty, but it was then that my composure started to slip. Tears formed in my eyes, but I blinked furiously, successfully ebbing the tide that would have ruined my painted face.

"Be strong, Dympna," I told myself, blanking out everyone and concentrating on the long walk, remembering to synchronize my steps with John's. Instead of "Here Comes the Bride" for the processional music, I'd selected "Jesu, Joy of Man's Desiring," a wonderful choice, it turned out. The few times I looked up and met people's glances, I saw no dry eyes. I didn't dare look at Mama when I approached the front pew where she stood, afraid that her tears might become my own.

John put my right hand in Charles and then lifted the veil that covered my face before he took his seat beside Mama. When the bishop, officiating at the ceremony, asked who was giving me away, my titular father, John, approached and gave his final seal of approval to the union. After reciting my lines, I started to feel giddy about the ceremony. And when the bishop pronounced us "man and wife," I felt a surge of ecstasy. It might just have been immense relief that it was over and I could go on with my life, but more likely the complex combination of my Ibo-ness, Christianity, and womanhood all kicked in at the same time, and I knew I was on my way to a truly fulfilling life. Whatever it was, I felt more pleasure than I had in many months.

At the conclusion of the ceremonies and the signing of documents, we marched out to a celebratory version of "Joy to the World," complete with trumpets, which rang throughout the cathedral and had people cheering and shuffling to the beat. I remember a moment of brightness and heat as we stepped out of the shaded cool church, and then the crowds of people were on me, with everyone insisting on hugging me. The pictures seemed to take hours; everyone wanted to be photographed with the bride and groom, some insisting on more than once.

What I remember of my wedding reception was the long line of guests who waited by the dais for an opportunity to speak. I didn't understand it completely then; I was incredulous that anyone would want to extend an already long affair just to repeat what many others had said already. Their speeches were the same old song and dance: "The success or failure of any marriage rests in the woman's hands." Many speakers couldn't resist adding that they hoped that they would be reinvited in nine months to celebrate an addition to the new family.

I fidgeted throughout, exhausted from lack of sleep and all the anticipation. But weeks later, when the videotape of our wedding became available, the motive was quite obvious. As news spread, the "speakers" thronged to our home, with their friends in tow, to view themselves on television. We replayed that tape hundreds of times and paused over and over to allow viewers ample opportunity to see themselves. Our wedding was the first, at least in Nsukka, to be videotaped, and as soon as the guests figured out what the video cameras were all about, everyone wanted to be featured in it. It was the topic of conversation for a long time.

Wedding guests followed us home to my in-laws' home as was still the tradition. About a block away, I climbed out of the car and a large group of women surrounded me, singing Ibo marriage songs while we gradually made our way to the house.

"*Meyelu ya uzo, meyelu ya uzo na onatago; chinye ya key, na onatago* (Open the door for her, open the door for her; hand her the keys to her place [kitchen] for she's home)." When we got to the double doors leading to my father-in-law's parlor, he and my mother-in-law handed me a set of keys, not keys to any room in particular, but a symbolic gesture of my acceptance into their household. A cheer that could be heard miles away went up when the keys exchanged hands. The women formed a circle and danced around me, their arms flailing, their hips grinding.

The ceremony after the reception threatened to be even grander than the earlier ones. The large crowd jammed the front and back yards, which had been converted into a banquet hall, complete with canopies and rented seats; people danced with abandon to both the traditional drums and blasting Western music. I was expected to change into a George, a ceremonious two-piece wrapper, worn with a lace blouse and an elaborate head scarf. But I had purchased a spaghetti-strapped, floor-length burgundy dress during my shopping spree in America that I was determined to wear. I knew that the clingy dress was the antithesis of my virginal wedding gown, but I wanted it that way. It was another opportunity for those who may have missed it, prior to the wedding, to see me in my element. It must also have been my long-suppressed rebellious side insisting on a last hurrah, even if the dress was a tad inappropriate for the occasion. Food and drink flowed abundantly and Charles' sisters led me from table to table so guests had a chance to hug or touch me.

On a platform were my *idu-uno* accoutrements, which stayed on display throughout that night and for two days afterwards. No one had ever seen such extravagance and my two families exploited the situation to their greatest advantage. To this day in Nsukka, mothers-in-law chide their sons' wives by comparing what their families brought on their wedding day to what mine gave me.

Then, Mama and John invited the guests to the platform where I was formally presented with the gifts from my family. As is the custom, they started with the inexpensive but indispensable tools of a woman's household. John picked up a broom, handed it to Mama, and Mama put in my hand. I was asked if I knew what the broom was for, and when I answered in the affirmative, I was told by an elderly woman that a good woman befriends her broom and makes it her close and trusted companion. Next were the pots and pans, which solicited the longest lecture. "A good wife always provides hot meals for her master, even if he does not provide money for the food or the household. You should scrounge, steal if necessary, to ensure that your husband has food on the table, even if he has eaten elsewhere. This is what being a good wife is all about," the elderly woman concluded. Someone else added, "Let his stomach always guide him to your home. He can give other women his heart, but be sure to keep his stomach." I was presented then the pestle and mortar and told to fix my husband pounded yam every day.

Gradually, we worked our way to the large items, and when an older male cousin pointed to the king-sized bed, the crowd hollered and not even my dark skin could hide my blushing.

"In the bedroom, your husband's wishes must be law at all times, no matter what he does, no matter how angry you may be with him. Always remember that if you deny him something that's rightfully his, another woman out there will give it to him more than willingly," the spokeswoman instructed. I knew what was coming. "We're all expecting that in the not-so-distant future, nine months at the very most, we'll be invited again for a celebration even greater than this one, to welcome your new child." The crowd roared their approval.

At that point, Mama began to cry. At first, I thought she would regain her composure quickly, but she didn't. Since she could no longer speak, John finished the presentation, hastily. My sisters, then cousins and aunts, joined Mama in tears, and soon almost every woman present was crying. People still remember that evening as strange, for the crying did not pass quickly, as it should have on the happy occasion. It lingered; some women had to sit down while others huddled, their arms clasped across their chests, their faces wet and shiny. Mama, inconsolable, had to be led to a seat away from the gathering, where close friends and relatives took turns holding her and crying with her. I remember one relative asking Mama in a stern voice, "Why do you cry as if your daughter is marrying someone you don't approve of? You should be dancing and accepting well-deserved accolades." But Mama's tears continued to flow unabated the entire evening. It looked and felt as if someone had died, and a dark cloud seemed to have settled. People departed quietly, and soon only the two families were left. Finally, my own tears started. I'd fought bravely all day to control them, but once the dam burst, there was no stopping the flood till the next day. I couldn't bear it when my family began to say goodbye. I cried as I watched my sisters, both very pregnant, hug their children to their bodies and walk away. I was sobbing quite loudly as John embraced me for a long time, then whispered that he and Delia would see me the next morning, before mass. Everyone walked to where I stood beside Charles, tears in their eyes, doing all they could to restrain themselves. Then it was over and I watched them file out of the house, none daring to look back at me. Although I was surrounded by people I had known all my life, I felt completely alone.

My in-laws had planned an all-night celebration. All the children and grandchildren were on hand to embrace their new wife, but it was not meant to be. Try as I might, my body shook from more sobs than I thought any body could contain. To this day, I don't know if what I felt was resentment for having been the sacrificial lamb or just plain separation anxiety, but whatever it was ruined our first night of marriage. Charles was too upset to be angry with me for spoiling his wedding evening and for embarrassing him in front of his brothers and sisters. He joined me in our room and after watching helplessly for a long time, offered a solution.

"Come, I'll take you back home," he said. I looked up in surprise: how could he say that? We were married and home was with him and his family. I couldn't tell if he was testing me, angry, or trying to help. I stayed where I was, my tears rushing down my face. "Let's go before it gets too late and your mother has gone to bed."

"But Charles, it doesn't look good," I managed through my tears.

"It looks worse to watch you cry all night. Let's go." He took my hands, and I followed him. It could have just been that I was too exhausted to reason properly, but I allowed him to lead me past his relatives, who were still sitting awkwardly in the parlor, through the front door, and into the car. A part of me knew that I was violating an unvoiced but sacred Ibo rule, but my hunger to see my family was so intense that I was willing to endure any punishment just to see Mama one more time. Later, I convinced myself that I was driven by my concern that Mama would be totally devastated and that I needed to tell her I would be all right.

Mama was as shocked as everyone else to see us that night. "Did you forget something, a night dress, something that couldn't wait till the morning?" She sounded very clear for someone who had been sobbing. But I understood her completely: Mama, ever the traditional woman, so mindful of appearances. I knew from the concern on her face that I had done the unthinkable. It was a first, as the stories later told it— the young bride who, on her wedding night, preferred her mother's company to that of her husband and his family. My visit at least accomplished one thing: Mama was so flustered by my impulsiveness that she immediately suspended her tearfest and hustled me into her room to plot how to contain the damage.

"Here," she forced a dress that one of my sisters retrieved from my old room into my hands. "Tell them you forgot to bring up the dress that you planned to wear to church tomorrow."

"But I'm not going to wear this dress to church," I protested.

"It doesn't matter. Just get going before they have a chance to notice that you're gone. Everything will be all right," she said, shoving me in the direction of the door.

Charles and I drove silently, and when we pulled into the walled compound, everyone stood on the verandah, as if they were looking for us. Charles hurried out, and when I heard him announce that he had taken me for a ride to get some air, I left the dress in the car and

walked out slowly. I resumed crying when we went to bed and continued to cry until early the next morning when Charles, maybe tired
from listening to my whimpers or just out of the goodness of his heart,
made me a promise that he swore to keep for the rest of our lives.

"Dympna, if you stop crying, I'll do whatever it takes to make you
happy."

I said nothing, and he misunderstood, believing I hadn't heard him.

"I promise to take care of you and do my best to guarantee your happiness," he said louder. I kept my silence, but my movement assured
him that I had heard. "I really mean it," he said.

"No matter what I do?" I said in my cracked, barely audible voice.

"No matter what happens, I will always try to be supportive of you,
if you do the same with me," he insisted. He was by then sitting, his
back supported by the wood headboard.

"If I offend you, will you give me a chance to make it up to you before being angry with me?" I ventured, rising from my lying position
and inching closer to his position.

"I promise to try," he assured me. Then he reached out to hold me,
and he gradually rocked me until I fell asleep. Our marriage night
would not be remembered for its passion, for it was just before we rose
that we finally got to the business that marriage nights are known for.
It was a quiet, reassuring union, and both of us desired and sought the
other with the familiarity of an old married couple. It was comforting,
because I could see ourselves that way in the future, still together, still
married, still supportive of each other.

We did not plan to go on a honeymoon. There was too much to do,
and John and his family were still visiting. I treasured the time I spent
with them and couldn't bear to be away when they only had a few
more days with us before their departure. But it was for more practical
reasons that we did not go anywhere.

You Go Wherever Your Husband Goes

Charles and I did not have a place to live and we had not made a final decision about where to set up a household. He was a resident at the University of Nigeria Teaching Hospital in Enugu, forty miles away from Nsukka and the university where I was a professor. Naturally, I wanted to live in Nsukka, not only for convenience to my job, but also to be close to Mama and nearly everyone that I cared for. Charles preferred to live in Enugu. He argued that his job took preference over mine. He was the man, the husband, and in spite of my high-powered position, I was still just a woman, his wife. I fully understood the implications. No self-respecting Ibo man would allow his wife or her pursuits, professional or not, to dictate his actions, and Charles would be no exception.

"It's absurd that you would even consider his moving to Nsukka so your life would be easier! Have you gone mad?" Mama told me when I sought her counsel. Hers was not a lone voice, either; others who heard what I was contemplating offered their unsolicited advice, "Today's children! Next you'll be asking him to help out in the kitchen! Where is this world heading to?" My mother-in-law found out about our tug-of-war and marched right up to me. "I will not let you turn my son into a woman's wrapper! He will not be the laughing stock of everyone in this town."

No one, not even my friends supported me. Instead, I was told I was seeking the impossible, that a good woman should follow a man wherever he went, without reluctance. It did not seem to matter to anyone that I had a more stable job than Charles or that I earned more money than he did then. What was important, as I was so poignantly reminded over and over, was our gender difference—that he was male and I was female, he the husband and I the wife.

I laid down my arms and began make preparations for moving to Enugu. I dutifully followed him to a flat, provided by the teaching hospital where he was employed. Our four-bedroom flat was one of nine occupied by Charles' fellow residents, some of whom were newlyweds like us. I felt somewhat detached from the person who mechanically arranged our possessions, most of which were part of my *idu uno* loot.

We settled into a routine, similar to the one my sisters had with their husbands and Mama probably had with my father. There were differences between my marriage and all the others around us, however. The most striking was that I dared call my husband by his name, instead of favoring one of the many preferred nicknames for one's "master." I was never one for nicknames and had resisted every attempt to shorten my name in favor of "D" or "Dee Dee" or something equally cute. I insisted on calling people by their given names and did the same with my husband.

The first few times, people within earshot actually cringed, and if they were light-skinned, their faces turned red in astonished embarrassment. Women simply do not call their husbands by their names. It's viewed as a serious transgression, similar to taking liberties with one's superiors. The seriousness of the matter is not hard to understand when viewed in the context of the real relationship between husband and wife. In the eyes of our culture, husbands and wives are not equal. How could they be when the man pays a bride price on the woman's head? My mother has told me more times than I can remember that my husband owns me—in plain terms, that I belong to him to do as he pleases. In such a system I dared call my husband by his name.

My mother-in-law calls my father-in-law "*Nna Anyi* (our father)." My mother refers to my father (dead thirty-eight years) as "Master." My sister Virginia did not call her husband anything until she gave birth to her first child; then he became "Papa Uzo" (father of Uzo). My other sister Martha called her university professor husband *Onye-nkuzi* (Teacher) until her first child was born and he graduated to "Papa Ogo." The list is endless, even among Ibos living in the United States. I've heard terms such as "Mine," "Darling," anything to avoid saying the man's name.

My cousin Eddie was concerned enough to call my attention to it. "Dympna, I know you don't mean it that way, but people are simply going to read it as a sign of disrespect, that you think very little of your husband."

When I asked Charles what he preferred, he said it was up to me.

We arrived at a compromise: I would continue to call Charles by his name at home, but in public I would act differently and treat him like a husband was supposed to be treated. If I could not come up with a fitting nickname, I would call him nothing at all. I could not come up with an appropriate nickname, so I simply didn't call his name in public. The girl who had lived in America and filled her head with liberal nonsense and even briefly flirted with feminism was gone, seemingly forever.

Charles and I never discussed the rules of the household, but I knew my place very well. How could I forget, with my mother-in- law barely an hour's drive way and more than eager to remind me of my wifely roles? Mama provided me with two house girls, less fortunate cousins of mine, who did the cleaning, the laundry, and the more menial housework considered below even a wife. I resisted at first. I felt that it was just Charles and me, and that together, we could tidy up the apartment in no time.

I learned differently and understood why maids are a necessary part of Ibo households. In spite of my long commute to Nsukka several times a week, I was still expected to do all the work in the house and wait on my husband. Charles told me repeatedly that he did not mind doing the work, but that he was concerned about how it would look if anyone found out about it. Sure enough, his mother found out that Charles did laundry, and that was the last time he helped.

I was terribly upset by that incident early in the marriage. Charles was washing out his clothes, not mine or household items, just his pants and shirts, when his mom walked into our apartment through the kitchen doors that were permanently unlocked. If she had entered through the front door, Charles would have seen her in enough time to arrange a cover-up. But she walked straight into the room where her first son was stooped, tackling a large basin full of his clothes. She let out a loud wail, startling both Charles and the neighbors who were home. "What has she done to you? You've been married only a few weeks and she has you washing her underwear!" Of course that was not the case; it is the greatest insult to ask a man to wash a woman's under things, and I had never done that. My mother-in-law knew that as well, but she was aiming for the greatest impact.

Charles tried to quiet his mother, to no avail. She sprawled on the floor of our living room where she held court with the curious neighbors who listened intently. I was later told that she gave her audience a history of our two families, and wondered aloud whether she'd made a big error by encouraging her son to go ahead with the marriage, even though she had recognized signs that I was not the same girl who left for America several years earlier. No one challenged anything she said; I was tried and judged a bad wife.

That same day, I stopped over at my in-law's house after finishing my lectures, before I returned to Enugu. When I walked into the house, my mother-in-law, in a very exaggerated fashion, turned away and clucked at me. Unaware of what had transpired, I curtsied and greeted her as I would ordinarily. She rose from her seat and spat on the vinyl floor before walking away, making sure that she slammed the door as she exited.

My father-in-law informed me of my sins, but unlike his wife, he did not feel that my offense was unforgivable. "You know, left to me, these things don't matter, but others feel differently, so you have to be very careful."

But then my mother-in-law re-emerged. "You've turned my son into your maid! No wonder you refused your mother's and my offer for househelp. You had made up your mind to use Charles as one! My son is in hell, and I'm the one who put him there."

Nothing I said made any difference, and I realized that insisting that they listen to me would not change a thing. I sat silently, under a barrage of insults. I only had myself for an audience. "Does it matter," one of me said to the other, "that they were his things, not mine, that he washed? Does anyone care that I left home at six o'clock in the morning to get to my job as a university professor? Can anyone hear me when I say that I didn't even know Charles was doing his own laundry?"

I decided as I rode back to Enugu that maybe I was not quite ready for marriage and that I was going to ask for a temporary separation while I reassessed my situation. I never took that step, for by the time I got home, Mama was waiting for me with two maids in tow. She was determined that her youngest daughter would not bring shame on the family name and that housework was not going to be an issue in the marriage. She told me that I was going to stay married to Charles, even if it killed me.

I knew it was futile to fight, so I finally settled into a wifely routine. Charles and I never discussed that incident or even alluded to it. We played our assigned roles. I did all the cooking and cleaning. It was a life very similar to that of all the women around me. No one who didn't know would have guessed from my manner or airs that I had an education, a university education, an American university education. I was simply "Charles' wife" if anyone asked. And to top it off, sixty days and two menstrual cycles later, I was already obsessed with my lack of fertility. The horrible truth was that my womb was still bare. And there was no way to hide that fact.

Part VI
Making My Life Whole

A Life Worse Than Death

Life has no meaning for an Ibo woman without a child. Every Ibo female knows this to the depth of her being. I'm sure I was aware of the consequences of barrenness before I could speak complete sentences. Through my childhood, I knew a handful of women who had no "issues"; yes, issues was the preferred term. What I remember about those unlucky women was the aura of sadness that followed them everywhere they went. One could identify them from far away or in a crowd, from the heavy burden they carried. They might as well have worn marks of their failure on their foreheads. Even as a little girl, I recognized it from the women's demeanor, from their walk to their speech. They lived and breathed their shortcoming.

When I look back to my childhood, the women I remember most were of childbearing age—women who lived in Mama's yard, women who belonged to Mama's church groups, mothers of my friends. They were either swollen with pregnancy or carried their infants strapped on their backs, their fertility flaunted for all to see. Even when women with children left their homes unaccompanied, I could tell a fulfilled from an unfulfilled woman just from one encounter. And it remains true today. The one with children sways her hips and swings her arms in an exaggerated fashion that calls attention to herself. Her walk says it all: "Look at me; I'm accomplished." She's light on her feet, her head is held upright, and she often breaks into a trot, cupping her milk-laden breasts as she does, fully expecting someone to call to her any minute to make inquiries about the children she left at home. No one, not even a stranger, needs to be told that the woman in question possesses the secrets of an Ibo woman's joy. And passersby do call to her, even if they have no prior knowledge of her situation. *"Nne Nwa, dalu"*—literally, "A child's mother, thank you." ("Thank you" in Ibo is a salutation, equivalent to "hello," and should not be confused with the English usage of it.)

The barren woman, on the other hand, is careful not to claim more space than her lowly position deserves. She places one calculated step ahead of the other, her arms close to her body, not swinging like the fertile woman's. Her eyes are cast down to the ground always, for as she reminds herself daily and is told by everyone, "What's there to look up for? The sun? The moon?" She moves like a shadow and often prefers to throw a second wrapper over her hunched shoulders, as one would a blanket. Her smile is as guarded as her speech, for what could she possibly say about anything? Everyone who passes knows her plight, and kind ones offer words of encouragement. No one inquires about her *umuaka* (children), although they may refer to her *ndibe* (household).

Two months before my marriage, I ran into a girl I had been in convent school with. In my excitement over seeing her, I asked about her children. How was I to know that she was without child? She had eagerly introduced her husband of seven years. She was dressed in Western clothing as I was; she was considerably larger than I remembered from our school days. So I blundered. The gasp that escaped from those that listened to our conversation screamed my insensitivity, but it was too late.

"I'm so sorry," I muttered, though no words could ever soothe the pain I knew I had created. "I didn't know," retreating from what was an exuberant reunion only a few minutes before, chastising myself for not noticing the obvious signs of her misery.

Our culture has not figured out a way to accommodate a woman who does not fulfill that for which she was born. In spite of growth in other areas, a woman is still measured by her motherhood. In years past and to some extent even today, women are married early, "before their unborn babies are wasted in monthly flows." Then they begin to bear children and continue to do so until any one of a number of outcomes occurs.

In a great number of cases, the women die during childbirth. Though this isn't as common as it used to be, childbirth-related complications continue to be the leading cause of death for Ibo women. If Ibos are told that a young woman is dead, the most logical question is: was she having a baby?

Another reason that women stop having babies is that they fall out of their husbands' favor, and the men devote their love and attention to younger, firmer-bodied, fuller-breasted wives or lovers and shun their wives' beds, making it impossible for the women to conceive or bear children. A woman whose husband refuses to bed, in most cases, has the sympathy of the community and can appeal for the intervention of some wiser men to prevail upon her husband to fill her with his seed. The man is accused of *ikpochi nwa na afo* (locking her children in her tummy), thereby denying her the greatest pleasure on earth—motherhood. He could be ordered to make "restitution," which most often involves drawing up a sex schedule that accommodates her needs, even if it kills him.

In some instances, women continue to bear children until menopause sets in. Then the woman, caught in the web of biology, walks around telling her woeful tale to anyone who will listen.

In rare cases, a woman is prevented from procreating because her son is already married and trying to get his own wife pregnant. It is taboo for a woman to continue to bear children after her daughter-in-law begins to do the same, but mercifully, this rule applies to male children, not to females. The logic behind it is that daughters begin to procreate early, too early, in fact, for their mothers to stop bearing children. But male children start later, often in their twenties or thirties, when their mothers are usually past childbearing anyway. A woman who insists on continuing to bear children after her own daughter-in-law is in the family way is believed to be stealing babies out of the younger woman's tummy.

Barrenness is an Ibo woman's single worst fate. Women have announced, in public, that they would prefer to be dead, to have never been born, than to live without the experience of birthing and raising a child. I was recently called by an Ibo woman who reported that the life of a friend of hers was devastated; she had lost a child right after birthing him. While discussing the ways to console her bereaved friend, the woman told me of another experience in her life, involving her best friend, who had been in a marriage for ten years, ten long years without a child to show for it. With no warning, just as she had resigned herself to her hopeless state, going as far as offering to marry another wife for her husband, she discovered that she was pregnant. Her joy knew no bounds, and she carried her gift child gingerly, but with a definite upward turn to her chin. She smiled, for her maker had finally given her something to smile about. Neighbors could at last converse with her without the awkward guardedness that had marked prior contacts with her. All waited for the child.

But it wasn't meant to be. The baby died as he struggled through the birth passage. He uttered no cries after he emerged, and his mother waited and waited for wails that never came. She was understandably inconsolable, to have been denied for ten years, and then have a child dangled before her eyes, almost within her reach, and then taken from her again. She lunged for her kitchen knives, but someone was always there to shield her. She held her breath, fully intending to end her miserable life. "Why does God let me live? Of what use am I if I can't bear a child?" she uttered. Then my acquaintance said she had told the stricken woman, "Look at you! Don't you see how much God has done for you? Were you at this point last year? Stop shedding tears and smile. No one can laugh at you and call you a man. You've proven to the whole world that you're a woman."

There are many others like her, all connected by their tragic fate. My family had a few infertile women. Aunt Monica, who raised Martha, was not afforded the joys of motherhood, so she spent all her energy on Martha, her foster child, and treated her like the child she would have had. We all believed that it was not Aunt Monica's fault that her marriage was not fruitful; after all, her husband's sister did not bear children in her own marriage. "It must be in their blood," we concluded. When Aunt Monica died, her childlessness stared us all in the face. Her burial ceremonies lacked the pomp that marks the passing of a woman, as it was when my grandmother died, as it will be when Mama dies.

At Grandmother's farewell, all her children, in-laws, and grandchildren attended. Each of our arrivals was heralded by the music troupe that accompanied us and the cheers drawn from the crowd of mourners who congratulated us on the size of the cow or goat each of us was obligated to bring to present to the villagers. Aunt Monica, on the other hand, was buried quietly. Those who sat around her death bed were her relatives, not daughters and daughters-in-law as is the custom. Our tears were bitter ones, for there was no one to cry "Mother, great mother," as she was lowered into the ground. Although she was as much a mother to Martha as Mama was, everyone knew she wasn't Martha's real mother, and people stated it. "So what if she gave the world to Martha? Does that make her Martha's mother?" In all the years that Martha lived with her, she never once called her "Mama." She was "Auntie," even as Martha sat by her gravesite, weeping uncontrollably. Also, Ibos sadly cling to the adage that "A child is asked who gave birth to you, not who raised you," and that whatever is done for another's child is a waste.

My mother's sister Mama Ngbada (the mother who lives down the hill) was also cursed with childlessness. She died in 1990, and throughout her life, her sister was her life. By extension, we could not escape Mama Ngbada's suffocating warmth. Mama Ngbada was unfortunate in marriage, and again, as was the case with all our barren relatives, we blamed her husband for possessing headless male seeds that couldn't see where they were supposed to go and traveled down instead of up. As she got older and was widowed, all of Mama's relatives and their children pulled together and built a house for Mama Ngbada. It was something that her own child was supposed to do for her, but Mama Ngbada had only her kin to keep a roof on her head. We returned the favors she gave us in our early lives and equipped her home with fineries that she never learned how to use.

I was absent on the day she died and when she was buried. Mama wrote a detailed account of the ceremony. "Dympna, everyone who came congratulated us on the great job we did. They said, 'If we didn't know her, we wouldn't have believed she didn't have a child of her own—to accord her all this'."

The issue of child-bearing is as important today as it was in my mother's generation, and it will be for my daughter if she chooses to marry an Ibo man. It was under such pressure that I lived right after marriage while I tried to have a child.

Waiting to Have a Child

I had all of three menstrual cycles between my wedding and my first pregnancy, but the time felt like all eternity. The four days that my period lasted each month were like a lifetime. I now believe I lost my mind temporarily as I lived and breathed my "barrenness."

My unpregnant state was not for lack of trying! So anxious were we that we never missed an opportunity to "baby hunt."

In retrospect, it seems ridiculous that I had been married less than three months, but felt that our lives were empty because I did not conceive a child immediately. I was so nervous that I became incapable of holding any food down. As my weight declined, my anxiety increased. Restlessness ruled me.

Mama asked what was wrong, but I put up a brave front and told her nothing. To talk about it, at least in my warped way of handling the situation, was to admit that my childlessness was an issue. "You know, people are beginning to ask what's wrong with you," she said. I let her have the last word, but all day long, as I lectured students or chatted with colleagues, Mama's question played over and over again in my mind. "How can I explain my barrenness? What am I supposed to say to friends and relatives? Why am I being punished by God for a crime I'm not even remotely aware of?"

I did a lot of soul searching during those days. I replayed my life in America—every party, every man I looked at or danced with, every touch I savored or encouraged, every thought and regrettable act. I began to pray, more furiously than ever before, for God's forgiveness. How fervently I begged God for a child, or just a pregnancy, even if it never went to completion. I wanted my community to see that I was capable of conceiving. That was the extent of my desire, and I dared not hope or ask for more.

I can still remember in graphic detail my pain on each of the three occasions when my period started. When I noticed the first trickles of reddish discharge, the symbols of my shortfall as a wife, I locked myself in whatever room I discovered the sign, crying desperately, like one whose life had come to an end. My heart always fell to the pit of my stomach and I had to grasp my middle tightly, gasping to catch my breath, to will myself the courage to face the world again. Every cramp, every discomfort I experienced during those days, felt magnified. But unlike previous periods when I took pain remedies and complained to all who would listen, I sought no relief and suffered silently, feeling myself deserving of it. Charles discovered me the first two times and spoke soothingly, assuring me that everything would be all right if I allowed myself and my body to adjust to my new situation—marriage. But by the third evidence of my failure, he too had become sufficiently concerned to suggest that we see a doctor "to get to the root of the problem."

Even if I had been able to live with my obvious and immediate failure, my community—relatives, well wishers, detractors—would not let me be while I tried to get pregnant. I was confronted with the same question everywhere I went. "What are you waiting for? Why aren't you pregnant yet?" Many would refer to my "tiny waist" to the amusement of a room-sized audience. Some demanded that I offer some explanation for my still-unpregnant state. Others offered unsolicited advice on how best to attain that which eluded me. As always, I bore the humiliation and listened to the nonsense. "You must eat only beans." "Bathe in cold water only." "Do not release your husband's you-know-what too soon after intercourse. Be sure to lie prone for at least an hour afterwards." In my hysteria, I took every bit of advice seriously and practiced it religiously. Who knows? I rationalized.

My obsession began to affect the way I perceived of myself and life in general. I started avoiding gatherings and places where I was likely to be accosted. I even delayed enrolling as a member in The Christian Mothers Group, an absolute necessity for any woman married in the church. Both my mother and mother-in-law hounded me about becoming a member. "It's not for today, Dympna," Mama said. "If, God forbid, anything should happen to you or one of your own, you'll be all alone. No one will come to your side." My mother-in-law's angle was, predictably, how my non-membership reflected on her son. "Charles' wife thinks she has all the answers."

I desperately wanted to belong to the group that my mother, sisters, and every woman I knew was part of, but I simply preferred to wait until I was deserving of the term "Christian Mother." I would not be the object of ridicule. I refused to be pitied. I refused to hear women whose entire perspective on life was limited to an area not larger than a forty-mile radius snickering behind my back, laughing if I stood up to make a point, or even screaming out my unhappy state. I knew what they would say. "Look at that one; just look at that one. Do you think this group is called 'Christian wives'? Why don't you reserve your comments until you're really qualified to be one of us?"

When my period failed to come in the fourth month, I dared not hope that it was what I prayed for. I literally held my breath, knowing and believing that each additional day without it offered me a new lease on life. I spent more time in the bathroom than out. Every discharge, every pain I felt, was mistaken for the start of my period. I would rush to the closest bathroom, slam the door behind me, and rest my head against the door. "I knew it! How could I even allow myself to think that I'm pregnant? How stupid I am." It would be several minutes before I dared peer into my panties and another few minutes before I could collect myself and walk out of the bathroom.

Three weeks later, my period still hadn't come, and Charles' friend, a lab technician, performed a urine test to determine if I were pregnant. He arrived late the next day with the results. Charles was not home when he showed up, and I knew it was not my place to probe him about the reason for his visit. He was my husband's friend, another man, and I was not supposed to discuss certain details with him. Instead, we engaged in meaningless small talk. I offered him drinks and endured more than an hour of the torture. I fidgeted nervously, my anxiety almost getting the better of me. One part of me screamed for the answer, while the other part of me dreaded what it might be. He readied to leave without referring to the issue at hand, and I watched, helpless. I said to myself, "Surely, if there was anything to it, he would have said something. It is all a hoax, a cruel hoax." At the door, I could feel my hot tears of disappointment collecting, stinging my eyes, when he turned to me and mumbled in a voice so low that for days I wondered if I had heard him correctly. "Tell Charles the test is positive." Then he walked out.

My body was invaded by a combination of emotions: relief, joy, triumph. I was not sure whether to scream and jump or just crawl into bed and savor my victory. My restlessness got the better of me and I paced the floor of our apartment, replaying the lab technician's words in my head, wanting and craving so desperately to be held by someone, to be cuddled until I calmed down. But Charles was out with his friends, and by the time he returned I was asleep, my excitement somewhat abated.

Charles warned me over and over that I should not tell anyone I was pregnant until I was past the first trimester, "to contain the gossip and disappointment if you should lose it." So then I was saddled with the additional fear that the pregnancy was precarious and could cease to exist at any moment. It's likely that this anxiety caused my sickness throughout the first trimester. I could barely get any food down and when I did, it was a struggle to keep it down. No one had ever seen a less healthy-looking new bride. Mama attributed my state to my misery that I had not accomplished what I was created for. On the days that I visited with her after my lectures at the university, she would not let me get a minute's rest. Instead, she placed one nausea-inducing plate of food after another before me, urging and cajoling me at the same time. "Look at you, my daughter! You've disappeared completely. Is your husband doing something to cause this? Does he beat you? Does he go after other women? What could be so bad as to have this effect on you?"

"It's none of that, Mama."

"But why else would you look like this? Of course! My poor child, how could I have been so blind? You're worried about your state. You have to believe that God will smile on you, if it's his will."

Finally, no longer able to contain my happiness and weary from her relentless probing about visible signs of my supposed happiness, I shared my good news with Mama. "Mama, I'm pregnant."

She stared ahead, blank faced, no response.

"I'm expecting," I stated, more confidently.

"Who told you? How do you know you are? Are you sure?"

Her expression of doubt irked me. "Of course I know!" I longed to yell, "I'm a twenty-five-year-old woman with an extensive education, I should know if I'm pregnant!" But no. I maintained my cool demeanor and told her the whole story, including the confirming pregnancy test.

"How long have you known?" She focused her full attention on me, and I realized it was one of those trick questions, that no matter how I answered, Mama would find fault with it. Just like clockwork, Mama and I got into an argument about how long I'd known I was pregnant without telling her. Any other time, I'd have resented her for raining on my parade, but this time, I knew immediately I'd been wrong. How? Because as soon as I told her, I started to calm down. It was important that Mama know what I had accomplished, that I was pregnant, poised to have a child. The more I thought about it, the better it made me feel. I knew that Mama would disseminate my good news, if only in her quiet subtle way. Her sprightly new walk and carriage and the angle at which she would hold her head would suggest more than words and cause a stir; everyone would know that Mama Edoga had something to celebrate. Inevitably, it would be traced back to me. Even if the pregnancy ended, Mama would be in a position to vouch for my womanhood.

One night during my twelfth week of pregnancy, I was startled by a familiar warm wetness between my legs which I had not felt for a while. My heart started racing, and the possibilities crowded my mind, temporarily crippling me. Without looking, I knew without a doubt that what I felt was blood and that its mere presence threatened not only my pregnancy, but also my precarious emotional state. As in many difficult times in my life, the stronger of my two personas emerged and stated bluntly, "The deed is done; there's nothing you can do now." I continued to lie there for what seemed like eternity, cursing the warm dampness that was gradually depriving me of my unborn child and crying softly, so quietly that not even Charles who slept beside me could hear. I mourned my yet-unborn child, but it was for myself that I cried, for what people would say. My mind played out the whole scenario, exactly as it would play when stories began to circulate that I had miscarried. Some would be genuinely concerned and urge me to "Let no time pass. Start tonight to make another one." Others, especially women, would add, "We hope the doctors cleaned out your womb really thoroughly, to wash out the evil one, so that it does not torment the ones that follow." But it was the other anticipated voices that caused me more pain that night. I could clearly hear the mockery in their voices. "She really thinks she can fool us. How can she miscarry a pregnancy that never was? She still has not told us what sins she committed in America all those years."

When I finally made it to the bathroom, my worst fears were confirmed, and I decided to wake Charles. He was as alarmed as I was at first, but he girded himself and calmed down enough to hold me when I started to bawl. He got me to stay in bed that morning until the bleeding trickled to spotting. Despite Charles' explanations that what I experienced was natural and happened to many women, I was convinced that my child was lost and there was no hope of saving the pregnancy. I prayed harder than I thought was possible, and because Charles held out hope, I too dared to believe that all was not lost.

I was immobilized for about a week, then gradually returned to my normal existence. There was no way of verifying if the pregnancy remained intact because at that time the University of Nigeria Hospital where Charles was a resident did not have sonogram equipment or anything that could have allayed our fears by confirming the existence of a heartbeat. We simply had to wait to see if the pregnancy continued to grow. What an agonizing wait it was.

With each day that passed, the pregnancy moved away from the first trimester, which raised my hopes. I felt at ease enough with the situation to want to talk to Mama about my anxieties. I sought answers to things I did not understand about the changes in my body. "Did you feel discomfort in your back? Did you hate the smell of food?" Mama always dismissed me with, "how would knowing how mine happened help you? Everything's in God's hands." She only affirmed what I already knew, that she was not at all comfortable discussing her body or mine, that such things were better left untouched. It was bad enough that both of us knew how pregnancies resulted, so we couldn't pretend mine came from something I had eaten! So for answers, I devoured books on pregnancy, but none provided the reassurances that my mother could have easily provided by allowing me insight into her own pre-natal experiences.

Much to my chagrin, my tummy wouldn't bulge, even long after I was assured that the pregnancy was once again on a firm footing. It remained flat, and I was able to wear my tightly fitted skirts well into the sixth month. Curious neighbors continued to chide me about my supposed inability to conceive a child. I was approached and told, "Nne, if there's a problem with conceiving, you should do something now before it's too late." I played along, feigning sadness and throwing my hands up in the air, "Please pray for me," I urged all my well-wishers while I could barely contain myself until they left my side. I longed to return to the United States to bear my child there. I was most compelled by my fear about delivering the child safely, but a part of me also wanted to share that exciting moment in my life with John and his family. I wrote them a letter detailing my plans and their response came quickly; they were thrilled that I wanted to have the child with them in the United States. Charles was in full support, but my in-laws pointed out that it looked suspicious, "As if you have something to hide." My mother-in-law said, "It's my first son's first child, and you want to go to America, a distant land, to give birth? Women have children every day in Nigeria," she added, discounting my expressed fear that something would happen to me or the baby.

But I was convinced that something would happen to the baby if I had it in Nigeria. I continued making my plans and left Nigeria when

I was in my eighth month. I arrived on a fall morning to John and Delia's warm embrace, and they took over the pregnancy in a display of generosity that astounded even me. I was spoiled and pampered while my brother and his family waited impatiently for the birth. Away from Nigeria and the pressures, I actually relaxed and enjoyed the pregnancy. I was no longer consumed with fear that something would happen; instead, I felt what every expectant mother feels—joyful anticipation. Delia delighted in purchasing the baby's layette. She was still in possession of her children's crib and furniture, which we set up for the child that was due any day.

It's a Girl

I don't know why I assumed that I would bear a baby boy first, but throughout the pregnancy, I did not have one doubt about the sex of the child. In my mind, it was the only right thing to do, and I was determined to provide my husband that which would guarantee my place in his life.

Neither Charles nor anyone in our two families said or did anything that could be misconstrued to suggest that they wanted a boy, but nothing needed to be said. I'm as Ibo as any other Ibo, and I knew their unvoiced desires. So I marched along through the pregnancy, convinced that the child I carried was male and would finally earn me well-deserved acceptance in my community.

"Look at that Edoga girl," I imagined our neighbors would say. "She succeeds in everything she attempts. See how she manages to deliver a bouncing baby boy to her husband less than a year after her wedding. Someone surely looks out for her."

My labor started around four o'clock in the morning of the expected date of delivery. The protracted contraction that woke me from sleep also caused my bag of water to break. I luxuriated in the warmth of the water that gushed out of me. I couldn't wait to meet my son. Although the frequent contractions kept me flinching with pain, I waited till morning to alert John's household, and when Delia came into my room as she did every morning, she was shocked to see me dressed and sitting up in bed.

"Wake up, everybody!" she screamed when I told her. "Dympna's having the baby!"

In the chaos that followed, I was mobbed by my nieces and nephew, who refused to go to school that day, believing as I did that the baby would be out shortly. When we got to the hospital, the doctor pronounced everything perfect and predicted that the baby would be born before the end of the work day. How wrong he was.

I made fast progress at first, but then, somewhere between four and five centimeters, I got stuck, and the doctor gave me a labor-inducing drug to move me along.

If someone had told me that there was that much pain anywhere on Earth, I would never have believed him. In spite of my firm resolve, I started to cry for my mother. I desperately wanted her there even though both John and Delia never left my side. In the hour and half between the start of the strong painful contractions and when I was given an epidural, I gained a new respect for Mama, especially in the way she endured everything life dealt her.

In my pain, everything became blurred and merged: Mama's own childbirths, her marriage, her widowhood, and everything that happened to her after her husband died. How excruciating the pain must have been for the fourteen-year-old child-mother who bore her first child, Charles. I've been told by reliable sources that Mama never cried out once in all the times she labored to have her children, and that no one could tell anything from her expressionless face. Most times, I was told, her midwives had no way of knowing how much progress she was making. I, on the other hand, basked in the midst of family and technology, yet I thought the pain would rip my soul apart, until the epidural. The relief was instant, the difference in my demeanor as stark as day and night, and a smile found its way back onto my face. I voiced my relief: "It's a wonder women have other children after experiencing labor."

All we could do then was wait for the child to be born. Between conversations, I napped or read from the novel that I brought along. The afternoon and evening came and went and we were no closer to our destination. Then, a flurry of activity around me suggested that something could be wrong. I saw my obstetrician whispering to John, and soon I was surrounded; someone told me they had to draw blood from the baby's scalp, raising my own anxiety level. I knew it, I said to myself. How could I ever have thought I could escape my destiny? How am I going to explain it to anyone back home?

It must have been a combination of things—my crying, John's and Delia's pacing back and forth in the tiny labor room, plus a team of residents and nurses that hovered over me—but at eight o'clock, the doctor told us that if the baby was not out by ten, he would deliver it by caesarean section. I was completely dilated, but the baby was stuck in a face-up position and no one could predict if and how long it would take it to completely turn around. We prayed fervently while the nurses readied me for whatever the next move turned out to be.

Everyone who worked on me was mindful of not offending John, who was an attending surgeon at Morristown Memorial Hospital where I lay. Since then, I've occasionally wondered if I was not inadvertently affected by his presence, by becoming a victim of too much attention. Mama told us all our lives, "Too much of anything—good or bad—is bad." I felt that my reproductive organs had become the New Jersey Turnpike. What seemed like a parade of people passed through the room, donned their gloves, and did their own examinations, to recheck my cervix for confirmation that I had done my own part and that what remained was the baby's. I even overheard what appeared to be an argument between two residents on how dilated I really was. I remember it all in still images, but the extensive medical discussions around me were all jargon to me then. My immediate concern was that the child I carried was stuck in me and was unwilling to exit gracefully.

I started to cry in earnest when I looked at the clock in my room and saw that it was nine-forty-five and still there was no change in the baby's position. "How could it be?" I cried to Delia, "How can I end up like this?"

"All you want is a healthy child, isn't it?" she said, her face puzzled by my outburst. I turned my pain inward; Delia couldn't possibly understand the significance of what was about to happen to me. I, Dympna, the last of Mama's daughters, the one who without doubt got the best of everything handed to her all her life, was about to be delivered of a child in a way that no woman in our family (neither maternal nor paternal) had ever done before. What will my mother say? What will people at home say when they hear of it? Hadn't my own mother delivered all her children, including two sets of twins (one set in breech position) naturally? Hadn't my own sisters delivered their babies in very deprived conditions?

I imagined Mama seated in her parlor, surrounded by relatives, as is normal, when the letter of the delivery of my child was read to her. "Dympna had her baby..." the reader would pause for the cheer that was sure to erupt, but knowing Mama as I do, she would hush everyone in the standing-room-only gathering and urge that the letter be completed, "...by caesarian section."

Even as I was wheeled to the delivery room, I could feel the awkward silence that would follow that revelation in Mama's parlor. It would be so disconcertingly quiet that neighbors who'd come to find out the cause of the earlier applause, would ask if anyone died. Mama would start to cry silently, and everyone would join her, and soon everyone would forget there was something to celebrate. All anyone remembered would be, "Dympna had a caesar." No one would dare make a derogatory remark while Mama stayed in the parlor, but after she'd exhausted herself from crying and retreated to her room, someone would glance over her shoulder to ensure Mama was not within earshot and say, "Didn't I always insist that that child should never have been allowed to fill her head with all that knowledge. Look what she did now." Others would nod their assent furiously, and another relative would comment, "She has roomy hips like all of us, and she couldn't push the baby out? America has made her too soft for her own good."

Neither my mother nor mother-in-law knows that my first child was delivered in any way other than the natural way. My sisters don't know. I didn't tell anyone. I'm sure that if I had confided in Mama, she would have told me to guard the secret. I might have told someone about it, but my next-door neighbor had given birth in my absence and almost everyone who came to see me when I got back to Nigeria told me of her near catastrophe. "But for the grace of God, they almost gave her a caesarean section," I was told. Her baby was badly positioned, as mine was, but when her doctor recommended that hers be resolved like mine, she and her whole family had been adamant and held out.

Caesarean sections are simply not an acceptable form of delivery, and women who go through it are considered less than women. I'm reminded of a close friend who delivered her two children via surgery and her subsequent attempts to give birth the natural way. Claiming she could no longer deal with the name-calling (such as *awalawa*—she who's cut up), she was determined to find a doctor who would let her "push the baby out" like a real woman. I was one of the dissenting voices that called her attention to her two lovely children, adding that she and the baby she carried could be hurt.

She told her story of how she was a laughingstock and had to prove herself. Besides, she whispered, she had two daughters, and was aware that if she continued to deliver by caesarean section, she was limited to four children. "What if there's no boy among the four? What would I do then?" Unable to stop her, she settled for a doctor in Nnewi whose credentials were dubious, but who guaranteed every woman who walked into his clinic a natural birth. My friend went into labor, but could not deliver the baby. She was rushed to a hospital where there were facilities for surgery, but by the time the baby was delivered, it had suffocated, kept too long in his mother's birth canal. My friend, who was looking for an opportunity to have many more, lost one of her four chances, and it was a boy. I don't know if she's exercised her last option yet.

In my case, I was delivered of my first baby at ten-thirty-six at night on Tuesday, November 23, 1982, twelve days shy of my first wedding anniversary. I stayed awake through the delivery and felt the tug as the baby was pulled out from my belly, and then my heart stood still, waiting for the pronouncement.

"It's a girl," the doctor announced, and as photos were snapped and the baby was placed in my arms briefly, I remember feeling slightly disoriented at first. In fairness to myself, my first conscious concern had not been the baby's sex as much as its health, but my pink newborn daughter was the picture of perfection, and when I heard her pronounced so, I started to feel let down. I felt like a child who, on Christmas morning, is laden with toys but does not find the particular one she's hoped for all year long. My whole being longed to scream, "Is that all?"

I've since read that it is natural for a woman to feel depressed after giving birth, but at the time, I was consumed by sadness. It wasn't because I did not feel immense love for the child I had, but because of a feeling that I got less than I expected. I had every intention of doing it right, of presenting my husband a boy first, a child to carry on his name, like my own mother had done for my father. I fell asleep on the night my daughter made me a mother feeling grossly inadequate. Not only had I fallen short of a routine womanly task, but I had a girl.

Delia Virginia Nneka Ugwu-Oju

I loved my baby daughter; there was no doubt in my mind about that. How could a good mother not love her child? But I was surprised that I was not overcome by my feelings for her, that I felt disappointment at the hand that I was dealt. I'm not exactly sure that I understand it completely, even to this day. My sadness stemmed from a fear, irrational though it seems now, that having given birth to a girl, I would have one daughter after another and not produce a son to carry on my husband's name, and thus we would perish. I don't know why I was consumed with such fear. Mama had four sons before she bore a daughter, but my two sisters had one girl, followed up with boys in record time. John and Delia bore two girls before their son. Mine was therefore not unusual, but that knowledge did nothing to reassure me. I had set my heart on having a boy first, not necessarily because I preferred boys to girls, but to get the pressure to bear a son out of the way, so that it would not be the driving force of my married life.

Ibos do not hide their disappointment with women who deliver one female child after another. She's told as soon as she delivers one child that she has a lot of work ahead of her, that her job isn't finished until she's given birth to a *real* child. One of Mama's earliest trainees (before I was even born) is unfortunately one of such female-filled women. She gave birth to eleven girls! In earlier pregnancies, her husband had held out hope that God would at last smile upon them, but after the sixth child, he stopped hoping for any miracles. I remember the haggardly thin woman even in the last stage of her pregnancies, and her anxiety that eventually condemned her to a psychiatric institution. Somewhere during her marriage, her husband decided to bring her to Nsukka to deliver her children under Mama's care. There was a good reason behind it; the woman needed to be restrained from hurting herself and the newborn after each birth. Mama was one of the few people that could calm her and give her the encouragement she needed to go on and try again. I was old enough to know something was amiss when she gave birth to one of her babies. Mama slept beside her in her hospital bed, keeping an all-night vigil over the newborn girl. When they returned from the hospital to our home, the woman and her new baby shared Mama's room and I recall stumbling upon her hunched in grief, her shoulders trembling, her face contorted in pain.

"When will you let me smile, Lord?" she whispered over and over, "When are you going to allow me a place in my husband's heart?"

Still, once my child was born, there was no doubt in my mind about what she would be called. I had long decided that our first child would be named either after my brother John or his wife Delia, in recognition of their contributions to my life. Charles readily agreed that if it turned out to be a girl, I could name her anything I wanted. But he had not shown the same carte-blanche magnanimity for a boy. He held out until I was in the final days of my pregnancy before acquiescing to naming the child after my brother. Charles' letter of authorization finally came; yes, his son could be named John. But he insisted on choosing his Ibo name, *Tobenna* (Praise the Lord).

The pain I felt following the birth was three-fold, stemming from the incision, the afterbirth, and my disappointment over the outcome of the pregnancy. None showed any signs of lessening in the first few days, and they became my excuse for not getting out of bed. The nurses tried without success to get me up from bed the first two days. Then my obstetrician literally dragged me to my feet and forced me to walk up and down the hallways of the maternity ward. I cried a lot those days from causes that I was not even aware of. "It must be the pain," I insisted to myself. "Why else would I cry?"

I was in the room alone when I was brought the form for my child's birth certificate. Without hesitation, I filled in DELIA VIRGINIA UGWU-OJU as her name. But the longer I stared at the form, the more inadequate the names looked. While they had strong sentimental value, they contained no real meaning, the way Ibo names do. I wanted to add one that reflected how I was feeling at that particular time, a name that would be significant years from that moment. In the little space left, I squeezed in *NNEKA* (Mother is Supreme) without any thought. It was almost as if someone else guided my hand and printed the letters. But having written it, it seemed so appropriate, in fact, the only name that would have sufficed. It spoke my heart, told the story of my life, of my mother's, of my grandmother's.

Mother is Supreme indeed. The name was a tribute to myself, for the pain I suffered even as I penned it and for the immense trials I knew I would go through as my daughter's mother, but mostly, Nneka was a tribute to my own mother, for her endurance and support all our lives. Today, no one really calls Delia by her Ibo name, but it is there nevertheless, and remains as much a part of her as she is of me.

I took my daughter home to her father in February 1983, when Delia, at three months, was old enough for the long journey. The celebrations that greeted us rivaled those that heralded my return to Nigeria with my master's degree. Charles met us at the airport in Lagos and we journeyed to Enugu together to eager relatives. Both Mama and my mother-in-law came for the *omugo*, the traditional visit to a new mother.

An *omugo* visit usually commences as soon as a woman gives birth and her mother is informed of it. The older woman pays attention to every detail in her preparation, for whatever she brings to her daughter will be a subject of discussion and legend for years to come. It will be compared with what other mothers brought their own daughters in similar circumstances. Under such pressure, the visiting mother buys only the largest yams and the tastiest smoked fish and meat, although she herself may not have ever been able to afford such luxuries for her own household. She selects fruits and other perishables early on the morning of her departure, and when she arrives at her daughter's house, she leaves her gifts intact until both her daughter and in-laws have assessed them. In fact, many families go into debt for their daughter's *omugo*, because of the repercussions of taking her too little. Ibos take this visit very seriously; they use it as a gauge of how highly the married girl is valued by her own family, as well as the extent to which the girl's family goes to please the in-laws.

I've witnessed numerous incidents where one *omugo* deeply affected both a daughter's marriage and her relationship with her parents. In one such case, the young woman's mother did not have the means to be lavish in the gifts she bore. She was a petty trader and could barely afford even the items she purchased. Besides, she reasoned, her daughter and her husband were very successful, owned two cars, and lived in abundance. What difference would a basket of goods make? It made a big difference, and brought much misery to her daughter's life.

I was at the daughter's house to view her young child on the day that her mother arrived. One of the servants announced that her mother had come for the *omugo* and my friend ran out, excited to see her mother and to show off her new child. She shouted her pleasure for all to hear as she followed the help downstairs. "My mother has come to take care of us! Everyone come see." She ran into her mother with such force that the two women lost their balance. Invariably my friend's eyes were drawn to her mother's luggage, sitting nearby. Everyone heard her gasp, and all eyes came to rest on the four wretched wrinkled tubers of yam, which looked more like cassava roots. Beside the yams was a gallon-sized container of palm oil and a polythene bag containing condiments. The young woman's eyes started to cloud, and I watched her initial enthusiasm for her mother's visit drain from her face and her body.

"Look how my mother has shamed me," she cried as I led her back to the flat. Nothing I said soothed her pain, even though I brought up her mother's financial hardships and her own affluence. "Your mother brought what she could afford."

"It would've been better if she never came at all," she insisted.

The pressure is not only on the mother to lavish gifts on the daughter's family. It's also on the in-laws to send the mother home with goods of an equal, if not greater, value." In my extended family, we've had numerous *omugo* mishaps, but they didn't stem from the mothers (my aunts and cousins) bringing their daughters inadequate gifts. The Edogas strongly advocate impressing one's in-laws, even if we have to go into debt in the process. The disappointments were caused by in-laws not reciprocating in kind when the visiting mothers were returning home. My cousin, Jacinta, who refused to marry the man we all agreed was best for her, had a baby with her chosen, and her mother, my aunt, traveled all the way to Lagos for the *omugo* visit. For a woman of my aunt's very limited resources, it was an immense task, but family rallied around, and she was able to buy yams, fish, and meat that were fit for an obedient daughter. She stayed with her daughter for three months to help Jacinta return to work and her normal routine. Our quarrel started when my aunt returned and presented what she was given by the same in-laws for whom she went into debt. Jacinta and her husband paid my aunt's transport back and bought her a six-yard piece of fabric. That was all, although my aunt had given up her savings and three months of her trading time. My cousin and her husband had not considered the curious neighbors and friends whom my aunt would be faced with, that she'd have nothing to show for her daughter's first child, a boy at that.

When Auntie returned home, neighbors gathered to hear stories of her daughter and the new child, and, most importantly, to view the gifts she was laden with. In these spontaneous celebrations, the new grandmother presents all who gather a container of baby powder with which to paint their faces, and then she parades one gift after another to cheers and songs. None of the gathered leaves emptyhanded, for the mother returning from *omugo* usually brings inexpensive favors like onions, oranges, bar soap, as a small symbolic gesture of sharing one's good fortune. My aunt, however, had nothing to share, and her lack of enthusiasm and teary eyes told her story more eloquently than words ever could. Neighbors dispersed quietly, certain to spread the tale of the woman who returned from her daughter's *omugo* with nothing.

Even though our anger was directed at Jacinta, we blamed my aunt for not stopping at a market to purchase something that she could pretend was given to her by her in-laws, to save face back home. When my cousin Jacinta delivered another child, a second son, her mother sat in Nsukka with no desire to make an *omugo* visit to her daughter in Lagos.

For my first child's *omugo*, Mama outdid everyone's expectations. In addition to the tubers of yam, fish, dried meat, and condiments, Mama brought a huge live goat to welcome Delia. In addition, she visited my in-laws' home with twelve other relatives, each bearing yam, fish, and meat to make additional presentations. Mama did the same for all her daughters, at least with all our first children. She had to tax herself to pay for the lavish occasions, but she felt it necessary, for her daughters' sakes, just as she did with the *iduno* (after marriage) to keep them on a pedestal in their husbands' homes. To this day, when people in my husband's village refer to Charles' wife's *omugo* gifts, they always end with, "We don't see how anyone can outdo that one."

Similarly, on the occasion of Mama's return to her home (she spent two weeks with me each time), Charles and I presented her with several high-quality items of clothing. In addition, Mama and I took a special trip to the market where she bought the loot to share with the crowds when she got home. With my other children, Mama came with a smaller group of people, but even more impressive gifts, for on those occasions I had borne boys and given everyone real reason to celebrate.

My parents-in-law welcomed Delia's birth with all the rituals. She's their first son's first child, and they spared nothing to commemorate her birth. Planned and spontaneous parties erupted after my arrival in Enugu. Then, Delia had to be taken to Aku, our ancestral village, to be received by her people. Assorted foods were served to the large crowd; palm wine and beer flowed freely, so that by the time we got to the ceremonial part, no one was feeling any pain.

Just before sundown, the large crowd assembled in a circle in my parents-in-law's front courtyard. An elder, who remained in the middle, ordered that my three-month-old daughter be stripped and handed to him. I had known it would happen, for I had witnessed many *ivu ndu* (giving life) rituals. But I took in the man's grimy hands, his dirt-caked loin cloth that barely covered his manhood, and the snuff-tinted fluid that dripped from his nose, and the last thing I desired was to hand my baby girl to him. For an instant, I was taken back fifteen years to little Umebe's clitorectomy, and I held fast to Delia. Of course, Delia was already too old to be subjected to circumcision, and my enlightened father-in-law would not have permitted its practice in his home.

But grimy old man or not, what happened to Delia was not my decision to make, and another woman grabbed the baby out of my hands before I had time to react. She passed her to the elder for the required task. Delia was thus laid on the damp mud floor, and my protests that the cold ground would sicken the child fell on deaf ears, while the man and other villagers chanted. It's a ceremony that I had watched numerous times before, though I was more relaxed watching someone else's baby lying on the floor and stepped over. My daughter, as I was told is the case with every child, was reminded of her human frailty and informed of virtues that would serve her well in life. Then, a cousin of Charles was asked to choose a name for Delia. The woman took a few dance steps and sang a few tunes, in appreciation of the honor bestowed upon her. After consultations with others, she called out the name, Ifeoma (A Great Thing Has Happened to Us), which also happens to be my own Ibo name. With its announcement, a cheer went up and an impromptu song, using Delia's new name, ensued. Women danced to their heart's desire.

After dark, with the courtyard sparsely lighted by the conversation-swallowing power generator, my own relatives, led by Mama, went onto the dance floor. My sister Virginia held Delia up, in a position where she was visible to all present, and they sang about their daughter's perfect child. At that moment, my father-in-law began to distribute the *omugo* gifts to my relatives, honoring in turn all the women who'd honored me by bringing gifts right after the baby was brought home. Because I was a university professor and Charles was a medical doctor, we went beyond the requirements of custom and gave each woman a six-yard piece of *abada*, an expensive print manufactured in Europe. Mama and my sisters received even more expensive Georges.

As each of my relatives departed, she sang the praises of my in-laws, a song that we knew would continue until she arrived at her own home, a song that would certainly call attention to herself and the gift she bore and would, more likely than not, spark a minor celebration of its own. Each woman would wear the clothing proudly, and since these wrappers never go out of style, she would wear it for the rest of her life. Each time, she would tell the story of how their daughter and her illustrious husband saw fit to bestow such an honor on her humble self.

Making My Life Whole

I wish I could say that giving birth to Delia allowed me to savor motherhood and enjoy my child in the way I wanted to, that my life was significantly better or that the pressure to prove my womanhood lessened.

On the contrary, the pressure to conceive and bear a son for my husband started as soon as those at home were notified that I had given birth to a baby girl. I got many congratulatory letters from friends and relatives, and all seemed genuine in their expression of joy about my safe delivery. However, almost every letter included an addendum that called for my return home so I could "begin making another child," with the unwritten understanding that it be male.

On the day I returned to our apartment in Enugu from the U.S., one of those who met us downstairs was the woman who lived in a flat adjacent to mine. As we walked up the stairs to my second-floor apartment, in a voice loud enough that the throng of others following heard her clearly, she said, "I hope you don't mind that you had a girl." She said it without malice, but it irked me that she voiced it out loud.

"Why should I mind? I'm grateful for whatever God gives me."

Many of the numerous visitors who came to see Delia repeated the suggestion that I pursue real fulfillment. "Don't wait. Start right away, while everything's still open from your daughter's birth."

Because I had decided to conceal the way my daughter was delivered from everyone except Charles, I could not tell my advisers that my obstetrician counseled that I wait a whole year before becoming pregnant.

Others lectured me on the Billings ovulation method, a highly acclaimed system for sex selection that was, among other things, approved and recommended by the Catholic Church. My oldest sister, Virginia, who at that point had four sons and one daughter, whispered, "How do you think I had all my boys?" That's when I found out luck had nothing to do with it; it was all about planning. Do it, I was told time after time. "You don't want to give birth to two girls in a row, before any boys; once the anxiety sets in, it's nearly impossible to conceive and carry a boy."

I allowed myself to be swayed, and I became pregnant when my daughter was eight months old. With the pregnancy came the anxiety. "What if it turns out to be another girl?" I knew that in spite of how carefully I had studied my body to predict the exact moment of my ovulation and the highest likehood of conceiving a boy, there were no guarantees.

A few days past the fourth month, I began to spot, then bleed, and was admitted into the hospital for bed rest. My feet were elevated as I lay flat on my back for three weeks straight, but as my mother told me, we cannot ever expect to have control over our lives. My carefully planned and conceived boy fetus was miscarried.

I don't remember feeling much pain or loss at that time; instead, I kept telling myself, "It worked; I can do it again." When people came to commiserate with us, they asked, "Did you see the sex?" to which I or whoever was with me replied, "It was a boy." My sympathizers would clasp their arms across their chest or sigh loudly; some even mustered some tears. "Oh, why didn't he stay?" Their expressions said it all: there was no time to lose in the pursuit of a live male child. I was pregnant again in less than two months.

If I had been capable of rational thought at the time, I would have ignored the insinuations and waited for my body to heal before con-templating another child. But I vowed to give my husband a son in no time. In fairness to Charles, he said that we should wait for several months to pass, but I was adamant. Charles did not have to live with the unsolicited advice I was given by strangers. But my male child again eluded me, for I miscarried in my seventh month. The baby's sex stared me in the face, mocking me. I watched him as he struggled for life, his tiny body writhing, my son leaving me to the stories I knew would follow the mishap.

This time, I was inconsolable and mourned my son, whom I named Uchechukwu (The Will of God), for weeks. I could not figure out what I had done wrong to be denied the one thing I sought with every breath I took. I often wondered, as I still do, if my pain was more because the child I lost was a boy. Would I have cried as loudly or refused nourishment for as long as I did if it had been a girl? My depression lasted, and several times I wished for death.

Mama brought me back to my senses. "You have one live child. God has his reasons and you can't question Him." She stayed with me while I healed, and she filled my days with stories—of my Grandmother, who carried more than twelve pregnancies but only had five children live past infancy; of herself, her first child, Charles, her golden boy, who was taken from her suddenly one afternoon. She reminded me of my oldest sister Virginia, whose first pregnancy had resulted in the still birth of a set of twins, a boy we called Julian and a girl Juliana. Martha as well, Mama said, lost a child in her eighth month, a boy too. She reminded me of the three babies Mama Li had lost right in our household as we grew up. "Don't you remember any of them?"

I shook my head no, although I remembered young Cy, named for my uncle Cyril, who died after we couldn't stop his fever-induced convulsions.

She mentioned other women I knew and reminded me of their stories too. "It's every woman's fate; it's God's way of making us stronger." But the fact that Mama was present in my home without a new child to nurture was a constant reminder of my failure.

I allowed some time to pass before Charles and I made another attempt at a male child. In the interim, I went to several gynecologists for some explanation of my problem. "What's wrong with me? Why can't I carry a male child?" Their assurances that nothing was wrong fell on deaf ears. I asked anyone who would listen and gathered tons of stories from women who'd had similar experiences. Many told me that I was probably afflicted with *ukwu-oku* (literally, hot pelvis), a condition that causes the woman to miscarry male children. The only remedy, I was told, was to douche with herbs, only prescribed by native doctors. Since Charles was vehemently opposed to it, I turned to praying to God. I told everyone to offer novenas for me. Meanwhile, I requested masses for divine favor. When I became pregnant again, I was gripped with fear. I felt no joy when the pregnancy was confirmed, for I fully expected to miscarry that child also. There I was, a twenty-eight-year-old woman with a two-year-old daughter and two miscarriages, and I felt that my time was quickly running out.

My doctors, for I was then being seen by several, recommended that I spend the entire pregnancy in the hospital. "Let's take no chances," they warned. I've never prayed as hard or wished as much for anything as I did for that child. Each anxiety-filled day came and went, and the hours dragged. I literally watched the hands on the clock moving, celebrating each hour that passed and moved me closer to my destination. The months till delivery turned to weeks, and when I was four weeks away from my due date, the doctors felt the risk of miscarrying was over, and I was discharged from the hospital.

Returning to America

During that pregnancy, my husband began making plans to continue his residency in the United States. By the time I went into the hospital, Charles had taken and passed the very difficult American licensing exams and was waiting to hear from the numerous programs to which he'd applied for a position. John came to the rescue once again and invited Charles to come to the U.S. so he could better assess the situation.

Charles was reluctant to go because of his concern about me lying in the hospital, and about Delia, who would be left without either of us. I convinced him to go: I was adequately taken care of by the hospital staff and relatives who hovered, eager to meet my every need; Delia was in the care of my sister-in-law, Priscilla, and she seemed happy with the arrangement.

With John's help, Charles secured a position in the surgical residency program at Morristown Memorial Hospital where John is an attending physician. Charles returned only a few days before I was discharged from the hospital, but he had less than two weeks to return to America and start the residency. Ironically, the news I'd eagerly awaited for so long did not give the pleasure I'd always expected it to.

I had pressured Charles to pursue his training in the United States because I felt it would present immense opportunities for all of us. I wish I could claim that I was motivated by a desire to escape my restrictive society, but that was not the case. I simply wanted Charles, the children, and me to have a better life.

Nigeria was a shambles. Nothing worked the way it was supposed to. We lived in our flat for four years, and not for one day did we have running water. We relied mostly on water purchased from tankers and from sources we were not sure were safe. We were lucky if we had electricity once a week, so although we had both a refrigerator and a freezer, we could not preserve perishable food. We resorted to a lifestyle that was similar to our grandparents'. Our telephone was broken more than it worked. We were ecstatic if we heard a dial tone.

The economy was a wreck. Workers went for months without paychecks. In spite of our jobs and earning potential, we were barely able to make ends meet. If we needed extras, we asked for help from Charles' parents or Mama.

Roads simply did not exist. It was nearly impossible for me to commute to work. The drive between Enugu and Nsukka was on a stretch of uninhabited areas with clusters of bushes and tall grasses flanking the two-lane highway. There were no traffic regulations or anyone to enforce whatever rules that did exist. Drivers of all sorts of vehicles, including large trailers, terrorized others on the road. It was common to see cars on the wrong side of the road or even in the middle of the two lanes. Sometimes armed robbers blocked the road and held motorists hostage for as long as they wanted. Who was there to stop them? I can't recall a week when I didn't see dead bodies on the sides of the road, either murdered or killed in car accidents. I drove alone, which made me an easy target, and we knew it was a matter of time before my luck would run out. Amazingly, people were content to live their lives that way. If anyone complained, the answer was invariably, "It's God's will."

Still, when our dreams became reality, I was hesitant to make the move. It had been five years since my initial return from America, and in spite of the logistical problems we faced in Nigeria, I felt well adjusted, almost grounded, in the Ibo tradition. I was reluctant to disrupt my life, and I dreaded the nightmare when Charles completed his training and wanted to return home and set up his practice in Nsukka or Enugu. I could have lived with a permanent move, but Charles would not commit to settling in the U.S. I felt it unfair that I would be forced to repeat the emotional and cultural roller coasters of the past years.

If I stayed in Nigeria while Charles lived in the United States, Ibos would have seen nothing unusual in that arrangement. Husbands and wives live separately if there is an understanding that it is for the good of the family. Many spouses and children of Ibos living in the United States stay at home in Nigeria or in separate cities and states within the United States. If asked, these Ibos are likely to say, "*Anam eri ya eri?* (Is he/she food that I need to eat every day?)" The physical separation does not affect the dynamics of the relationship in any way, and the man continues to rule his household from afar. Without doubt, Charles, his parents, and siblings would have continued to maintain tight control over my life if I had remained in Nigeria.

How strange, I was told, that I, the American-trained spouse with greater exposure to Western culture and more to gain by moving back to America, was the more reluctant to plunge into the American opportunity we were given. Charles gave me hundreds of reasons why we should go to America. But I held out, reminding him of my very fulfilling career as a professor at the University of Nigeria; the children and I would visit during vacations. Mama was solidly behind my resistance. "If you go, you'll lose many crucial years, not only at your job but in our community. You'll have to start over again when you return. Prevail upon him to go alone."

Charles' parents also supported my position that the children and I remain in Nigeria, but for completely different reasons. My parents-in-law thought that Charles would be reluctant to return to Nigeria if I were there with him, that I would trap him into staying permanently in America like my oldest brother John. They wanted me to be their bait to lure him home where he belonged.

Charles finally asserted himself and put his foot down. "You're my wife, and you go where I go. I want you beside me, and I don't want any more arguments." My resistance buckled, and again I remembered that it was not my decision to make in the first place. It was settled that Charles would leave first and that I, Delia, and the child I would bear, God willing, would join him as soon as the baby could travel. Once the decision was made, everyone reminded me of how lucky I was that my husband wanted me to be with him at all times. "He could allow you to stay in Nigeria, so he can seek his pleasure with other women." As my mother says, behind every dark cloud is a bright sun.

Charles' departure was not celebrated as mine had been the first time I left home. A few close friends visited us and spoke words of encouragement, but all implored him to return to his country when he finished his training, and not join the hordes of other Nigerians who were "living like people without a homeland" in America. On the night before he was to leave, it suddenly dawned on me that I would be completely alone as I bore the child I carried. Charles would be thousands of miles away, same as he was when our first child was born.

It was my destiny, I consoled myself, to go through major events alone. At least with my first child, John and Delia had been by my side. This time, although Mama, my mother-in-law, and my sisters were close by, I found no solace in their presence; I was constantly surrounded, yet I felt strangely alone and abandoned. My tears started to flow early the next morning as he prepared to depart and continued until hours after we had returned from the airport where we saw him off. Charles left on June 14, 1985, eleven days before his son was born.

I Have a Son

Like our daughter Delia, our first son, Chuka, was born on a Tuesday night. Unlike Delia, who arrived exactly on the day she was due, Chuka made his appearance three weeks early and without much trouble. It was as if my son decided that he had already caused enough trouble in keeping me immobilized in the hospital throughout the period I carried him.

With Charles gone, all my attention was turned toward my daughter and unborn child. My earlier anxieties returned as I approached the end. I knew that anything could go wrong. During my stay at the hospital, I witnessed firsthand the high rate of still births and maternal deaths. Maternal death is so common and widely accepted that we use the term *ozidago* ("she's climbed down from the mountain of death") to announce that a woman has given birth.

My doctors decided that the baby would be delivered by caesarean section to ensure that both baby and mother survive. My protests fell on deaf ears, and I was told, "You want to survive with a child, don't you?" Well, when put like that, I had no options but to ready for the scheduled delivery date. I had friends donate blood for my use and was ready to bear the humiliation, for the sake of my second child. I told only one close friend of the delivery situation. I didn't even tell Mama or my mother-in-law. I knew they would throw their arms up in the air and begin to cry, as if something terrible had happened to me. I decided that they would have plenty of time for crying after the baby was delivered. If God blessed me with a healthy boy, the snickering about my inability to push would be lessened. People would remember to add, "At least it was a boy."

My son spared me the agony and gossip. He made his entrance into the world quite suddenly, and had I wasted any time, he would have been born at home. I was sitting in bed around eight-thirty at night when my water broke. A neighbor, aware of what I had suffered for that baby, rushed me to the hospital. I still had not felt one contraction when the admitting nurse examined me and exclaimed that the baby's head was right there. His birth was a blur—before I knew what was happening, I was being told to push him out. I applied every ounce of strength I had, and he emerged at nine-fifteen. "It's a boy!" someone screamed, and everyone else began to shout out their congratulations.

I suddenly felt my body washed with joy, more than I thought was possible, more than I had ever felt in my life.

"But what if they were just saying that to appease me?" I wondered. I raised my upper body to catch a glimpse of him, to verify that it was the truth they spoke. Not even the stings from the episiotomy repair deterred me, as my gaze followed my prize child, wrapped in a blanket, to another table where his vital signs were checked.

"Are you sure it's a boy?" I asked no one in particular, and when my question was ignored, I called out again, "Can I see for myself?" My son was brought to my arms. I lifted the thin cotton blanket with which he was swathed and peered in to see the thing that elevated him above his sister, above me, above every Ibo woman anywhere on the planet.

"Thank you, God," I whispered over and over as reality set in. I had a son, my very own son. I had everything an Ibo woman could ever want.

I was carried away by my euphoria. When one of the nurses asked what I would call him, I did not hesitate one second before I called out a not-so-common Ibo name, *Chimezurum* (God Has Given Me Everything I Want). I felt incredible relief that it was over, not only that I had a live child but that the child was a boy. If I never had another child, I had fulfilled my duty to my husband, my role as a woman and wife. In the hours it took to resettle me in the maternity ward, I thought of nothing but my good fortune, and every few seconds, I checked the cot beside me to reassure myself that he was there and that it was not all a dream.

My son is not called by the name I gave him, the one that spoke my heart. As I was reminded, it was not my place to name the child I bore. Mama shook her head at my audacity when I told her his name.

"You can't give him a name. He does not belong to you."

I stopped calling my son Chimezurum when my mother-in-law arrived to view her first son's first son. With Mama's prodding, I asked my mother-in-law what she wanted the child named, and she called him *Chukwuka* (God is Supreme). Everyone calls my first son Chuka, for that's the name that's entered in all the official documents. But deep down in my heart, I feel that even "God is Supreme" is inadequate.

I think I know how to raise Chuka and his brother, Obi, in the Ibo tradition. That way of life holds no special challenges for male children, even in laid-back California.

But what should I do with Delia?

We'll have to see.

Part VII
Epilogue

Sherifa—and Twenty-Three Other Nieces and Nephews

On March 12, 1994, Sherifa Omade Edoga, John's first child, Mama's first grandchild, and my best friend, died from complications of heart surgery. Sherifa was twenty-three years old.

She was a Stanford University graduate, National Merit Scholar, Academic Decathlon gold medalist, women's and minority rights activist, actor, and writer. But suddenly, she was gone. All that brilliance and beauty gone.

I called Mama shortly after Sherifa's funeral and she expressed shock that we had returned to our normal lives in less than a week.

"She's barely gone; how could you forget her so soon? How could you go on as if nothing happened?"

When I said nothing, she pressed on. "Is there something about her death that you're not telling? Did she commit a heinous offense before her death?"

"This is America," I finally told her. "Life goes on as if nothing happened." But even as I uttered those words I knew mine couldn't go on, for I continue to feel that until we've grieved for Sherifa and sent her off on her long journey to eternity, we'll be stuck in our loss forever.

Sherifa's death and funeral have made me much more aware of the stark differences between my two worlds. They reminded me how much of an outsider I remain in this society, even though I've lived here most of my adult years. It made me wish that I were back home in Nigeria, in my hometown Aku, among people who understand the need to mourn a loved one, especially one who died so young. We would have wallowed in self-pity, sung her praises, celebrated her life. Ultimately, we would have released her. Let her go.

When Mama learned that Sherifa was gone, she did as I wish I could have done. Her wailing could be heard blocks away, beckoning her people, announcing the passing of so treasured a life. Neighbors and friends came in droves and sat with her, their voices joining hers. Their songs of death, I was told, were heard at the marketplace, several miles away. Market women hurriedly packed their wares and trooped to Mama's side, to offer their own voices and strength. Mama was surrounded the entire four weeks of her sitting for her grand-daughter. If she felt like throwing herself on the ground, she was not discouraged. "Let her cry," neighbors would whisper. "Let her get it out of her system."

For my part, when John called to tell me Sherifa died, I was all alone. There was no one to hold me while I struggled to catch my breath. I could not wail, for I had to be mindful of not disturbing my neighbors, people I barely knew. How I wanted to cry out, so my voice could be heard blocks away. I wanted all traffic to stop, my neighbor-hood food store to close, and my dry cleaner to lock his door. I wished for my world here to acknowledge and proclaim my loss, as it deserved to be.

My wails would not have been empty cries or without meaning, for they would have been sing-song melodies about my niece, her life, and the emptiness I knew she would leave behind. I would have told of her great beauty, her commanding presence, her royal car-riage, and the joy and pride she brought to all of us. I would have asked her why she couldn't stay with us longer and why her depar-ture was so sudden. But my unsung melodies are still within me and weigh heavily on my chest.

John, Delia, Tita, Che and I traveled from San Francisco, where Sherifa died, to Morristown, New Jersey, John and Delia's home. In the first hours of our return, we were joined by Anthony and his wife Felicia, and Ogbonna and his wife Elizabeth.

The days between Sherifa's death and her interment, especially the two days of receiving well wishers at the funeral parlor, were torture. We rose in the mornings, drank coffee, bathed our bodies, bantered about what clothes to wear, traded makeup secrets to camouflage our swollen faces, and actually laughed at times. We visited our Sherifa in a stranger's house, a place that she had never been in her life and which I'm sure she would not have liked.

Had we been home, Sherifa would have been dressed in her best regalia and laid out, not in a half open casket, but in her own bed, the bed that she slept in all her life, with her most treasured belongings surrounding her. She would have been attended by everyone who loved her. I would have been there to bathe and oil her, massaging her skin as I had done many times in her life. I would have had a chance to cradle her and smooth out the pains she must have felt her last days. Because she was not only my niece but my best friend, I would have sat at the head of her bed the entire night before she was laid to rest, singing to her and about her.

Here, though, my unsung words are still formed in my head and will not give me rest.

I would have been required to give Sherifa instructions for her life hereafter, to remind her that she was going where many in her family had gone already—that her grandfather, my father, Mama's Master, would await her and watch over her, that her great-grandmother, my grandmother, would cradle her and rock her as she did when Sherifa was a little girl. I would have told Sherifa not to be afraid, and to go with our love.

Mama's letter on ceremonies for Sherifa reported that all members of our family were present for the entire duration. Christopher and his wife Cecilia were at home with Mama when they got news of Sherifa's death. Virginia, who lives in a building adjacent to Mama's, had reportedly heard the wailing from several blocks away, at the school where she taught and, without knowing who had died, had started crying. Martha, who lives hundreds of miles away in northern Nigeria, was contacted by telephone, and journeyed home by bus the day after. The other passengers took turns holding her and crying with her.

Throughout the period, the womenfolk sat at home while the men hovered around, amidst friends, for a whole month. Life stood still while everyone mourned Sherifa. No one in my family was expected at their places of employment, nor were the Edoga grandchildren and cousins required to be at school, for that whole month. They sat, discussing little except their memories of Sherifa. No fires were lit in the kitchen of Mama's household, and everyone would have been appalled had they been. If anyone bathed or changed clothes, they did so discreetly, usually at night when they were not likely to be noticed by outsiders.

I've been told that each morning, right after cock's crow, a woman's voice—Virgy's, Martha's, Mama Li's, Mama's, or anyone of the tens of women that passed the nights with them—rang out, piercing the early morning's quietness, partly to keep count of how long it had been, and to remind the world of their immense loss.

"It's been four days, Sherifa. Four days is too long to still be asleep." The early-morning cries would alert everyone else to join the wailing, which lasts until all eyes are dry. Anyone who felt her heart breaking or just wanted to could start crying loudly at any time during the sitting, knowing that others' voices would join hers.

On the seventh day, Mama asked her grandchild, "Sherifa, is this it? Is this the end? Are you really gone from our lives?" The sitting lasted another three full weeks, allowing them to celebrate her life and to let her go. Sherifa's family in Nigeria departed the gathering ready to rejoin life.

Here, my own heart is still laden with pain.

Although Sherifa's body was not present, Mama and our family proceeded with a full traditional burial rite. On the night of the 16th of March, the eve of her interment, she was given a twenty-one gun salute. It was an honor she earned by her life and hard work. As is the practice, her death was announced over the local radio and television stations, and the obituary listed all those who survived her, including aunts, uncles and cousins, all who would be touched by her absence.

The day after the ceremonies were concluded, Mama and all others who wanted to offered their heads to be shaved and traded their colorful clothes for basic black. When she began to go out once again, her first few outings were orchestrated, and she was accompanied by friends. Strangers walked up to Mama, "Please accept our sympathy. We're so sorry about your loss."

But I, barely two days after Sherifa was buried, boarded my plane to return home, without fanfare, without anyone acknowledging my loss. Alone in my pain, I was just one of thousands of travelers at Newark International Airport. I said to myself, "Surely, someone must know. Someone in this vast airport is aware that my Sherifa is gone." But no one acted as if they knew. All were caught in the rush, as if nothing had happened, as if Sherifa were still alive.

I was angry, not because Sherifa was dead, but because life went on and dragged me with it. And I longed to be home where people who knew my pain would make life wait until I was ready to rejoin it.

John and Delia's other children, Miata (Tita) and Che, are doing well. Tita graduated from Williams in June 1994 and is now working as an actor in Los Angeles. Che is a sophomore at Skidmore. John is highly acclaimed in his field of vascular surgery and has a successful practice in Morristown, New Jersey. Delia recently closed down her law practice and is exploring her interest in art.

Anthony and his wife, Felicia, live in New Jersey. Anthony graduated from the University of Kansas with a degree in biology and is employed by the City of Morristown. Felicia, also from Aku, is a pharmacist. Mama arranged the traditional marriage before Felicia joined Anthony in March 1990. They don't have children yet.

Ogbonna's traditional marriage to Elizabeth was arranged by Mama in 1991. They have a one-year-old daughter, Emma Ijeoma, and live in Roanoke, Virginia, where Ogbo is a computer analyst. He graduated from the University of Pennsylvania, returned to Nigeria in 1981, but came back to the U.S. to settle in 1989. His wife, Elizabeth, is the youngest sister of Cecilia, my childhood best friend and co-flower girl.

My husband Charles has an OB/GYN practice in Madera in central California. Without doubt, I could not have asked for a better husband than Charles. I hope my daughter will find a man as good for her as her father is for me. We live in nearby Fresno, and our children are doing well in school. Delia is in seventh grade, Chuka in fourth, and Obi, our second son, is in second.

I teach writing at a local community college and have occasionally written articles for magazines and newspapers.

On the home front, Martha is a school headmistress. With my prodding, she enrolled in the University of Nigeria, Nsukka, and completed both a bachelor's and master's degree in foreign languages. Her specialty is French. Martha is the mother of seven children, ranging in age from twenty-three to five years old. Her oldest, Ogochukwu, married at seventeen and is the mother of Obumneme, Martha's first grandchild, and Mama's first great-grandchild. Her husband, Emmanuel Egbe, is a professor of education at the University of Jos in northern Nigeria.

Virgy's life followed a path that's parallel to Mama's. She bore eight babies (two, a set of twins, died in infancy) and is raising six children: from Uzoamaka, who's twenty-one, down to Chiedozie, who's nine. Like Mama, Virgy was widowed too early in her marriage. Her husband Godfrey Ezeora died in 1990, and Virgy and her children are now back at Mama's house, occupying one of the flats in the building where John's family stayed when they came for my wedding. Virginia completed her bachelor's degree in education and is a teacher in one of the public elementary schools.

Christopher and his wife Cecilia, who is also from Aku, have four children, aged eight through eighteen. Their first child, Ifeoma, is named after me. Christopher and his family live with Mama in the original house. His wife, who is also a schoolteacher, handles the day-to-day housekeeping of the house. Christopher works closely with

Mama and runs her businesses. He is also the man of the house and represents Mama in most of her dealings.

My parents-in-law, Felix and Esther Ugwu-Oju, are doing very well, and continue to maintain their strong friendship with Mama.

Cousin Mary lives in Nsukka with Augustine, her second husband, with whom she has four children.

Mama Helena, Mama's early mentor, died in 1992, at over eighty years old.

Mama continues to live in the first house she built. She's visited the U.S. three times and, with the exception of arthritis, is generally in good health. We speak regularly on the phone. Her church, which recently honored her with a life membership, continues to be at the center of her existence.

Index